TEACHER PREP

**MERRILL
PRENTICE HALL**

Teacher Preparation Classroom

See a demo at
www.prenhall.com/teacherprep/demo

Your Class. Their Careers. Our Future. Will your students be prepared?

We invite you to explore our new, innovative and engaging website and all that it has to offer you, your course, and tomorrow's educators! Preview this site today at www.prenhall.com/teacherprep/demo. Just click on "go" on the login page to begin your exploration.

Organized around the major courses pre-service teachers take, the Teacher Preparation site provides media, student/teacher artifacts, strategies, research articles, and other resources to equip your students with the quality tools needed to excel in their courses and prepare them for their first classroom.

This ultimate online education resource will provide you and your students access to:

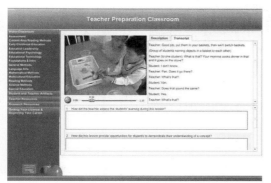

Online Video Library. More than 250 video clips—each tied to a course topic and framed by learning goals and Praxis-type questions—capture real teachers and students working in real classrooms.

Student and Teacher Artifacts. More than 200 student and teacher classroom artifacts—each tied to a course topic and framed by learning goals and application questions—provide a wealth of materials and experiences to help your students observe children's developmental learning.

Lesson Plan Builder. Step-by-step guidelines and lesson plan examples to support students as they learn to build high-quality lesson plans.

Articles and Readings. Over 500 articles from ASCD's renowned journal *Educational Leadership* are available. The site also includes *Research Navigator*, a searchable database of additional educational journals.

Strategies and Lessons. Over 500 research-supported instructional strategies appropriate for a wide range of grade levels and content areas.

Licensure and Career Tools. Resources devoted to helping your students pass their licensure exam; learn standards, law, and public policies; plan a teaching portfolio; and succeed in their first year of teaching.

How to ORDER *Teacher Prep* for you and your students:

- For students to receive a *Teacher Prep* Access Code with this text, please provide your bookstore with ISBN 0-13-222393-7 when you **place** your textbook order. The bookstore **must** order the text with this ISBN to be eligible for this offer.

Upon ordering *Teacher Prep* for their students, instructors will be given a lifetime *Teacher Prep* Access Code. To receive your access code, please email: **Merrill.marketing@pearsoned.com** and provide the following information:

- Name and Affiliation
- Author/Title/Edition of Merrill text

KNOWING AND SERVING DIVERSE FAMILIES

DIVERSE FAMILIES

Third Edition

Verna Hildebrand
Michigan State University, Emerita

Lillian Aotaki Phenice
Michigan State University

Mary McPhail Gray
U.S. Department of Agriculture

Rebecca Peña Hines
Healthy Family Initiatives, Inc., Houston, Texas

PEARSON

Merrill
Prentice Hall

Upper Saddle River, New Jersey
Columbus, Ohio

Library of Congress Cataloging-in-Publication Data
Knowing and serving diverse families / Verna Hildebrand . . . [et al.]. — 3rd ed.

   p. cm.
Includes bibliographical references and index.
ISBN-13: 978-0-13-228544-5 (pbk.)
ISBN-10: 0-13-228544-4 (pbk.)
1. Family services—United States.   2. Family social work—United States.
3. Multiculturalism—United States.   I. Hildebrand, Verna.
HV699.K59 2008
362.820973—dc22

                    2007021610

Vice President and Executive Publisher: Jeffery W. Johnston
Publisher: Kevin M. Davis
Acquisitions Editor: Julie Peters
Editorial Assistant: Tiffany Bitzel
Production Editor: Linda Hillis Bayma
Production Coordination: Thistle Hill Publishing Services, LLC
Design Coordinator: Diane C. Lorenzo
Photo Coordinator: Sandra Schaefer
Cover Designer: Ali Mohrman
Cover Image: Jupiter Images
Production Manager: Laura Messerly
Director of Marketing: David Gesell
Marketing Manager: Amy Judd
Marketing Coordinator: Brian Mounts

This book was set in ZapfHumnst BT by Laserwords Pvt. Ltd. It was printed and bound by R.R. Donnelley & Sons Company. The cover was printed by R.R. Donnelley & Sons Company.

Part opener photo credits: p. 1, Valerie Schultz/Merrill; p. 61, Todd Yarrington/Merrill; p. 205, PhotoDisc/Getty Images; p. 355, Getty Images–Stockbyte.

Additional photo credits: Photos on pp. 15, 73, 112, 146, and 244 supplied by the authors.

Pearson Prentice Hall™ is a trademark of Pearson Education, Inc.
Pearson® is a registered trademark of Pearson plc
Prentice Hall® is a registered trademark of Pearson Education, Inc.
Merrill® is a registered trademark of Pearson Education, Inc.

Pearson Education Ltd.
Pearson Education Singapore Pte. Ltd.
Pearson Education Canada, Ltd.
Pearson Education–Japan

Pearson Education Australia Pty. Limited
Pearson Education North Asia Ltd.
Pearson Educación de Mexico, S.A. de C.V.
Pearson Education Malaysia Pte. Ltd.

10 9 8 7 6 5 4 3 2 1
ISBN-13: 978-0-13-228544-5
ISBN-10:   0-13-228544-4

Preface

Knowing and Serving Diverse Families, Third Edition, is designed to expand your knowledge of diverse families beyond your own homes and neighborhoods. Consequently, this text puts you, as a new professional, in a frame of mind to interact with families in the world of human services, including education, during your studies and beyond graduation. The authors come from diverse backgrounds and experiences in family studies and child development. For many years, their expertise has helped professionals serve families in need of assistance.

The authors examine families from an organized approach to help you work with children and their families, both individually and in groups. You'll begin to recognize how you might gain insight into understanding an individual child or family. Of course, you learned early in your studies that each family, like each child, is unique. However, as a developing professional, you may also ask what logical generalizations your studies allow you to make.

Broadly considered, family professionals meet and work with children in schools, child-care centers, health or human service agencies, and the like. At other times professionals meet with parents in social service agencies to help with a family or child issue or challenge when the parents need assistance. It may be a school, a church, or an agency offering social or health services for individuals and families that brings you, the professional, and the family together.

Most education and other human services professionals realize that to help children, they must know about and help parents. You must be able to see both the generalizations and the uniqueness of families and apply your skills to help parents learn to be independent decision makers. The fields of human development, psychology, sociology, legal services, medicine, economics, and so forth, will be applicable as you become a helping professional.

As a practicing social scientist, you will also increase your own understanding of the sciences while matching the concepts presented in this text with your goals to service families and their children. It is a major undertaking for you, and we hope you'll enjoy the venture you've begun! Remember, as you are always learning, no two individuals or families are exactly alike, so you need to think broadly to serve them best.

ACKNOWLEDGMENTS

We would like to thank the reviewers of this edition of the text for all helpful comments and suggestions: Jerold P. Bauch, Vanderbilt University; R. Eleanor Duff, Southeast Missouri State University; Carol Gestwicki, Central Piedmont Community College; and Sharon Rosenkoetter, Oregon State University.

The authors dedicate this book to students and professionals who help implement the vision of a world supporting healthy families.

Brief Contents

PART I INTRODUCTION 1

Chapter 1
Knowing and Serving the Human Family: An Introduction 3

Chapter 2
Serving Individuals and Families: Equal Protection 21

Chapter 3
Systems for Knowing Families 41

PART II ETHNIC DIVERSITY AMONG AMERICAN FAMILIES 61

Chapter 4
African American Families 63

Chapter 5
Hispanic American Families 84

Chapter 6
Asian American Families 111

Chapter 7
Arab American Families 145

Chapter 8
Native American Families 164

Chapter 9
Amish Families 187

PART III LIFESTYLE VARIATIONS AMONG U.S. FAMILIES 205

Chapter 10
Teenage Single-Parent Families 207

Chapter 11
Divorced Single-Parent Families 243

Chapter 12
Stepfamilies 273

Chapter 13
Families with Children with Special Needs   297

Chapter 14
Gay and Lesbian Families   330

PART IV   CONCLUSIONS   355

Chapter 15
Serving Families   357

References   370
Name Index   394
Subject Index   402

Contents

PART I   INTRODUCTION   1

Chapter 1
Knowing and Serving the Human Family: An Introduction   3

Families in Your Career   6
Diversity Makes Life Interesting   7
Serving Unique Families   8
Families   11
Out of Many, One   14
Building on the Ideal   14
Your Membership in a Minority Group   14
Peaceful Accommodation   16
A Global Community   17
Conclusions   18
Study Questions   18
Applications   18
Volunteering   19
Media Resources   20
Key Internet Resources   20
Further Reading   20

Chapter 2
Serving Individuals and Families: Equal Protection   21

Stereotypes   22
What Is a Family?   24
Diverse Workforce   25
Effects on Home Life   27
Serving Families   28
Rights of Individuals and Families   29
Federal Laws   30
Examples of U.S. Laws That Apply Widely   31
State and Local Laws   34
Your Career Goals   34
Being Professional   35
Family-Related Sciences   35
Strengths of Families   36

Conclusions   *37*
Study Questions   *38*
Applications   *38*
Media Resources   *39*
Key Internet Resources   *39*
Further Reading   *40*

Chapter 3
Systems for Knowing Families   41

Which Families Shall We Study?   42
Using a Systems Approach   43
Communication for Helping Professionals   44
A Systems Approach to Studying Families   45
Adaptation   48
Values   49
Philosophy of Empowering Families   50
Family Functions   52
Human Capital   54
Application to Diverse Families   57
Conclusions   *58*
Study Questions   *58*
Applications   *59*
Key Internet Resources   *59*
Further Reading   *60*

PART II   ETHNIC DIVERSITY AMONG AMERICAN FAMILIES   61

Chapter 4
African American Families   63

Historical Background   65
Demographic Information   66
The Ecology of African American Families   68
African American Values   71
African Americans and the Educational System   72
African Americans and the Health Care System   74
African Americans and the Governmental System   76
African Americans and the Criminal Justice System   77
African Americans and the Economic System   77
Helpful Techniques for Serving African American Families   79
Conclusions   *80*
Study Questions   *81*
Applications   *81*

Additional Resources   *82*
Media Resources   *82*
Key Internet Resources   *83*
Further Reading   *83*

Chapter 5
Hispanic American Families   84

Brief History of Three Major Hispanic Groups   85
Who Are the Hispanics?   88
Hispanics: Likenesses and Differences   90
The Ecology of Hispanic American Families   92
Religious Foundation of Hispanic Families   92
Hispanic Family Structures   93
Male Roles in the Hispanic Family   94
Female Roles in the Hispanic Family   95
Children's Roles in the Hispanic Family   96
Prominent Values of Hispanic Families   98
Hispanic Families and the Governmental System   103
Hispanic Families and the Economic System   104
Hispanic Families and the Health Care System   105
Helpful Techniques for Serving Hispanic Families   105
Conclusions   *106*
Study Questions   *107*
Applications   *107*
Media Resources   *108*
Key Internet Resources   *108*
Further Reading   *109*

Chapter 6
Asian American Families   111

Who Are the Asian Americans?   113
The Ecology of Asian American Families   115
Asian American Family Values   116
Asian American Families and the Educational System   117
Asian American Families and the Health Care System   119
Asian American Families and the Governmental System   120
Asian American Families and the Economic System   121
Japanese American, Vietnamese American, and Korean American Families   122
The Ecology of Japanese American Families   122
Families and Acculturation   125
Selected Japanese American Traditional Family Values   129
Japanese American Families and the Educational System   130

Japanese American Families and the Health Care System   130
Japanese American Families and the Governmental System   131
Japanese American Families and the Economic System   131
The Ecology of Vietnamese American Families   132
Vietnamese American Families and the Educational System   135
Vietnamese American Families and the Health Care System   135
Vietnamese Americans and the Governmental System   136
The Ecology of Korean American Families   137
Korean American Families and the Educational System   139
Korean American Elderly and the Health Care System   139
Korean American Families and the Religious System   140
Helpful Techniques for Serving Asian American Families   140
Conclusions   141
Study Questions   142
Applications   143
Media Resources   143
Key Internet Resources   144

Chapter 7
Arab American Families   145

Who Are the Arab Americans?   146
The Ecology of Arab American Families   150
Arab American Values   156
Arab American Families and the Educational System   157
Arab American Families and the Health Care System   158
Arab American Families and the Governmental System   159
Arab American Families and the Economic System   159
Helpful Techniques for Serving Arab American Families   160
Conclusions   161
Study Questions   162
Applications   162
Key Internet Resources   163

Chapter 8
Native American Families   164

Who Are the Native Americans?   165
The Ecology of Native American Families   168
Cultural Expressions of Values   174
Native Americans and the Educational System   175
Native American Families and the Health Care System   177
Native American Families and the Governmental System   179
Native American Families and the Economic System   179
Helpful Techniques for Serving Native American Families   182

Conclusions   183
Study Questions   184
Applications   184
Media Resources   185
Key Internet Resources   185
Further Reading   185

Chapter 9
Amish Families   187

Who Are the Amish?   188
The Ecology of Old Order Amish Families   191
The Amish and the Educational System   198
The Amish and the Religious System   198
The Amish and the Health Care System   199
The Amish and the Governmental System   200
The Amish and the Economic System   200
Helpful Techniques for Serving Amish Families   200
Promoting Respectful Relationships   201
Conclusions   201
Study Questions   202
Applications   202
Media Resources   203
Additional Resources   203
Key Internet Resources   203

PART III   LIFESTYLE VARIATIONS AMONG U.S. FAMILIES   205

Chapter 10
Teenage Single-Parent Families   207

Societal Concern and Debate   208
Never-Married Parents   209
Trends in Numbers   211
Sociocultural Foundations   219
Economic Status   220
Changing Roles of Women   222
Changing Roles of Men   222
Socialization of Children   224
Demographics   225
Education   225
Religion   226
The Health Care System and Teenagers   226
Economic Factors   229
Housing   230

Governmental Policies and Agencies   231
Kinship Networks and Interactions   232
Change and Adaptation   233
Helpful Techniques for Serving Teenage Single-Parent Families   235
Conclusions   238
Study Questions   239
Applications   240
Media Resources   241
Key Internet Resources   241
Organizations   242
Further Reading   242

Chapter 11
Divorced Single-Parent Families   243

Historical Background   245
No-Fault Divorce   245
Property Settlement   245
Children's Experience in Divorce   246
Sociocultural Foundations   248
Socialization of Children   253
Ecological Factors   256
Kinship Networks and Interactions   264
Helpful Techniques for Serving Divorced Single-Parent Families   267
Conclusions   269
Study Questions   269
Applications   270
Media Resources   270
Organizations   270
Key Internet Resources   271
Further Reading   271
Further Reading for Children Coping with Divorce   271

Chapter 12
Stepfamilies   273

Complex Structure of Stepfamilies   274
Historical Background   276
Changes as Children Age   282
Socialization of Children   283
Roles of Grandparents and Others   284
Ecological Factors   284
Family Interactions and Kinship Networks   289
Change and Adaptation   290
Helpful Techniques for Serving Stepfamilies   291

Conclusions   293
Study Questions   294
Applications   294
Organizations   295
Key Internet Resources   295
Further Reading   296

Chapter 13
Families with Children with Special Needs   297

Partnering with Parents   298
Historical Background   300
Sociocultural Foundations   304
Demographics   309
A Deficit Model   311
Aesthetics   312
Education   313
Religion   314
Health Care System   314
Economic Factors   315
Family Interactions and Kinship Networks   318
Changes and Adaptations   319
Helpful Techniques for Serving Families with Challenged Members   321
Conclusions   325
Study Questions   325
Applications   325
Media Resources   327
Organizations   327
Key Internet Resources   328
Further Reading   328

Chapter 14
Gay and Lesbian Families   330

Family Definition Revisited   331
Gay and Lesbian Families   332
Historical Background   332
Sociocultural Foundations   335
Changing Roles of Females   342
Changing Roles of Males   343
Socialization of Children   345
The Role of Grandparents and Others   346
Ecological Considerations   346
Changes and Adaptations   349
Helpful Techniques for Serving Gay and Lesbian Families   349

Conclusions   *351*
Study Questions   *351*
Applications   *351*
Media Resources   *352*
Periodicals   *352*
Organizations   *353*
Organizational Resources   *353*
Key Internet Resources   *353*
Further Reading   *354*

PART IV   CONCLUSIONS   355

Chapter 15
Serving Families   357

Remembering Goals   359
Fostering a Sense of Community   359
Giving Service   359
Welcoming Diversity   360
Applying Ecological System Concepts   361
Focusing on Economic Concerns   362
Acting with Humility   365
Being Honest   365
Being Energetic   366
Acting with Dedication   366
Being Flexible   366
Using Advocacy   367
Correcting Problems of Discrimination   367
Conclusions   *367*
Study Questions   *368*
Applications   *368*
Key Internet Resources   *369*
Further Reading   *369*

References   *370*

Name Index   *394*

Subject Index   *402*

Note: Every effort has been made to provide accurate and current Internet information in this book. However, the Internet and information posted on it are constantly changing; so it is inevitable that some of the Internet addresses listed in this textbook will change.

I

INTRODUCTION

1

Knowing and Serving the Human Family: An Introduction

→ **Key Concepts**

- Human Rights
- *E Pluribus Unum*
- Pluralistic
- Synergy
- Diversity

Pearson Learning Photo Studio

Recognition of the inherent dignity and the equal and inalienable rights of all members of the human family is the foundation of freedom, justice, and peace in the world.
—UN Universal Declaration of Human Rights

Globalization is predicted to be the watchword of the twenty-first century, just as it became popular during the later years of the twentieth century. The term *globalization* is used in discussions of everything from accounting to zoology, and globalization has itself reached the far corners of each continent. We wear clothing from the Far East, eat foods from Russia, and serve wines from Europe. Our farmers, once a group slow to change, now favor globalization because it means markets for their grain. Globalization may have unintended consequences, such as apparent exploitation of poor people—especially women—in the developing countries where many exports are produced. Jervis (1997) suggests in his book, *System Effects: Complexity in Political and Social Life,* that any step the country takes may have a number of consequences—many unforeseen.

Václav Havel (1994, 1997), president of the Czech Republic, was the first democratically elected president after communism fell in the old Czechoslovakia. He writes,

> Precisely because of this globalization, our planet is in graver danger today than ever before. For just as the benefits of civilization are global today, so are all the dangers of that civilization, be they economic, social, demographic, ecological, or any other. In short, all of

humanity is in the same boat, and almost everything that happens anywhere directly or indirectly touches everyone (p. 155).

He says further,

[I]f our world is to face up to the great threat looming over it, we must find within ourselves the strength for a new type of global responsibility. The climate of multicultural coexistence, if it can be created, could be the first expression of this new responsibility, and could at the same time provide a proper environment for its development (p. 159). (These remarks are from Havel's address to the Indian Parliament on February 8, 1994, on being presented with the Indira Gandhi prize).

Globalization, of course, goes far beyond business and trade as some think of it. Cross-governmental organizations are helping bring order to international discourse. The United Nations (UN) meets in New York with a full agenda of programs that serve needs around the world. The officials who represent their country in international bodies help teach people at home how democracy works. Thus the fabric of democracy is being strengthened in many countries around the world. Rights for minority persons and for women are increasingly widely accepted, although still not universal at this writing. American families adopt infants and children from all around the world.

Globalization has come to those professionals who have interests in families. Children's and women's programs in particular are making inroads into the needs of families globally. For many years various governments have made efforts to help the needy in their own countries with aid of various types. Professionals working with families have certainly done their part. Andrews (2003) discusses these programs, saying,

[P]rofessionals located throughout the world have been building human and social capital in all the societies in which we work. As an informal network of peers and mentors, we have assisted one another, shared information and strategies, and influenced actions on behalf of children, youth, families, households, and communities both in our own homelands and on the international stage. Whether our need for understanding is of a technical, environmental, social, economic, or spiritual nature, we have talented people with the sensitivities, competencies, and connections that make things happen.

Scientific knowledge is breaking down barriers as scholars exchange information, read each other's journals, and help people solve problems in many countries beyond their own. Scholars study where the cutting-edge information is being discovered largely without being deterred by national boundaries. Much of the U.S. space exploration program includes international scholars. When an epidemic occurs, scientists and aid program leaders often converge to help wherever there is a need. Natural disasters bring scholars from many countries to view the situation and advise local officials. Over recent years, such help has become more and more commonplace.

The Internet and computers have greatly increased the amount and speed of international communication and discourse. Of course, international scholars use technology as widely and efficiently as Americans do. The exchange of information and ideas is so rapid that an old-time scholar who once waited months for letters and for journals to arrive from overseas can hardly believe it.

Traveling for international meetings held in many remote parts of the world has become commonplace for scientists, scholars, and members of international organizations—from teachers, to physicians, to farmers, or labor union members—they all can learn from each other. International travel simply for pleasure has grown by leaps and bounds in recent years.

Transportation has advanced, making rapid movement of people and products possible. Communications, too, have made rapid strides in very recent years. The Internet has brought high-speed contacts and a common denominator for many during the last few years.

As college and university students, many of you will plan for careers that are related specifically to the global arena. Others will learn how each specialty has global effects or is affected by global conditions. Many of you will take part of your education abroad—an almost commonplace experience today compared to only a few years ago. Your college or university likely has an international studies program or has an adviser willing to help you gain international educational experience. If not, then the neighboring college down the freeway undoubtedly does. The international aspects of life are recognized by far more schools than only the elite Ivy League schools that once planned international study experiences. Such studies cover every profession within the university.

Many students have taken the opportunity to participate in the Peace Corps, the program instituted by President John Kennedy. This program includes people of all ages in many parts of the world.

Most higher education science programs give insights into the global environmental aspects of our own industrial complex. You've learned about the effects of population growth, a distant volcano, the ramifications of providing the goods and services of modern life for all those around the world who aspire to a modern standard of living, and America's trade with other countries.

The new information presented in this volume and this course is from the perspective of families—those who receive the services of professionals like many of you expect to become, who are players in the drama of globalization, and whose condition offers additional perspectives on our studies in, for example, science, business, or humanities.

The United States and its people and careers will be the focus of your course. However, the broader perspective is understanding the world—its people and human systems—which you will meet in the years to come.

FAMILIES IN YOUR CAREER

Providing service to people is the hallmark of many careers today. How can you, as a future helping professional, best serve individuals and families? This book focuses on the diversities inherent in families and reveals ways of relating to family members who may differ from you in age, race, ethnicity, economics, and family form.

It is clear that there is a need to think about the professional challenges that lie ahead in your career. Preparing to work with individuals and families is a long-range educational objective requiring much of your attention during your entire educational program. Proper study and experience now will ready you to serve families following graduation with skills that cannot be easily learned the day before your first job begins.

As professionals in careers ranging from accounting to zoology, you will deal with individuals or customers and, either directly or indirectly, their families.

Talk It Over

What is your definition of a family? Explore this concept with your classmates. On what points do you agree? Many families, if not most, may differ radically from the family and the community in which you grew up.

You may question the importance of a course that emphasizes families when your future career requires only that you relate to individuals. Experience shows, however, that individuals are best served by professionals who understand the family, social milieu, and personal dynamics of their individual client, customer, patient, or student.

DIVERSITY MAKES LIFE INTERESTING

Diversity is exciting. You may know people who travel, study abroad, or read and ask questions to become aware of the ways people are alike and how they differ from themselves. Listen when a friend meets a foreigner and begins talking about how "we" do something here in the United States. Your impression may be that your friend is self-centered. However, good conversationalists often consciously seek common ground with other people, a technique that can lead to interesting ideas and friendships.

A close look at our own hometowns, where much common ground exists, will reveal that individuals and families are unique and different from us as well as each other. How can you prepare yourself to serve those in your hometown, as well as people on the other side of the world?

Perhaps you've had the experience of relating a problem to a friend, then having that person suggest solutions that would never work for you—mostly due to your individual family circumstances. You may have been prompted to comment, "That would never fly in my family." Such experiences point to our need to learn more about the differences that exist in and among families.

Talk It Over

List the characteristics of three families that you know best. What are the ages of members? How many years apart, and of which gender, are any children? What are their goals, values, and economic and other resources? From your analysis draw conclusions regarding their diversity.

SERVING UNIQUE FAMILIES

> A family is like no other family,
> Like some other families, and
> Like all other families.

These assertions will help you think about the many facets of your education concerning families, and each will be examined briefly.

Like No Other Family

By now you have learned that individual people are unique. No two are alike! In the same way, individuals both come from and form families that are also unique and unlike any other family. Think of the fact that the 6.1 billion people in today's world came from approximately 1 billion families. Or, think of the prediction that by the year 2010, the world will contain 6.9 billion people and that, by the year 2025, that figure will increase to 7.8 billion (Population Reference Bureau, 2002). This rich diversity is amazing and makes for a much more interesting world than if we were all similar.

The population of the United States is expected to increase from 281 million people in 2000 to 346 million by 2025 (Population Reference Bureau, 2002). The U.S. map in Figure 1.1 shows which states had increases in population and their changes from 1990 to 2000. The states shown in black had the greatest increases in population and thus received additional seats in the U.S. Congress. The first Congress using the new data was seated in January 2003.

Learning to appreciate the trends is important. Statistics can be confusing. We've done our best to use the latest figures available and to interpret them clearly. One important bit of advice is that when you read a percentage change, ask yourself, what is the previous or basic figure? For instance, one group has a large percentage increase, but the reported population is the smallest. Thus the number of persons is actually relatively small compared to the other groups.

Table 1.1 shows growth of the U.S. population from 1950 to 2000 and projections for 2025 and 2050 by sex and race. There is some question about certain of these census data because the 2000 questionnaire allowed the respondent to check multiple racial

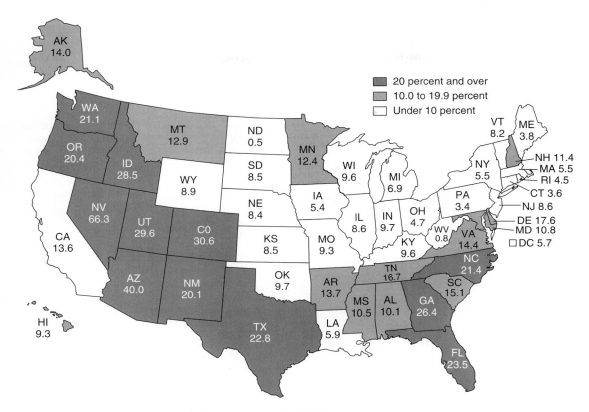

Figure 1.1   Percentage Population Change, 1990–2000

Source: Chart prepared by U.S. Census Bureau; for data see Table 18. U.S. Census Bureau, *Statistical Abstract of the United States: 2001.*

Table 1.1   Resident Population—Selected Characteristics, 1950–2000, and Projections, 2025 and 2050

[In thousands (75,187 represents 75,187,000)]

Date	Sex		Race				
	Male	**Female**	**White**	**Black**	**American Indian, Eskimo, Aleut**	**Asian, Pacific Islander**	**Hispanic origin**
NUMBER					NA Not available		
1950 (Apr. 1)......	75,187	76,139	135,150	15,045	(NA)	(NA)	(NA)
1960 (Apr. 1)......	88,331	90,992	158,832	18,872	(NA)	(NA)	(NA)
1970 (Apr. 1)[2]......	98,926	104,309	178,098	22,581	(NA)	(NA)	(NA)
1980 (Apr. 1)[3,4]......	110,053	116,493	194,713	26,683	1,420	3,729	14,609
1990 (Apr. 1)[3,5]......	121,284	127,507	208,741	30,517	2,067	7,467	22,379

(Continued)

Table 1.1   Resident Population—Selected Characteristics, 1950–2000, and Projections, 2025 and 2050 (*Continued*)

[In thousands (75,187 represents 75,187,000)]

Date	Sex		Race				
	Male	Female	White	Black	American Indian, Eskimo, Aleut	Asian, Pacific Islander	Hispanic Origin
NUMBER							
2000 (July 1)[8]	134,511	140,619	226,232	35,307	2,434	11,157	32,440
2025 (July 1)[8]	165,009	172,806	265,306	47,089	3,399	22,020	61,433
2050 (July 1)[8]	197,047	206,640	302,453	59,239	4,405	37,589	98,229
PERCENT DISTRIBUTION							
1980 (Apr. 1)[3,4]	48.6	51.4	85.9	11.8	0.6	1.6	6.4
1990 (Apr. 1)[3,5]	48.7	51.3	83.9	12.3	0.8	3.0	9.0
2000 (July 1)[6,7]	48.9	51.1	82.2	12.8	0.9	4.1	11.8
2025 (July 1)[8]	48.8	51.2	78.5	13.9	1.0	6.5	18.2
2050 (July 1)[8]	48.8	51.2	74.9	14.7	1.1	9.3	24.3

Source: U.S. Census Bureau, *U.S. Census of Population, 1950,* Vol. II, part 1; *1960,* Vol. 1, Part 1; *1970,* Vol. 1, Part B; *Current Population Reports,* P25-1095; "National Estimates, Annual Population Estimates by Sex, Race, and Hispanic Origin, Selected Years from 1990 to 2000": published 26 May 2000; <http://www.census.gov/population/www/estimates/nation3.html>; and "National Population Projections-Summary Tables"; published 13 January 2000; <http://www.census.gov/population/www/projections/natsum-T3.html>.

groups, which was not allowed previously. For instance, when comparing the 1980 or 1990 census with the 2000 census that asked the racial question differently, what do the new data tell us? Keep these problems in mind. Look for further analysis of the census of 2000 during the whole decade.

Table 1.2 shows resident U.S. population by sex and age groups. The most startling information here is the numbers of "75 to 84 years" and the "85 and older" citizens. People are indeed living longer, according to the census, and likely your family has some evidence of this among your relatives. These data explain the increase in numbers of nursing home facilities currently being built and the related need for skilled nursing home employees. These data will also help you understand the political discussion focusing on medical and drug benefits for senior citizens. It will also make you appreciate the need for developing good plans for retirement benefits for your generation, assuming the aging trend keeps increasing.

Table 1.3 shows household composition. Of the 105 million households, only 34.5 million have children under age 18. Further analysis shows 54.5 million married couples with 24.8 million having children under age 18. There were 12.9 million female-headed households with 7.5 million having children under age 18. Nonfamily households account for 33.5 million households. The Statistical Abstracts of the United States: 2000 also show data for each state.

Table 1.2 Resident Population by Sex and Age Group, 1990 and 2000

[248,710 represents 248,710,000. As of April 1, 1990 data are uncorrected counts. Minus sign (-) indicates decrease]

Characteristic	Number (1,000)		Percent Distribution		Percent Change, 1990–2000
	1990	2000	1990	2000	
Total population. . . .	248,710	281,422	100.0	100.0	13.2
Male.	121,239	138,054	48.7	49.1	13.9
Female.	127,470	143,368	51.3	50.9	12.5
Under 5 years.	18,354	19,176	7.4	6.8	4.5
5 to 9 years.	18,099	20,550	7.3	7.3	13.5
10 to 14 years.	17,114	20,528	6.9	7.3	19.9
15 to 19 years.	17,754	20,220	7.1	7.2	13.9
20 to 24 years.	19,020	18,964	7.6	6.7	-0.3
25 to 34 years.	43,176	39,892	17.4	14.2	-7.6
35 to 44 years.	37,579	45,149	15.1	16.0	20.1
45 to 54 years.	25,223	37,678	10.1	13.4	49.4
55 to 59 years.	10,532	13,469	4.2	4.8	27.9
60 to 64 years.	10,616	10,805	4.3	3.8	1.8
65 to 74 years.	18,107	18,391	7.3	6.5	1.6
75 to 84 years.	10,055	12,361	4.0	4.4	22.9
85 years and over.	3,080	4,240	1.2	1.5	37.6
Median age (years).	32.9	35.3	(X)	(X)	(X)
18 years and over.	185,105	209,128	74.4	74.3	13.0
Male.	88,655	100,994	35.6	35.9	13.9
Female.	96,450	108,134	38.8	38.4	12.1
65 years and over.	31,242	34,992	12.6	12.4	12.0
Male.	12,565	14,410	5.1	5.1	14.7
Female.	18,677	20,582	7.5	7.3	10.2

X Not applicable.

Source: U.S. Census Bureau, "Table DP-1 Profile of General Demographic Characteristics for the United States"; published 15 May 2001; <http://www.census.gov/Press-Release/www/2001/cb01cn67.html>. U.S. Census Bureau, *Statistical Abstract of the United States: 2001.*

FAMILIES

The sciences devoted to the study of individuals include genetics, psychology, and human development. Each family's uniqueness occurs because individual family members contribute to the distinctiveness of the whole family. Thus each family constellation differs. For example, every family is unique in the ages of the partners, the number and gender of any children, the years between siblings, the unique characteristics of each individual, the variation in structure of the family, and many other aspects.

Table 1.3   Family Households: 2000

[105,480 represents 105,480,000.]

State	Households (1,000)									
	Family Households							Nonfamily Households		
		Total[1]		Married Couple		Female Family Householder[2]				Average household size
	Total	Total	With own children under 18 years	Total	With own children under 18 years	Total	With own children under 18 years	Total	House-holder living alone	
U.S.	**105,480**	**71,787**	**34,588**	**54,493**	**24,836**	**12,900**	**7,562**	**33,693**	**27,230**	**2.59**

[1] Includes male family householders with no spouse present, not shown separately.
[2] No spouse present.
Source: U.S. Census Bureau, *2000 Census of Population and Housing, Profiles of General Demographic Characteristics*. U.S. Census Bureau, *Statistical Abstract of the United States: 2001*.

If individuals and families are so unique, how is it possible to develop sufficient background to serve them in a professional capacity? The answer is that your understanding of families will be a long-range proposition to be gained both from your education and your experience. Through your formal and informal studies, you will begin to understand characteristics that are especially unique to the family groups you will be serving. You will develop a certain sensitivity and learn how to search for facts about new individuals and their families when you encounter them.

Actually, some of the very experience you'll need can be gained by taking every opportunity to volunteer in community agencies while you are still enrolled in college. By doing so you'll learn how individuals and families pursue their lives and solve problems. You'll also be making an important contribution to your community. Later, you'll draw on this rich reservoir of experience with individuals and their families when you become a new professional.

For example, volunteering in Head Start—an early childhood education program—will give you opportunities to meet the parents of the small children you serve, which will give you confidence in dealing with those parents you meet when you attain your full professional degree, even though you are not a parent yourself. To help you search for volunteer and, sometimes, paid experiences, the end of each chapter of this book contains suggestions for application or volunteer experiences to consider. You can research your own community for volunteer possibilities, through such organizations as United Way funded agencies or a community volunteer office. Be sure to keep a record of the name of the organization, dates and hours worked, types of activities engaged in, and your supervisor's name to add to your job résumé later on.

Like Some Other Families

In certain respects, your own family is like other families. For example, we are somewhat like our neighbors, simply due to the fact of being born and reared in similar communities within the same country. As Americans we live under the same Constitution and the same laws, giving us shared values of freedom and liberty. Americans have many common experiences such as voting, education, and popular culture. We learn some common assumptions, such as knowing we have a right to be heard at a public meeting, and have access to some common resources, such as schools and communication media. Foreigners even say we have some common personality traits! These commonalities make individuals and families in a community more like each other than they are like families on the other side of the country or the world.

These shared characteristics are called culture and are studied in the social sciences we know as sociology, social psychology, cultural psychology, and family studies. Culture is continuously in a state of slow change. Throughout your education you will come to know the many factors that contribute to our shared values and characteristics. Also, you will learn to argue different viewpoints to remind others that there is another view or additional fact to consider before coming to any conclusions.

Like All Other Families

With the help of the social sciences of archeology and anthropology we know that we are part of the human family and members of the human species. This fact gives each family characteristics in common with families from the farthest reaches of the world.

Human beings have common patterns of genetics, biology, physiology, reproduction, growth, development, speech acquisition, problem solving, aging, and the like. For example, researchers have even found commonalities in how children learn languages around the world (Slobin, 1972). Your task will be to learn as much as you can and gain different perspectives from those who study families in detail. In fact, from his studies, linguist Pinker (1995) writes,

> Children develop these complex grammars rapidly and without formal instruction and grow up to give consistent interpretation to novel sentence constructions that they have never before encountered. Children must innately be equipped with a plan common to the grammars of all languages, a Universal Grammar, that tells them how to distill the syntactic patterns out of the speech of their parents. (p. 22)

Talk It Over

Suggest ways that separatism is alarming and dangerous for a peaceful, just, and happy human community. What actions have been taken in your college or larger community to bring people together? State some steps that persons in your future profession can take to end separatism.

OUT OF MANY, ONE

E Pluribus Unum (Out of many, one) is the motto of the United States. This motto, which appears on our coins, states one of the values of the founders of our democratic form of government. When foreigners arrive on our soil, it isn't long before they begin to think of themselves as Americans, rather than French, or Haitian, or Irish, as they might if they had immigrated to some other countries. Americans have developed a pluralistic society. That is, people with differing backgrounds have come together to form a society in common, the United States of America.

BUILDING ON THE IDEAL

What are some steps that we, as helping professionals and today's citizens, can take to build on the ideal of *E Pluribus Unum* and help end the cycles of misunderstanding, conflict, and violence among families and individuals in the United States and within and among countries of the entire world? In a world full of many diverse cultures and countries, are there ways families and individuals can more effectively seek peaceful, democratic, and pluralistic means of living together in harmony with all human beings?

YOUR MEMBERSHIP IN A MINORITY GROUP

Like every citizen, you are a member of a minority group. If this sounds far-fetched to you, consider that, according to some estimates, there are about 5,000 distinct ethnic groups and about 1,000 languages in the world. Taking a global perspective, with a total human population of over 6.1 billion diverse peoples, it appears, by various definitions, that there is no majority race, culture, or lifestyle. Consequently, each of us has a vested interest in minority rights. Minority rights are those basic human rights of equal protection and equal opportunity enshrined in those cherished U.S. documents, the Constitution, the Bill of Rights, and other amendments to the Constitution. These rights and values are the glue that holds this nation of diverse peoples together. Laws, regulations, and agreements at the local, state, national, and international levels help provide additional glue, making it possible for peoples of all backgrounds to cooperate. A selection of these laws and two special amendments are described in Chapter 2.

It is essential to prepare professionals to serve and promote harmony among diverse families if improvements in relations are to be significant and rapid. Avoiding oppression and victimization and providing equal protection and equal opportunity for every individual becomes crucial to every one of us. Cross-cultural contacts, study, interaction, cooperation, and service seem necessary if bridges of understanding and friendship are to be built in the ongoing American and global experiments of learning to thrive within—and gain from—multicultural and other forms of diversity.

PEACEFUL ACCOMMODATION

Peace is cheaper than war or strife in terms of costs, whether in lives or materials. Peaceful resolution of difficulties of many kinds often results from free competition in the marketplace of ideas—from discussions by "friend" and "foe" alike. The role of freedom of expression and freedom of inquiry in producing healthy change merits serious attention in the new millennium.

Decades ago, President Woodrow Wilson said, "I have always been among those who believed that the freedom of speech was the greatest safety, because if a man is a fool, the best thing to do is to encourage him to advertise that fact by speaking" (Dority, 1992, p. 31).

Exposing bigotry concerning any minority group is best done by debate and reason. The answer to a poor idea is a good idea that can be arrived at best by more, not less, free speech. Discrimination against any ethnic group or culture must be exposed to enlighten people. Bridges can be built between cultures, races, and religions. Free speech, and thus the free exchange of ideas, provides a peaceful way of achieving perpetual revisions and improvements in the light of new understanding. In a democracy, dissent is not viewed as treason, heresy, or disloyalty. Thoughtful opposition is preferred over thoughtless agreement. Reform is a never-ending process and requires constant discussion.

If two people each exchange a good idea in a discussion, they have doubled their wealth of useful knowledge. Indeed, synergy often occurs, with the result becoming greater than the single contribution of each party. Furthermore, new insights may also be stimulated by the exchange of ideas. For example, an issue may arise in a discussion group that might cause you to think and later alter your perspective.

Talk It Over

List and give details of some recent national or international dialogues between historically hostile groups or countries that give the world hope of peaceful reconciliation. How did these breakthroughs happen? What role do you think free speech played?

With many cultural variations on national and global levels, peaceful accommodation becomes essential. Different ethnic and cultural groups often choose different ways in which to live. A pluralistic society with a pluralism of values can contribute greatly to progress as continual discussion is stimulated. Diversity can be a strength. Although each of us views a situation through eyeglasses colored by the culture within which we were born and reared, understanding gradually comes through cross-cultural contacts, studies, and observations, and a more enlightened and objective view generally develops. Harmful separatism or tribalism can gradually be replaced by a general bonding among the human species, a bonding transcending borders surrounding each group of seemingly diverse people. A wider cooperating community of diverse peoples will be the result—perhaps best summarized as a "community of communities."

A GLOBAL COMMUNITY

More people are becoming aware of the global nature of our lives. Markets are global, and even the plague that struck India in 1994 was said to be related to a similar outbreak in the United States a year earlier. Many different forms of communication are now instantaneous, and rapid modes of transportation move individuals from one continent to another in a matter of hours. English has become a language utilized by commerce and governments in many areas. Even so, many more Americans in our global economy are feeling the need to learn other languages.

The UN is one major global attempt to build bridges connecting all countries of the world. As indicated in the opening quotation of this chapter, the UN provides a forum for developing a global respect for human rights. It is hoped that, through efforts like these, the future will hold no place for unjust oppressors or suffering victims. Humans seem to be learning through trial and error that differences among individuals need not make a difference. Diversity enriches our lives, for example, through art, literature, and music, and need not divide people.

Strangely, the human species is the only animal species known that systematically wages wars to destroy its own kind on a massive scale! After billions of years should the human species contrive its own self-destruction? One great strength of the UN is that people in countries outside specific local, regional, cultural, or lifestyle conflict generally are able to take a more rational and objective perspective than those directly involved in a conflict. This follows because people and countries outside certain areas of conflict are less likely to be captives of or subject to the same current or historical societal conditioning or emotional pressure. The many diverse people of our planet have the power to develop new visions, to make changes, and to remove destructive myths or superstitions that have kept us apart.

Cooperation, friendship, safety, and perhaps even love, will develop as we learn to share and enjoy life together. That is the civilized way. Violent bloody conflicts and wars are too deadly to tolerate. Global institutions of governance to help settle disagreements peacefully and with justice are a vital worldwide resource. Although the merits of such organizations as the UN, the World Court, and the UN peacekeeping units are recognized, the supervised disarming of opposing forces and the overseeing of honest and peaceful elections will need skillful international negotiation.

✧ CONCLUSIONS

Think of your career path and begin to prepare yourself by taking advantage of experiences with many different individuals and families. In a real sense you are a minority person in certain environments. You can surely recognize a self-serving interest in being respected and treated with respect for your intellect and ability. However, the modern idea that all human beings are born equal and should, as global citizens, enjoy basic liberties and rights is gaining wider acceptance. With the foundation given in this book, the authors believe that respect, hope, self-esteem, and development for every member of the human family will be stimulated. Our world, at times referred to as "a global apartment house" because we live so closely together in terms of time, can be made safe not only for participatory democracy, but, also, safe for diversity where families of all kinds are welcomed, valued, and even cherished.

✧ STUDY QUESTIONS

(Reviewing the Study Questions for each chapter will help you focus on particular concepts presented in each chapter and clarify the ways in which the authors apply those concepts.)

1. Name the organization that sponsors the Universal Declaration of Human Rights.
2. The present population of the world is _____. In 25 years the world population is expected to reach _____. How will the racial and ethnic mix in the United States change in the next 25 years?
3. What does the statistic termed *dependency ratio* show? How does that ratio relate to a study of families?
4. According to the latest census reports, what was the percentage of U.S. children living in single-parent homes in 1990? What has been the trend since 1990?
5. List three sciences that focus on individual development.
6. List the social sciences that study groups of people and families.
7. *E Pluribus Unum* is the motto of the United States. Given its meaning, how does it apply to your study of families?
8. What does *pluralistic* mean? How is it applied in your text?
9. What does *synergy* mean? How is it applied in your text?

✧ APPLICATIONS

(Students: Each chapter contains a list of Applications, encouraging more in-depth study of concepts learned earlier. Complete one or several of these suggestions to gain experience applying concepts discussed in each chapter. The purpose of the Applications is to make the chapter more relevant to your particular situation. The exercises are open ended and individual, and the answers will vary. Discussing them with your class-mates will aid in learning how each of the Applications relates to the topics.)

1. Write out and discuss your definition of a family.
2. List the characteristics of three families you know best. What are the ages of each family member? How many years apart and of which gender are any children? In describing themselves, do they use racial or ethnic characteristics? What can you conclude about your sample of three families?
3. In considering the population and demographic statistics provided, list statistics that apply particularly to your home community. Were there any surprises? If so, what are they?
4. As you consider your future career, write a one-page essay about the types of in-dividuals and families with whom you expect to interact. State how you are preparing or expect to prepare yourself for this interaction.
5. Suggest ways that separatism is alarming and dangerous. What steps have been taken in your college or community to bring people together? State what people in your future profession can do to end separatism.
6. List and give details of recent national or international dialogues that have taken place between historically hostile groups and give the world hope of peaceful reconciliation. State some ways your personal interests might be affected by these dialogues.
7. Write a one-page essay of your thoughts on controversial points of view, and then prepare to discuss them in your class.
8. Write a one-page essay on how the UN facilitates understanding among the peo-ples of the world.
9. Talk to three persons, on or off campus, whom you recognize as being different from yourself. Ask their views on current issues, families, and the relationship of families to their career. Summarize in a two-page report the three views and your own view on the topics.

✦ VOLUNTEERING

Canvass your community for an opportunity to volunteer to work with people on a weekly basis to have relevant personal experiences you can apply to your courses. Ask your local United Way for a list of agencies needing volunteers. Your instructor can also guide your search and selection of a volunteering site. College credit is sometimes at-tached to a specific volunteering experience, so it might be worth your while to look into it.

Keep a daily log or diary of your work, complete with time spent, dates, names, and addresses of supervising personnel. At graduation, this record can help you de-velop an item on your employment résumé or vita to substantiate your volunteer ex-perience. A record of volunteer experience is viewed favorably by most employers.

✦ MEDIA RESOURCES

Videos

Culture: Alive and well and living in the workplace. 60 minutes. Human service leaders discuss culture and meeting the challenges of diversity in the workplace. (Available from National Association for the Education of Young Children, 1313 L Street NW, Suite 500, Washington, DC 20005, 800-424-2460).

Teaching tolerance. (2002). (Available from Southern Poverty Law Center, Box 548, Montgomery, AL 36104. Also: www.tolerance.org; www.splcenter.org; www.teachingtolerance.org)

✦ KEY INTERNET RESOURCES

National Center for Health Statistics
www.cdc.gov/nchswww/products/pubs/pubd/netpubs.htm

PopNet (Population Reference Bureau)
www.popnet.org

Population Index (Princeton University)
http://popindex.princeton.edu

Population Reference Bureau
www.prb.org

U.S. Bureau of the Census
www.census.gov

✦ FURTHER READING

Aronson, S. (1996). *Trade and the American dream.* Lexington: University of Kentucky Press.

Coles, R. (1997). *The youngest parents: Teenage pregnancy as it shapes lives.* New York: Norton.

Eldering, L., & Leserman, P. (1993). *Early intervention and culture.* The Hague: National Commission for UNESCO.

Ferencz, B., & Keyes, K., Jr. (1991). *Planethood.* Coos Bay, OR: Love Line Books.

Gonzalez-Mena, J. (2007). *The child in the family and the community.* Washington, DC: The National Association for the Education of Young Children.

Lawton, M. P., & Salthouse, T. A. (Eds.). (1998). *Essential papers of the psychology of aging.* New York: New York University Press.

McCracken, J. B. (1993). *Valuing diversity: The primary years.* Washington, DC: The National Association for the Education of Young Children.

Jones, J. (1998). *Four centuries of black and white labor.* New York: Norton.

Kotlowitz, A. (1998). *The other side of the river: A story of two towns, a death, and America's dilemma.* New York: Doubleday.

Riley, N. E. (1997). *Gender, power, and population change.* Washington, DC: Population Reference Bureau.

→ 2

Serving Individuals and Families: Equal Protection

→ **Key Concepts**

- Stereotypes
- Defining a Family
- Legal Rights
- Being Professional
- Strengths versus Deficits

PhotoDisc/Getty Images

An African American family was involved in a car accident on a highway near a small midwestern town. The accident victims were moved to a small hospital nearby for observation and treatment. Later, the mother wrote to the head nurse, thanking the nurse and the staff for their caring attitude toward her and her family. "Our greatest fear was that we might be refused desperately needed services," the mother wrote.

The helping professionals in this small hospital are remembered for their quick, professional, and nonprejudicial service to this family. The mother's statement shows that she is fully aware that in some localities her family might not have received the prompt, thorough treatment needed. Mistreatment or nontreatment may have been her prior experience.

STEREOTYPES

The word *stereotype* generally applies to social situations in which a static picture is held of a person, group, race, or issue. A stereotype often represents an oversimplified view based on limited information. Many stereotypes are generally considered harmful.

Yet stereotypes might sometimes be considered helpful. For example, when the fire alarm rings, you respond in a stereotypical manner without asking why—until later. In social situations today, the ideal is to go beyond stereotypes. This means using prior knowledge and new ideas to judge a situation or a person. This is not always the case, however. It is likely that each one of you belongs to a group where you've been judged prematurely and stereotypically.

Talk It Over

In your own life, where have stereotypes been applied? How have stereotypes affected you or others you know? Discuss with one or more classmates. Write down five conclusions.

In Figure 2.1 consider the pairs of concepts that are stereotypes in some locales. Imagine yourself on one side or the other and how you might feel.

**Figure 2.1   Common
Stereotypes**

Male	⟷	Female
Old	⟷	Young
Slim	⟷	Fat
Tall women	⟷	Average women
Short men	⟷	Average men
Black	⟷	White
Foreign born	⟷	Native born
Straight	⟷	Gay or lesbian
Plain looking	⟷	Beautiful
Good hair	⟷	Bad hair
Good health	⟷	Poor health
Rich	⟷	Poor
Blue-collar work	⟷	White collar work
Salaried	⟷	Hourly
One religion	⟷	Another religion
Small family	⟷	Large family
Rural dweller	⟷	City dweller
Married	⟷	Single
"Traditional" family	⟷	"Other" family form
House living	⟷	Apartment living
Suburb	⟷	Inner city
Good grammar	⟷	Poor grammar
Well educated	⟷	Poorly educated
Well traveled	⟷	Nontraveler
Club member	⟷	Non–club member
Car travel	⟷	Public transport
Air travel	⟷	Car travel
Military veteran	⟷	Nonmilitary

WHAT IS A FAMILY?

Most people have their own definition of a family, and it is likely to coincide with the family in which they grew up. Most young children believe their family is like everyone else's family. To some, the family is a place as well as a group of people. One young man wrote, "A family is where, when you go there, they have to let you in."

Diversity is one thing to be aware of in serving families. Even your particular family is diverse within itself. At any one time, a given family can differ from one to several members, with people of different ages and with differing relationships. Diversity is a vital part of families, even families in your particular town, state, region, or nation. Families are far from being all alike.

There are legal definitions, political definitions, sociological definitions, and personal definitions of the family. Family scholars Bubolz and Sontag (1993) have developed the following inclusive definition:

> We define families in an inclusive sense to be composed not only of persons related by blood, marriage, or adoption, but also sets of interdependent but independent persons who share some common goals, resources, and a commitment to each other over time. (p. 435)

Using the Bubolz-Sontag definition of the family you would include many individuals today living in social groups, whether they are a couple in the family formation stage or a grandparent in his or her waning years. The family is the most common social group among the world's peoples. Note the important features of the preceding definition: composition, goals, resources, commitment, and interdependent but independent people.

Current news stories often discuss employment and mothers with dependent children. Figure 2.2 shows that the labor-force participation of married mothers with dependent children is about the same as the labor-force participation of unmarried mothers with dependent children today. Percentages have increased steadily over 25 years.

The "Welfare Reform Law" of 1996 (see later in this chapter) provided for child care and education to help mothers on welfare to become employed. The high costs of welfare drove this decision. Reports are coming out that the improved self-esteem of these newly employed women is helping their children see a purpose for education and training for themselves. These families will be clients for many helping professionals in the years ahead. They are discussed in detail in Part II of this text.

Talk It Over

Are college roommates a family? Is an unmarried couple without children a family? Is your elderly great-grandparent who lives alone a family? Is a single parent rearing a child a family? Is a parent who lives with a son and his family part of the son's family? Discuss.

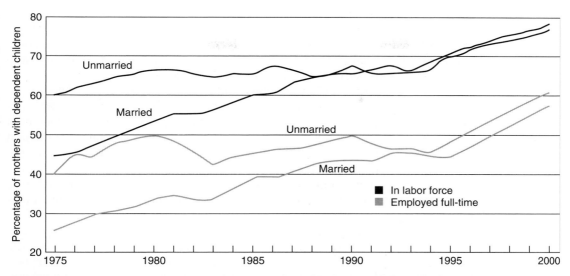

Figure 2.2   Employment Rates of Married and Unmarried Mothers with Dependent Children, 1975–2000

Source: U.S. Census Bureau, *Statistical Abstract of the United States: 2001*.

DIVERSE WORKFORCE

"Managing Cultural Diversity—On the Pitcher's Mound," shouted the headline in the *Wall Street Journal* (1998, September 30, p. B1). Editors found it newsworthy to report that the New York Yankees' manager had something rivaling the UN in the pitching staff he managed every day: an Australian, a Cuban, a Japanese, two Panamanians, plus several U.S. pitchers. Such is the scene in nearly every walk of life in the twenty-first century.

You'll meet people who differ from you everywhere you go today. People in communities everywhere are learning to interact with people in more open and accepting ways than might have been true some decades in the past.

For example, integration has been an ongoing objective of school systems since *Brown v. Topeka Board of Education* found "separate but equal" schools unacceptable. The ruling by the U.S. Supreme Court in 1954 was the landmark case that brought minority and majority children and teachers together, perhaps for the first time. Thus, because you've been in school since this time, it is likely that you've had some experience with diverse people. In more recent years the law spelling out rights for people with disabilities has come into effect. You can reflect on how you've felt as you've learned to meet and interact with people who look different from you. In the long run you'll feel more capable of meeting the demands of twenty-first century life if you use democratic and open reasoning in meeting new groups.

The result of more integrated elementary and high schools has been followed by increased integration of both students and faculty at the college and university level. With more highly educated minority students the work force has begun to include a wider group of graduates, and workforce diversity has been heightened. People from nearly all diverse groups have been drawn into workplaces.

Historically, women, racial minorities, and homosexuals have been the victims of discrimination in many workplaces. Some of this overt discrimination has subsided as people have become more familiar with each group and with settlement of court cases against many public entities, corporations, and universities over the past 30 or so years. There is, of course, still room for improvements, but today we can anticipate having highly qualified minorities, homosexuals, and women in any workforce. Thus, as students, you will all be helping the move toward a more diverse society as you graduate, no matter where you go. How you will fare may be a question you ponder.

Ageism, another stereotype, is a growing concern as the whole population ages due to medical success in keeping people alive and healthy. As youthful graduates, you may sometimes be frustrated that the positions you desire are still being filled by persons who have worked in those jobs for many years. Many senior citizens are encouraged to remain on the job past minimum retirement age for several reasons: Skilled labor is in short supply, seniors are still healthy and desire to keep their positions, and they also wish to continue contributing to their pension plans.

Newly trained and younger managerial personnel are learning new ways to provide leadership for these older workers. Discrimination is illegal, and managers must keep their employees performing at top-quality standards. Thus they must motivate older workers to learn new skills unknown to those individuals when they began their careers years earlier. Midcareer workers are being given incentives to retool continuously so they can continue to serve their employers. Continuing education is a fact of modern life—to keep workers attuned to new ideas and new ways to do things. The pace of change is expected to continue accelerating. This fact works against a parent who wishes to stay home for a few years for child rearing. It is hard to be up-to-date later on when wanting to return to the workforce.

Every age citizen is being confronted with new types of people serving in "traditional" roles. Take the 90-year-old Mrs. K in an assisted living environment. When she rang her buzzer and said she needed help to go to the bathroom, she reported being "shocked" to see that they'd sent a male worker. Mrs. K's age-old stereotype held that nurses and health workers were all women. Probably anticipating some resistance among the patients, a female supervisor accompanied and introduced the man, who was training to become a registered nurse. Together they helped Mrs. K, who grew to appreciate the man, especially his physical strength. Later on she showed preference for him after getting over her initial shock. Perhaps, men's physical strength was one of Mrs. K's stereotypes. That is, was he actually stronger than the female helpers?

A variation on this dilemma is the librarian who is asked by a minority student for certain occupational materials. In one era the librarian might have discouraged the student with the information that a particular field was "difficult to get into." Or, he might have suggested a field more in line with where he knew that minority persons work. However, in the present day the librarian would not want to prejudge that student's ability or later success in any field. Legally, occupations are expected to be open for qualified persons of each gender and every race and ethnic background. For instance, since higher education came under the civil rights legislation, professional schools, such as schools of veterinary and human medicine, engineering, and law, have increased their enrollments from a few percent women to 50 percent or more women—using equal opportunity standards. A record number of women in the list of honors graduates indicates that they have done exceptionally well as a group. The U.S. military forces include women in virtually all ranks and services.

EFFECTS ON HOME LIFE

The new type of workforce affects very directly the homes and families of workers. It also affects the individuals interacting with employees and students in these newly integrated work environments. For example, children who feel accepted in a new school may act happy both at home and at school. Adults whose sexist or racist humor is no longer accepted due to its prejudicial connotations may feel thwarted, with that feeling being transferred to the home.

Women who watch as male colleagues group together and go out to lunch feel frustrated. Women realize that even when they have scaled the high employment wall and have finally been hired, they may not easily be welcomed into the working environment or rise to higher levels—the so-called glass ceiling is in effect. They wonder whether they will ever be welcomed on projects requiring collaboration—as modern projects often require. A child or worker in difficult situations may bring home problems that come directly from the discrimination felt in the outside world.

Home and family life are affected by the new roles of women and men and even children. Egalitarianism gets greater discussion in homes today than in earlier times. Home roles are shifting, too, in case you haven't noticed.

School officials have responded to some in-school conflicts by training children to be playground or classroom arbitrators—helping reduce tensions when certain events occur. Children are trained to aid in conflict resolution to keep problems from getting worse and out of hand. Some school districts have adopted uniforms for children to wear at school, having discovered that clothing was the problem in some cases of friction.

Talk It Over

Reflect on your own experience of being part of a recently integrated school, neighborhood, workplace, or business. What happened? What were some pleasant positive experiences? What were the more difficult ones? Recall discussions in your school, neighborhood, home, or family that helped you through that period. List examples that include you or others. Discuss.

SERVING FAMILIES

Some agencies and programs are developed to be support services for families. Child-care centers, for example, are developed to help families care for and educate their children while parents are working. For families to remain strong, society must have high standards of care with regard to children's centers, so that children will develop appropriately. These are the formative years for young children and less than high-quality care could have damaging effects. Current professional efforts are devoted to improving standards for child care. Child care, formerly referred to as day care, has been available in the United States since the 1800s and thus is not a new support service for families. Today there are many types of child care, ranging from family child care in homes, to nonprofit centers, to centers operated by industries for their employees' children. The concept of dependent care during the day is also used to provide care for the elderly and is a growing service available to American families. Occasionally, the child and elder care are in the same facilities.

If your future work involves adult educational programs, you may be involved with individuals who must arrange your program around the needs of their family. A program leader must be sensitive to family demands of participants when setting location, needs for child care, and times for meetings. Certain programs are currently being designed to help unemployed parents obtain job training for future employment. Helpful attitudes toward family circumstances on the part of directors and instructors in such programs will largely determine whether the participating parent succeeds or fails in the new schooling endeavor.

Children's needs are a priority for parents taking classes. Having a babysitter cancel on a class night or having a sick child at exam time are devastating situations for any parent. Patience, understanding, helpfulness, and procedures that accommodate these emergencies are hallmarks of good service in those who work with parents, particularly parents with young children.

Being "family friendly" has become a mark of excellence for some American corporations. These companies have developed programs that help their employees deal with family concerns while interfering little with their work. For example, numerous on-site child-care centers have been established in industries across the country. With flextime, employees are able to select a work schedule different from the typical 8 to 5, and this has become a possibility in cooperation with other employees. Some people may begin working at 7 A.M. and leave at 4 P. M. Others may work 10 hours a day for four days a week, rather than 8 hours for five. Two people may actually fill one position, or "job share." Through the use of interactive communications and computers, many employees are able to conduct a part, perhaps even a substantial portion, of their work from a home office. Family friendly employers are being recognized for encouraging parents, both mothers and fathers, to use their family leave when an infant is born or adopted. You may already be part of an organization that is considered supportive of families. Or, you may want to select your professional career from such a family-friendly setting. Each fall *Working Mother* magazine identifies family-friendly corporations and workplaces.

Whatever your career choice, you'll surely have contact with families, if not in your job, perhaps in your neighborhood or in your own extended family. Many careers involve opportunities to serve individuals who are part of families. Other careers may serve the whole family as a unit. Whether serving individuals or families as a whole, being informed about families can only contribute to your success.

For instance, you'll likely have immediate interaction with parents if you are a teacher of children, a physician maintaining the health of children, or a law enforcement officer taking juveniles into custody. You can logically assume that these children or youths have parents who are expected to be responsible for them and whom you'll need to contact. Indeed, in the first two cases, parents are likely to contact you.

Suppose that your career deals with products; for example, engineering or agricultural products. Although you may actually be designing structures or producing various products, people in families will use them. And people from families will help produce them. You may serve in your spare time on a school board or on a Chamber of Commerce committee where service to the community's families is a goal. Also, your employees, friends, neighbors, coworkers, and others generally live in family groups. This course will aid you in understanding families of different kinds.

RIGHTS OF INDIVIDUALS AND FAMILIES

The U.S. Constitution provides the very foundation for the rights or protections for individuals and, therefore, their families. Any professional interaction as well as other interpersonal relationships with individuals and families must conform to these constitutional protections. Two amendments stand out as being significant for everyone. These are the first and fourteenth amendments.

First Amendment

Congress shall make no law respecting an establishment of religion, or prohibiting the free exercise thereof; or abridging the freedom of speech, or of the press, or the right of the people peaceably to assemble, and to petition the Government for a redress of grievances.

The First Amendment instructs us as citizens to allow others to have their say and to exercise our own rights to speak up for the good of all. The organization you become involved in must assure people that they can exercise their freedom of religion and be confident that it neither gains them favors nor causes them to be excluded.

Planning for the free exercise of these rights needs to be part of any organization's bylaws, policies, and practices.

Fourteenth Amendment

. . . No state shall make or enforce any law which shall abridge the privileges or immunities of citizens of the United States; nor shall any State deprive any person of life, liberty, or property, without due process of law; nor deny to any person within its jurisdiction the equal protection of the laws. . . .

Talk It Over

Discuss specific ways the First Amendment applies to you and your family. Recall any instance in your community or in a news story where an individual tested this amendment. Discuss why Americans might accept these rights casually.

Talk It Over

What due process procedures exist to protect your rights in your college or in your housing arrangement? Discuss.

Most organizations have written bylaws, policies, and procedures for providing due process to those they serve or hire. That is, if a problem occurs on the job or with regard to the service, there is an established written procedure for the individual or family to express their concern and an opportunity for those responsible to make constructive suggestions and work out acceptable remedies. Without proper procedures within the policies of businesses, institutions, and other organizations, the courts become the last resort for due process, as legal action is taken.

FEDERAL LAWS

A number of federal laws, in addition to the Constitution, offer various protections to individuals and directly or indirectly to families. A few of the primary laws will be described briefly. Your librarian can help you gain more information about a specific law or a certain type of legal protection. Laws of this type are continually being evaluated and may be amended. As professionals you must become aware of the laws that apply within your professional arena. Certain laws are usually on the books that authorize the service in the first place. You should know about those laws and read the standards for your particular service and discuss them with your supervisor, especially any laws or standards you do not understand. You are obligated to follow the laws governing your service.

Later, as a professional, you may be in a position to make recommendations for changes in laws. The laws listed and briefly described here are the more prominent ones. However, there are literally hundreds of laws that affect individuals and families in their homes and places of work. Your librarian can help you find out details of laws on any topic, as well as the history of the legislation, including the social conditions that led to the passage of the laws.

EXAMPLES OF U.S. LAWS THAT APPLY WIDELY

1. *Civil Rights Act of 1964—Title VII (amended in 1972 and 1978)*. This act, when passed, was the most comprehensive civil rights legislation in U.S. history. It contains provisions for parity in the use and enjoyment of public accommodations, facilities, and education as well as federally assisted programs and employment. It prohibits discrimination because of race, color, religion, sex, or national origin (*The Guide to American Law*, Vol. 2, pp. 339–349). The Pregnancy Discrimination Act of 1978 was an amendment to the Civil Rights Act, Title VII, that prevented the practice of firing workers because of pregnancy (*The Guide to American Law*, Vol. 4, p. 334).

2. *Voting Rights Act of 1965 and Voter Registration Act of 1993*. The 1965 Act established guidelines for courts to follow in cases involving voting rights discrimination. It provided that no policy or procedure may be adapted or maintained by state officials for discriminatory purposes (*The Guide to American Law*, 1987 Supplement, p. 334). The 1993 act allows a citizen who has reached age 18 or older to register to vote while obtaining a driver's license or to send in a voter registration by mail (*The Guide to American Law*, 1994 Supplement, p. 475). Both acts help individuals gain fuller access to the voting process, one of the hallmarks of a democracy.

3. *1968 Fair Housing Act*. A fair housing program was part of the Civil Rights Act of 1968 that focused on discrimination in public housing and created the mandate for equal access to housing for persons and families regardless of race, color, creed, sex, or national origin. Efforts to reach this goal still continue, including a ruling in 1991 that pertained to advertisements in the *New York Times* for rental or sale of housing stating that it was unlawful to "publish any . . . advertisement, with respect to the sale or rental of a dwelling that indicates any preference . . . based on race" (*The Guide to American Law*, 1992 Supplement, pp. 308–309). Accepting diversity in housing has been a long time coming in America.

4. *Equal Pay Act of 1963*. This act requires equal pay for men and women performing similar work (*The Guide to American Law*, Vol. 9, p. 230).

5. *The Fair Labor Standards Act of 1938 (1972 amendments).* Often referred to as the "Wage and Hour Law," the act established a minimum wage, equal pay, and recordkeeping requirements. It forbade the use of child labor under the age of 16 and prohibited the use of workers under the age of 18 in those occupations deemed dangerous (*The Guide to American Law*, Vol. 5, p. 137).

6. *Vietnam Era Veterans' Readjustment Assistance Act of 1974.* Prohibits job discrimination and requires affirmative action to employ and advance in employment qualified Vietnam veterans.

7. *Executive Orders 11246 and 11375 (of President Lyndon Johnson).* Both executive orders relate to providing equal opportunity in employment. This mandate began with employment in federal government positions, over which President Johnson had the most control, and expanded over the years. The executive orders listed here require an affirmative action program by all federal contractors and subcontractors with a contract of $10,000 or more (Johnson, 1964–1965, p. 334, and p. 684).

8. *Rehabilitation Act of 1973 (amended 1974).* Prohibits job discrimination because of disability and requires affirmative action in employing and advancing in employment qualified workers with disabilities. The amendments of 1974 required modification of public buildings or facilities financed by federal aid to provide individuals with physical disabilities with means of access to them. This act is a forerunner of the 1990 Americans with Disabilities Act (*Guide to American Law*, Vol. 6, pp. 3–4).

9. *Education for All Handicapped Children Act of 1975.* This act provides the incentive for making available to individuals with disabilities the opportunities formerly denied to them. A "free and appropriate public education" must be available to children with disabilities comparable to the educational opportunities provided to other children in the public schools (*Guide to American Law*, Vol. 6, pp. 3–4).

10. *Social Security Act (Social Security Act of 1935 and Federal Insurance Contributions Act).* Provides retirement, disability, burial, and survivor benefits to eligible employees and self-employed individuals. In 1939 Congress created a separate benefit for the dependent wives, children, widows, and parents of wage earners—to soften the economic hardship created when a family loses a wage earner's support. Today, fathers left with dependent children may receive the benefit, too. In 1935 the law reached only workers in industry and commerce; however, in the 1950s the act was extended to most self-employed individuals, and nearly all jobs are covered by Social Security today. The spouse of a retired worker who reaches 62 can receive benefits equal to half of the worker's benefits. Supplemental Security Income (SSI) provides extra payments for those who are blind, over 65, or disabled (*The Guide to American Law*, Vol. 9, pp. 286–298).

11. *Occupational Safety and Health Act of 1970.* Requires that employers furnish employees a safe place to work. Under this act, standards are promulgated, penalties are established for noncompliance, and investigations of hazardous working conditions are made (*The Guide to American Law*, Vol. 7, p. 37).

12. *The Age Discrimination in Employment Act of 1967 (amended 1978).* Prohibits discrimination against persons 40 to 70 years of age in any area of employment (*The Guide to American Law*, Vol. 4, p. 337).

13. *National Research Act of 1974.* An act requiring anyone doing research with human subjects of any age to obtain informed consent without undue influence, force, or deceit (*The Guide to American Law*, Vol. 8, p. 151). This act requires a board to screen all research projects to assure that an individual's rights are protected.

14. *Americans with Disabilities Act of 1990.* Title I prohibits discrimination against individuals with disabilities by requiring equal employment opportunities.

    Title II requires equal availability and accessibility in state and local government programs and services, including transportation.

    Title III prohibits discrimination in public accommodations and services, such as hotels, restaurants, grocery stores, retail stores, service establishments, and other public facilities.

    Title IV addresses communication, particularly telecommunications.

    Title V contains miscellaneous provisions regarding the continued viability of state or other federal laws providing people with disabilities with greater protection, various generally applicable rules, and provisions of the Architectural and Transportation Barriers Compliance Board (Cross, Cantwell, & Summers, 1993).

15. *Family and Medical Leave Act of 1993.* The act permits workers to take up to 12 weeks of unpaid leave of absence each year for family illness, childbirth, or adoption, and it requires employers to maintain workers' insurance benefits and assure their job after their leave. This act is considered a significant advance in employee rights and the strengthening of families, and it places workers somewhat on par with families in other advanced industrial nations (*The Guide to American Law*, 1994 Supplement, p. 455).

16. *Government in the Sunshine Act.* This act requires that boards of public decision-making bodies give adequate public notice of the forthcoming meetings of these committees, councils, and the like, and conduct their meetings in public. This act has brought many decisions out in the open when formerly they might have been made secretly in political deals. More democracy, fairness, and representation have thus become available to all citizens (*Federal Register*, 1992).

17. *Personal Responsibility and Work Opportunity Reconciliation Act of 1996.* This law (PA 104-193) became known as the welfare reform law. It makes sweeping changes in the program of federal assistance for families in poverty. Aid to Families with Dependent Children (AFDC) was replaced. Block grants to the states put the monies closer to home with local decision makers. The law reduces by large sums spending for federal welfare. Training programs for parents are coupled with child-care grants to support getting parents trained for jobs, into paying positions, and off welfare. Stringent rules were established to keep recipients on a track of progress toward self-sufficiency and off assistance in the future (U.S. Government Printing Office, 1996).

STATE AND LOCAL LAWS

Laws vary considerably among the various states and localities. These laws must extend federal benefits and not provide less than the federal legislation and the rulings of the U.S. Supreme Court designate. For information or free brochures regarding protections under your local or state laws, contact your local and state governmental agencies.

Talk It Over

Considering these laws and amendments, are there any that you think are unnecessary? Discuss a law that you have had personal experience with.

As a professional or a citizen affected by any of these laws, you can make a contribution by recommending amendments to or enforcement of laws. Your local or state bodies will hold hearings when new amendments are offered to laws or new laws are being discussed. You are welcome to attend such hearings. You can learn about the hearings through the appropriate legislative committee. Also, you are free to testify in the time allotted for testimony if you have information that would be helpful. Students often find such hearings very informative.

YOUR CAREER GOALS

Sometimes students, upon graduation, expect to return to their own communities and serve. Of course, this goal can indicate a personal dedication to service and an understanding of the needs in their own communities. However, it can also indicate a desire for a safe haven, a place where clients will be more like them. Remember, even in your own hometown, you'll find diversity among families. Very few families could be expected to have your exact background. Each professional with a career in a helping profession will be a member of some minority group that some clients won't readily identify with. Additional information about families will be essential to your service, even in your hometown. A broader professional career objective would be to serve families in a culturally sensitive manner, regardless of any particular individual characteristics.

Knowledge, skill, and professional expertise are paramount in any career. Surely another goal is to be accepted as a professional, offering expertise to families without necessarily having the personal experience. For example, a single person can be called on to serve married persons. A person of one race or religion can be called on to serve persons of other races or religions. Persons from cities can work with people from rural areas and vice versa. Individuals without children can serve those with children, and so on.

At a recent university graduation when the medical school degrees were presented, a member of the audience whispered to her friend in the next seat, "I wouldn't want to go to them." "Why?" asked her friend, wondering if it was because many were women. "Because they are so young," came the reply. If such a biased attitude prevails, new young physicians have much work ahead of them to gain the confidence of the older people many will serve.

BEING PROFESSIONAL

Being both professional and excellent in your specialization requires objective, yet empathetic, controlled, yet emotional responses to a client's needs. You'll need methods, sensitivity, and experience to be both empathetic and professional simultaneously. When an individual needs a professional service, the diversity between himself or herself and the professional sought should matter little. For example, like the employees in the hospital emergency room described in the opening anecdote, all professionals need to fulfill their responsibilities in rapid sequence without regard for the racial, ethnic, or other characteristics of those individuals needing emergency care. Close family members or friends may display emotion, but professionals must be in control of their emotions and proceed quietly, methodically, thoroughly, and objectively in performing the services for which they were trained and licensed.

Families and individuals have many legal protections as they seek the services of professionals. Through study and experience you'll learn to recognize and appreciate the differing characteristics of individuals and families and be better able to help them obtain the services needed.

Many professionals are doing an excellent job today serving as role models for preprofessionals like yourself who are preparing to join them in the workforce. Many professional organizations have worked hard for years to bring more equity and diversity into their workplace. There is still much to be done before the goal of equity is achieved. The role you will play is an important one.

FAMILY-RELATED SCIENCES

A variety of family-related sciences will help provide the information you will receive in this course. We draw on scientific studies, our own professional experiences, and those of professionals in many fields. Our goal is to help you study, analyze, and understand more fully the wide variety of families you may encounter in your career. This course will teach you frameworks for looking at each family and ways of analyzing any new type of family that presents itself. With your greater understanding, your services will reach more families successfully and have a positive impact on society. As a result, you will find satisfaction in the services you are able to render.

STRENGTHS OF FAMILIES

Your study will focus on the strengths of families. This approach contrasts with a tendency to focus on the pathologies or deficits of certain families, implying that the pathologies are associated with the entire group.

Talk It Over

What are the strengths of the family you grew up in? How did those strengths facilitate your entry into college?

"What are family strengths?" you may be asking. Strengths might include the family's willingness and ability to manage limited resources tightly to make them cover essentials. Or, a strength can be a family's mutual love and respect for each member. Parents sacrificing for their children's education might be another strength. Another family strength would be parents who exercise strong control over their children's whereabouts, education, or goals. Still another strength might involve the cohesion within the family and the extended family, exhibiting shared effort among family members, perhaps of several generations.

"What are family deficits or pathologies?" The deficit or pathological approach might focus on the family's impoverished situation, an absent parent, lack of job skills, or poor housing.

Funding agencies, attempting to fix certain problems, may pressure professionals to use a so-called pathological approach to any problems. For example, a Mexican American educator was asked to participate in a study that focused on the deficits of people in her community. She asked the psychologists why they could not focus on the strengths the people brought to their families. The psychologist replied, "Because you can't get funding for that type of research." The woman's professional experience showed her that many of the families had strengths, which, if documented, could lead to positive suggestions for the troubled families of the community.

Another project used a door-to-door survey to describe the characteristics of an inner-city neighborhood. When the results were presented, the negative, or problem, statistics were emphasized. Yet, looking at the data, one could see that a sizable percentage of people were making it in that community. Why not ask, "How do these people make it? What are their strengths?" The answers to these questions may give clues to help those who fall by the wayside.

Talk It Over

What are pathologies of a family you know or have recently read about? Have those pathologies hindered the family members from meeting goals? (To protect privacy, avoid using any real names in your discussion.)

Biographies are good sources of success stories, giving insights into the strengths of individuals, often showing the family support, and sometimes sacrifice, that helped the individual persevere to greatness. You can ask your own professors, for example, about any mentors who made a difference in their careers. Behind their cloak of prestige often lies a very humble beginning with key models or supporters encouraging them along the way.

✧ CONCLUSIONS

Families differ widely throughout our country, primarily because they are composed of groups of unique individuals that do not fit some preconceived model. The U.S. Constitution and many laws are designed to protect individuals and families from discrimination. Professionals must be conscientiously aware of these legal protections and must be ready to defend them when necessary.

As you discuss issues presented in this chapter, you may find you disagree with your classmates or the instructor. In a democracy, dissent is not treason. However, learning to disagree agreeably and respectfully is essential. Like your senator on the floor of the Senate, learn to argue with decorum. The person you disagree with today may be a powerful ally tomorrow. What is needed is an orderly, thoughtful discussion of the various ideas, the separation of facts and myths, and a sharing of views concerning the many issues on the table. Those of you who have had the experience of taking various sides in debate classes or on debate teams can help your classmates learn the technique of effective debating.

Clearly, the need to discuss diversity and discrimination is immediate, and the responsibility for serious thinking and the development of some creative solutions rests on us all. Let your study of knowing and serving families with their many ethnic and structural variations proceed rapidly, thus preparing you to help solve pressing societal problems.

✦ STUDY QUESTIONS

1. Define a family.
2. Define and discuss stereotyping.
3. Make a list of 10 ways different professionals help families.
4. (a) Write down the First Amendment to the U.S. Constitution.
   (b) Think about, then explain, how this amendment relates to family rights.
5. (a) Write down the Fourteenth Amendment to the U.S. Constitution.
   (b) Think about, then explain, how this amendment relates to family rights.
6. (a) List the 17 federal laws described in the chapter that assure special rights to individuals.
   (b) Paraphrase the essential right provided by each one, especially how each law applies to a family. Describe family life without this protection. Share your views with your classmates. If you have had special experience with a law, be sure to share your experience with others.
7. Indicate the positive and negative aspects of the statement, "I want to work with my own people."
8. List 10 major characteristics of a professional. Star those that you have achieved. Place a # symbol before ones you are working on presently. Discuss.
9. (a) Think of a family you know. Write a paragraph differentiating between studying that family from a *strengths* perspective and studying that family from a *deficits* or *pathological* perspective.
   (b) Give examples of how a deficit usually does not include the whole person or a whole family and why this fact can be a strength.
10. (a) Describe how our senators and congressional representatives argue with decorum.
    (b) Explain how this style can facilitate class discussion. (Watch a session of C-SPAN television for examples.)

✦ APPLICATIONS

1. Analyze the features of the Bubolz-Sontag definition of family. Select your own or another family you know well and, using pseudonyms, state
   (a) Who makes up the family?
   (b) What would be "common goals and resources"?
   (c) What would be "commitment"?
   (d) What does "over time" mean?
   State your definition of family. Discuss how the Bubolz-Sontag definition differs or agrees with your own definition.
2. (a) State your present proposed profession or career.
   (b) Write a two- to three-page analysis of how a person in that career or profession will have contact with or serve families or individuals who are part of

families. State at least three laws that would be prominent in your work with families. Describe a typical work day for a person in your profession.

3. Reread the First Amendment to the U.S. Constitution quoted in the text. Write a two-page essay on how you think that amendment applies to the content of this book. (See the Table of Contents, Dedication, and Preface.)

4. Reread the Fourteenth Amendment to the U.S. Constitution quoted in the text. Write a two-page essay on how you think that amendment applies to the content of this book. (See the Table of Contents, Dedication, and Preface.)

5. Reread the sample of laws relating to individual rights. Select one law and write a 100-word essay on how it affects families.

6. Interview three people from three different families. Ask them to evaluate their contact with a helping professional in recent months. Using pseudonyms, write a two-page report on the positive and negative aspects of what these people encountered in their contact with professionals and the help or lack thereof they received. Discuss.

7. Take, from a newspaper or magazine, a story involving a family or individual *and* a professional person. Describe the interaction with the professional depicted in the article. Write down your own opinions regarding the interaction, and connect your views with those mentioned in the chapter.

✦ MEDIA RESOURCES

Videos

Seeds of Change—Leadership and Staff Development. Video, 30 minutes. Professional development of teachers in structuring ways schools and communities help children. (Available from National Association for the Education of Young Children, 1509 16th Street N.W., Washington, DC 20036-1426, Phone 1-800-424-2460)

✦ KEY INTERNET RESOURCES

American Family Rights Association
   www.familyrightsassociation.com/

Child Welfare Information Gateway
   www.childwelfare.gov/systemwide/laws_policies/federal/index.cfm

FindLaw for the Public
   http://family.findlaw.com/

Talking About Stereotypes
   www.familyeducation.com/article/0,1120,24-6364,00.html

→ FURTHER READING

Blank, R. M. (2002). Fighting poverty: Lessons from recent U.S. history. *Journal of Economic Perspectives, 14*(2), 3–19.

Blank, R. M., & Haskins, R. (Eds.). (2001). *The new world of welfare*. Washington, DC: Brookings Institution.

Brooks-Gunn, J., Duncan, G. J., & Aber, J. L. (Eds.). (1997). *Neighborhood poverty: Context and consequences for children* (Vol. 1). New York: Russell Sage Foundation.

Danziger, S. H., & Haveman, R. (Eds.). (2002). *Understanding poverty*. Cambridge, MA: Harvard University Press.

Dorris, M. (1990). *The broken cord*. New York: Harper Perennial.

Duncan, G. J., & Chase-Lansdale, P. L. (2002). *For better and for worse: Welfare reform and the well-being of children and families*. New York: Russell Sage Foundation.

Edin, K., & Lein, L. (1997). *Making ends meet: How single mothers survive welfare and low-wage work*. New York: Russell Sage Foundation.

Ehrenreich, B. (2001). *Nickel and dimed: On (not) getting by in America*. New York: Metropolitan Books.

Katz, M. B. (1997). *In the shadow of the poorhouse: A social history of welfare in America*. New York: Basic Books.

Keister, A. (2000). *Wealth in America: Trends in wealth inequality*. Cambridge, England: Cambridge University Press.

Landes, D. S. (1999). *The wealth and poverty of nations: Why some are so rich and some so poor*. New York: Norton.

Lichter, D. T. (2002). Welfare reform: How do we measure success? *Annual Review of Sociology, 28*, 117–141.

O'Connell, M. (1993). *"Where's papa?" Fathers' role in child care*. Washington, DC: Population Reference Bureau.

Pruett, K. D. (1987). *The nurturing father*. New York: Warner Books.

Stier, H., & Tienda, M. (2001). *The color of opportunity: Pathways to family welfare and work*. Chicago: University of Chicago Press.

Wu, L. L., & Wolfe, B. (Eds.). (2001). *Out of wedlock: Causes and consequences of nonmarital fertility*. New York: Russell Sage Foundation.

3

Systems for Knowing Families

→ Key Concepts

- Intercultural Communication
- Family System
- Family Ecosystem
- Principles of Empowerment
- Human Capital
- Family Functions

Pearson Learning Photo Studio

WHICH FAMILIES SHALL WE STUDY?

Families, like individuals, come in many varieties because of member ages, genders, and numbers. How do we begin this study to help us as we begin our work with families? Should we look at families like some of the following families?

Family A: Is our family like the farmer's family—twelve girls and one boy—the result of the parents' intense desire for a male heir that drove them to keep trying for a boy until one finally arrived?

Family B: Is our family a two-child family, preschoolers—one boy and one girl two years apart—with both parents employed outside the home, or is one parent a stay-at-home dad—or mom?

Family C: Is our family a widow or a widower with two dependent children under school age living on one low income and using public child-care services?

Family D: Is our family an elderly couple trying to manage their affairs independently and wondering how they will manage financially if one becomes ill and cannot be cared for at home?

Family E: Is our family an immigrant family straining to become skilled in English and wanting their two children to become part of the mainstream by attending school and speaking English?

Family F: Is our family one with multiple health problems, with worries about finances and mobility for the four children and the parents?

Family G: Is our family one with four children headed by the mother who is attempting to become trained for a viable job to get off welfare and into the mainstream?

Family H: Is our family an upper-income family where the adults focus on earning money and pay scant attention to their two teenagers, a boy and a girl?

Family I: Is our family one that focuses on youth sports or Scouts to the point that every extra moment is devoted to their two sons and to helping in that organization or in practices or travel to the next tournament?

Family J: Is our family a young college student couple recently married and setting up their first apartment on the beginning wages of the two?

Family K: Is our family a middle-age couple with a moderate income and house and includes the mother of one of the adults—as is typical in that partner's culture?

Family L: Is our "family" a single elderly woman—the fastest growing segment of society—living alone with little to moderate actual financial support from savings or programs?

Family M: Is our family a divorced couple with an out-of-the-home nonsupportive husband—presenting evidence of mental illness and homelessness—who occasionally visits the boy and girl of school age in the home paid for by the mother and who makes elaborate promises, some of which are inappropriate and others that he can't or won't keep?

Family N: Is our family a single pregnant 18-year-old trying to finish high school and to establish stability for herself and her forthcoming child, hoping the child will have the opportunity and stability she's never had?

****

Here we have 14 examples of family configurations that might be considered typical as a cross section of any American community where you might be hired to work professionally following graduation. Given your type of family professional expertise, how will you begin to figure out how to approach your professional service tasks?

Kim went out to the garage to start her car for the 20-minute trip to work. The car failed to respond to the touch of the key in the ignition. "Now what's wrong?" exclaimed Kim in a panicky voice. After trying the lights, Kim made a quick diagnosis: "The battery is DEAD!" Kim's quick test showed that the car's electrical system was without energy.

USING A SYSTEMS APPROACH

Investigating various systems is routine in diagnosing mechanical difficulties in equipment and even social problems in modern society. A *system* is defined as *a group of devices or an organization forming a network for a common purpose.* For instance, a secretary congratulated herself on how much work she had accomplished one morning and realized that there had not been the usual telephone calls that interrupted her work. Picking up the phone, she heard no dial tone and concluded that the telephone system was not working. "No wonder things were quiet," she exclaimed. The telephone is an important part of a modern communication system.

When the telephone, water, or electrical system temporarily fails, we realize how dependent modern society is on various systems that are all linked together in a maze of interconnections. Individuals and families confront many such systems every day of their lives.

Your body has numerous systems as well. You know that there are interconnections between systems from your study of the skeletal, respiratory, reproductive, and cardiac systems in biology class.

As you go about your daily routine, take time to think about the various systems you use each day. Knowing about a system helps you learn how to get the most out of that system and how to fix it if problems arise. For example, the starter on Kim's car responded when she properly attached jumper cables from another car's battery to her car's battery. This activated the electrical system to start the car.

COMMUNICATION FOR HELPING PROFESSIONALS

Communication with diverse individuals and families will become a necessity as you move into your volunteer and career roles in the helping professions. Communication is a two-way street between you and your clients, customers, patients, students, or others. Communication probably requires some reorientation and new learning for you, as it does for most persons who branch out to serve others in the helping professions. Recall that, in a certain sense, we are all minorities to some of those we will serve; thus bridging the communication gap is essential.

Intercultural communication has become an important science as business and political leaders have moved into the international arena. The skills they are learning have meaning for any of us working with people who are different from ourselves.

Striving for *shared meaning* will be our goal. Shared meaning involves understanding each other in both written and spoken language, in body language, and in concepts. Achieving shared meaning will take time and effort on your part. Even if we speak the same basic language, we may not fully understand another person. Humor is a case in point. With shared meaning we can laugh heartily; without shared meaning many things are simply not funny. However discouraged we become, we must still keep trying to communicate. Meanings are in people, and striving for shared meaning is fundamental to building positive relationships.

Every act of communication is in some sense an intercultural one, according to Sarbaugh (1988), a specialist in intercultural communication. Studies show that the more alike you and another person are in terms of feelings, beliefs, materials, helping with tasks, or working together on a common activity, the more positive the relationship will be perceived. Thus being aware of the differences between yourself and another individual or family will encourage you to work hard to create a positive relationship and arrive at shared meanings. Rather than give up your personal integrity, you increase it as you develop new ways of interacting with and understanding others.

Studying communication and racism, Teun (1987) found that persons within a group tend to stress differences between themselves, whereas when talking to or discussing members of other groups, people stress similarities or common ground. The in-group members tended to minimize differences between ethnic groups and between ethnic group members. That is, Asian Americans might discuss their similarities to Hispanics, and note their differences among all other Asian groups.

In studying new information of any kind, individuals who discriminate typically tend to look for *similarities,* but when looking at members of their own group tend to look at the *differences,* according to Teun (1987). For clearer reciprocal interaction, it is necessary to observe both the similarities and differences you find in your clients, customers, patients, students, or the like.

A helping professional must look beyond the social, cultural, selective-focusing and attention-getting veneer of a new client or even a coworker, and attempt to understand what is really going on. A thorough and critical look at one's own biases is a necessary step. To this end, some organizations have routine workshops to help people discuss their own ethnic, racial, gender, or age biases so they can move on to new levels of service.

Old stereotypes and ethnocentric ideas often get in the way of progress. Some of these are reinforced in the media. The most subtle stereotypes provide models of ethnic groups in negative behaviors or situations. Classic examples are the social topics of urban decay and rundown neighborhoods. Indirectly, this negative image is attributed to a given ethnic group. As you study many aspects of American life, you'll learn that stereotypes are often unfounded. The effort you'll make in this course will be an important step in overcoming stereotypical biases.

Communication is a two-way street where you can learn something every day and still have much to learn. Many clients may speak languages other than English, so you'll have additional avenues to explore to be able to communicate with them effectively. Learning to communicate in another language is a long-range effort that is worthy of your time and attention. If you have the interest and take time to learn a single word or phrase, that effort will be rewarded by someone longing for empathetic support.

A SYSTEMS APPROACH TO STUDYING FAMILIES

A number of approaches are used in understanding and describing the family. The *functional family* is one defined by shared activities: shared household living, shared responsibility for daily life, and shared child rearing. The *legal family* is defined by legal structures that are altered by divorce or adoption of children. The *biological family* is defined by blood relationships between parents and children, between siblings, and between and among blood relatives of present and former generations. The *interpersonal family* is defined by the perceptions of its members.

A *systems approach* for studying the family uses an integrative method that is holistic, dynamic, and adaptable to change. A systems approach can be used with any of the definitions of the family. The main reason for studying the family system, for you as helping professionals, is because the family is assumed to be economically responsible for and socially and emotionally influential in the care, treatment, and education of its individuals. A good plan for regaining the health of an individual can become sidetracked if the family does not understand the plan or is unable to follow through. Or, in contrast, the family can be so successful with a plan that recovery is swift and thorough.

System Effects

Various scientists are studying the systems of their particular field of inquiry. They find that systems are linked with a larger whole. According to Jervis (1997), there are *system effects* that occur as the larger system is studied. Within systems are found other systems linked together in an interdependent relationship so that any change in any one system will have an effect on all other related systems. Jervis shows how several system effects must be considered; there are interconnections within a system, and indirect and delayed system effects. He says that human systems can have an important and often overlooked effect on social and political life. For example, in their original family system, when the couple adds an infant, many changes in the family system occur. The couple's developing system of interacting, eating, financing, scheduling, even sleeping, may change radically. The system will increase in complexity as additional children are added to their family system. System effects must be considered and accounted for in any analysis.

When a government makes an effort to help a segment of its families, the system effects will have ramifications for other segments of the populace. The 1996 legislation known as welfare reform (see Chapter 2) required many system changes. For example, changes occurred within the social welfare system, the immigration system, the food stamp system, the economic system, and the child-care and adult education systems. Of course, many changes were occurring within the individual family systems being affected. Also, you can imagine the effects of this one piece of legislation on the local, state, and federal government offices across the nation and on charitable systems related to the social welfare system.

Feedback within the system's parts must be taken into consideration. Feedback can be negative or positive. Both kinds of feedback are to be expected and should be looked for, even though predictions from it can be imprecise. The more complex the system, the more difficult the feedback predictions will become.

The Human Ecological System

The *human ecological system* is a holistic approach to studying the family system. Psychologist Urie Bronfenbrenner (1979) viewed the individual as being linked to the family and the community. There is reciprocal influence of each on the other. He described four entities or systems that influence individuals: *microsystems, mesosystems, exosystems,* and *macrosystems.* These systems are envisioned as concentric circles around the individual, the community, and the larger environments. The closest are *microsystems,* the immediate settings containing the individual, such as the family. The *mesosystems* consist of the various microsystems regularly involving the individual. For example, for a school-age child the family microsystem and the school microsystem are linked together as the mesosystem of the child. However, for the family members who are not regularly involved in the school, the child's mesosystem becomes an *exosystem.* The *macrosystem* refers to the outside institutions of the culture, such as religious beliefs and practices, and the political and economic influences of society. These four systems form the "context" in which the individual and child function. Bronfenbrenner advocated analyzing the total context when planning programs for or facing difficulties with children.

The individual's and family's interactions with the physical-biological and the sociocultural environments make up the *human ecosystem.* For example, in the human ecological approach, the teacher or physician planning strategies for helping a child must connect with the parents who are responsible for the child and who will, in all likelihood, be in charge of carrying out the plan. Social scientists studying and serving humans have borrowed the concept of ecology, meaning the relationship of an organism with its environments, from natural scientists to show the extent to which the individuals (organisms) are in a relationship with the environment.

The Family as an Ecosystem

The *family as an ecosystem* is a conceptual framework for studying the family that builds on Bronfenbrenner's human ecological approach and on other approaches from natural science. Hook and Paolucci (1970) emphasized the mutual transactions that link people and environments, and the creative decisions families make to adapt to the environment and to foster human development. The family ecosystem is an *open system* with interactions flowing between and among (1) the *natural physical–biological environment,* (2) the *human-built environment,* and (3) the *sociocultural environment.* The family interacts with and is interdependent on the total environment (Bubolz and Sontag, 1993, pp. 419–448).

Families have many uncertainties that require far more understanding than a car. Family scholars Griffore and Phenice (2001) suggest using the *family ecological system* in thinking about advising families because this system includes ways to think about and analyze human–environmental relationships, including the human interactions and distinct factors that go on within families (pp. 9–12).

Natural Physical–Biological Environment.   The natural environment includes the climate, rainfall, water, land, forests, plants, animals, minerals, and other physical–biological resources available to the family or influencing the family's economic situation through the type of jobs available for the family's livelihood. The natural resources available will affect the family and the systems that serve families. One example might be a small village where most people make their living working in a gold mine in round-the-clock shifts. The big concern for such a village is what to do for a livelihood when the gold ore has all been processed.

Human-Built Environment.   The human-built environment includes all alterations made by people and transformations of the natural physical-biological environment over the centuries as they have served human needs, Urban settlements, buildings, cultivated land, medicine, and material artifacts such as school books are only a few examples of alterations and transformations made over time to the natural environment by human beings. Every community is now becoming aware of the toxic by-products from these alterations and transformations of the environment. The problems created by these changes, such as polluted air and water, have become prominent social issues demanding action.

Systems have been developed in every segment of life, for instance, in agriculture, transportation, education, medicine, business, government, and religion. Such systems have altered and transformed the natural physical-biological environment over the centuries. The early American pioneers, for example, strongly supported the establishment of schools for their children. Schools were often created as soon as a settlement was staked out. In many instances, one pioneer mother or daughter served as a teacher in a simple one-room school built by neighbors out of local materials.

Sociocultural Environment.   The sociocultural environment includes the other human beings, community organizations, language, laws, values, and patterns of behaviors. It also includes human population levels, family size, family structure, and the communications among family members, kinship groups, and the greater society. In the family ecosystem approach, understanding situations facing families contributes to the success of any venture purporting to improve life for children.

You can think of the three environments just described as three concentric or embedded circles with the family at the point enclosed by each of the three circles. This conceptualization indicates that each of the three environments affects the family and, also, that the family affects each of the three environments. Imagine a water bed as you think of these interacting forces. Any pressure at one point will cause movement in other parts of the system.

ADAPTATION

Individuals and families interacting with and modifying the environment in which they function can help create an improved quality of life. Individual values and goals are often framed and reframed as people strive together to invent ways to address family concerns. As in a natural ecosystem, the family adapts and changes the state or structure of the family system. According to Bubolz and Sontag (1993, p. 433), the family modifies its environment to meet goals, detect information, select from a range of possible alternative responses, and respond. Through feedback, the family modifies its structure and organization. This requires knowledge, commitment, creativity, and energy from family members.

In human systems, constant exchanges are going on. Exchanges of energy, information, matter, and resources come into play. *Negative feedback* and *positive feedback* occur continuously in families as they deal with exchanges. That is, experienced individuals may know when something might work and when it might not work based on feedback or prior knowledge or experience (Griffore & Phenice, 2001, p. 23).

Talk It Over

Write down, and then prepare to state for your own parents, or a family you know well, from what sources information comes into the family. What information is unsolicited, and what information is available for the asking? What information is reliable? Or unreliable? What are positives and negatives when using Internet information sources? State specific examples.

VALUES

Values are defined as those things you hold most dear. They are conceptions of what is good, right, or worthwhile, and they direct your actions as well as those of other family members. When you hear someone say, "You ought to . . ." you are hearing them state a value.

Talk It Over

Write down the "ought to" statements you have heard your parents or others make. What "ought to" statements are easiest for you to follow? Discuss.

As you study families throughout this course, think about your own family as a system and the various systems within which the members of your family interact. You can think about your family's values—those things you hold most dear. How do these values guide your behavior and the behavior of your parents? You'll begin to recognize how families use their values, goals, and human and nonhuman resources to make decisions and fulfill the objectives they set for their family members individually and for the family collectively.

As you begin your interaction with families, you can diagram their ecosystem to consider methodically the various environments that affect their behavior. This analysis will help you design a process for interacting with the family members.

PHILOSOPHY OF EMPOWERING FAMILIES

Many of you are studying for professional careers involving service to people. Or perhaps you are already working with families. That is one reason you've embarked on reading this book. Or you may be interested on a nonprofessional level, expecting to apply the ideas to your own family or neighborhood.

The *empowering philosophy* is this book's philosophy. *Empowering* means helping individuals and families take charge of their future by encouraging their decision-making confidence as they weigh the alternatives available to them. We developed this philosophy over the years while working with families and individuals. Using this philosophy in dealing with individuals and families can help create healthy families that can impact their systems. Many of the careers of the twenty-first century are focused on keeping people healthy, responsible, and fully functioning.

Principles of Empowering Families

As a helping professional, there are four simple principles to consider in the empowering philosophy. The principles, which permeate many of the following chapters, include the following:

1. *The professional's task is one of identifying a family's strengths and building on those strengths for the good of the individual family member as well as the family as a whole.* As you work with individuals and families you will find some successful families that, by all odds, should have problems. As one divorced mother said of her family, "I insist we do not have a 'broken home,' whatever that means. We are stronger than ever." She had marshaled the family's resources and worked on relating to her two children consistently and comfortably so she could make this statement with assurance.

   The empowering principle can be contrasted with one that focuses on the family's problems or deficits; for example, a family's homelessness or ill health. Typically, if a problem exists in a family, the family members are seldom the entire cause of the problem. The cause of the problem lies partly in another system, perhaps the economic system. When families recognize their own strengths and realize they can make a difference through their efforts, they are empowered to act and to carry out plans for making changes within their own family system, in their interaction with other systems, and within other systems.

2. *The methods and strategies selected by professionals to achieve goals will enable and empower families to make informed decisions themselves.* Differences in cultural background and the adults' stage of life within a family may have an impact

on how problems are understood, faced, and solved. Solutions that fit one type of family may be wrong for another type of family. An example is the housing expert who, speaking to a group of women senior citizens, told them how families could make furniture out of boxes or purchase it at garage sales. Had the professional considered the backgrounds of the women in her audience, she would have realized that these women were sizing down their households, giving away furnishings accumulated over many years. They needed helpful information on how to divide up their treasures fairly among family members wanting their antiques.

As a professional who is new to a community of families, you can learn from other more experienced professionals which methods and strategies they find most useful within the community. You also can find ways to learn from the families themselves regarding their needs. Then, by using your experience and professional knowledge, you can help families develop meaningful programs to fit their needs. Solutions must be developed with the full participation of the family. Understanding the diverse cultures of different families is necessary to deal most effectively with the complexities of each community of families.

This empowerment principle contrasts with one where the professional makes people feel incompetent or fails to develop their decision-making ability by making decisions for them. To succeed with any program for families, the professional must take the time and have patience while learning the values, goals, and interaction processes typical of the cultural group. Competent professionals treat clients—young or old—as equals with valuable opinions. Choices are established clearly so that families or individuals can make informed decisions.

3. *The approach will be one of a cooperative partnership with families, as families recognize their own needs and decide what steps they want to take to fulfill their needs.* Encouraging families to state what *they* need and exploring ways *they* might fulfill those needs fit this principle. When future problems arise, the family will have learned an improved method of analysis and decision making. This principle contrasts with one where a professional assumes an authoritative role and decrees what must be done without consulting the family.

4. *The goal is to strengthen the available human and material resources in the total community—within the individual, family, school, service clubs, religious organizations, and neighborhood.* There is a Chinese proverb that says, "Give a man a fish and you feed him for a day; teach him how to fish and you feed him for a lifetime." Teaching skills to help people cope with their problems is an important role for the helping professional. Additional resources can be provided at minimum costs. Many a service club has cleared a vacant lot for a baseball diamond or put up basketball hoops to provide young people a healthful place for recreation (Dunst & Trivette, 1987).

As you study the following chapters focusing on families with their various ethnic and structural characteristics and challenges, consider how the four principles of empowering families apply. Positive relationships with families that help them feel strong and able to act wisely are important, not only to the families, but also to the future of the society on the local, national, and global levels.

Professionals must work on the assumption that if they are truly successful, the families they help will be able to continue progressing alone. The autonomy of families in their communities is a major objective. Also, the notion of continuing or lifelong education should be stressed to families to help them accept the idea of progressive learning throughout life. With the fast pace of modern life, each person must be prepared to retool from time to time. Professionals can expect to complete their jobs with particular families and turn their attention to other families in need.

FAMILY FUNCTIONS

What functions do families perform? You might ask, "Where among these functions would a helping professional serve?"

The family is viewed as being part of the social system. As such, the family is expected to contribute to society by performing the following functions:

Reproductive Function

The family unit is responsible for perpetuating the human species. Small families and thoughtful family planning are considered essential by demographers to preserve the quality of life for future generations. The developed world has been criticized often for using more than their share of the world's natural resources and fostering pollution. Many helping professionals assist families with family-planning information, decisions, and services. These decisions have important ramifications for the child, the family, the society, the environment, and the balance of productive resources relative to population in each country throughout the world. Some couples may choose not to have children or to use their energy to support and care for children in their communities or in their extended family.

Socialization and Caregiving Function

The family is responsible for the physical care and nurturing of children and family members. The family unit is expected to socialize children to interact appropriately in kinship groups and in the larger society. Because of rising economic and other pressures for both parents to work outside the home, large numbers of children are also cared for by others—often in infant, toddler, and child-care centers. In addition, families with school-age children often seek the help of professionals as they guide the education and care of their children. This natural linkage with families must be facilitated by teachers, aides, and administrators of every school group from infant care through high school. In addition, this socializing and caregiving function must be supported by the community in a demonstrable way to help stem the violence being fostered when children are neglected by families and others.

The care of the elderly will be an increasing family responsibility as our population ages in the coming years. Like child-care centers, elder-care centers are becoming more widespread in some localities. Protected environments allowing elderly citizens to remain self-sufficient in their own homes, with assistance from health care workers with regard to personal care and medications, offer another alternative. These tasks promote careers for a new group of health care workers.

Emotional Support Function

The family is expected to foster the healthy emotional development and emotional ties among family members. Family members all need trust, love, security, and safety. The family home is expected to be a private secluded environment for individual expression of affection and for protection at all times. Assisting in maintaining the emotional health of families is one role the professional can play. Helping some families find the appropriate therapeutic service and aiding with that treatment at times may be another essential function of the professional. Family goals of strengthening emotional ties between family members are achieved gradually. Any stigma attached to seeking professional help should be removed, especially at crucial transition times, such as birth, divorce, remarriage, retirement, and the like.

Economic Function

The family's economic function is ever present. Families need jobs to survive. Jobs are directly related to both the natural and human resources available. The family of today buys most items it consumes. Historically, the household was largely a self-sufficient production unit, producing many of the personal and household items needed for daily living. Even today, many families could thrive better economically if they had the skills and motivation to do more production within the home. Making nutritious meals, caring for clothing, doing home repairs and renovation, or raising vegetables are examples of home production. One important economic skill today is the family's ability to make decisions based on a selection of needed and desired goods and services and their relationship to family goals.

Talk It Over

Consider what preparation you received in your own family for learning to become an economic support person for a family. What small steps and large steps were part of your family experience? What did adults tell you and what did their behavior show you? Discuss.

In fulfilling its economic function, the family is expected to prepare its members to contribute to the economic life of society. Families need jobs, skills for job advancement, and the cultivation of appropriate job behaviors. All of these may require help from professionals, who can teach adults and adolescents methods of searching for jobs as well as counsel them about future jobs. Professional help may be essential to prepare families to confront gender or racial discrimination.

Depending on your professional specialty, you may be called on to serve families or individual family members concerning one or more of these four family functions—reproductive, socializing and caregiving, emotional support, or economic. How will you go about it? What useful skills are you learning now?

HUMAN CAPITAL

The concept of *human capital* is useful for helping professionals as they appeal for financial support and carry out programs to serve individuals and families. As an economic concept it may attract an audience of funders who might not otherwise find an argument for equity in human development appealing.

Human capital includes the knowledge, skills, abilities, and attitudes that we each possess to enable us to function in society and to produce needed goods and services. Such services range from a personal level of self-care to helping one's children acquire the skills and attitudes necessary for life outside the home, as well as the development of skills and knowledge that are economically valued in the marketplace (Schultz, 1994).

Human capital contributes to a country's economic development as surely as physical capital or natural resources contribute to the overall economic health and wealth of a country measured by the gross domestic product (GDP).

Educating the New Hands

You will often hear the statement that each new person contributes a new pair of hands for working. Yet we must consider that long before the infant's hands become a worker's hands, the family, the school, and the community must develop the infant's inborn potential to become a worker by nourishing, caring for, and educating the child at home and at school. Large costs are connected with this health and education service. Some societies are more able and willing to assist families to do their part than others. The effort to transform an infant into a worker demands tremendous physical capital outlays (money and materials), as well as the skills of many parents, teachers, and others. The community and nation must be willing and able to make this investment. Human capital development is severely hampered when large numbers of births outstrip the funds available for human capital investments in families and schools. This fact is evident today in the developing world where in some countries the population is doubling in less than 20 years.

The United States, for example, had a period of population pressure on resources for developing human capital that occurred following World War II in 1945. Because all available resources were directed toward the war effort, the United States had to catch up from about a decade of being unable to build schools. Los Angeles, for example, experienced a period of rapid growth that necessitated the building of numerous schools.

A large number of people had migrated to the region during the Great Depression of the 1930s and during the war to work in war industries. The postwar baby boomers were reaching school age in 1945 to 1950. The city reportedly was dedicating a school nearly every day of the year in those postwar years.

Of course, the high costs of building and staffing all those schools were borne by the taxpayers and were considered, overall, essential. The investments in education and other human services contributed to the economic progress that followed. During that time, the educational program known as the GI Bill gave World War II veterans an opportunity to further the schooling they were deprived of because of their required military service. The government invested heavily in the human capital of its youth and young adults. This cadre of well-educated, former military-service people who were now trained to take jobs that needed doing encouraged the out-migration from agriculture that was necessary for economic growth after the war.

Talk It Over

What might have happened if U.S. taxpayers had not shouldered the burden of funding schools, teachers, and the GI Bill after World War II?

In an agrarian developing country, the family was able up until fairly recently to teach children what was necessary to know to carry on the family work in the future. However, in today's world, most parents are unaware of the needs of the next decade, let alone the next three decades. And parents usually do not have the technical knowledge, skills, or materials necessary to prepare their own children. This is as true among poor Americans as it is among poor people in many other countries. Thus all parents need community support to succeed in developing their children's human capital. Parents' own human capital must also be updated in most societies today because of the rapidly changing employment scene.

Nutritional Improvements

T. Paul Schultz (1994), of Yale University, in analyzing worldwide studies of human capital, indicated that mothers with schooling are able to provide more adequate nutrition for their children than mothers without schooling. Because child care is the province of women in most societies today, male education does not show the same statistical connection to children's well-being as does female education, Schultz claims. Yet many societies place high priority on the education of sons. In addition, mothers who have had some schooling have fewer children and experience fewer infant deaths. Of course, adequate nutrition is essential for life as well as for a sustained level of child growth and development and employment later as adults. (Schooling in Schultz's studies refers to minimal levels of literacy in developing countries, pp. 50–51.)

Life Expectancy

Another human capital statistic analyzed by Schultz (1994) is the longer life expectancy of females than males. Since about 1930, female life expectancy has improved as families in many countries moved to urban centers from rural areas. The urban environment provides females increased opportunities for schooling, as well as opportunities to enter the labor force and earn money for their own care and the care of their families. Females also have benefited from improved health services, including family-planning services, more readily available in health centers located in urban areas. Fertility control, which is in part responsible for the reduction in maternal deaths, also makes a significant difference in female life expectancy statistics (p. 18). That is, if birth spacing occurs, if mothers with problem pregnancies can prevent them, and if women can stop having babies when they have reached their desired family size and their older ages, their health and life expectancy improve. By avoiding frequent pregnancies, women can devote more of their own human capital and family resources to educate and nurture current children.

Human capital is first developed in the families of the world as children are cared for by parents and others in the community. The analysis done by Schultz (1995) found that the investment in women (who have been woefully neglected in some societies) who in turn can nurture children adequately is an excellent long-range economic investment. Mothers with an education are more likely to see that their children become educated than women or men without an education.

Most countries and families have a history of dedicating more resources to educating males than females. This is especially true where education is not compulsory, children need to work, and costs are a private expense for the family. The Schultz (1994) analysis showed that:

Social subsidies for investments in female children and adults may be justified by:

1. efficiency, such as high individual private market returns;
2. social externalities, such as reduced child mortality and [female] fertility;
3. intergenerational redistribution, such as better health and education of children and a slower growth in population; and
4. equity, that is, an increase in the productive capability of poorer individuals relative to richer individuals. (p. 48)

The Equal Pay Act of 1963 makes an equity argument in stating that males and females should be paid the same wages for doing the same job. The Schultz (1994) analysis shows that the long history of lower investment in female education is largely responsible for females topping out in low-paying positions. Statistics from the 1970s showing the percentages of women and men admitted to a given class in professional schools of law or medicine can be compared to statistics on 1998 admissions for two stark examples. Only since the 1970s has a legion of female students entered many of the higher paying professions. Thus, for generations, females have missed out on state subsidies for their educations that males have long enjoyed, not to mention the traditional private family contributions of greater subsidies for sons than for daughters. The same would likely be true if an analysis were done of minorities and education in the United States. White Americans have received governmental subsidies for their educations for generations, which explains the lower wage categories for most minorities, at least up until 1972 when the Civil Rights Act began to take effect in higher education.

Higher rates of investment in the human capital of females by a widening circle of industrially developed countries show that these countries have been more successful in stimulating modern economic growth, even though most adult women's wage rates are still far below male rates. Furthermore, placing emphasis on the education of females provides many external benefits to society, as measured by reduced child mortality and morbidity, improved child nutrition and schooling, and decreased fertility and population growth. Schultz's (1994) studies show a shortfall in female education and health services compared to that of males, particularly in South and West Asia and in Africa. He believes that in these areas of the world, the family decision-making process and parents' own traditionally defined interests attach less value to the future productivity of daughters than sons. (Recall this finding when the preference for sons is discussed in later chapters.)

Talk It Over

Select a family you know and list examples of human capital development that you think occurred within the family. Give examples of parents of friends as mentors for the children.

APPLICATION TO DIVERSE FAMILIES

The Schultz (1994) analysis of the differences in human capital investment between women and men suggests that females be given adequate schooling and health supports as efforts are made to render our society gender neutral, as well as racially and ethnically equal. Additional investments in girls' and women's education and health care will create human capital and are certain to produce monetary and private and social returns needed by society.

In later chapters, we present American family groups with varied ethnic backgrounds and family structures and challenges. You can develop a process of analyzing family characteristics based on the family ecosystem framework, the empowerment model, the family functions, or the human capital concept. Thus, as a helping professional encountering a family, you can select a system for planning your interaction with its members. Think of your family analysis as descriptive, instead of either good or bad, or right or wrong. The question to ask yourself is, "How can these family members be empowered or find the strengths to achieve goals on their own?"

Talk It Over

In considering male and female children of all racial and ethnic groups, do you think the argument that "equity in subsidies improves economic efficiency" would be heard more favorably in the halls of Congress and legislatures than the argument that "equity is desirable because it is right"? Discuss your arguments in class or in a written paper.

✦ CONCLUSIONS

Several analytical frameworks have been presented for you to use in working with families in your professional career. The ecological system, the four major family functions, the four principles for empowering families, and the concept of developing human capital are all frameworks that a helping professional can use in analyzing situations facing families. These frameworks should be kept in mind as you study families and their ethnic, racial, religious, and family structures. There is no one best approach to use in helping a particular family. Remain sensitive to the fact that families change over time and will require new approaches as family members gain experience and reach new stages in their life cycle. The empowerment of families is your objective.

✦ STUDY QUESTIONS

1. Define a systems approach to studying families. Give examples of systems and system effects.
2. Explain the human ecosystem as identified by Bronfenbrenner and Griffore and Phenice.
3. Identify the three parts of the human ecosystem as defined by Bubolz and Sontag. Explain in your own words the relationships among the three environments.
4. Define the role of adaptation in a human ecosystem.
5. State the four principles of empowering families and give examples.

6. State the four major functions of families and give examples.
7. Define human capital.
8. Describe the findings of the T. Paul Schultz analysis with regard to investment in women and how it impacts the economic development of a family or a country.
9. How does the Schultz analysis give substance to the statement "When you educate a female, you educate a family"?
10. Discuss findings of studies by Teun and Sarbaugh on intercultural communication.

✦ APPLICATIONS

1. Using the three environments of the human ecosystem, diagram your own family and label the various parts of the system. Discuss adaptation among the environments as you analyze your family.
2. Using the human ecosystem framework, diagram the interaction that a family with two young children might have with the systems outside the family.
3. State the four principles of empowering families, and give an example of each principle in relation to some interaction you experienced at college. Discuss.
4. Look up statistics of women entering the professional fields during the late 1970s in the United States. Compare your data with statistics from a decade earlier. How many more women were admitted to professional schools such as law and medicine in the later decade? What does this suggest about family and governmental subsidies for education and the differences in availability to women and men?
5. Discuss with your classmates the Talk It Over questions in the chapter.
6. Reflect on someone you've known a long time. In describing that individual, would you describe similarities or differences with yourself? Reflect on someone you've met recently who is very different from yourself. How would you describe that person? How does your behavior fit Teun's research described in the chapter?

✦ KEY INTERNET RESOURCES

Collaborating with Families
www.afec.org/tipsforteachers/tips_e3.html

Family Structures and Communication
http://novaonline.nvcc.edu/eli/spd110td/interper/relations/Linksfamilystructure.html

✦ FURTHER READING

Aronson, S. (1996). *Trade and the American dream.* Lexington: University of Kentucky Press.

Brown, L., Gardner G., & Halwell, B. (1998). *Beyond Malthus: Sixteen dimensions of the population problem.* Washington, DC: World Watch Institute.

Coles, R. (1997). *The youngest parents: Teenage pregnancy as it shapes lives.* New York: Norton.

Davis, M. (1998). *Ecology of fear: Los Angeles and the imagination of disaster.* New York: Henry Holt.

Jones, J. (1998). *Four centuries of black and white labor.* New York: Norton.

Paolucci, B., Hall, O. A., & Axinn, N. (1977). *Family decision making: An ecosystem approach.* New York: Wiley, 1977.

Rehm, M. L., Allisson, B. N., Darling, C. A., & Greenwood, B. B. (2002, April). Insights and understandings of diversity: Family and consumer sciences educators' life experiences. *Family and Consumer Sciences, 94,* 48–57.

Rothenberg, D. (1998). *An oral portrait: The hidden world of migrant farmworkers today.* New York: Harcourt Brace.

Schultz, T. P. (1994, August). *Human capital and economic development.* Presentation to the International Association of Agricultural Economists, Harare, Zimbabwe.

Schultz, T. P., & Tansel, A. (1992). *Measurement of returns to adult health: Morbidity effects on wage rates in Cote d'Ivoire and Ghana* (Discussion Paper No. 663). New Haven, CT: Yale University, Economic Growth Center.

Schultz, T. W. (1967). The rate of return in allocating investments to education. *Journal of Human Resources, 2*(3), 293–309.

II

ETHNIC DIVERSITY AMONG AMERICAN FAMILIES

→ 4

African American Families

→ **Key Concepts**

- Reductionist
- Ethnic
- Minority
- Oppression

Corbis Royalty Free

Langston Hughes, the award-winning African American poet, understood too well the often-insurmountable obstacles and prejudice faced by Black people and their families. His poetry, however, was filled with hope and encouragement. He deeply believed that if African Americans learned to accept themselves as beautiful and proud, and celebrated their own individuality, their resilience and self-reliance would enable them to achieve their potential despite great adversity.

African Americans represent the second largest ethnic minority group in the United States. The term *ethnic* is used in the sociological sense of common ancestry, being born in a particular community or culture and following a particular social pattern that gives one a sense of belonging, such as speaking a particular language or dialect of a language. According to Mindel, Habenstein, and Wright (1988), an ethnic group consists of people who share a historically unique social and cultural heritage that is passed on from generation to generation. The term *minority* is also used in the sociological sense and refers to unequal access to power in relationships, which translates into access to opportunities, such as having less political and economic power than the majority (Wilkinson, 1993).

This chapter offers an overview of African American family relationships as depicted in a variety of family patterns and individuals. As we look at these families, we touch on the complex web of relationships that exist between them and their environments. As in all human systems, specific African American family structures arise from their interactions within and interdependence on their environments. As in all families, the overview represented here may reflect that of the more public family, which is more easily studied and understood than that of the private domain of family life. Therefore, it must be understood from the outset that any data and information reported of Black families may only represent a small portion of the picture, although this *reductionist* view of Black families can still be useful, and may, in some cases, be necessary. However, reductionism and *holism* are complementary approaches and, when used in proper balance, help us obtain a deeper knowledge of the life of the African American family.

HISTORICAL BACKGROUND

For African American families, the painful legacy of oppression and racial discrimination from more than 200 years of slavery in the South has marked their existence in the United States and cannot be adequately addressed here. Their despicable treatment by White Americans highlights their heritage in the history of the United States, but they have adapted, evolved, and survived in spite of historical and statistical distortions that systematically segregated and discriminated against them. Since the mid-1960s, a national effort has been made to dismantle institutional forms of discrimination. However, the process has been slow, and unfortunately, discrimination is still a part of the African American's experience (Schafer, 1993). Conditions that exist for many in accessing adequate housing, employment opportunities, good education, good health care, and other social systems have been the result of years of experiencing institutional barriers that have denied them equal access.

For many years, the use of racial labels perpetuated and emphasized the skin color of African Americans as though they were a people without a country of origin. Being Black held many negative stereotypes that date back as far as the 1600s, when Blacks were described as suffering the "curse of God" (Jordan, 1968). Deprived of heritage, where they came from, and burdened with stereotypes, many African Americans are concerned about the future of their community. John McAdoo and Julia McAdoo (1994) suggest that scholars spend less time in labeling and placing blame and spend more time finding positive solutions for positive role functioning in families (p. 295). The authors emphasize the use of an ecological approach to present family roles and functioning from an Afrocentric perspective (p. 289).

Billingsley (1968) identified four distinct cultural traits that separated African Americans from other immigrants to the United States and helped define their special sense of peoplehood: (1) African Americans came from a country with norms and values that were different from the American way of life; (2) African Americans came from different tribes with different cultures, languages, and traditions; (3) African American men came first, without women; and (4) African Americans came in bondage.

Much has been written about the destruction of the family as a result of slavery and the consequent weakening of the man's traditional functions. There are also scholars who support the notion that the family, as a social unit during slavery, provided an important mechanism for survival. The family was the haven for companionship, love, empathy for one's suffering, and the socialization of the children.

Billingsley (1968) noted that a significant mistreatment of Black families by social scientists in the past contributed to the negative and distorted image of African American families in America today. Because family behavior patterns were seen as different from the majority, the behaviors were often described as deviant. He suggested that the misinformation generated and perpetuated by social scientists is partially responsible for the self-fulfilling prophecy found among the youth of today. Historical evidence indicates that earlier survey research data gathered about African Americans was driven by the need to compare them to Whites. Prior to the 1980s, only three of nine studies attempted to reach a cross section of African Americans. The other studies collected and reported data that only sampled a select region or community. The data were generalized as representing African Americans. This practice by social analysts led to the oversimplification of differences among African Americans (A. Wade Smith, 1998).

We strongly encourage you to read further about African American families. The resources suggested at the end of the chapter provide a short list of worthwhile, available information. While reading, study the research data, historical information, articles, and books from the viewpoint of the applied major theoretical approaches that have, historically and currently, influenced the field of social science in the study of African American families.

DEMOGRAPHIC INFORMATION

In 2000 there were 34,679,000 African Americans in the United States. This represents 12.3 percent of the total population, the second largest ethnic minority group in America, the first being that of Hispanic origins (U.S. Census Bureau, 2000). During the 1950s through the 1970s, African Americans made gains in education, health, living conditions, political access, and income. According to all demographic and economic indicators (U.S. Census Bureau, 2000), African Americans were on an upward climb. In the 1960s, the poverty rate was at 55.1 percent; in 1990, 30.1 percent of African Americans, and in 2004, 24.7 percent, were in poverty. Recent indicators are that this upward trend may be reversing itself. For example, the poverty rates rose for Whites, whereas for Blacks, the 2003 poverty rate of 24.3 percent was approximately the same as in 2002. According to the U.S. Census Bureau (2004), Black households had the lowest median income of $30,134, which was 62 percent of the median for non-Hispanic White households ($48,977). Included is the U.S. Census Bureau's Official Weighted Poverty Thresholds in 2004 by the size of family. You can access this information by referring to www.census.gov/hhes/poverty/povmeas/papers/orshansky.html.

	(Dollars)
One person	9,645
Two people	12,334
Three people	15,067
Four people	19,307
Five people	22,831
Six people	25,788
Seven people	29,236
Eight people	32,641
Nine people or more	39,948

At the same time, the middle class earning $50,000 or more includes 1 out of 7 African American families, whereas in the early 1960s this ratio was closer to 1 out of 17. The widening gap between the affluent and the poor presents a difficult problem for the African American community; there are families who have gained access and others who still struggle for it. The movement of middle-class African Americans to the suburbs has been on the increase as well. This trend has created an isolated and poorer inner-city community with insufficient material, human resources, and institutions to support families adequately. Most African Americans live in large metropolitan areas such as New York, Chicago, Detroit, Philadelphia, Los Angeles, Houston, Baltimore, and Washington.

In 1990, 84 percent of African Americans lived in metropolitan areas. There is much concern about an increasing number living in high poverty areas with associated high crime rates and other social ills (O'Hare, Pollard, Mann, & Kent, 1991). With the decline of manufacturing and blue-collar jobs in inner cities, many urban poor face even more isolation and unemployment, further undermining the strength of the African American family. By not participating in the labor force, the poor are often marginalized into nonadaptable patterns within the African American community. According to Aguirre and Turner (1998), many enter into a lifestyle that is difficult to change.

The median age of the African American population is 29.7 years, whereas that of the total U.S. population is 35.4 years. With higher birthrates of 2.4 children per woman, compared with 1.8 per White woman, there is a momentum for future population growth as the large number of African Americans of childbearing age continues into the twenty-first century.

Birthrates for unmarried women increased dramatically in the 1980s. In 1988, 64 percent of African American infants born during that year were born out of wedlock—many to teenage mothers (U.S. Census Bureau, 1990). Within a decade, however, we have seen the rate of infants born to teenage mothers on a decline. According to the National Institutes of Health (1998), this represents a significant change in teen pregnancies among African American youth. Whereas low-weight infants were a major cause of high infant mortality rates among African Americans because of malnourishment, inadequate neonatal care, and poverty, it is anticipated that a decrease in births (especially among young mothers) will lessen this impact.

An African American male child born in 1990 can expect to live an average of 66 years, about 8 years less than an African American female child. In comparison, an average White male child born in 1990 can expect to live an average of 73 years. Since 1985 there has been documented decline in life expectancy for African Americans, especially males, whereas Whites continue to gain life expectancy. At every age, African Americans die at higher rates than Whites (National Center for Health Statistics, 1991). These differential death rates, such as reported here, often indicate the existence of societal inequalities. Some individuals are born into privilege and others into deprivation. There are differences in diet, health care, schooling, and circumstances that can influence resilience and the desire to persevere.

A particular problem facing the African American community is the unbalanced sex ratio with more females than males, which is not the result of more girls being born but a serious indication of social and environmental injustices. The young adult man experiences an environment that challenges his right to survive. The African American male homicide rate is over 10 times the White rate. Other statistics are equally staggering. For example, 499,000 African American men are in prisons. According to Mauer (1994), this is 40 percent of all prisoners in the United States, more than the number of African American men in higher education. There are over 30 percent more health-related occurrences of heart disease, cancer, and stroke among African American men than among their White cohorts (Jaynes & Williams, 1989). The consequences have resulted in creating competition for mates among women. This will continue to deny large numbers of African American women suitable mates.

THE ECOLOGY OF AFRICAN AMERICAN FAMILIES

Using the ecological system framework presented in Chapter 3 helps us look at various systems that influence families. Systems will include those within and outside the family, and those impacting families.

Family Structure

"The Black Family Nobody Knows," an article published in *Ebony* magazine by Massaquoi (1993), states that, "Despite the fact that most Black families are close-knit, loving, hardworking, law-abiding, and stable, there is a widespread tendency to write

Black families off as dysfunctional . . . and in disarray." What is often not reported is the fact that "the Black family has survived and continues to survive" (pp. 28–31). In A. Billingsley's (1993) book, *Climbing Jacob's Ladder,* he debunks some of the most commonly held beliefs, stereotypes, and misinformation written about the African American family. Stable Black families are found in all economic classes; however, the largest group of predominantly stable families is the "non-poor working class." Billingsley identifies this group as the economic, social, and political backbone of the Black community. Andrew Billingsley's, *Black Families in White America* describes the importance of the African heritage of the extended family and the ethos of collectivism, which was never destroyed despite slavery and segregation.

However, change is a cultural imperative, and, like families of other ethnic groups, African American families have undergone dramatic evolutionary changes. Although the traditional family, consisting of a married couple and children, is prevalent, there are other types of relationships that constitute a family and a feeling of belonging. More and more African American families are opting to remain childless to pursue their dual-career goals.

Approximately 5 percent of African American adults are living together, without marriage, in stable, economically viable relationships (Massaquoi, 1993). Some of these relationships are a prelude to marriage and others are a substitute for marriage. Such living together has been rapidly increasing among African Americans, reflecting a general trend in America.

The African American community is experiencing dramatic and fundamental changes, with a growing number of female-headed households and many living in poverty. According to a study by Lindblad-Goldberg (1986), African American single-parent households that function well have a number of characteristics in common, such as these:

1. More internal organization, with the single parent being clearly the one in charge
2. More response to children's need for authority
3. Less conflict between individuals within the household
4. A view of themselves as quite adaptable to the ways of the outside world
5. Cohesiveness and integration in their relationships with each other
6. Having control over their life space and asserting control over their living environment.

According to Lindblad-Goldberg, well-functioning, single-parent families see that the most important source of income for the family is employment. According to Sudarkasa (1993), African American women have adopted unique family forms of organization in response to the demographic, economic, and political realities of life in America.

Family scholars have argued that the weak structures of African American families have always differed from traditional European American families and should not be expected to conform to the nuclear couple pattern. Some analysts argue that this is a result of the legacy of slavery when marriages among Blacks were not legally recognized. Other social scientists trace some of the family structure back to ancestral homes in African countries (Farley & Allen, 1991). An aspect most scholars agree on is that kinship structures are interdependent and multigenerational. According to H. McAdoo (1979), African American families are characterized by involvement with each other and adhere to a set of unwritten obligations and reciprocity to relatives, regardless of age. Manning Marable (1994, p. 74) states, "research on Black male-female relations tells us what our common sense should have indicated long ago—that the essence of the Black family and the community life has been a positive, constructive, and even heroic experience."

Gender Roles

There is a growing trend among African American women to remain single, and the statistics indicate an unprecedented number of single African American women. According to Staples (1988), the institutional confinement of many men is one factor in this growing trend, and other sociocultural factors have impacted the relationship between males and females. Staples (1988) argues that the conflict between African American men and women is traced to incompatible roles. The societal prescription is for Black women to be passive and Black men dominant. However, Black women resist Black men's dominance. Often Black men, who wish to be accorded the superior male role, cannot fulfill the economic provider role because of unemployment.

It is known that income superiority helps support the dominance of men in American families. However, for African American families, their history has been a legacy of mutual cooperation and unity. Marable (1994) believes that men and women must come together and forge a new and equal alliance. This unity can be achieved when African Americans overcome the inherent and ingrained stereotypes of sexism that prevail in society. African American men and women are working toward a similar goal of eradicating social injustice, and together they can achieve Black freedom.

According to Coontz (1992), African American working women have made the largest income gains relative to men of any ethnic group, thereby producing new options for women both inside and outside of marriage. African American women with good jobs are more able to define their own status and gain more independence. Many are models of strength, courage, and independence.

African American Children

Examples abound throughout history of the impenetrable bond between the African American mother and her children (Bell, 1971; Brown & Forde, 1967). Rooted in African heritage, a mother's children hold a special value because they represent the continuity of life. Most mothers share a similar desire to give the very best to their children. All mothers want their children to grow up in a safe environment, get a good education, and make a contribution to their community and society. However, African American parents realize that for an African American child to survive and achieve there are other socialization requirements. The child must develop an extensive set of different behavior patterns regarding social relationships. According to McAdoo and McAdoo (1985), African American children's interactions are very complex because they need to interact in many different environments, each with differences in values, social expectations, and social relationships. For example, as a young African American child enters a school environment, it may take the child more time to observe and assess what is being required of him or her. African American children must be able to demonstrate flexibility in many situations. Pierce and Profit (1994) encourage African American parents to teach their children:

1. To look for more options and opportunities
2. To have more nonverbal awareness, such as when to take an offense and how and when to counter an offense
3. To feel needed by starting to give them small repetitive tasks and progressively more responsibilities as children mature
4. To think of what can be done rather than what can't be done
5. That they will live longer, a message of hope that may be necessary, given the demographic situations that African Americans presently face.

The child-rearing techniques of African American parents are often designed to prepare children to survive in environments foreign to most middle-class Americans. According to Staples (1988), African American parents are more likely than Whites to use physical punishment rather than verbal reasoning to enforce discipline. There is also currently considerable debate on the effect of the absence of a positive male role model for a majority of African American children today. However, studies fail to support a direct relationship between a father's absence and children's problem behaviors. Many African American children experience growing up without a father living in the home, yet many are in contact with warm, nurturing male role models among relatives and friends in the extended family system.

For generations, African American families taught their children to be polite and submissive and to always conform to the larger society. To conform to the expected social behaviors, they were taught to be very observant of their environment. African American children are highly observant of nonverbal behaviors. This is reflected in the outward appearance of a lifestyle, such as in choice of clothing. These behaviors, according to Pierce and Profit (1994), are statistically evident in African American men, who talk more about clothing than any other group.

Today, more and more African American families are challenging their children to take risks, accept their past heritage, and push for improvements in racial equality. Some parents place extraordinary demands on their youth to question and challenge the role society plays concerning their struggles against marginality. African American parents are finding it important to help their child feel needed and wanted. The earlier patterns in childrearing of talking about "race" and "what can't be done" are being replaced with "race" and "what can be done."

AFRICAN AMERICAN VALUES

According to Guess (1990), the progress of African Americans has been attributed historically to the role played by the African church and the influence of Black ministers. Even today, we hear the calls of ministers like E. Edward Jones, President of the National Baptist

Convention of America (1993), who reminds the community that "Black people need to come back to the Church where family values and morals are extolled" (p. 98). The Black church is a by-product of slavery and has been considered the backbone of African American families.

According to Franklin Frazier (1932), during slavery any African who was baptized was not considered a slave but an indentured servant. However, this practice was quickly abandoned as a result of laws passed and decisions passed down by the courts. It was declared that there was no relationship between acceptance of the Christian faith, baptism, and the conferring of free status on Africans. Today, many believe that Christianity is a liberating theology and that, with God's help, Black people can endure and overcome life's pains.

For African Americans, religion is and has been one of the strongest institutional systems of support. Disturbingly, from January 1990 to February 1996, 45 southern African American congregation churches were affected by hate crimes. Between 1995 and 1996, 73 African American churches were burned ("Black Churches on Fire," 1996). Investigations show that approximately a quarter of these burnings may have also been motivated by hate and anger. The cost of replacing a church building is minor in comparison to healing the weakened trust between the African American community and its neighbors.

Endurance of suffering while moving ahead is a major theme found in African American families. This theme is eloquently portrayed in the poem "Mother to Son" by Langston Hughes, the noted prize-winning Black poet. Many social scientists agree that various themes give coherence to African American families. The synthesis of these themes forms unique constellations of African American families and includes the following:

1. Strong kinship bonds among a variety of family households
2. Strong work, education, and achievement orientation
3. High level of flexibility in family roles
4. Strong commitment to religious values and church participation
5. A humanistic orientation for perceiving the world and relationships

Many cultures share similar values; however, each ethnic group expresses them in its own unique way. There really is no single right or wrong way.

AFRICAN AMERICANS AND THE EDUCATIONAL SYSTEM

For many African American families, the message is clear: Education, even in times of economic uncertainty, will enhance the quality of their lives. From the first legal Supreme Court victory of *Brown v. Board of Education of Topeka, Kansas* (1954), (Kluegel, 1975) there has been a strong belief among African American families that education in the long run can eliminate discrimination and provide a certain measure of economic security.

Today, African American children make up about 16 percent of the nation's public school students, and they are the majority in a number of our largest school districts, comprising as much as 90 percent in cities like Atlanta, Detroit, and Washington, D.C. Although educational levels have risen for African Americans, they are more likely to drop out of school than Whites but less likely than Hispanic youth, except in suburban areas where the dropout rates are nearly equal (National Center for Education Statistics, 2003).

Studies show that students are more likely to drop out of school when their grades are poor or when they are older than their classmates. They are also at higher risk of dropping out when they come from single-parent households, live in the center of metropolitan areas, or have parents who never finished school themselves. All these factors have been attributed statistically to poverty.

Coontz (1992), in her book, *The Way We Never Were,* asks ironically, "Why launch new school reforms when . . . the real key to educational performance is whether a child comes from a two-parent family? Why experiment with new anti-poverty programs when . . . the most important indicator of poverty is whether there are two parents at home?" When this argument is used, blame is placed on the single-parent family. The solution is simple. "Marriage is the ticket out of poverty" (p. 256). This prevailing attitude does not address the success of the increase in educational attainment of Black children and youth. For example, in 1990, individuals with some college or with an associate's degree totaled 2,952,000, whereas in 2003 the number had almost doubled to 5,625,000. The same can be said of receiving a bachelor's or advanced degree—in 1990, 1,890,000 versus 3,558,000 in 2003 (U.S. Census Bureau, 2004–2005). Despite existing evidence suggesting that the prevailing negative social climate of schools can lead to good students performing below their ability and poor students being discouraged from improving, many Black children are overcoming these conditions. Although complex social issues and unequal access to quality learning environments in the home, neighborhood, and school are sometimes overlooked as possible reasons for poor academic achievement and low graduation rates, the degree that African Americans tend to cluster in inner cities where residential isolation and lack of financial resources create unequal access to decent schools and public services, African American children persevere and demonstrate resilience as witnessed by the changing data over the last 10 years.

Some find themselves unable to escape what Kunjufu (1982) calls a discrepancy between what the inner-city African American male learns in his neighborhood environment and the required behavior for success in the educational system and workplace. Kunjufu states that a number of young men have skills that serve them well on the streets but poorly in the rest of society. For example, aggressive interpersonal skills necessary for street survival contribute to high rates of suspensions and other disciplinary actions in school. The results are often lower academic achievement or high dropout rates. However, there is a trend toward a decline in the dropout rate of 0.95 in 1990 to a low of 0.65 in 2003 (National Center for Education Statistics, 2003).

Meanwhile, African American women tend to be more educated than African American men at all levels, except at the doctoral level. According to the U.S. Census Bureau (2003), African American men continue to lag behind African American women educationally. Achieving a higher level of education has helped women become involved in the workplace and has placed them at an economic advantage. The service and high technology sectors of the U.S. economy are continually growing, and African American women are becoming more competitive in the expanding economy.

However, African American men with generally less education than women are often unable to secure employment in a shrinking industrial marketplace. The immediate challenge is to increase the number of men in higher education. There is also a need to support the historical Black colleges that emerged in the 1800s to educate young African Americans who were excluded from private and state colleges in the South. These institutions were the primary source of higher education for African Americans in the South.

AFRICAN AMERICANS AND THE HEALTH CARE SYSTEM

If we were to look at the estimated life expectancy at birth in years by race, we must conclude that there has been an increase in the quality of life for Blacks. For example, a Black person born in 1941 would have expected to have lived until the age of 56.3

for women and 52.5 for men, whereas if born in 2002, the life expectancy for women is 75.6 years and for men, 68.8. Although the gap between Black and White life expectancy is narrowing, there are alarming indications that certain health risks are increasing. Today, the 10 leading causes of death and disablers of African Americans are cardiovascular disease, cancer, cerebral vascular disease, diabetes mellitus, unintentional injury, homicide, HIV, and chronic lower respiratory disease (National Center for Health Statistics, 2002). Ten years ago the eight major killers were cardiovascular disease, cancer, diabetes, substance abuse or chemical dependency (including heavy alcohol use and smoking), violence (homicide and suicide), accidents, infant mortality, and AIDS (Goodwin, 1990). Noticeable differences exist in the ranked list of the top 10 types of health risks found 10 years ago versus today. Missing from the top 10 are deaths by substance abuse or chemical dependency and infant mortality. This is a clear indication that Blacks are moving toward less self-inflicted health risks. However, increases are seen in cancer rates for African American men and women that are higher than the rates for White counterparts. The cancer rate is 17 percent for Black men compared to 5.9 percent for White men, and 8.3 percent for Black women compared to 6.5 percent for White women (National Cancer Institute, 1986).

Harold Freeman, president of the American Cancer Society, estimates that approximately a third of African Americans either don't have the money or insurance to see a doctor or are so fearful of cancer they are likely to put off a physical exam until it is too late (Barrow, 1990). The uninsured rate and number of uninsured for Blacks are 19.7 percent or 7.2 million. This figure has remained unchanged from 2003. About 13 percent of Black children are uninsured. The likelihood of being covered by health insurance rises with incomes over $25,000 (U.S. Census Bureau, 2004–2005).

The elderly, who form the fastest growing segment of the African American population, are undergoing a crisis in medical care. The Black elderly are more likely to be sick and disabled than the White elderly. They have higher rates of chronic disease, functional impairment, high blood pressure, and other indicators of risk. The problem is compounded when research data indicate that elderly African Americans have different patterns of gaining access to the health care delivery system and different utilization patterns. These different utilization patterns are often based on mistrust of the health care system. In the infamous Tuskegee syphilis study, African Americans were victims of medical experimentation from 1934 to 1972 (Thomas & Quinn, 1991). Medical records also show a legacy of being used as specimens in medical schools for teaching medical, surgical, and pathological examination procedures in the nineteenth century (Gamble, 1993). Historical events such as these are not easily forgotten and lead to generational mistrust of the medical system, especially by the elderly. Even today, it has been found that once Blacks are hospitalized, institutional racism often dictates the quality and nature of the services rendered (Edmonds, 1993).

A large portion of elderly African Americans no longer live in the same city as relatives and thus they are deprived of needed in-home care and support. There is the ideal notion that the Black elderly will be taken care of by relatives and never need to be placed in a nursing home. The use of nursing homes may seem relatively new; however, nursing home care for the African American elderly has been around since the slave era. According to Barrow (1990), there have been between 200 and 300 homes for the Black aged established since 1860. Even so, there is a shortage of African American professionals in the field of gerontology.

One of the most disturbing differences between Blacks and Whites is the fact that the Black infant mortality rate is 2.5 times the rate of White infants in the United States (Collins, David, Handler, Wall, & Andes, 2004). Although there was a 24 percent increase in receiving prenatal care in the first trimester of pregnancy from the 1990s to 2002, the results demonstrate limited impact in birth outcomes. Prenatal care definitely is important; however, there are larger issues related to social and contextual factors that must also be taken into account in the equation of preventative care. Much of this disparity is associated with low birth weight, placing infants at higher risk of death. Low birth weight is attributed to poor nutrition, poor health, poor prenatal care, smoking, preteen and early teen pregnancy, and other harmful lifestyle habits of mothers during pregnancy. The birth of low-weight infants in the African American community is a significant factor hampering healthy development and survival of infants and mothers.

AFRICAN AMERICANS AND THE GOVERNMENTAL SYSTEM

Prior to the passage of the Voting Rights Act of 1965, African Americans, especially in the southern states, were discouraged and even barred from voting in elections. Poll taxes and literacy tests were both used to discourage or actually prevent Black voter registration. Today, all African Americans, at all levels, are free to vote. In fact, Blacks are becoming more involved in politics, running for office, getting elected, and serving in government at all levels, including the president's cabinet and the Supreme Court. In some states, African Americans constitute a significant number of voters, largely supporting the Democratic Party and African American candidates. An example of the strength of the collective Black and liberal vote was witnessed recently in Virginia where Lawrence Douglas Wilder became the first African American elected governor of any state in the history of the United States. More recently, Condoleezza Rice, a conservative Republican African American woman, has risen to the top position of secretary of state in the second term of President G. W. Bush following her predecessor, Colin Powell, a distinguished Black American four-star general and a moderate Republican.

To diminish discrimination, the unequal treatment of individuals or groups on the basis of an attribute such as race, ethnicity, religion, age, or sex, the civil rights laws of the 1960s, as interpreted by Executive Order 11246, required organizations doing business with or receiving funds from the government to increase minority representation (Jaynes & Williams, 1989, p. 316). These affirmative action policies were rigorously enforced in the 1970s and the early 1980s. In recent years, public ambivalence and the courts' contradictory decisions have weakened its impact. Some states are challenging the policies of affirmative action, and, in several cases, these policies have been overturned by popular vote.

AFRICAN AMERICANS AND THE CRIMINAL JUSTICE SYSTEM

A vast majority of the African American community believes that the criminal justice system discriminates against its members, especially against the Black man. For example, in Maryland from 1995 through 1997, 70 percent of the drivers whose vehicles were searched by state troopers were African American. Several studies carried out by the nation's leading foundations, including the Ford Foundation, the MacArthur Foundation, and the Rockefeller Foundation, report that "Justice Is for Some" (www.accessmylibrary.com/comsite5/bin/comsite5.pl?page=document_print&item i. . . .)

According to published reports, African American youth are 16 percent of America's youth population. However, 26 percent of youth arrests, 44 percent of youth detained after arrest, 46 percent of youth committed to public facilities, and 58 percent of youth admitted to adult prisons in America were Black youth (Schiraldi, 2006). These rates of overrepresentation in the criminal justice system are much more pronounced for Black youth than for White youth. There is enough evidence to indicate that young people of color are more likely to be arrested, jailed, tried in juvenile or adult court, and convicted than White juveniles for the same crime. This calls for further investigation, and social scientists interested in social justice need to explore the probability of institutional racism within the various levels of the judiciary system. A higher value should be placed on the lives of young Black boys and men so they are not lost in the shuffle and bureaucracy of the judicial system. The criminal justice system must reflect justice for all.

Americans are confronted daily with numerous negative stereotypes labeling and demeaning the status of African American men. Stereotyping and profiling perpetuate the destructive images reflected in society. Often neglected and forgotten are the majority of Black men who are contributing to the well-being of their families, communities, and society. The question that must be asked is why? Why are Black men overrepresented in the data reflected by our criminal justice system? Why is the Black man perceived as a competitive threat to individuals, communities, and society?

AFRICAN AMERICANS AND THE ECONOMIC SYSTEM

During the period 1997 through 2003, African Americans made tremendous progress toward becoming active participants in the economic system of the United States. African American–owned businesses increased from slightly over 800,000 firms to over 1.2 million firms during this 16-year period, generating nearly $89 billion in business revenue (U.S. Census Bureau, 2006). In 2002 approximately 4 in 10 firms operated in health care, social assistance, and other services. Many of these businesses were small firms; larger firms (about 969) employ 100 people or more. There are 10,716 African American–owned companies with receipts of $1 million or more. These account for 1 percent of the total number of Black-owned businesses.

More than 3 million individuals are in management, professional, and related occupations. This amounts to 25.2 percent of its population, with another 22 percent
employed in service occupations, 27 percent in sales and office occupations, with others
in various jobs such as in construction, transportation, fishing, farming, and maintenance. Approximately 59.4 percent are found in the civilian labor force, and another
0.8 percent in the armed forces for individuals over 16 years of age.

Approximately 15 percent of African American families had incomes of $75,000
or more during the 2000 census, with 1 percent having an income over $200,000. In
1989 one in seven Black families, about a million, had a yearly income of $50,000 or
more, whereas in 2000, tremendous progress was made as approximately 2.5 million
families had incomes beyond $50,000.

Top-level Black executives in corporate America have found that beyond the glass
ceiling there are still barriers, but not as many as during the previous decade, as reported by Graves (1993). There are still forms of intimidation and unjustified denial of
credit-worthiness when applying for mortgage, business, or personal loans. The public's perception of African Americans is troubling, as reported by the Federal Reserve
Board of Boston by Smith (1992), which showed that Blacks were 60 percent more
likely than Whites to be rejected for bank loans. To overcome this roadblock, affluent
Blacks are pulling together to create a banking system founded by Black enterprise to
better meet the needs of their community.

Over the past decade, African American workers are losing economic ground and
are facing the future of possible high unemployment, intermittent work, and low pay.
Many workers are overrepresented in low-paying service jobs. Conditions affecting
economic opportunities include the following:

1. A decrease in skilled and semiskilled blue collar jobs in the economy
2. An increase in immigrants who compete with workers and small business owners
3. A decline in membership in industrial union power
4. Movement of employment opportunities from inner cities to suburbs
5. A resurgence of conservative beliefs about government and its role in solving economic
   problems (Aguirre & Turner, 1998, p. 78)

There are loud warnings about social and economic isolation of urban African
Americans. Most Blacks live and work in large cities across the United States, so they are
disproportionately vulnerable to the next urban calamity because of their lack of access
to services, institutions, and economic opportunities (http://www.prb.org/template.cfm:
template=InterestDisplay.cfm&InterestCategoryID=247). For example, this sporadic
work history often leads to lack of health care and adequate retirement benefits for
African Americans. Older Blacks often live in poverty, retire early because of poor
health, or work past normal retirement age to maintain some economic security (Allen,
1988). Elderly African Americans earn approximately a third less retirement income
than the majority of Americans. According to researchers, elderly Blacks see themselves
in three groups: (1) workers 55 and over who are working 20 or more hours a week; (2)
retirees who are not working at all or working less than 20 hours a week; and (3) non-
retirees, those not working or those working less than 20 hours a week but who do not

see themselves as being retired (Allen, 1988). Those particularly disadvantaged are the so-called nonretired, who are financially less secure, less educated, and less healthy. A significant percentage of nonretired African Americans are female heads of households who tend to live in rural areas.

Between 1990 and 2000, African Americans comprised up to 20 percent of the new entrants into the labor force. This labor force is divided along educational and socioeconomic lines. If present trends continue, a disproportionate number of African Americans will form an underclass, lacking the educational training required for upward mobility and remaining in low-paying jobs, such as those found in the service sectors (O'Hare et al., 1991; U.S. Census Bureau, 2000). The inappropriate early tracking of many African Americans into dead-end jobs often produces low-paid workers and low-income retirees.

According to a study by Joe and Yu (1984), the decrease of African American men of working age in the labor force corresponds closely to the percentage increase of African American women heading families alone. In 2000 the African American median income for women working full time, year round, was $25,000, whereas the median income of African American married couple families was $33,255. These data show that full-time employed women's income has markedly risen from income reported in 1990, which was $11,600 compared to married family income of $30,700 (O'Hare et al., 1991).

HELPFUL TECHNIQUES FOR SERVING AFRICAN AMERICAN FAMILIES

As helping professionals in your chosen career, you will meet many African American families. With the increase of African Americans in higher education, many Black professionals will be working side by side with you. Racial labels such as *colored* and *Negro* are considered derogatory and should never be used. Whether one prefers being called Black or African American should be explored. The term *African American* does not emphasize skin color but includes reference to a cultural heritage and formalizes a connection to Africa. For many Blacks, there is a sense of their group's history and for some it has become an integral part of their personality. Because helping professionals serve many clients of all diverse groups, it is important to realize that your clients' decisions made at the present are sometimes influenced by the events of the past. You must be sensitive to the social, cultural, and environmental context of families and individuals. Every member of a family has a different story to tell, especially if they are from different generations. It is mandatory that the performance of professional ethics be of the highest standards to build trust through expressive body language and effective communication.

Cooperating with African American churches, sororities, fraternities, and a variety of other organizations will facilitate service to African American families. The majority of African Americans belong to the Baptist and the African Methodist Episcopal churches. Therefore, explore the role of the church in the lives of your African American families.

Many community groups are willing to contribute services, mentoring, and money to help African American youth. In part, your role will be one of activating various community resources.

According to Ho (1992), a consequence of a legacy of slavery and racism has been the development of a thriving, cultural paranoia phenomenon. This phenomenon of suspicion of others with different values and colors must be challenged with cultural sensitivity and through communicative exchange. Often, if the professional is African American, she should not assume that the other is less suspicious and guarded because of their similar ethnic heritage. Remember that nonverbal communication is a critical means of gaining information and is worthy of consideration. Trying too hard to understand African Americans can be as much a problem as being too distant. For example, this statement is to be avoided: "Let me help you with your problem."

When helping African American families, concentrate on the strengths of the families. Assist individuals and family members in gaining information and skills necessary to make decisions and solve their own problems. Reinforce and emphasize empowerment through ethnically sensitive practices and by creating opportunities for others to make their thoughts and feelings known. You can start by assuming that others have useful ideas and information, and by paying attention and not interrupting.

✦ CONCLUSIONS

African Americans are continuing to make remarkable gains in every generation. No other ethnic minority group can claim the achievements made in this short time. However, what does the future hold? There are many indications that African American families will become bipolar in economic distribution; that is, the span between the affluent and poor is widening, with little evidence of a growing middle class bridging the gap.

A majority of African American children live in one-parent households. The income available to these families is often insufficient to move them out of poverty. Especially vulnerable is the young African American male who is struggling to achieve a higher quality of life without good strategies for success. However, even with many odds against them, many African American children from poor families become successful adults. Educational attainment data show an increasing number of young men and women are going on to college. The likelihood of increasing life expectancy for these young people indicates a movement toward the "mountain top."

Derrick Bell (1992) leaves us with a powerful message in his national best seller, *Faces at the Bottom of the Well:* "We yearn that our civil rights work will be crowned with success, but what we really want—want even more than success—is meaning. . . . It is a story less of success than of survival through an unremitting struggle that leaves no room for giving up. We are all part of that history and it is still unfolding" (pp. 198, 200). Many of us cannot see the world around us because of our limited perspectives from the bottom of the well. We must climb out of the well and see there is more than one way to be, act, and think.

✦ STUDY QUESTIONS

1. Define the terms *ethnic, minority, discrimination, prejudice, holistic, segregation,* and *affirmative action.*
2. Billingsley believes social scientists have misrepresented African Americans. List three of his reasons.
3. List at least 10 demographic findings from census data about African American citizens and African American families.
4. Describe African American gender roles as described by researchers.
5. State evidence of African American family values.
6. List 10 findings from studies of African American children and adults in the educational system.
7. Summarize the findings regarding the health and involvement of African Americans in the health care system.
8. List findings regarding elderly African American people.
9. List evidence of African Americans' involvement with the governmental system.
10. List findings from data showing participation of African Americans in the economic system.

✦ APPLICATIONS

1. Is it true that the best studies of African American families have been done by African American scholars? List five reasons why you believe this statement is true and five reasons why it is not true.
2. Assume that you and your children are recipients of unequal treatment. Write a one-page essay stating how you would feel and how you would react as a parent.
3. List five examples of practices and behaviors that demonstrate institutional racism. State in a one-page essay how each institution in question should correct the behavior.
4. Check your library and review an encyclopedia of prominent African Americans. Select one individual, and write a one-page essay on the factors that contributed to that individual's success.
5. Dr. Martin Luther King, Jr., was the most famous leader of the civil rights movement. However, women leaders also played key roles. Select one individual, and write a one-page essay on either Rosa Parks, Daisy Bates, Ella Baker, Constance Motley, Diane Nash, or Autherine Foster.
6. In learning about an ethnic group, the best way is to operate with guidance and cooperation. If possible, to experience another ethnic culture, ask to be invited as a friend or guest by a member of that group who will agree to act as your guide.
7. Who you are is determined by many factors. The following activity will help you understand some of the things that influence who you are. Fill in the blanks and compare this with someone from another ethnic group.

Objective: To deal directly and specifically with apparent discrepancies.

My nationality is:
My ethnicity is:
My race is:
My religion is:
My favorite food is:
My age is:
I live in a _____ city_____ suburb_____ rural area
Family born in United States:
_____ parents _____ grandparents _____ great-grandparents
Languages I speak are:
My career choice is:
My birth order is:

What four choices from the preceding list adequately define who you are?

✦ ADDITIONAL RESOURCES

A tour of Colonial Williamsburg, Virginia, would be of help in understanding the African American family during the period of slavery. In 1979 the African American historical and cultural experience was introduced into the historical replica of colonial Williamsburg. The museum tour, called "The Other Half," depicts the daily life of slaves and freed Blacks and how they lived during that period. Lectures on the slave trade, urban and rural slavery, education, religion, and music are also introduced.

In recognition of Black History Month, *Underground Railroad: First Person Narratives of Escapes to Freedom in the North* is a powerful book to read.

Dyson, M. E. (2004). *The Michael Eric Dyson reader.* New York: Basic Vivitas Books.

✦ MEDIA RESOURCES

Videos

A Question of Color. (1992). 16 mm film, 58 minutes. (Available from Resolution, Inc., California Newsreel, 149 Ninth Street, Suite 420, San Francisco, CA 94103)

Black History: Lost, Stolen, or Strayed. (1965). Video, 60 minutes. (Available from Insight Media, 2162 Broadway, New York, NY 10024)

I'll Fly Away. PBS Television Series, Video. (Available from some libraries and from local TV stations; Washington Educational Television Association, Box 2626, Washington, DC, 703-998-2600)

Encarta Africana, CD Encyclopedia. Also in book form, Perseus Books. This encyclopedia on disc was largely financed by Microsoft.

✦ KEY INTERNET RESOURCES

National Black Child Development Institute (NBCDI)
   www.nbcdi.org/Welcome/

National Coalition African American Parent Involvement in Education (NCAAPIE)
   www.ncaapie.org/HOME.asp

✦ FURTHER READING

Dyson, M. E. (2004). *The Michael Eric Dyson reader.* New York: Basic Civitas Books.

Graham, L.O. (2000). *Our kind of people.* New York: Harper Perennial.

Jackson, J., Chatters, L., & Taylor, R. (Eds.). (1992). *Aging in Black America.* Newbury Park, CA: Sage.

Majors, R., & Gordon, J. (Eds.). (1994). *The American Black male.* Chicago: Nelson Hall.

McAdoo, H., & McAdoo, J. L. (Eds.). (1985). *Black children.* Beverly Hills, CA: Sage.

Ploski, H. A., & Williams, J. (Eds.). (1989). *The Negro almanac: A reference work on African-Americans* (5th ed.). Detroit: Gale Research.

5

Hispanic American Families

→ Key Concepts

- Hispanics
- Anglos
- Three R's of Hispanic Values

Six-year-old Gloria skipped into her grandfather's tiny grocery store in the barrio of a small Texas town. She carried her first reader under her arm, embraced her grandfather, and exclaimed in Spanish, "¡Abuelito, Abuelito, I learned to write my name today!" Grandfather Martínez stopped arranging shelves and embraced Gloria, saying in his native Spanish, "¿De veras? Muéstrame aquí." ("Is that true? Here, show me.") He tore a corner off some butcher paper and handed her a stubby pencil he carried in his grocer's apron. Gloria wrote the letters G L O R I A in her 6-year-old's script and proudly showed Abuelito. "¡Qué bien!" ("How great!"), he exclaimed, admiring her work. Then he opened his wallet, tucked the scrap of paper in for safekeeping, and carried it for many years. Gloria felt the warmth of her grandfather's love and his appreciation of her success for all her growing-up years.

Family support for education, as indicated in this story of Gloria and her grandfather, is evident in many Hispanic parents and grandparents. They are often even more overtly persistent in their encouragement of education for their children and grandchildren when they themselves have missed out on educational opportunities.

BRIEF HISTORY OF THREE MAJOR HISPANIC GROUPS

Three national groups comprise the majority of Hispanics in the United States: Mexican, Puerto Rican, and Cuban Hispanics. Combined, these groups make up 79 percent of all U.S. Hispanics (Figure 5.1). The remainder of Hispanics comes from Central and South American countries, the Caribbean, and Spain. Hispanics are an ethnic group, not a distinct racial group. Thus Hispanics can be of any race (U.S. Census Bureau, 2000).

Figure 5.1   Percentages of Hispanics in the U.S. by National Origin

Source: Adapted from U.S. Census Bureau, *Current Population Survey*, March 2000.

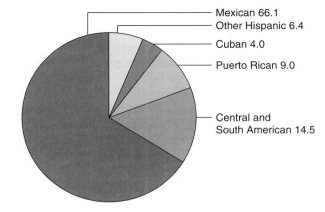

Mexican 66.1
Other Hispanic 6.4
Cuban 4.0
Puerto Rican 9.0
Central and South American 14.5

Geographically, Hispanics live in every corner of this nation (Figure 5.2). However, heavy concentrations can be found in certain regions: Puerto Ricans in the Northeast (New York); Cubans in the Southeast (Florida); and Mexicans and South and Central Americans in the Southwest and West (Texas, California). Census 2000 data show that although over half of all Hispanics live in just two states—Texas and California—more and more states are reporting significant increases in Hispanic numbers. Additional states that

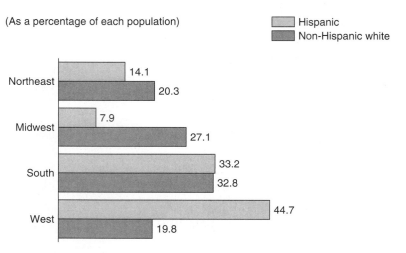

Figure 5.2   Distribution of Hispanics and Non-Hispanic Whites by U.S. Regions

Source: Adapted from U.S. Census Bureau, *Current Population Survey*, March 2000.

report increases in Hispanic population since the 1990 census, for example, are Wisconsin, 107 percent; Iowa, 153 percent; and Minnesota, 166 percent.

Population Data

It is clear that, of all the racial and ethnic groups profiled by the census, Hispanics are the most dynamic, not only in terms of increase in their numbers but in many other demographic characteristics as well. During the decade of the 1990s, more than 10 million immigrants came to the United States. By way of comparison, statistics show that during the decade of the 1960s, the largest number of immigrants (40 percent) were of European descent. During the 1990s, however, 52 percent were from Latin America and 30 percent were from Asia. The Hispanic population exploded by 68 percent, from 22.4 million in 1990 to 32.8 million in 2000. Over 62 percent (20.6 million) of the 32.8 million Hispanic immigrants are of Mexican origin. Factors causing this migration include primarily economic conditions and political turmoil, as well as, in some instances, religious intolerance in the countries of origin (Falicov, 1998; Stavans, 2001). In 2000, Hispanics comprised 12 percent of the total population of the United States. Fully two thirds of Hispanics in the United States are immigrants or children of immigrants (Martin & Midgley, 1999).

Assuming moderate fertility rates, which are highest among Hispanic immigrant women, the prediction is that the number of Hispanics living in the United States will soar from 12 percent of the total population in 2000 to 24 percent in 2050. Comparing Hispanics to non-Hispanic Whites or *Anglos,* the U.S. Census Bureau (2000) reports that, on the whole, Hispanics are younger and less educated than non-Hispanic Whites (Figure 5.3). The median age for Hispanics is 26 years, and for Anglos, 37 years.

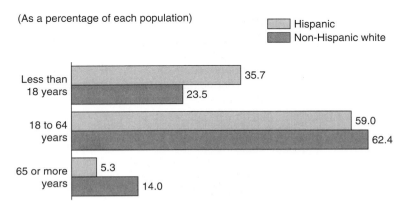

Figure 5.3   Percentage Comparison of Hispanics to Non-Hispanic Whites, by Age

Source: Adapted from U.S. Census Bureau, *Current Population Survey,* March 2000.

More than 36 percent of the Hispanic population is under 18 years of age, compared to 24 percent of the Anglo population. Only about 5 percent of Hispanics are over 65, whereas 14 percent of non-Hispanic Whites are 65 or older. Educationally, 57 percent of Hispanics ages 25 and older complete high school, compared to 88 percent of Anglos. Some large U.S. cities, like Houston, Texas, report high school dropout rates nearing 50 percent or higher. Hispanics with associate's or bachelor's degrees number less than 11 percent, as compared to 28 percent for non-Hispanic whites. By and large, of all Hispanic national groups, Cuban Hispanics achieve the highest levels of education (U.S. Census Bureau, 2000).

WHO ARE THE HISPANICS?

Hispanic Americans' roots are related to Spain. The people of that country, in the fifteenth century, discovered and exploited the New World, especially southern parts of Mexico, Central America, South America, the United States, and the Caribbean islands. This chapter focuses primarily on Hispanics whose ancestral roots are in Mexico, Cuba, Puerto Rico, and Central and South America. These groups tend to have a common experience in the use of the Spanish language and their status as a minority. However, the notable diversity among the groups is grounded in their different points of national origin, immigration history, and social class backgrounds (del Pinal & Singer, 1997).

As early as 1565, Spanish explorers and colonists settled in parts of what is now Florida. Spanish-speaking peoples also were the first to migrate into the Great American Southwest, settling there even before the founding of the Plymouth Colony by the Pilgrims in 1620. They came by way of Mexico during Spain's colonial expansion, occupying land mainly in what is now New Mexico, Texas, Arizona, California, and Colorado. In a historical sense, settlers of Hispanic descent predate the settlers of Anglo-European origin, populating what is today the southwestern United States.

Soon after the original 13 colonies gained their freedom from British rule, massive migration began across the continent and into the Spanish-owned Southwest. After Mexico gained its independence from Spain in 1821, the government encouraged migration into its sparsely populated territory to the north and promised land to those willing to settle there.

After many years, those settlers became increasingly difficult to govern, and many perceived the Mexican government as being so unjust and intrusive that they were driven to declare their independence from its oppression. In 1836, against what appeared to be insurmountable odds, Texans united, fought, and won their freedom in the decisive Battle of San Jacinto. Thus Texas became a free "republic" for a brief period of nine years. The new republic encompassed the Great American Southwest, a conglomerate of original Spanish settlers, pioneering Anglo-Americans, as well as Native American Indians. In 1845 Texas joined the United States as a state.

During the ensuing decades, migration from the south and the east continued at a swift pace. People seeking freedom from the bondage of oppression often brought with them a legacy of poverty. Mexicans, desirous of better economic and social environments, traveled north to settle and start anew. They entered the new republic freely—with no legal restraints—to join relatives, find work, and thus create a better existence. They came seeking a new and better life, often at the cost of great personal suffering and risk.

Occurring simultaneously with the Spanish invasion of the mainland in the 1500s was the invasion of the Caribbean island now known as Puerto Rico. Spanish conquerors brought their language, literature, food preferences, and life values with them. They brought African slaves to the island to work in the production of sugarcane. Over time, the native Taino Indian way of life became inextricably meshed with Spanish and African influences.

Another invasion of Puerto Rico occurred in 1898 when the island became the property of the United States as a result of the Spanish-American War. In 1917 Puerto Ricans were granted U.S. citizenship, which greatly facilitated migration between the island and the mainland. It is believed that the strong influence of colonization by the United States, and the ease of passage between the two lands, has greatly affected the lack of stability in Puerto Rican family life.

The Caribbean island of Cuba, like Puerto Rico, was also invaded and colonized by Spanish conquistadors in the 1500s. Unlike Puerto Rico, Cuba was able to gain independence from U.S. rule resulting from the Spanish-American War, and until the Cuban revolution in 1959, Cuba remained tied to the United States only through limited political and economic interest.

The course of economic development in Cuba since its independence resulted in the bulk of its wealth being in the hands of a small percentage of its citizens. After decades of exploitation, a large underclass was ripe for revolution and triumphed under Fidel Castro's socialist leadership (Stavans, 2001). An immediate exodus from the island by the elite class ensued, with thousands choosing to migrate to the state of Florida, just 90 miles across the water.

Cuban migration to the United States has occurred over many decades, but the vast migration after 1959 consisted of the well-educated middle and upper classes. At that time, Americans openly welcomed Cubans because they were fleeing from communism. Additional but smaller waves of Cubans immigrated in 1980 and later during the 1990s.

Prejudice

The reception of later Hispanic arrivals by the original settlers was less than enthusiastic, however. The newcomers were unwelcome and treated with disdain and intolerable prejudice. Today, it might seem unthinkable that human beings would begrudge other human beings the right to pursue a better existence for themselves and their family. But Mexicans and other immigrants were—and, in many instances, are still today—scorned by those who arrived here first. Discrimination seems to be a common plight of new immigrants. Perhaps the fact that some migrated from Mexico, a country with which the United States had had military conflicts, or the fact that many immigrants were so culturally, ethnically, and linguistically distinct, encouraged the prejudice toward immigrants arriving in the "new republic."

Today, throughout the land areas that border Mexico, prejudice persists in various forms and degrees, not only toward Mexicans, but toward other Hispanics who immigrate from Central and South America as well. There is often an unspoken fear that immigrants come to take jobs and other benefits that rightfully belong to U.S. citizens and legal residents (Cozic, 1997; Martin & Midgley, 1999). It is today ironic that some Hispanics who have become citizens and acculturated often speak against the immigration of others, even those from their own country of origin.

Additionally, pressure exerted by the majority culture on immigrants to become assimilated into a homogeneous national culture is pervasive, and not always subtle. Many Hispanics—superbly proud of their roots and distinct national heritages—tenaciously resist the pressure to assimilate. Unlike Anglo-European Americans, Hispanic Americans sustain and reinforce their culture largely because of the geographic proximity of their ancestral countries and islands (Stavans, 2001).

HISPANICS: LIKENESSES AND DIFFERENCES

Even though differences among Hispanic groups are sometimes as great as the similarities, many Hispanics attest to the fact that they are more alike than different in the areas that really matter. Although fiercely proud of their diversity, Hispanics have in common several salient cultural characteristics that seem to cut across lines of national origin, and, for that reason, will allow themselves "with inclusive pride" to be grouped and referred to as Hispanics. Hispanic is a government-imposed label that to many implies political conservatism. The term *Latino* seems to be the label of choice for those who tend to be advocates for the enhancement of economic and political rights of the group. A survey conducted in 1996, however, indicates that 58 percent of persons of Hispanic/Latino background prefer the term *Hispanic* to 12 percent who prefer *Latino* (del Pinal & Singer, 1997).

These inclusive labels notwithstanding, most Hispanics prefer to be identified and called by their country of origin, such as Mexican American, Cuban American, Spanish American, and the like. This may indicate the various groups' strong desire to maintain a tight grip on their respective roots. Many Mexican Americans prefer the term *Chicano* because it is a self-chosen identifying term that connotes pride in the unique bicultural heritage of an American of Mexican descent. *Boricua, Latino*, and *La Raza* are also words by which Hispanic groups identify themselves. The personal decision of how to refer to the different groups lies ultimately with the individuals and their distinct preference. Some may prefer to be called Americans. Of course, a large percentage have been born in the United States and are Americans; others are in various stages of becoming American citizens in the legal sense.

The Spanish Language

The Spanish language is one of the most salient characteristics of all the Hispanic people whose roots are ultimately from Spain. The beautiful, melodious Spanish language has been preserved by many American Hispanics, making Spanish one of the proud characteristics that the various Hispanic groups hold in common (Stavans, 2001). One's native language is an intimate, integral, and very personal part of the self. To have it recognized and valued is a boost to one's self-esteem. Conversely, to have one's language discredited or negated can be an assault on one's sense of identity.

The language of the home is the thread that tangibly connects individuals to loved ones. Weakening of the mother tongue may contribute to the weakening of the family (Stavans, 2001). Disparaging a person's language may add to the alienation of the individual. To eradicate the language, or even to suggest such an action, can have immediate—as well as long-term—deleterious effects on individuals and families (Fillmore & Britsch, 1988). To be stripped totally of one's mother tongue and culture is tantamount to negating one's personal identity—alas, one's very own personhood. Although some would deny this, obliteration of one's native language should not be sought or expected of any cultural group or individual. Many more life choices exist for those with the ability to use more than one language (Garcia, 1997).

It is incumbent on educational institutions, particularly those serving the young, to value and help preserve students' mother tongues, even while encouraging children to learn English. Non-Spanish-speaking helping professionals should try to learn and use at least a few common Spanish phrases. Sincere attempts at using the language go a long way in establishing warm relationships that are so important to Hispanics.

The Spanish language, of course, is a language spoken by about 500 million people in Spain and in the Western Hemisphere. There is a large body of Spanish literature spanning many centuries. Until 1967, when the Bilingual Education Act became law, children were penalized in schools if they spoke a language other than English. Despite the educational intent of this practice, it served to discourage most children and to plant doubts in their minds about the value of their mother tongue, sometimes resulting in their partial or total avoidance of Spanish.

Since the implementation of the Bilingual Education Act, schools have provided teachers who can help children build on their native language while learning English. Integrating the children's cultures as well as their languages into the school and class environment is a more appropriate approach in a multicultural world. Under the old system, many Hispanics never learned to write or read Spanish or to understand its structure, even though they used the language in their most intimate associations. Modern educational approaches expect schools to maintain the Spanish language and value the cultural backgrounds of the children. However, the extent to which this is reality may vary significantly from school to school.

In contrast, some Hispanic parents still insist that schools teach their children English, and only English, unaware of the effect on the child's self-image and overlooking the advantages of fluent bilingual abilities. Parents may equate proficiency in English with success in obtaining good jobs in the future. Some will even ask that no Spanish at all be spoken to their children in school, and they will not allow their children to be placed in a bilingual class, fearing their learning of English will be impeded. Many Hispanic immigrants come to this country with the express purpose of accessing an education for their children and having them become English proficient. Although many parents want their children to maintain and preserve their native Spanish, they see

Spanish proficiency for their children as a responsibility of the home, not of the school. Parental attitudes may be colored by their own struggle to learn English and their inability to obtain better jobs because of a lack of English-language proficiency. Professionals can help children by working closely with parents to clarify the immediate and long-term benefits of being bilingual and bicultural in today's world (Stavans, 2001).

State and national efforts to legislate "English-only" as the "official language of the government" tend to surface occasionally. Although the intent of such bills may be to speed the learning of English, to expedite assimilation of language minorities into the mainstream culture, and to maintain the efficiency and cohesiveness of a single common language, they are considered by proponents of bilingual education to be restrictive of the civil rights and opportunities of non-English-speaking Americans, as well as unnecessary (Lyons, 1993).

THE ECOLOGY OF HISPANIC AMERICAN FAMILIES

Although there is significant diversity among Hispanic Americans, certain important values are held in common by all groups. By and large, Hispanics are traditional in orientation and affiliative in nature. This seems particularly true of the most recent arrivals to the United States. Values rooted in the Judeo-Christian religious tradition strongly affect male and female roles and how these roles are played out within the family. Many Hispanics' views of work, people, and life are affected in many of the same ways as other similarly rooted traditional cultures.

RELIGIOUS FOUNDATION OF HISPANIC FAMILIES

Hispanics have lived and functioned with the pronounced influence of Judeo-Christian principles on family roles and interpersonal relationships. Spaniards first introduced the Roman Catholic faith to the indigenous peoples of the New World. Through the centuries, a mingling of the Old World religion with the beliefs of native peoples resulted in Christian converts who practiced the religion but still held on to some indigenous beliefs, such as *mal de ojo* ("evil eye") and *brujería* ("witchcraft") (Falicov, 1998).

When helping professionals learn of the beliefs held by clients they serve, it is important to withhold judgment and avoid making insensitive comments, no matter how unusual or different the belief may be or how much one disagrees with it. A nonjudgmental attitude on the part of the helping professional allows a rapport to develop, which, in turn, facilitates a better understanding of the individual's functioning.

Catholicism is the professed religion of the majority of Hispanics, even though many do not actively practice the faith. Today, however, significant numbers of Hispanics are leaving Catholicism to join Protestant denominations and evangelical churches (Stavans, 2001). A small but growing number are embracing the Muslim faith. Many Hispanics are simply rejecting religious affiliation altogether. The appeal of some

Protestant denominations to Hispanics is because the ministers generally come from a Latino background, speak Spanish, share the daily hardships of the community, and provide more of an egalitarian, or more democratic, church life based on scripture. The fundamental, traditional aspects of the Muslim faith seem to attract more traditionally minded Hispanics.

Today, the Catholic Church is facing many changes. In 1993 a committee of U.S. Catholic bishops developed a document on marriage that encourages Roman Catholics to move beyond the sexual stereotypes they grew up with and to strive toward equality of the sexes. Declaring that "marriage is a partnership of man and woman equal in dignity and value," the statement was developed for presentation at the annual meeting of the National Conference of Catholic Bishops (Briggs, 1993).

As change takes place, many Hispanics profess to be Catholic as an automatic response, instead of a practicing reality in their lives. As individual Hispanics consider traditions and practices that tend to bind more than liberate, they may choose from other belief systems or religious options, including the option of practicing no formal religion at all. This, however, seems to be more the exception than the rule for the majority of Hispanics.

HISPANIC FAMILY STRUCTURES

In searching for new economic opportunities and accepting new realities, Hispanics endeavor to maintain close ties with their families of origin. The sanctity of the family is particularly emphasized in traditional Hispanic culture. It is within the context of the family that the individual finds security and emotional strength (Olmos, Ybarra, & Monterrey, 1999).

"There's No Question: Family Comes First," declares a newspaper headline about Chad Richardson's (1993) research on Mexican families living in northern Mexico along the U.S. border. Adults in these families enter the United States daily to work. In search of employment, some venture deeper into the United States and stay longer, leaving family behind. "Most people in Mexico do not want to leave their families, their homes, and their country behind," says Dr. Richardson, a sociology professor and director of the Border Life Project at the University of Texas at Brownsville. "Awfully strong pressures, economic and otherwise, force them to go," he states. He continues, "The family is much more important in Mexico than in the United States" (p. 10).

Financial needs often force children to drop out of school to help support the family. Individual goals become subordinated to the needs of the family. Likewise, Mexican Hispanics, especially the more recent immigrants, are oriented strongly toward the family, which is considered to be the dominant source of advice and support for the family unit as well as for the individual (Rumbaut, 1997).

Although the notion that Hispanics are more family oriented than Anglos has been a consistent theme in the social science literature for decades, the recent rise in the number of disrupted families headed by women is seen as an outcome of highly stressful environments (Frisbie, 1993). Census data show that between 1970 and 1995, the percentage of persons older than 18 years who were divorced doubled. Nearly 26 percent of all Hispanic families are headed by single women, as compared to 13 percent of White families. The percentage of single-parent families among Puerto Rican Hispanics is 50 percent, or double the total Hispanic percentage, and almost triple the Anglo average of 13 percent. The number of households made up of intact families is highest among Mexican Hispanics, at 84 percent, as compared to the 73 percent of all other Hispanic groups combined (U.S. Census Bureau, 2000).

Specifically, among Mexican Americans and Cuban Americans, statistics show that marital stability is inversely related to educational attainment. That is, the more education achieved, the less marital stability. Among Puerto Rican Hispanics, however, marital stability increases with educational attainment (Frisbie, 1993). Mexican Americans have the highest fertility rate, and Cuban Americans, who are more highly educated, have the lowest fertility of all Hispanic groups. Statistics show that for all groups, poverty and lower educational levels are positively correlated with higher fertility rates (U.S. Census Bureau, 2000).

To be sure, Hispanic families have not escaped the societal assaults that negatively impact families of all cultural groups today. Divorce has taken its toll on Hispanic families and has seriously challenged the traditional, strongly held concept of family as a sacred institution and marriage as a lifelong proposition (del Pinal & Singer, 1997).

MALE ROLES IN THE HISPANIC FAMILY

The authority of the husband as head of the wife and household is defined in the Bible, and it is literally lived out in the traditional Hispanic nuclear family unit, particularly in the most recent immigrant arrivals. The authority of the husband and father is seldom questioned or disputed. The father's role is expected to be one of breadwinner and protector of the family. He provides for the family's physical needs and monitors and controls all members' participation in the world outside the home. This sovereign role is often perceived by the society at large as macho, or chauvinistic, and extremely undemocratic. However, in the Hispanic culture, machismo refers to a role that carries major responsibility for others, namely the family (Olmos et al., 1999). The concept of *manliness* is more synonymous with *macho* for most Hispanics. Such a definition is devoid of arrogance or chauvinistic characteristics often ascribed to the term by mainstream society. To Hispanics, the male role commands respect and significant regard, not because of the individual who plays the role but because of what the role involves.

The Hispanic father is viewed as the provider of income and sustenance for his family. His involvement with his children, particularly the younger ones, is often very limited or nonexistent. The rearing and care of the children is regarded as primarily the mother's role. Once the children grow into adolescence, however, the father is often called on to exert his authority as head, particularly in matters of discipline. The lack of earlier bonding and rapport may make this role very difficult for the father to play and difficult for the teenager to accept. Continued parent–child conflict often is the cause of youth leaving their families to affiliate with gangs.

Talk It Over

Mr. Santos, appearing upset, requested a conference with Mrs. Angela, the teacher of his 4-year-old son, Jorge. While talking with the teacher, Mr. Santos thanked her for all she had done for Jorge since he enrolled in the preschool only six months before. The boy was now speaking English well and seemed to be on his way to becoming thoroughly bilingual. But the fact that Jorge had learned a great deal did not detract from Mr. Santos's distress. He wanted to address the gnawing concern that was on his mind. He was disturbed as he watched his son "playing house" in the home center of the classroom. It seemed that Jorge enjoyed dressing up like a "Mommy" as he played with the other children. "What are you going to do about it?" he emphatically asked the teacher.

Mrs. Angela, the teacher, believes that children gain perspective and understanding by playing out many roles in the classroom. She was now challenged by the traditionally oriented father to explain why. What would you say and do if you were the teacher?

FEMALE ROLES IN THE HISPANIC FAMILY

The Hispanic woman's self-sacrificing, self-effacing role as wife and mother is derived from the strict, traditional biblical interpretation of submissiveness. In this light, the woman is expected to serve her husband and nurture her children, often at the expense of her own needs and desires. It is her role to see about the needs and activities of the children. As mentioned previously, although the father may be well aware of all of the family's goings-on, his actual involvement is limited at best. Throughout most of the Hispanic world, the role of mother is venerated as the giver and perpetuator of life and love within the family.

Like the male role, however, the Hispanic married woman's traditional role is affected in the United States by values of individual equality regardless of gender and by tremendous societal pressures and opposing expectations. Women of today are educated and expect to be equal in power within as well as outside the family. Thus the greater the degree of cultural assimilation that characterizes the Hispanic family, the greater the likelihood that egalitarian roles will exist within the family unit.

Societal factors that impact male and female roles—such as the need for women to work outside of the home—have confronted the Hispanic family with an often unwelcome need for change. The family's resistance to such fundamental change has resulted in difficult struggles. From all sides the message seems clear: The traditional

Hispanic way of family functioning is at odds with the American way of life. Thus a cultural dilemma arises for the traditional Hispanic family. Economic pressures alone are often great enough to cause the mother to work outside the home, something diametrically opposed to strongly held convictions about obligations to home and family. Both males and females of younger and older generations are learning to adjust to prevailing social forces.

As the Hispanic woman goes to work outside the home, she usually does so with much ambivalence about leaving her children in the care of others. Doubts about the decision are minimized when the caregiver happens to be the grandmother. However, more and more, grandmothers are unavailable because of their own need to be involved in the workforce or because families live long distances from members of the extended family.

Working outside the home is advantageous if the family's economic situation requires it and the woman can command a decent salary. Lack of skills and education often limits the Hispanic woman's chances for a well-paying job, however. Unless the woman has sufficient education and qualifications, any wages that are earned may merely cover the cost of paid child care. But educated or not, for many Hispanic women, to work outside the home when children are young is a very difficult decision to make. Generating income in her own right, which can cause a woman to expect to have more power in the family, often conflicts with the traditional role of the woman as nurturer of the family and the man as the provider and authoritarian head of the household.

CHILDREN'S ROLES IN THE HISPANIC FAMILY

Children are highly valued in traditional Hispanic families, especially at younger ages. As infants, children are indulged, not only by parents but by older siblings and relatives as well. As children grow, however, they are expected to contribute to the family by performing chores, running errands, accompanying parents on shopping trips to help with English interpretation, and caring for younger siblings. Teens and young adults are expected to contribute financially to the family by working after school and on weekends. Such family obligations may interfere with the child's full participation in school, thereby resulting in poor academic performance. Poor school performance may contribute to the child's dropping out of school to work full time to help the family. Until they marry and leave the home, young adult children are expected to work and contribute some or all of their earnings to the family.

Children at School

In the school, the Hispanic child seems acutely sensitive to social and psychological cues in the environment. This style of learning has been referred to in the literature as a "field-sensitive" style (Hudgens, 1993). Studies conducted in classrooms with significant proportions of Hispanic children have shown that working with peers in small groups or pairs and receiving individual attention from the teacher are methods that facilitate learning. An environment that is psychologically cold, detached, and extremely task oriented may actually impede Hispanic children's learning. In contrast, an accepting atmosphere that enhances rapport between child and teacher and fosters supportive peer relationships is more likely to result in effective learning.

At school and through the media, children learn about democracy and how that philosophy plays out in day-to-day life in mainstream society. But the democratic way of life that influences children outside of the home often causes parent–child conflicts within some Hispanic authoritarian homes. Participation in support groups where parents can feel safe to explore issues that affect family functioning within this democratic society may contribute to a more sound family life.

Educators and community leaders can invest their energies and lend their expertise in motivating students to achieve and reach educational goals through such successful efforts as the YES Charter School, the KIPP Academy, and Project GRAD, all located in Houston, Texas.

Obligations to the Extended Family

Caring for family members, including extended family, such as grandparents, aunts, uncles, and cousins, is a priority in Hispanic families. The extended family functions as support and a stabilizing force for individual members. Placing elderly parents in nursing homes or centers for the aged is virtually unknown. To do so may be looked on as abandonment or rejection of a loved one and as a serious shirking of family responsibility. The wisdom of elder family members is highly respected, sought, and valued. Children demonstrate respect for the authority of elders, whether related or not, by referring to them as "aunt" or "uncle" and demonstrating the same deference they would give to family members.

Many Hispanics in the United States, particularly the more recently immigrated, seek out and live in *colonias* or *barrios*, where the majority of residents may be of a common national origin. Family members, relatives, and other members of the community often share responsibility for the upbringing and socialization of the children. Close-knit communities collectively watch over their children by taking an interest in and participating, not only in accepting and nurturing them, but in guiding and disciplining them as well. Out of care and concern, even neighbors assume the role of "family" (Falicov, 1998) and may report to parents any observed inappropriate behavior or social infractions, causing children and youth to behave more circumspectly than they might otherwise.

The birth of a child is a cherished event celebrated by the family and community. In the Roman Catholic faith, the christening of the infant child is cherished as well. The adults chosen to be the child's godparents literally become a second set of parents for that child. They assume a significant role in the upbringing of the child and vow to take full and complete responsibility for the child if the parents die. For the older child, religious and nonreligious events, such as confirmation and the *quinceañera*, which is a coming-out event for adolescent girls, are significant and often celebrated by the community.

PROMINENT VALUES OF HISPANIC FAMILIES

Cultural groups possess many *characteristics* that can be considered to be neutral, positive, or negative in terms of value; all cultures possess all three types. These characteristics distinguish groups in unique ways. Such characteristics may include artifacts and traditions such as foods eaten, manner of dressing, special holidays observed, and, in many cases, language.

In contrast, cultural *values*, by definition, are enduring, positive attributes that are held in esteem by the group and are practiced, consciously or unconsciously, in everyday life. Cultural *values* dictate people's day-to-day actions and decisions about life. They are passed down from generation to generation and are slow to change. Strong, positive cultural values are such an integral part of a group's identity that to be forced to change or pressured to relinquish them can be at best demoralizing and even psychologically detrimental.

It is more beneficial to build on the strong values of a culture than to dwell excessively on what has often in the literature been referred to as "problems" or "deficits." Therefore, only the strong, positive values held by most Hispanics are addressed here. A better understanding of Hispanics can result if significant values that seem to cut across the socioeconomic boundaries and national origins of the various Hispanic groups are examined more closely.

This author believes strongly that focusing on the positive, strong values of a people can work to counteract the prevalent negative, debilitating, deficit-oriented perspective where Hispanics are depicted as problematic and as an enigma to society. America is a conglomerate of diverse cultural groups from all over the world. Indeed, it is this rich diversity of people that contributes to the very strength of the nation. When each group lends its strongest, most positive values to the whole, something like a rich tapestry is created, woven in a beautiful, unique pattern to be admired, enjoyed, and valued. It is in this spirit that the salient values that Hispanics hold dear are addressed here and offered for consideration and appreciation.

Before proceeding with further discussion, we must focus on the fact that as a whole, Hispanics comprise a disproportionate number of the poor in the United States. The various national groups that make up the Hispanic Americans are differentially poor as well. Keeping in mind that poverty is an economic condition and *not* a cultural value, this chapter emphasizes the attributes that make the Hispanic culture special and considers the positive contribution Hispanic values can make to a society that often seems insensitive, materialistic, and elitist.

The Three R's of Hispanic Values

Personal *relationships, respect,* and *responsibility* are three values that Hispanics hold most dear, and are referred to here as the three R's of Hispanic values. More than other values, these seem to cut across nationalities, as well as across all the socioeconomic levels of Hispanic groups. Two related values are *cooperation* (as opposed to competition) and *other-centeredness* (as opposed to self-centeredness).

Some social scientists say that the Spanish language is the glue that binds Hispanics to one another, and that may well be true. Clearly, the magnetism of the language seems to draw speakers of Spanish to each other, establishing an instantaneous rapport and connectedness between them. However, as strong as the language bond is, family *relationships, respect,* and *responsibility* are so important that even when language has been forgotten, abandoned, or inadvertently lost, the internalization of these values by the individual may result in a manner of "being Hispanic" that is not easily altered or discarded.

In mainstream society, where competition and rugged individualism are prevalent, the values of relationships, respect, and responsibility offer such contrasts to the mainstream way of life that Hispanics may find it difficult to adjust. Further discussion of how these values are lived out in everyday life may result in a better understanding.

Relationships in Families.   First, among most Hispanic groups, family *relationships* are very important. Reported high divorce rates notwithstanding, Hispanics make decisions based primarily on how they will affect the family. In the last two decades, assimilation and other societal pressures have caused an increase in family disruption, but, by and large, family still takes priority above all else. No sacrifice is considered too great to make for one's family. For example, it is very common for more recently immigrated families to spend all their hard-earned savings to travel great distances for extended visits to family members, particularly to see parents, siblings, and grandparents. Furthermore, so valued are family relationships, that if the choice is between spending money to purchase much-needed furniture for the home and making a trip to visit family, the latter will always win out. In such cases as this, there is hardly a choice involved. For Hispanics, "people before things" seems to be the operating principle.

The valuing of human relationships is clearly demonstrated by parents over and over in daily family life, in big and small ways. Children learn early and firsthand that people matter, above all. All children—but particularly very young children—are treated with great affection and attention. Much demonstrable affection is exhibited among family members such as greeting each other with a hug and/or kiss. There are frequent visits and get-togethers of the immediate as well as extended families. This affection creates strong emotional ties that transcend even great geographical distances. A feeling of belonging and strong family ties helps sustain many Hispanics through life's difficult and trying situations. An appropriate phrase to describe this phenomenon may come from the popular song: "People who need people are the luckiest people in the world."

Loyalty to family is demonstrated by and expected from all family members. For example, older children may be kept home from school to help care for ill siblings or parents. Teachers may find that older Hispanic students who are frequently absent from school may be attending to family obligations, such as accompanying a parent on community shopping trips or medical appointments to help with language interpretation, or going on regular, extended, out-of-town visits to the grandparents' home. Likewise, adult wage earners may risk losing their jobs when they fail to return to work on time because trips to visit relatives had to be prolonged for reasons deemed important to sustaining family ties and providing family support. The laborer's attitude that often prevails here is "there are always other jobs to be had." Teachers and employers may be hard-pressed to understand how to deal with this phenomenon, as it may appear to be in opposition to the goal of "getting ahead" in American culture. If close, trusting relationships exist, employers and teachers may succeed in helping families see that striking a balance between meeting family obligations and fulfilling work and school expectations is critical to achieving a successful life in the United States.

The high value placed on family relationships also affects how individuals relate to those outside the family. Most Hispanics relate to the world from a familiar and comfortable people-oriented framework. They demonstrate gentleness and respect, and they expect it in return. If this response is not reciprocated, they are likely to withdraw psychologically or avoid similar, seemingly degrading situations. Barriers are created, negatively affecting any future interaction.

Respect.   To Hispanics, *respect* means something quite different from what it means to the majority culture. To Anglos, to respect means to admire someone who is considered superior, to treat someone on an equal basis, or to grant others equal opportunity. To Mexicans, to respect means to show affection, to love someone, and to give and receive protection. Mexican psychologist and medical doctor Rogelio Díaz-Guerrero and American researcher Robert Peck examined the concept of respect as perceived by the Mexican and American cultures. A list of 60 different roles typically held by individuals in society was presented to 298 Mexican students and to 340 American students. The various roles included professional and educational occupations, as well as roles played within the family or other societal institutions, like the church. It also included personal attributes such as age and sex. Students were asked to indicate the people to whom the word *respect* might apply. The results showed significant differences between the cultures as to which roles in society or which stations in life are worthy of respect. For example, Mexicans respect people at the extremes of age, whereas Americans seem to respect youth. Beggars and poor people are more highly respected in Mexico and receive only medium respect in the United States. Thus, in the Hispanic culture, respect is not only demonstrated but expected from each family member toward others, not for *what* they are but merely for *who* they are as human beings.

In summary, Díaz-Guerrero and Peck concluded that in American society, respect is accorded on the basis of "what individuals perform or produce, and in Mexican culture, respect is bestowed on the mere basis of a person's humanity or for just being" (Díaz-Guerrero & Peck, 1976). Stated another way, a person's station in life has little or no bearing on the degree of respect that he or she might command in society. The famous Mexican leader and president Benito Juarez spoke of respect saying, *El respeto al derecho ajeno es la paz* ("Respect for the rights of others is peace").

Responsibility.   The third value that typifies Hispanic Americans is *responsibility*. Responsibility toward the group is instilled diligently and early. The individual is expected to contribute to the group in whatever ways are appropriate to age and gender. For example, the father's responsibility to provide for his family by honest work constitutes the model for other male family members. Work is viewed as a utilitarian function that enables one to provide sustenance for the family and for self. One does not work for the sake of working but to provide for those for whom one is responsible. Among Hispanics, so-called workaholism, or an enslavement to work for work's sake, is not likely to occur. The accumulation of material possessions is not the Hispanic's primary motive for working. Rather, it is to meet family responsibilities.

The Hispanics' spirit of *cooperation* is related to the sense of responsibility. All family members work together for the good of the group and not for individual gain. If the individual achieves in any area, the group receives the glory. An example may be swimmer Pablo Morales, the winner of the Olympic gold medal, who dedicated his gold medal to his mother, who died of cancer just prior to the 1992 Olympics. Morales publicly attributed his drive and motivation to his mother's strong and persistent support. Touching scenes of demonstrable family closeness and pride were televised worldwide as Morales triumphed in Barcelona. In similar fashion, young children may decide to behave or do well at school to please their parents. The family's blessing and sanction are very important to the Hispanic child. In educational settings, teachers will do well to encourage cooperative group learning where individuals feel that their contribution enhances the group and makes a difference.

Education

Education is highly valued by Hispanics. Parents will immigrate to this country and soon bring their children to join them so they can access more free education than they could otherwise have in their country. Although they desire educational success for their children, parents are often unaware of their role in relation to the school. They may fail to realize that their continued involvement in and with the school is often key to their child's achievement and long-term educational success. School personnel may also fail to encourage the parents' involvement because of their uneasiness with cultural and language differences. It is incumbent on the school to put forth exerted efforts to make the parent feel welcomed and needed. A better understanding between the school and the Hispanic home is critical to the child's educational success. As mentioned earlier, trusting, warm relationships between educators and families, as well as demonstrated respect, is critical in bringing about successful home–school collaboration.

Valued as education is, if it is perceived by the family to contradict or come between the individual and his or her allegiance to the family, it may be promptly relegated to a low-priority status. Education is valued only to the extent that its attainment will enhance the family group, not merely for how it will aggrandize the individual. The well-known Spanish proverb, *La escuela instruye mientras el hogar educa*, or "the school instructs while the home educates," well illustrates the order in which priorities are held. Stated differently, the individual who is *bien educado*, or "well educated," is not the one who is clever and quick with book-learned facts and intellectual rhetoric. Rather, it is the child who is respectful and responsible, first to his or her family and then to others as well. These behaviors are learned in the Hispanic home, where the most important "education" is believed to take place.

Most Hispanics believe that if the instruction of the school causes the individual to put on airs, to consider oneself better than others, or in any way to exhibit conceit or vain behavior, then the school has failed in its purpose. Should a person's educational pursuits—as laudable and valued as they might be—cause her or him to disregard family, that individual is regarded as one whose priorities have gone awry. It is then incumbent on the person to demonstrate convincingly that family loyalties can never be displaced. When an educated or schooled family member is able to maintain an acceptable balance between educational attainment and familial attentiveness, this individual is considered worthy of praise and emulation.

The apparent conflict between educational dedication and family attentiveness can pose quite a dilemma for the Hispanic individual. Is family being deliberately disregarded? The family may perceive it as such. For some individuals, it may be a difficult, but not impossible, challenge to strike a balance between the two values of family and education. Educators should capitalize on the notion that education is a family affair that involves not only the child but the parents as well. Meaningful involvement of Hispanic parents in the educational process will be a fruitful strategy once a level of trust and comfort is established with program personnel. Valuing lifelong learning by all family members is key to breaking the cycle of poverty and low achievement that characterize so many Hispanics.

Higher Education

Opportunities, economic and otherwise, increase greatly for Hispanics who hold college degrees. Hispanics' participation in higher education, however, is disproportionately low, compared to the overall growth in their numbers. Statistics show that 10 percent of all Hispanics hold associate's or bachelor's degrees as compared to an average of 29 percent of non-Hispanics. In 2000 about 55 percent of Hispanics who graduated from high school enrolled in college. Of those attending an institution of higher learning, only about 11 percent graduated. Census data show that 23 percent of Cuban Hispanics, 13 percent of Puerto Rican Hispanics, and 7 percent of Mexican Hispanics hold bachelor's degrees (U.S. Census Bureau, 2000).

Not only is the lack of financial resources the most significant deterrent to the attainment of a college education, but also, for many Hispanic students, such an accomplishment may necessarily result in being separated from family by great distances. Lucrative jobs and prestigious opportunities often require the individual to locate far away from the immediate and/or extended family, not a desired outcome of many

Hispanic parents for their children, and especially for the female offspring. Pursuit of these appealing opportunities may be perceived by some Hispanic families as increasing their vulnerability to the dangers of excessive assimilation into the mainstream, the loss of cherished values, and thus a loss of a genuine Hispanic identity.

Bicultural and Bilingual Attainment

It is very difficult emotionally for the Hispanic family to be deprived of the proximity and loyalty of its young offspring who leaves to pursue education and subsequent economic opportunities far away from home. The goal here, then, is *not* for the individual to make the values of family and educational attainment mutually exclusive, but to help him or her attain a balance by embracing both the values of education and family simultaneously. The ideal solution, then, is for the individual to become *bicultural*— that is, to develop the skills to be able to function with ease and comfort in two largely distinct cultures. Being bicultural means that the individual embodies the unique blending of two cultures, without sacrificing one for the other. He or she moves easily back and forth between and within the two cultural worlds. As a prominent author expressed it, "bilingual/bicultural . . . implies and demands a synthesis, a coming together of opposite cultures and languages out of which emerges a third enriched reality that was not there before," thus *biculturalism* (Chavez, 1991).

For many Hispanic youth, achieving biculturalism for themselves may seem problematic and may appear to be quite an impossible task. They may conclude, albeit mistakenly, that living out one cultural value system is necessarily at the expense of or to the exclusion of another, making biculturalism, for them, quite unattainable. Students may not feel valued for who they are and may be made to regard their backgrounds as inadequate or even inferior. They may perceive subtle messages such as, "Change who you are and become who we say. Discard all the values and characteristics you bring and take on new ones." For educators, helping students see the advantages of becoming truly bicultural is doing them a great service (Stavans, 2001). To help them examine the two cultures critically and to integrate the best of both into their own unique lifestyle is the most desirable solution for the individual and for society as well. In the schools and in our communities, distinct cultures can exist successfully side by side. Fortunately for Hispanic students, the number of Hispanic bicultural professionals is growing and providing observable models for children, parents, and others.

HISPANIC FAMILIES AND THE GOVERNMENTAL SYSTEM

Hispanics value highly the American protection of rights and the freedoms afforded to the individual under the U.S. Constitution. A desire for less oppressed lives and economic opportunity are primary reasons for Hispanic immigration. Many Hispanic citizens are enjoying the right to vote and are even running for public office. More than ever before, Hispanic names are appearing on election ballots, thanks to the redistricting brought about by more accurate accounting for Hispanics in the 2000 census. A noted Hispanic asserts that, "Hispanics stand on the verge of making a quantum leap into [the] realm of political participation" (Rodriguez, 1993, p. 10).

New immigrants to the United States, however, often lack knowledge of how the system works and how they can make the system work to their benefit. They may not know their rights under the Constitution and thus may find themselves being taken advantage of where they live or in the workplace. Language barriers and lack of knowledge of the mainstream culture place them at a disadvantage in their efforts to get ahead and to make it in their new adopted land. Attaining citizenship and subsequently the right to vote often eludes them because mere day-to-day survival within the new culture becomes an overwhelming priority. Helping professionals and educators can lend support by directing individuals and families to support services and resources that exist for the express purpose of facilitating the newcomers' adaptation to their new homeland.

HISPANIC FAMILIES AND THE ECONOMIC SYSTEM

Perceiving the United States as a land of opportunity, Hispanics view the abundant resources as blessings to be shared, not hoarded. Although poor in material possessions, Hispanics sincerely say, *Mi casa es su casa* ("My house is your house") and really mean it. They offer the humblest of possessions, including their own home, to guests, as a gesture of generosity. But their generous nature notwithstanding, Hispanics do not readily accept handouts and often refuse to seek out needed social support services to which they may be entitled.

The most recent statistics show that slightly over 41 percent of Hispanic laborers are in service, agricultural, factory, and construction jobs, compared to 23 percent of non-Hispanics in similar positions. Hispanics fill only 14 percent of managerial or professional occupations, whereas non-Hispanic whites hold over 33 percent of such jobs. (U.S. Census Bureau, 2000) Heads of households often hold down several low-wage jobs to make ends meet. In 1999, 23 percent of Hispanics earned more than $35,000 annually as compared to 49 percent of non-Hispanic White families. About 23 percent were living below the federal poverty guidelines as compared to only 8 percent of non-Hispanic families. Less than 10 percent of Hispanic households had annual incomes above $50,000 (U.S. Census Bureau, 2000) as compared to over 27 percent for non-Hispanic Whites. Despite the significant very low-income percentage, the ever-increasing number of Hispanics is creating a buying power that is growing three times the rate of inflation. Proud of their self-sufficiency and belief in hard work, Hispanics accept responsibility in the economic arena. They labor with diligence and integrity.

The Cuban experience has made that group of Hispanics unique in America. In the 1960s the educated elite left Cuba to escape the Castro regime. With their higher levels of education and skills, they have prospered economically in Florida and in many other parts of the United States. As a group, their income has been and remains at substantially higher levels than other Hispanics, according to the most recent U.S. Census Bureau statistics.

HISPANIC FAMILIES AND THE HEALTH CARE SYSTEM

Many Hispanics, especially recent immigrants, often do not take advantage of available health care services. This may be primarily because of language, economic, and other reasons, such as inconvenient location of services and the impersonal and frustrating treatment they often receive at public clinics. In 1995, 9.5 million Hispanics were not covered by private or government medical insurance (del Pinal & Singer, 1997).

High rates of unimmunized children and poor prenatal care are very common among Hispanics, particularly among recent immigrants. A recent study shows that 17 percent of the nation's patients with AIDS are Hispanics, and that they are contracting the disease faster than any other ethnic group (Office of the U.S. Surgeon General, 1993). Health care professionals with a real desire to serve Hispanics need to involve the family, speak Spanish when essential for real communication and understanding, meet people in their own communities, and foster participation of Hispanics in the health provider organizations and agencies (Falicov, 1998). In a barrio in Houston, Texas, for example, mobile dental and medical clinics are brought to a community social service agency weekly on Fridays. Hundreds of low-income adults and children are able to access the convenient services right in their own familiar neighborhood.

HELPFUL TECHNIQUES FOR SERVING HISPANIC FAMILIES

Throughout this chapter, suggestions are offered that should ensure success in working with Hispanics. In this section, some of those suggestions are reiterated and additional ones offered. Working with children and families of Hispanic descent will be a beneficial and rewarding experience if you are willing to *get to know the people and their culture in more than a superficial way. This approach builds good relationships, which facilitates rapport building. Valuing and appreciating the people and their culture intimately, in word and action, are keys to success.*

If you speak Spanish, you'll feel at home with Hispanics, even though many of them will speak English as well as they do Spanish. However, if you don't speak Spanish, you can *start learning the language to gain rapport with the people* you hope to serve. It bears repeating that rapport-building behaviors and attitudes contribute to the development of warm relationships that are highly valued by most Hispanics. Ask Spanish-speaking friends for help in making word and phrase lists; develop techniques for remembering them, and then work hard to learn more. Hispanics will appreciate your efforts to learn. Many of them are working very hard to learn English, and your effort to learn Spanish can help you appreciate the complexity of their task. Furthermore, newly immigrated Hispanics are learning many new things about a new culture. It is true that many Hispanics, although fluent in Spanish, may not be able to read or write Spanish, not having had the educational opportunity to learn these skills. They are not to be considered any less Hispanic because of the lack of skill in reading and writing the language. When addressing a bilingual speaker, you can simply ask which language he or she prefers to use without making assumptions either way.

In today's society where everything is mechanized, computerized, and depersonalized for efficiency's sake, respect and meaningful relationships are rare commodities. Environments that are solely production and/or task oriented are not conducive to relationships unless care is taken to make them so. Hispanics thrive and respond positively in environments where the cultural values—relationships, respect, and responsibility—are understood, affirmed, and practiced. Rapport between Hispanics and helping professionals can be more readily established if respect and regard are demonstrated in warm person-centered surroundings. Condescending or prejudicial attitudes build barriers to relationships and breed disrespect. The implied message in such an approach is "things above people," and nothing discourages Hispanics more than this mode of thinking. Depersonalized treatment alienates Hispanics, making it impossible to establish rapport. At every opportunity, *greet people cordially*, even when such individuals are strangers. In familiar settings, *ongoing dialogues should be maintained* whereby professionals and Hispanic individuals demonstrate personal interest in one another, and, in a sensitive manner, share their diverse perspectives and establish common ground for fruitful and beneficial relationships.

Within educational settings, this back-and-forth, give-and-take dialogue can occur with students of all ages. Persons in the helping professions will do well to familiarize themselves with, as well as *appreciate and value, the unique traditions and practices of individual Hispanic families*. This should result in an understanding of the Hispanic's frame of reference. Keep in mind that although Hispanics may have some common cultural values, each individual family unit has its own unique culture as well. This uniqueness should be acknowledged and appreciated as you deal with individual families and their children. Valuing the Hispanic child's family and home enhances the child's positive feeling about herself or himself. A strong, positive self-identity will be the bedrock of the child's future success as a member of this diverse society. The child's cultural values and traditions must be preserved and built on. The development of personal abilities that help to preserve the best of the family's culture while adding on the best of the majority culture must begin in the earliest educational experiences. In this way, the strengths of true *biculturalism* emerge.

In summary, Hispanics thrive in warm, nurturing environments. In places characterized by sensitivity and acceptance, and by respectful relationships, the message is strong and clear: "People matter here; I am valued." Only by living in a society that encourages and supports their cultural uniqueness can Hispanics preserve their dignity and achieve success.

✦ CONCLUSIONS

Knowing and serving Hispanic families will be an enriching and fulfilling experience for persons who understand and value—through word and action—the strengths and uniqueness of the culture and individuality of Hispanics themselves. Demonstrating warm respect and sincere interest will likely result in mutually beneficial interpersonal experiences that contribute positively to people's lives and, ultimately, to stronger communities.

✦ STUDY QUESTIONS

1. List historical facts about the three major groups of Hispanic families in the United States. Explain how the accident of history affects the three groups today.
2. Study the statistics given in the chapter, and list at least two statistics that apply to each of the three main Hispanic groups.
3. What is meant by the terms *bicultural* and *bilingual?* List the benefits of being one or both.
4. What were the provisions of the Bilingual Education Act?
5. What is meant by "English-only" legislation?
6. Name and describe the predominant family structure of Hispanics.
7. Tell how the religious system affects a majority of Hispanic families.
8. Tell how the government system affects Hispanics.
9. Contrast male and female roles in the Hispanic family.
10. Tell how the economic system affects the three Hispanic groups.
11. State the statistics for the three Hispanic groups that show the relationships between education and fertility and between education and marital stability.
12. State the primary arguments for helping people maintain their mother tongue.
13. What are the three R's of Hispanic family values?
14. What attitudes are important for helping professionals to develop in working with Hispanic families?

✦ APPLICATIONS

1. Focus on the word *Hispanic*, and write down the first 20 words that come to mind.
2. Relate the word *stereotype* to the list you have made for item 1. Are there harmful or prejudicial words in your list? What would happen if you acted on those stereotypes?
3. Write a description of a Hispanic friend or acquaintance of yours (or a Hispanic public figure if you do not personally know any Hispanics). Tell how that person is bicultural and/or bilingual. Interview that person by telephone or in person if possible. Ask questions to learn about early history of family and education and of career goals. Write a two- or three-page report.
4. Read newspapers and magazines to discover names of two Hispanic contemporary artists, authors, or musicians. Research the figures in appropriate periodicals, and write a one-page essay on the early life, education, and experiences of each one. Conclude with one or two paragraphs about how you think their early life affected their art form.
5. Read a major newspaper in your state or inquire through a politician's office in your state to learn about what is being done legislatively to ensure that Hispanic children's educational needs are being addressed. Citing your sources of information, write a two-page report.

6. Interview a person who came to the United States and learned English. Learn all you can about the person's age, motivation, obstacles or opportunities, and outcomes. Giving references, write a report, drawing your own conclusions.

7. List the values a large majority of Hispanics hold in common, regardless of socioeconomic status. Discuss variations you have read or heard about.

8. Write a two-page report addressing this question: Why do Hispanic Americans face a difficult adjustment to the larger society? Make five recommendations that you think would help.

9. Make a list of 10 commandments for non-Hispanics to follow to help Hispanics of all ages adjust to U.S. society more successfully. Use your own career area if you'd like.

10. Write an essay on how the cultural traits of the Hispanic culture can contribute to our global perspective today.

11. Write a two-page report on information resources on a topic of interest regarding Hispanics. Some examples might include bilingualism, immigration, international trade, liberation theology, the Spanish Inquisition, Cuban or Mexican Revolution, and Agency for International Development. Question your librarian for appropriate sources to research.

12. Suppose you were going to visit a Hispanic majority country for a summer service/educational experience. List in chronological order the tasks you would need to accomplish in order to prepare yourself to leave next June. State the country or region you'd visit and your primary goal. Conclude by giving your rationale for your list.

✦ MEDIA RESOURCES

The Status of Latina Women. (1993). Video, 26 minutes, color. (Available from Films for the Humanities & Sciences, Inc., P.O. Box 2053, Princeton, NJ, 08543–2053, 800–257–5126 or 609–275–1400).

✦ KEY INTERNET RESOURCES

Hispanic News Online Newspaper
www.hispanic.cc/culture_and_traditions.htm

Dr. Amado M. Padilla, Stanford University, Hispanic education
www.stanford.edu/~apadilla/

✦ FURTHER READING

Cafferty, P. S. J., & Engstrom, D. W. (Eds.). (2000). *Hispanics in the United States: An agenda for the twenty-first century*. New Brunswick, NJ: Transaction.

Cintron, R. (1997). *Angel's town: Chero ways, gang life, and rhetorics of the everyday*. Boston: Beacon Press.

Cruz, J. (1998). *Identity and power: Puerto Rican politics and the challenge of ethnicity*. Philadelphia: Temple University Press.

De Anda, Roberto M. (Ed.). (1995). *Chicanas and Chicanos in contemporary society*. Boston: Allyn & Bacon.

De Varona, F. (1996). *Latino literacy: The complete guide to Hispanic American culture and history*. New York: Henry Holt.

Díaz-Guerrero, R., & Díaz-Loving, R. (1996). *Introducción a la Psicología: Un enfoque eco-sistémico* (Segunda Edición). México, D. F.: Editorial Trillas.

Fitzpatrick, J.P. (1997). *The stranger is our own: Reflections on the journey of Puerto Rican migrants*. Princeton, NJ: Theological Book Service.

Flores, W.V., & Benmayor, R. (Eds.). (1997). *Latino cultural citizenship: Claiming identity, space, and rights*. Boston: Beacon Press.

Fox, G.E. (1997). *Hispanic nation: Culture, politics, and the constructing of identity*. Tucson: University of Arizona Press.

García, I. (1997). *Dignidad: Ethics through Hispanic eyes*. Nashville, TN: Abington Press.

García, I. M. (2000). *Viva Kennedy: Mexican Americans in Search of Camelot*. College Station: Texas A & M University Press.

Gracia, J., & De Greiff, P. (Eds.). (2000). *Hispanics/Latinos in the United States: Ethnicity, race, and rights*. New York: Routledge.

Hogue, C. J. R., Hargraves, M. A., & Collins, K. S. (2000). *Minority health in the United States: Findings and policy implications*. Baltimore, MD: Johns Hopkins University Press.

Isasi-Diaz, A. M. (Ed.). (1996). *Hispanic/Latino theology: Challenge and promise*. Minneapolis: Fortress Press.

Kanellos, N. (1994). *Handbook of Hispanic cultures in the United States: Sociology*. Houston, TX: Arte Público Press.

Kanellos, N. (1998). *Thirty million strong: Reclaiming the Hispanic image in American culture*. Golden, CO: Fulcrum Press.

Lorey, D. E. (1999). *The U.S.-Mexican border in the twentieth century: A history of economic and social transformation*. Wilmington, DE: Scholarly Resources.

Lynch, E. W., & Hanson, M. J. (1998). *Developing cross-cultural competence: A Guide for working with children and their families* (2nd ed.). Baltimore, MD: Paul H. Brookes.

Macule, D.R. (Ed.). (1996). *Chicanas/Chicanos at the crossroads: Social, economic, and political change*. Tucson: University of Arizona Press.

Maldonado, C., & García, G. (Eds.). (1995). *Chicano experience in the northwest.* Dubuque, IA: Kendall/Hunt.

Moráles, E. (2002). *Living in Spanglish: The search for Latino identity in America.* New York: St. Martin's Press.

Portales, M. (2000). *Crowding out Latinos: Mexican-Americans in the public consciousness.* Philadelphia: Temple University Press.

Ramos, J. (2002). *The other face of America: Chronicles of the immigrants shaping our future.* New York: HarperCollins.

Rodriguez, R. (2002). *Brown: The last discovery of America.* New York: Viking Penguin.

Ruiz, V. L. (1998). *From out of the shadow: Mexican-American women in the twentieth century.* New York: Oxford University Press.

Spain, D., & Bianchi, S. M. (1996). *Balancing act: Motherhood, marriage, and employment among American women.* New York: Russell Sage Foundation.

Trumbull, E., Rothstein-Fisch, C., Greenfield, P. M., & Quiroz, B. (2001). *Bridging cultures between home and school: A guide for teachers.* Mahwah, NJ: Erlbaum.

Valle, I. (1994). *Fields of toil: A migrant family's journey.* Washington State University Press.

Vento, A. C. (1997). *Mestizo: The history, culture and politics of the Mexican and the Chicano: The emerging Mestizo-Americans.* Lanham, MD: University Press of America.

→ 6

Asian American Families

Key Concepts

- Angel Island
- Chinese Exclusion Act
- World War II Detention of Japanese Americans
- Issei
- Nisei
- Amerasians

The mountain moving day is coming.
I say so, yet others doubt.
Only a while the mountain sleeps.
In the past
All mountains moved in fire,
Yet you may not believe it.
Oh man, this alone believe
All sleeping women now will awake and move.

—Yasano Akiko (1911)

As Akiko, the Japanese poet, alluded to in the preceding verse, Asian women in the early part of the twentieth century were awaking from their traditional roles and moving to stand equally and strongly with men. So too are Asian Americans awaking and changing as they become aware of new opportunities and choices in American society. Their old, limiting perceptions, influenced by remnants of the patriarchal Asian family traditions and expectations, are undergoing radical change because of contact with Western culture. Although demographic data indicate an increasing rate of inclusion into the social systems of the United States, which may indicate an improvement in quality of life for a majority of Asian American families, a high percentage of Asian Americans are still living in poverty—as much as 40 percent of families (U.S. Census Bureau, 2000).

WHO ARE THE ASIAN AMERICANS?

The term *Asian American* is often used to refer to both Asians and Pacific Islanders. Asian Americans are perhaps one of the more diverse of America's major minority groups with people originating from over 26 countries. These include Bangladesh, Bhutan, Burma, Cambodia, China, Hong Kong, India, Indonesia, Japan, Laos, Macao, Malaysia, the Maldives, Mongolia, North Korea, South Korea, Nepal, Pakistan, Philippines, Singapore, Sri Lanka, Taiwan, Thailand, and many of the Pacific islands. Subgroups of the Asian American population, like the Chinese Americans and Japanese Americans, have been in the United States for at least five generations; others, including Koreans and Vietnamese, are more recent immigrants to America. Because each of these groups represents different cultural value systems and behaviors, their experiences in and acculturation to American society are unique. Although to many individuals not of Asian ancestry, Asian Americans may appear to be alike, they are certainly not homogeneous!

This chapter highlights some commonalities among Asian Americans and then focuses on three subgroups, Japanese Americans, Vietnamese Americans, and Korean Americans, to gain an understanding of the cultural differences among and within these groups.

Historical Background

Asians first immigrated to the United States at different times and for a variety of reasons. Many early Asian immigrants were fortune hunters, such as the Chinese who came seeking their fortune by working as sugarcane laborers in Hawaii, gold miners in California, and railroad workers across parts of the United States. Later, Chinese immigrants moved into the service industry as cooks, servants, and launderers (Mei, 1984). Of those Chinese who came to California, many were processed through *Angel Island,* and, according to Lai, Lim, and Yung (1981), they experienced a prisoner-like welcome in the United States. America's outstretched arms of welcome were not offered to these Asian immigrants as they were to the "huddled masses" of European immigrants entering Ellis Island in New York Harbor.

Shortly after the Chinese came the Japanese, Filipinos, Koreans, and South Asians, who were also attracted to the idea of economic prosperity in the United States. Because there was such a boom of Asian immigration in the latter part of the nineteenth century, the U.S. Congress felt compelled to pass restrictive immigration laws targeting Asians. For example, in 1882 Congress passed the Chinese Exclusion Act, which was the first law prohibiting immigration based on nationality (Takaki, 1993). This law allowed only Chinese scholars, diplomats, and merchants to come to the United States, obviously thought of by Americans as a more "valued" group, perhaps because they may have been wealthier, more educated, and even more "Westernized" than the laborer group, thus allowing them to acculturate more easily into American society. Almost a century later, in a belated step toward equal treatment, the 1965 amendment to the Immigration and Nationality Act reopened the door to large-scale Asian immigration. Currently, in the United States, Asian Americans enjoy a much higher degree of acceptance and respect, a phenomenon unheard of during those early hostile years (Chan, 1991).

Asian immigrants also came to the United States to escape political persecution and seek asylum, to get away from intolerable family pressure, and to fulfill personal ambitions. For example, many Chinese immigrated to the United States in the later 1940s to escape from Chinese communism, and, for similar reasons, many Vietnamese came to the United States during and after the Vietnam War. Many of the more recent Asian immigrants, such as South Asians and Koreans, however, have come bringing highly desirable professional skills and expertise to the United States, such as computer, engineering, and medical skills.

Demographic Information

Asian Americans are the fastest growing minority group in the United States. According to a U.S. Census Bureau press release in 2003, from January 2002 to April 2003 the number of people who are part of this group increased 3.8 percent, more than triple the growth rate of the entire U.S. population.

In 2002 approximately 13 million Asian Americans comprised 4.4 percent of the total population of the nation (www.census.gov/Press-Release/www/2003/cb03-html). The growth rate from 1980 to 1990 was 95 percent, surpassing all other minority ethnic groups in the United States. It is estimated that by 2025, Asian Americans will number 22 million or more (U.S. Pan Asian-American Chamber of Commerce, 2002). The top six Asian American populations are the Chinese, numbering 2.3 million, followed by Filipinos, 1.8 million; South Asians, 1.7 million; Vietnamese, 1.1 million; Koreans, 1.076 million; and lastly, Japanese at 796,000.

In 2001, 40 percent of all Asian and Pacific Islander families had incomes of $75,000 or more, and 17% had incomes of less than $25,000. This translates into 1.3 million Asians and Pacific Islanders (17%) who lived below the poverty level compared with 15% of non-Hispanic White families (U.S. Census Bureau, 2002). The annual median family income of Asian and Pacific Islander households is the highest of any racial group. This is 117 percent of the median income for non-Hispanic White households, which represents $57,518, and has remained almost unchanged since 2002, when it was $57,313. The median household income in the United States remained unchanged in 2004 from 2003 (U.S. Census Bureau, 2004). According to the Census Bureau, the householder is the person (or one of the people) in whose name the home is owned or rented and the person to whom the relationship of other household members is recorded. This means that only one person in each household is designated as the householder, and caution must be used when describing ethnic minority groups who often have more than one wage earner reporting household income.

For example, two factors unique to Asian American households were that their median income surpassed the median income for Whites in 1990 but dropped below Whites in 1994. It then surpassed Whites again in 2002. These factors contributed toward these findings: (1) in Asian American households, a larger proportion of both spouses work, and (2) Asian Americans tend to pool resources by living all together in large households where most of the family members work. This includes adult children, who often live with their parents. This strategy of pooling all the earnings is a common phenomenon among Asian Americans, resulting in their having a higher household income than other households although lower per capita income than the non-Hispanic White population.

Ninety-six percent of Asian Americans live in high-cost metropolitan areas, such as those in California, New York, Hawaii, Texas, and New Jersey. For example, Hawaii's Asian American population makes up 58 percent of its total followed by 12 percent of California's population. Population-wise, the highest number of Asian Americans live in New York City, followed by Los Angeles, San Jose, San Francisco, and Honolulu (www.census.gov/prod/2001pubs/c2kbr01-7).

Two distinct economic groups of Asian Americans live in the United States today. One group is well educated and advancing into the middle- and upper-middle class; the other group lacks the necessary skills and education to escape poverty. The poverty rate for Asian Americans was 17 percent in 2001, 11.8 percent in 2003, and 9.8 percent in 2004. This decreasing trend in the poverty rate for Asian Americans is not reflective of the increasing number of people in poverty witnessed for the rest of the population during the last four consecutive years (U.S. Census Bureau, 2004). There are strong indications that low-income Asian American households actively participate in governmental service programs, such as cash public assistance, Medicaid, food stamps, or low-income energy assistance.

THE ECOLOGY OF ASIAN AMERICAN FAMILIES

Family Structure

Family structure varies greatly among Asian American families; however, many are still strongly influenced by the male-dominated patriarchal Asian family traditions. There are 2.6 million Asian American families, and of these 80 percent consist of married couples. Among the married-couple families, there are those who remain traditional in their cultural beliefs of family and those who have acculturated characteristics of the larger society. Members of traditional Asian American families are expected to follow clearly defined positions in the family hierarchy, based on age and gender (Ho, 1990). Often the patriarchal lineage and hierarchical relationships, sometimes called *vertical relationships,* fall into the patterns of (1) father to son, (2) elder brother to younger brother, or (3) husband to wife. The only *horizontal* relationships, that of equal status, are those found between friends. Among the Chinese, such traditional practices are based on the teachings of Confucius, and in these households, fathers maintain a strict, authoritative, and aloof relationship with family members. Children often judge fathers to be somewhat stern and unapproachable.

Women in households following these ancient traditions are expected to play a passive role. This is particularly true of older Asian women and those born in their native land. The Asian American "foreign-born" population, as a whole, is 37 percent of the general population (www.census.gov/Press-Release/www/2003/cb03-100.html). Women are expected to be housewives and mothers who nurture and maintain the emotional well-being of the family. A mother forms a close bond to her children, with the eldest son being in the favored position rather than her husband. A husband is often closer to his mother than to his wife (Lee, 1982). Although the father is considered the head of household and the breadwinner, a large proportion of Asian American women are in the workforce as well.

Seventy-eight percent of Asian American children live with their mothers and fathers. Children whose parents are first-generation immigrants find that the challenge of acculturation and transition is usually greater and more frustrating than for those who live with third- or fourth-generation American-born parents. Balancing both worldviews has often led to compartmentalizing behaviors. At home a child may be an obedient daughter, but at school she may display a more assertive self.

Even among less traditionally based Asian American families there are intraethnic acculturation differences, but with each successive generation, Asian Americans are becoming more like the majority. For example, with each generation born in the United States, sons are no longer taking on the responsibilities as primary caretaker of aging parents, and daughters are equally relied on in this caretaking role, which is the predominant practice among the majority population. However, certain family traditions still are slow to change, such as young men who enjoy the privileges of being in the favored position of "number-one son," and expect younger siblings to defer to their family status. Younger, more educated Asian American men and women encounter problems with their parents, spouses, or other Asian Americans as they become acculturated in American ways that encourage equality between the sexes (True, 1990). By actively participating in the majority culture, they are sometimes deeply troubled about perceiving themselves to be unfairly treated at home. It is not uncommon to find that the younger generation is involved in dating non–Asian Americans, which is a topic of frustration for many traditional family members who openly prefer their children to date someone of their own ethnic subgroup.

ASIAN AMERICAN FAMILY VALUES

Historically, Asian people have been influenced by various religious beliefs, such as Buddhism, Christianity, Confucianism, Hinduism, and Islam. However, certain common value systems springing from these beliefs identify the group as a whole. Of course there are also distinct differences in behavioral interpretations of these characteristics among the various Asian groups. Some of the more distinctly similar characteristics are group orientation, family relationship and responsibility, self-control and personal discipline, emphasis on educational achievement, respect for authority, reverence for the elderly, and the use of shame as a behavioral influence (Chung, 1992; Tsui & Schultz, 1985). Although acculturation has been a powerful social force, there are indications that Asian parents tend to be much more structured in their discipline and maintain an ability to socialize their children to delay gratification. Asian Americans may believe that their children are not necessarily born gifted, but as parents, they admit that their children are raised to succeed.

These characteristics and values contribute to a strong sense of self-reliance and interdependence in Asian families and individuals. Evidence of traditional respect for family values and personal discipline could be an explanation for the low divorce rate found in the group, as compared to the rate of non-Hispanic Whites (U.S. Census Bureau, 2002).

ASIAN AMERICAN FAMILIES AND THE EDUCATIONAL SYSTEM

The current popular image of Asian Americans as hardworking and successful is quite different from earlier depictions of them as the "Yellow Peril,"[1] when they were seen by some as a threat to the American way of life. It wasn't until the 1960s that successful Asian Americans became the popular model of achievement. Protests by other ethnic minority groups seeking social justice were discredited by the majority society in its insistence on following the Asian American success pattern.

Asian Americans were viewed as a group who overcame racism and achieved success by hard work, uncomplaining perseverance, and quiet accommodation. Like any stereotype, this became an idealized view, to the extent that many Asian Americans themselves felt an obligation to live up to this prescribed American vision of the group. Asian Americans believe that with more education come higher career earnings, and those with only a high school diploma will only earn approximately half as much as someone with a college degree.

Today, Asian Americans have become the largest ethnic minority group in many career fields and at many elite colleges. In 1980, when Asian Americans comprised only 1.5 percent of the population, they consisted of 5 percent of all engineers and 8 percent of all doctors in the United States. Asian Americans, enrolled in elite colleges, show the most significant evidence of the importance of education. For example, in 1987 Asian Americans consisted of 13 percent of admitted freshmen at Harvard and 25 percent of freshmen at the University of California, Berkeley. Asian American women comprised 30 percent of entering female students at Massachusetts Institute of Technology (MIT) and over half of newly admitted women engineering students at the University of California, Berkeley (Hu, 1988). In 2003 a staggering 51 percent of Asian American men and 44 percent of women age 25 and older had a bachelor's degree or higher compared with 32 percent of non-Hispanic white men and 27 percent of

---

[1]*Yellow Peril* (sometimes *Yellow Terror*) was a racist phrase that originated in the late nineteenth century with immigration of Chinese laborers to various Western countries, notably the United States. The term, a color metaphor for race, refers to the skin color of East Asians and the xenophobia that the mass immigration of Asians threatened White wages, standards of living, and indeed, Western civilization itself. The phrase *yellow peril* was common in the newspapers owned by William Randolph Hearst.

non-Hispanic white women. The Asian American population has the highest proportion of college graduates of any race or ethnic group, and the corresponding rate for all adults in this age group is 27 percent (www.census.gov/PressRelease/www/2003/cb03-100.html).

There is a belief that Asian Americans experience no barriers to higher education, although it is misleading. Evidence indicates the existence of restrictive admission policies against Asian American college applicants. For example, Asian American applications to colleges increased by 70 percent from 1980 to 1990; however, the number of applicants accepted has decreased by almost 80 percent (U.S. Commission on Civil Rights, 1992). Republican and Democratic Asian American leaders are working together to address issues related to Asian American admission to institutions of higher education. Asian Americans perform so well on college entrance examinations that there is pressure to limit their admissions. Debate continues about appropriate measures to ensure all an equal access to higher learning.

Despite these institutional barriers, South Asians in the United States are particularly well educated, with over 58 percent of them college graduates (Barringer, Gardner, & Levin, 1995). Despite this high rate, however, some families must overcome obstacles in attending college. For those Asian American families with limited income, a strategy used to overcome institutional barriers or lack of educational funds is to have their young adults first enroll in a community college or junior college that has a formal agreement with larger in-state universities to accept qualified students, and later have them transfer to the larger and more established university. The cost for two years at a junior college is far less than that at a larger four-year university, so a family can spend less on their young adult by choosing this route.

Another obstacle that originates with certain families results in differences in educational levels by gender. Sometimes families make deliberate choices that show sons being favored over daughters. Men tend to receive a better education than women in most Asian American groups, except for the Filipino group, where a higher rate of completion is found among women. This may reflect the role of women in Philippine society. But the greatest gender disparity exists among Korean Americans, with 34 percent of men and only 22 percent of women completing four or more years of college.

Although Asian Americans have taken full advantage of the benefits of the American educational system, there are still problems for Asian American students who do not fit the stereotype created by society. It is a commonly known fact that most Asian American students major in engineering, computer technology, or science. What about those students who decide on careers in the social sciences or arts and letters? The Asian American community is also polarized along extreme ends of the continuum, with many students needing special assistance at one end and others exceeding all expectations at the opposite end, leaving few in the middle. On the needy end, during the 1980s to early 1990s, the dropout rates among Khmer, Hmong, and Laotian students approached a high rate (Hsia & Nakanishi, 1989). What was the cause of this? On the success end, recent data indicated that Asian Americans, except the Vietnamese, exceeded or equaled Whites in terms of high school completion and college completion (U.S. Census Bureau, 2004).

ASIAN AMERICAN FAMILIES AND THE HEALTH CARE SYSTEM

Health problems vary among Asian American groups. For example, Filipinos have a high incidence of hypertension, Southeast Asian Americans have a high prevalence of tuberculosis infection and hepatitis B, and Chinese, Japanese, and Filipino Americans have problems with cancer and cerebral vascular disease (Leadership Education for Asian Pacifics, Inc., 1993). In 2004 the uninsured health rate for Asian Americans decreased from 18.8 percent to 16.8 percent, whereas, for the majority population, the rates have remained unchanged since 2003. These data indicate that Asian individuals are better able to procure government health insurance programs, such as Medicare and/or Medicaid, or private health insurance.

The 10 top leading causes of death in the Unites States for Asian Americans have been as follows:

1. Cancer
2. Heart disease
3. Stroke
4. Unintentional injuries
5. Diabetes
6. Influenza and pneumonia
7. Chronic lower respiratory disease
8. Suicide
9. Nephritis and nephritic syndrome
10. Septicemia

Although more than a million families live below the federal poverty level, the Asian American population is bifurcated on the extreme ends of the socioeconomic and health indexes. Surprisingly, it has been found that Asian American women have the highest life expectancy of any other group (Office of Minority Health, 2006).

Access to adequate health care is fragmented in the Asian American population because of issues of language and culture, especially for the elderly, women, Southeast Asian refugees, and recent immigrants. Problems of communication go beyond language use and proficiency. Often the trust needed for this relationship to succeed is built from perceptions that, because of subtle verbal and nonverbal cultural styles, may develop more slowly.

Data suggest that Asian Americans frequently experience their psychological problems as physical complaints (Moor & Boehnlein, 1991; Nguyen, 1982; Nicassio, 1985). Incidences of peptic ulcers and hypertension are more common among second-generation Japanese Americans, whereas Sansei, or third-generation Japanese Americans, are more likely to complain about headaches, digestive troubles, insomnia, and backaches than their Euro-American counterparts. High incidence of somatic problems are also found among Vietnamese and Amerasian refugees (Uba, 1994).

Asian attitudes regarding mental health care are complicated by the belief that the problem is a result of separation between the physical and emotional self. In Western societies, it is generally accepted for people to seek mental health professionals when they encounter emotional issues. Among the Asian American population, however, the welfare of the family comes first, and to communicate with an "outsider" about problems is considered shameful or humiliating for the family and in direct cultural conflict with traditional Asian norms (Asian-American Family Services, 2006). However, growing evidence indicates that more Asian Americans are using mental health services. Such data indicate that Asian Americans are increasingly finding appropriate cultural and linguistic assistance at mental health agencies (True, 1990). At the same time, ignorance of Asian American cultural beliefs by mental health professionals can lead to misunderstandings at the mild end to a misdiagnosis of a severe problem at the worst end. For example, a Southeast Asian immigrant may talk to a professional about seeing and talking to her deceased son. This is reflecting a cultural belief, a normative behavior, in the supernatural, where spirits have rights, needs, and feelings, and it is not a delusion or psychosis (Uba, 1994).

ASIAN AMERICAN FAMILIES AND THE GOVERNMENTAL SYSTEM

Based on historical experience, relationships between the Asian American community and the various local, state, and national levels of government have not been harmonious, to say the least, but have been plagued by struggles of acceptance and rejection. Especially difficult was the relationship between Japanese Americans and the U.S. government following the bombing of Pearl Harbor by the Japanese on December 7, 1941. President Franklin Roosevelt signed Executive Order 9066, which allowed the legal incarceration of Japanese Americans into relocation camps. Many Japanese Americans had to sell their businesses, farms, personal properties, and homes for a loss. They were only allowed to bring to the camps what they could carry. Although their families were interned, many of the Japanese American young adult males, classified as enemy aliens, joined the U.S. Army to prove their loyalty to the United States (Kitano, 1988; Tsuchida, 1990).

Because of this experience of Japanese Americans during World War II, as well as similar experiences by other Asian subgroups, it has been a truism of the Asian American community for many years that if they maintained a low profile, they could live more harmoniously in American society, thus ensuring their survival. Therefore, for many years, Asian Americans were relatively absent from political offices, with the exception of the state of Hawaii, where Asian Americans are the majority population. The once passive role of Asian Americans in U.S. politics is changing, and they are becoming more active participants in the political arena, although they are not easily characterized on the whole as either Democrats or Republicans.

In 1992, 10 percent of the California population was Asian American, and the first Asian American was elected to a state position (U.S. Commission on Civil Rights, 1992). More recently, there has been an increase of Asian Americans elected to various offices, including those at the federal level. According to studies carried out at the University of California, Los Angeles, Asian-Pacific-American voters are almost evenly divided between the Democratic and Republican parties in their registration and voting behavior (Nakanishi, 1989). Both political parties have attempted to win Asian American voters to their side because many are major financial contributors. During the 1988 presidential election, approximately $10 million from Asian American contributors was evenly divided between the two parties. Today, 57 percent affiliate with the Democrats, 22 percent with Republicans and 21 percent with Independents. There is increasing indication of politicized consciousness (www.modelminority.com/printout41.html).

ASIAN AMERICAN FAMILIES AND THE ECONOMIC SYSTEM

Traditionally, running a small family business was common among Asian Americans living in the United States. For example, a Korean American family and their relatives might assist in running a small grocery store, Japanese American family members might own a grocery store or a truck farm, and Chinese American families might operate restaurants or laundries. During times of economic crisis, Asian community organizations pool their resources to bail out some of their members. As a result, many Asian American credit associations have been founded to provide loans for those within the community. Pooling resources may have contributed to the 913,000 Asian American–owned firms, which have generated a total of $306 billion in U.S. sales. It is estimated that Asian American–owned businesses employed more than 2.2 million workers in 2000. Today, Chinese Americans, once stereotyped as owners of dry cleaners and "mom and pop" grocery stores, are fully represented in all industries, including research, public relations, real estate, commodity brokers, and manufacturing. In fact, Asian Americans are represented in a majority of professions considered white collar. With the exception of Filipinos, women are less represented than men in these types of occupations, but they are overrepresented in service occupations. Without a doubt, Asian Americans are becoming a powerful force in the U.S. consumer market, with approximately $230 billion in spending power (U.S. Pan Asian-American Chamber of Commerce, 2002).

Leong and Hayes (1990) found that many Asian American students become engineers, mathematicians, and computer scientists. The presence of occupational stereotyping has created a social reality for the Asian American community. Over recent decades, the socioeconomic position of Asian American families in American society has improve because of a high investment in educational credentials. In 2004 approximately 7.6 percent of Asian Americans, as compared to Whites at 6.5 percent, had family incomes below poverty levels, and families with female-headed households, with no husband present, were at a level of 13.2 percent as compared to Whites at 21.7 percent (U.S. Census Bureau, 2004). Asian Americans believe that family members must work together and pool their resources for investing in higher education in order to achieve economic success.

Asian Americans are more likely than Whites to work in the manufacturing and trade industries and in professional positions, and they are less likely than Whites to work in blue-collar jobs. Studies show that Asian American men are often confronted with a glass ceiling in areas of promotion (Cabezas & Kawaguchi, 1988; Moore & Gunnison, 1994; Tang, 1991).

Immigrant women from Bangladesh, Burma, Cambodia, Pakistan, Sri Lanka, Thailand, Indonesia, India, and China often work in low-wage jobs in garment factories or electronic assembly lines (LEAP, 1993). More recently arrived immigrant women are clustered in some of these lower paid jobs. Their inability to speak the English language, their work skills and mastery levels, and a willingness to work at these low-paying jobs all contribute to this pattern.

JAPANESE AMERICAN, VIETNAMESE AMERICAN, AND KOREAN AMERICAN FAMILIES

In order not to mask the differences that exist among various subgroups, this section focuses on three Asian American communities: Japanese American, Vietnamese American, and Korean American.

The Japanese American community is made up of generations of mostly native-born Americans, compared to that of other Asian American groups. The internment of Japanese Americans during World War II, as previously described, provides evidence and a reminder that any person or ethnic group can be discriminated against unless there is vigilance in protecting basic human rights as enshrined in the U.S. Constitution. This historical lesson gives us insights into how and why assimilation strategies used by Japanese Americans have contributed to a unique cultural adaptation.

Vietnamese American families are examples of Asian Americans who immigrated to the United States for political reasons. Many are experiencing cultural conflicts and struggles as they accommodate and acculturate to the mainstream society. The question of balancing, staying true to one's culture while adapting to the American way of life, is the greatest challenge for many individuals in Vietnamese families. As children and parents acculturate and assimilate into American society at different rates, it is not uncommon for parent–child conflicts to emerge.

Korean Americans immigrated to the United States in one of two ways: An entire family immigrated or one member of a family immigrated and later sponsored members of the family to come over. Most contemporary Koreans have immigrated since 1965, numbering approximately 30,000 each year. Some Korean Americans adhere to traditional values more strongly than today's families in Korea; others are less traditional than they were in Korea.

THE ECOLOGY OF JAPANESE AMERICAN FAMILIES

To understand Japanese Americans, we must look at the human ecological changes throughout history from one generation to the next. Recall the discussion of human ecology in Chapter 2. According to Suzuki and Yamashiro (1980), different environments affected the Japanese ability to transfer an ethnic worldview from one generation to another. This finding is especially important given the nature of the Japanese personality and culture.

The Japanese have been characterized as a *situational* people, tending to accommodate to the present situation and make the best of it. According to Hall (1966, 1983), the traditional Japanese culture is considered a *high-context* culture. This means the context or environment in which the individual is living, working, and interacting is important in determining the adaptive strategy used in relating to others while still maintaining aspects of traditional values. The surrounding cultural and social conditions influence the life of the individual, organization, and community.

For example, the Japanese in Hawaii are embedded in an ethnically dominated geographic setting, whereas those in the continental United States typically reside within the majority community. Those who live in an ethnic community reinforce their cultural values and processes, whereas those residing outside the community find their values reinforced by a different system. The community environment influences a family's ability to instill particular values and practices.

Although the largest concentration of Japanese Americans is found in California, followed by Hawaii, the acculturation process for each group is uniquely different (U.S. Census Bureau, 2003a). The history of Japanese American life in Hawaii is different from that of Japanese Americans on the U.S. mainland. Keep in mind the contextual milieu of Hawaii and the West Coast of the United States at the time of the original immigration and the much later context during and after World War II. These two eras are significant in Japanese American history.

In Hawaii, most Japanese Americans were confined to the islands during World War II. Those who were interned were perceived as a potential threat to the U.S. government. Most Japanese Americans who lived in the western United States were treated as prisoners and forced into internment camps. The camps started in March 1942 and ended in January 1945. Although three years seems a comparatively short time, being viewed an enemy and put behind barbed wire was for Japanese Americans a period of great shame and disgrace. They somehow felt responsible for being put into one of ten camps in California, Arizona, Idaho, Wyoming, Colorado, Utah, and Arkansas. During the internment, most of the Japanese Americans lost their residences, businesses, and almost everything they owned. It has taken three generations, especially for the Sansei (Japanese Americans born in the United States), to speak out as true citizens. The Sansei have been responsible for initially bringing the internment experience before the public.

Family Structure

The first Japanese to come to the United States were students who arrived under two separate financial arrangements. One group was given scholarships to study in New England and Europe so they could return to the Meiji government and assume high government service posts. The other group consisted of private students who paid their own expenses. However, most of these students returned to Japan and are not considered the original pioneers (Ichioka, 1988).

Between 1861 and 1870, Japanese immigrants to the United States numbered only 186 individuals. Immigration increased after agreements were made in 1885 between the Japanese government and the Hawaiian sugar plantation owners. This agreement enabled Japanese contract laborers to leave their country to work in the sugarcane fields in Hawaii (Immigration and Naturalization Service, 1984; U.S. Department of Justice, 1964–1980). Many of these immigrants were young single men who came temporarily, fueled by dreams of making money and returning home to live more comfortably. Facing hardship and discrimination were perceived as short-term experiences, and many felt they could *gaman shi te* ("stick it out"). Over time, as some families adjusted to the culture, returning to Japan presented difficulties. Many families chose to remain in Hawaii.

Japanese immigration to the continental United States began in the 1890s. Most of the immigrants' work ranged from domestic and agricultural work to jobs in mining and logging. From 1880 to 1890, most of the immigrants were unskilled single men. In 1908 a "gentlemen's agreement" was reached with the Japanese government to restrict immigration from Japan. During the period 1907 to 1920, most of the immigrants were women who came as contractual "picture brides" for Japanese men already in the United States. With the 1924 Immigration Act, all Asian immigration to the United States was banned, leaving more than 42 percent of adult Japanese men without wives and with little hopes of marriage to Japanese women.

In 1940, 88 percent of the Japanese Americans on the mainland lived on the West Coast, with 83 percent in California. A small percentage lived in New York and Chicago. The Japanese attack on Pearl Harbor in 1941 was followed with the relocation of more than 110,000 Japanese Americans from the West Coast to concentration camp sites in Arizona, Arkansas, California, Colorado, Idaho, Utah, and Wyoming, with some being arrested and sent to prison camps as enemy aliens (Daniels, 1981). Only in 1992, 50 years later, did Congress attempt to correct this wrong by paying a token sum of $20,000 to each survivor of this World War II infringement on citizens' rights.

Some Japanese Americans experienced arrest. In camps surrounded by barbed wire, their individual freedom was restricted. People were policed by soldiers carrying guns and following official directives. According to Broom and Kitsuse (1956), priority in these sites was given to daily routine and little to long-term planning for the future. Many used their skills and creativity to grow vegetables and decorate their quarters. Scholars have suggested that individuals who are sustained in prison-like conditions later experience adaptive struggles once they leave the prison camp and enter society again.

After World War II came the second relocation of Japanese Americans, with the majority unable to return to their former homes. Reports show that 268,814, or 37.5 percent, were living in California; 9.4 percent were in the Pacific and Mountain states; 6.5 percent in the Northeast; 6.5 percent in the Midwest; and 6.6 percent in the South (U.S. Census Bureau, 1990). Today, the population numbers show an increase, with 1.14 million people (U.S. Census Bureau, 2000). Japanese American families faced the difficult task of rebuilding their lives as they experienced opposition and prejudice in the communities, but they used their initiative and energy to blend into society and live as inconspicuously as possible. Children were urged into educational achievements, and young adults were pressured into occupational mobility by their families.

FAMILIES AND ACCULTURATION

Today, Japanese Americans are generally perceived as successful middle-class people who have been well integrated into American society. This gradual acculturation and adaptation into American society is best seen in generational terms. Individuals are commonly asked, "What generation do you belong to?" The practice of naming each generation using Japanese terminology honors the original immigrants but gradually has lost significance with each successive generation.

Specific terms—*Issei, Nisei, Sansei,* and *Yonsei*—identify individual generations since Japanese families first immigrated to the United States. The first generation immigrating to the United States is called *Issei*. The firstborn or second generation in the United States is called *Nisei*. Offspring of the Nisei are called the *Sansei*. The fourth generation is often simply termed the *fourth generation,* although if one were to follow appropriate Japanese terminology, the term *Yonsei* would be used. By the fifth generation, most people see themselves as five generations removed from their immigrant ancestors and probably could not tell you the Japanese term for the fifth generation.

The Generational Model

Generational terms determine largely the degree of acculturation embodied by a Japanese American person. The first generation has minimal acculturation; the fourth or fifth generation is almost fully acculturated. The process of retaining the traditional culture or acculturating to the larger society depends to a large extent on whether an individual (1) seeks out other Japanese Americans, (2) lives in a rural or urban area, or (3) belongs to the first generation or subsequent generations.

Issei. Issei is the term for the first generation of Japanese individuals who immigrated to Hawaii in the 1880s and to the United States in the 1890s. The Issei usually began life in the United States as single young adult men who arrived with the intent of returning to Japan after accumulating some wealth (Kitano, 1988). According to Strong (1934), the Issei were ambitious, intelligent, and probably the only early American immigrant group with the equivalent of an eighth-grade education.

The Issei formed ethnic communities that were a mixture of Old World traits and accommodative and acculturative institutions (Marden, Meyer, & Engel, 1992). The community functioned as an extended family support unit. Investments, leisure activities, *Tanomoshi* (a credit system), restaurants, shops, real estate, and other businesses could all be found in the Japanese American community. The Issei community was tightly committed to the ways of Japan.

To begin families, the Issei men turned to their family, friends, and matchmakers in Japan to secure future Japanese wives. Thus the traditional Japanese custom of marriages arranged between households found its way to the United States. The practice of exchanging pictures of the prospective bride and groom was developed and added to the institutionalized and traditionally arranged marriages. The women were called "picture brides."

Although the marriage process was altered and hybridized, the concept of a patriarchal family and kin relationships continued unbroken from Japan to the United States (Yanagisako, 1985). Family rights almost always predominated over individual rights, and family loyalty, duty, and responsibility took precedence over personal desires. A high value was placed on prescribed roles for males and females, with variations depending on age, status, and gender. The family was hierarchical in structure, with husbands holding most of the authority. There was a strong preference for male heirs.

The social structure of families was based on traditional Japanese interpretations of Confucian ideals of the superiority of old over young and male over female regarding all interpersonal relationships. The practice of the eldest son inheriting the property and power was also a link to the old country.

The pre–World War II Issei generation established clear boundaries of who was inside the family and who was considered an outsider. The Issei family system was an extension of the ethnic community. The norms, values, and behaviors of families were reinforced by the ethnic community at large. These communities provided the family with socioemotional and economic support. Ethnic food stores, businesses, service organizations, newspapers, and other activities all helped create a secure familiar atmosphere for the Issei. Japanese American Issei families relied heavily on family customs concerning marriages, deaths, births, anniversaries, holidays, picnics, and recreation as a means of ensuring and solidifying Japanese family customs and traditions from generation to generation.

The phrase *kodomo no tame ni* ("for the sake of the children") (Ogawa, 1978) was a common Issei phrase meaning sacrificing one's needs for the children. High hopes and expectations for gaining success and acceptance were placed on the American-born children of Japanese parents.

With World War II and the evacuation of 110,000 Japanese Americans living along the West Coast of the United States, life drastically changed for Issei families. Families were forced into hurriedly built internment camps in isolated areas—often desert areas—of states such as California, Idaho, Utah, Wyoming, Colorado, Arkansas, and Arizona. According to Kitano, the Issei

> learned to live by official directives, learned to respond to announcements, and learned the importance of adjusting to the whims of government-appointed White administrators. . . . Families were housed in one room units in modified barracks . . . almost all noise could be heard throughout the unit. . . . Community mess halls, lavatories, showers, and washrooms meant adjusting to communal living (1988, p. 265).

The Issei family was severely challenged by being uprooted and incarcerated. Their freedom was taken from them, and they were placed in a cultural context that was completely alien. It was unlike their ancestral community, unlike their American ethnic community, and unlike the majority White community. It was an environment wrought with fear and crisis.

The first-generation (1800s) Issei could not marry a white person, according to family values as well as societal rules of disapproval. Neither could they own land after the Alien Land laws were passed in California and other states. They were limited in the types of neighborhoods in which they could live, the types of jobs they could hold, and the types of social and recreational opportunities available to them. The Issei were discriminated against and prevented from attending public schools. They had to struggle for the right to public education. These situations created great psychological stress for the Issei. They responded by resisting acculturation (Ichioka, 1988).

Nisei.   Nisei are the children of Issei. They are the second-generation Japanese Americans. The Nisei represented to the Issei what they felt they could not achieve: success through education.

Outside of Hawaii, many second-generation Nisei attained middle-class stature, moved out of the old Japanese ethnic neighborhoods into suburban America, and blended into the mainstream of social activity. Nisei were children and youth during World War II and spent years in the isolated environments of internment camps. One college-age Nisei student who was released from a desert-area camp to attend college told a seatmate on a long-distance bus ride, "You can't imagine how it makes you feel to have your loyalty to the United States questioned." Her seatmate, a majority college student, listened in shocked disbelief at the student's personal account of the internment.

Nisei assimilation into the majority culture was more common among mainland Nisei than among the more traditional Japanese Americans of Hawaii. The Nisei generation is now of senior-citizen age. According to Kitano (1988), the Nisei practiced American-type activities, such as dating, outings, retreats, conferences, and dances within their own peer group, and they were culturally closer to the American way of life than the Issei lifestyle.

The differences between the two generations are easily seen in the changes in marriage customs and rituals. For example, the Issei marriage was a model from Japan characterized by the following (Yanagisako, 1985):

1. arranged marriages
2. couples' interaction based on obligations
3. family bonds more important than spousal bonds
4. male domination
5. labor differing by gender
6. emphasis on compassion, respect, and consideration
7. expected emotional restraint and stability
8. little verbal communication between spouses
9. high family involvement in relationships

The Nisei had a choice between the opportunities presented by the American model and the traditional ways of the Issei. This meant freedom of choice in choosing a spouse, allowing for romantic love, greater equality of the sexes, more overt emotional expressions, more verbal communication between spouses, prioritizing the spousal bond as more important than the family bond, an attachment to family relationships defined as opportunity rather than obligation, and freedom from negative sanctions concerning marriage and family stability.

The Nisei adapted to the bicultural dilemma by incorporating some of the old traditions and some of the new ways. English was their first language. Each individual and family selected those ideals that best fitted their cultural experiences and context. Today there exists a variety of family forms and customs, ranging from the traditional ideals of the Issei to the American ideals of individual freedom of choice.

What has remained important to the generations is the family, its past, its present, and its future with roots in both the Japanese and American dreams. Family gatherings, such as New Year's celebrations, weddings, and funerals, are important functions that serve to rekindle the ties of the cultural heritage.

An example of this cultural synthesis is the mixture of the old traditional foods, such as mochi, rice cakes, sushi, and sashimi served along with American cookies, cakes, and soft drinks. Today monetary wedding gifts and bridal shower gifts are given. Envelopes containing a twenty-dollar bill as well as a sympathy card are considered appropriate for funerals. Such behavioral practices all create the delicate balancing act of the second generation of Nisei with the new times and the places in which they reside.

Sansei.   The third generation, the Sansei, is a mixture of holding and letting go of the ways of the older generations. Sometimes Sansei have been labeled "the bumblebee generation" because bees are striped with yellow and black and deliver a sting. The Sansei are like the fearless bumblebee that attacks when necessary. The yellow stands for being Asian; the black represents what was learned from the African Americans in their struggles for equal rights, and the sting to inflict pain in awakening the consciousness of the American people. The Sansei have brought to the nation's consciousness the human rights issues of the U.S. internment camps for Japanese Americans during World War II. Most Sansei have almost completely assimilated into the mainstream majority culture. They see no semblance of Japanese traditions in their own socialization or self-identity, except for their outward physical appearance.

The Sansei have integrated more American ways into the definition of self than the Nisei, just as the Nisei were more assimilated than the Issei. Thus, with each succeeding generation, acculturation to the American model becomes more widespread. Yet, according to Kitano and Daniels (1988), personality tests reflect scores that indicate that the Sansei generation shows more self-restraint, self-denial, submission, and deference to elders and those in authority than is found among majority individuals. This study shows that many Sansei still identify with their Japanese ancestry and take pride in traditional cultural values. However, there are those who believe that the Sansei may have acculturated, or Americanized, themselves to the point where it is impossible to permit effective ethnic recovery.

Many Sansei have lost their ethnicity in establishing their self-identity. Many first- and second-generation Japanese Americans would say that the Sansei have adapted to the values of the majority culture by being more independent. Yet although they have moved away from the value of family dependence, they prefer the value of indirect confrontation over direct confrontation. By preferring to be called Japanese Americans, the Sanseis have maintained a symbolic ethnicity, according to Gann (1979).

The Sansei generation participates in majority cultural activities with freedom and with fewer ethnic social controls than were found among the Issei or Nisei generations. The Sansei know little of Japanese cultural traditions and language, and they participate less in Japanese events and art forms. They frequently marry out of the Japanese American ethnic group. Biracial Japanese Americans identified less with being Japanese and were more acculturated in adapting to societal values and behaviors than other Japanese Americans (Mass, 1992).

It appears that there may be a generational difference in consciousness and adherence in ethnic identity. However, this is more complex than the simple generational explanations, for apparently several factors can influence this outcome. The Japanese American samples studied were taken from different areas of the country and at different times under different acculturative and racial pressures (Connor, 1977; Newton, Buck, Kunimura, Colger, & Scholsberg, 1988; Uba, 1994).

Role of Japanese American Women

Japanese American women are among the more highly acculturated Asian Americans. Possibly identification with their ethnic group can conflict with their sense of individuality and desire for individuality (Smith, 1983). Their intermarriage rate among Asian subgroups is the highest in the United States. This indicates a permeable boundary existing between Japanese Americans and the majority culture.

Role of Japanese American Men

Japanese American men today are freer of old obligations. They are in the mainstream of business and academic life because of their high regard for—and achievement in—higher education. They are accepting a more egalitarian role in their families, enjoying play with their children, for example, in ways that they never would have in the traditional home. Japanese Americans are the most acculturated Asian American group and, as a group, may have more resources available to them. Today, issues concerning a desire to intermarry present little, if any, problems for their families.

SELECTED JAPANESE AMERICAN TRADITIONAL FAMILY VALUES

Japanese Americans place significant value on family and community responsibility. This means carrying out obligations and showing respect for those in authority, those who are elderly, and other family members. According to Roland (1984, 1988), the familial self of the Asian contrasts sharply with the highly individual self of the American. The familial self includes the fact that Japanese Americans place significant value on family and community responsibility. This means carrying out obligations and responsibilities, and loyalty to one's family and ethnic group. Being a member of a family means enjoying privileges of trust, intimacy, and sharing. At the same time one is an extension of the family and, therefore, has obligations to contribute to the family so that even a child contributes by getting good grades in school.

Context refers to the collection of social and cultural conditions that surround and influence the life of an individual, a family, an organization, or a community. According to

Hall (1966, 1983), the Japanese American lives in a high-context culture as opposed to a low-context culture. For example, the Japanese pay much attention to the surrounding circumstances, or context, of an event. An example would be interpersonal communication, where phrasing, tone, gesture, posture, social status, history, and social setting are all crucial to the meaning of a message. In contrast, Euro-Americans, according to Hall, typically exist in the medium- to low-context culture, and their identity is rooted in the individual rather than the family. In short, Japanese Americans may see and hear nuances in events others seldom perceive, because they are so very alert to context.

Culturally meaningful behavior and standards are difficult to address in a rapidly acculturating ethnic group. Because Japanese Americans are socialized to pay close attention to the surrounding context, traditional values of importance are often obscured by the demands of the mainstream culture. However, there are indications that Asian parents tend to be a lot more structured in instilling discipline and an ability to delay gratification than American parents. There is a strong belief among Asian Americans that although their children are not necessarily born gifted, their children are raised to succeed.

A central theme of the Japanese and Japanese American culture is for people to be in harmony with their environment. Harmony is especially noticeable in Japanese art and gardens, and this concept extends to being in harmony with one's internal psychology and one's social relations. In behavioral terms this translates into not creating problems. Individuals are taught there are consequences for their behaviors. Actions can bring shame and embarrassment to the family or honor to the family, depending on whether one is cooperating with the norms of the ethnic group and imposing self-limits.

JAPANESE AMERICAN FAMILIES AND THE EDUCATIONAL SYSTEM

Japanese Americans have accepted the American view that education is the key to success—that it will ensure a good life. For example, results of a 1992 study comparing parental involvement of three generations of Japanese Americans, the Issei, Nisei, and Sansei, show that the ensuing generations of Japanese Americans become more and more active and directly involved in the education of their children. The researchers concluded that this evolutionary development was highly related to language communication and familiarity with the dominant culture (Shoho, 1992). Parents want their children to succeed in school. All evidence points to the fact that most Japanese American students work hard in their studies and their work and succeed at very high rates.

JAPANESE AMERICAN FAMILIES AND THE HEALTH CARE SYSTEM

The Japanese American population in Hawaii has one of the longest life expectancies of any large population subgroup in the United States, as well as the world (Curb, Reed, Miller, & Yano, 1990). The average Japanese American lives approximately

6 years longer than the average White person. It is thought that their good health may be related to a diet low in fats or a lifestyle moderate in the use of alcohol and other stimulants. With regard to health care, Japanese women, especially the elderly, prefer female doctors. Japanese Americans are typically served well by the health care system because of their economic affluence.

In the area of mental health, there are significant differences among interethnic Asian Americans and their severity of psychological problems. As a group the Japanese Americans have the least severe problems in contrast to the other Asian Americans (Gim, Atkinson, & Whitely, 1990). It is believed that as a group the Japanese Americans are the most acculturated and have the most resources available to them to counteract the waves of cultural stressors.

JAPANESE-AMERICAN FAMILIES AND THE GOVERNMENTAL SYSTEM

Most Japanese Americans, like other Americans, were totally bewildered by the bombing of Pearl Harbor and felt totally alienated from that act of aggression. Yet they were herded into concentration camps at the onset of World War II. Though citizens of the United States, they were denied due process of law as required by the Fourteenth Amendment to the U.S. Constitution. Not one case of espionage was ever found among the 120,000 people interned (Daniels, 1981).

Today, a few Japanese Americans are members of Congress. It is difficult to generalize about party affiliations for most of the Japanese Americans. There seems to be an even split among Democrats and Republicans, with generous monetary contributions going to both major parties. Senator Daniel Inouye from Hawaii, a wounded World War II veteran, has served in the Senate for many terms.

JAPANESE-AMERICAN FAMILIES AND THE ECONOMIC SYSTEM

Asian Americans were called a model minority in 1982, America's superminority in 1986; and in 1987, they were acknowledged in a television special presented on Asian American achievements and successes. Asian Americans have been held up as role models and are compared with and encouraged to compete against other ethnic minority groups. Ignored are the many important variables that overshadow these glowing accounts. For example, reported higher family income among Asian Americans is often reflective of more wage earners present in a family, rather than a higher income per worker (Cabezas & Kawaguchi, 1988). In 1988 the U.S. Equal Employment Opportunity Commission revealed discrimination patterns of low employment for Asian Americans in all occupations in private industry, with the exception of service work. According to Langberg and Farley (1985), Asian Americans still experience some degree of discrimination and segregation in society because of differences in racial and cultural background, despite high levels of education and economic achievement.

According to Jiobu (1988), it is clear that Japanese Americans are beginning to resemble the stereotype of a model minority as they assimilate socioeconomically and structurally. There are families who keep their Japanese cultural heritage symbolically and consciously but at the same time socialize their children to live in the culture of the dominant society. These are not people trapped as marginal, but people who have made choices to be dual cultured. As the Japanese American group succeeds, it can increasingly afford to maintain this duality.

Therefore, what may seem to be contradictory behavior to an outsider is really an expression of an adjustment to the perceived context. For example, when a majority person is invited to dinner, the dinner table appears similar to any other household in terms of food, tableware, manners, conversation, and so forth. If, however, a Japanese American person comes as a dinner guest, most likely there will be more ethnic foods served, the dishes and tableware may be very different, and sometimes people may sit on the floor at a low table to eat dinner. Noticeable are the conversation style and figures of speech reflecting the cultural heritage.

Depending on the particular household and the degree of conscious maintenance of its ethnicity, a Japanese American family member may seem completely acculturated to the dominant society. However, the identities of Japanese Americans often bear witness to the Japanese cultural heritage.

THE ECOLOGY OF VIETNAMESE AMERICAN FAMILIES

The end of the Vietnam War brought many Vietnamese individuals and families to the United States, predominantly as refugees. Many of the early refugees were Laotians (including the Hmong people) and those Cambodians who had helped the United States during the war and were literally rescued from Cambodia to save their lives. From 1975 to 1992, more than 856,500 Southeast Asians sought refuge in the United States. Most of the refugees were Vietnamese seeking asylum and fleeing from persecution. Those who could prove they were in danger, because they had aided Americans in the war effort, were airlifted out of the country. They were members of the South Vietnamese military or members of the elite who were fearful of the North Vietnamese invasion. The second wave of immigrants consisted mostly of Chinese Vietnamese who became known as "the boat people." Those who were able to leave the country were allowed into the United States by way of a third country only upon showing proof of relatives living in the United States. To seek asylum in the United States, policies exist that require time spent in a third country. Subsequently, it became more and more difficult for the Vietnamese to immigrate into the United States.

Initially, Indochinese refugees were dispersed across the country by the U.S. government in an effort to minimize their impact on local services and to aid in their rapid assimilation into the United States. Refugees were often sponsored by church groups and middle-class families (Barringer et al., 1995). Under no circumstances were they obligated to stay where they initially settled, and many moved to warmer climates, such as the South and West, particularly California. The first Vietnamese refugees of

1975 have adjusted quite well to the United States. They arrived with higher educational levels and more exposure to Western culture, compared to later immigrants.

Amerasians.   Amerasians are children conceived in Vietnam of Asian mothers and U.S. servicemen during the Vietnam War. Most have experienced years of rejection by the Vietnamese people, and many were totally unacknowledged by their American fathers. Amerasians were not allowed admittance into the United States before 1982 because of their illegitimate status. In Vietnam, due to the stigma attached to marrying an American serviceman, many mothers destroyed marriage licenses and birth certificates that would have given proof of their association with Americans. In the United States, many Amerasians suffered because of their mixed race, especially those whose fathers were African Americans.

In 1982 the Amerasian Immigration Act allowed only the children of U.S. servicemen into the United States. However, most Amerasians with any family were unwilling to leave them behind. Orphans and abandoned children generally had no monetary means of cutting through the enormous amount of red tape necessary to leave Vietnam. In 1982, of the total number of Amerasian refugees admitted to the United States, 50.1 percent were 19 years old or younger (Office of Refugee Resettlement, 1982). In 1987 Congress passed the Amerasian Homecoming Act, allowing relatives to accompany Amerasian children into the United States. These families have strengths and weaknesses similar to other Vietnamese families who have lived here for more than 10 years. Generally, the Amerasians arriving in the United States are 80 percent illiterate.

In spite of their high numbers, refugee youth have not been studied, and there is an absence of hard data and knowledge that also affects services for these young people and their families.

In 1990 the total number of Vietnamese Americans living in the United States was 614,547. This is an increase of 135 percent since 1980 (LEAP, 1993). The largest Vietnamese populations are found in Orange County, California, followed by Los Angeles, San Jose, San Diego, Houston, and Washington, D.C.

The Vietnamese American community is divided economically, with half earning more than $38,205 per household. The median household income in the United States is $35,000. However, 23.7 percent of Vietnamese American families live in poverty (the U.S. poverty rate is 13.2 percent). More recently arrived Vietnamese immigrant families experience a higher level of poverty and are four times more likely to receive welfare assistance (LEAP, 1993). They also have less education, less command of the English language, and fewer marketable skills.

Family Structure

Most of the Vietnamese immigrants came from rural areas of Vietnam that contain several ethnic minority groups, each with its own language and cultural practices. There are several religions; however, Buddhism is the most prominent.

The Vietnamese family consists of parents, siblings, and all relatives. Because the family is considered more important than the individual, the individual owes loyalty to the family before all else and holds the family interest above personal interest (Brown, 1988).

The traditional family is highly structured, with a hierarchy of priorities where parental ties are paramount. The family is the caretaker of its members' physical, social, and emotional well-being. Family members care for their families first and community second. The concept of "strangers" intervening does not exist in Vietnamese culture. There is great reluctance to admit problems to strangers. Well-intentioned interventions by helping professionals, for example, may be serious insults to the Vietnamese, who, out of politeness, will not reveal their feelings about the situation.

The Vietnamese family's social and economic status has undergone dramatic changes, especially those associated with family roles. It appears that the father is no longer the primary provider, and parents often depend on their children to interpret and help them cope with the American system. Children, who feel a strong sense of family obligation, have taken on an enormous responsibility for easing their parents' despondency by overcompensating behaviors (Uba, 1994). Overcompensating behaviors include trying to meet the economic and social needs of their parents, who are unable to speak English, cannot drive, and spend most of their lives at home. These situations create intergenerational conflicts as elderly Southeast Asian Americans find that in the United States being old makes it more difficult to adjust to American ways. The younger members often assimilate more quickly, thus assigned traditional Vietnamese roles become conflicted. This is especially true with the family's power structure. In the past, power was held by the elders; now power is mediated by the younger generations.

Vietnamese Male Roles.   A son's first obligation is to his parents, followed by obligations to his siblings. These are permanent expectations between parents, children, and siblings (Dillard, 1987).

The oldest man is the head of the family and has absolute power and responsibility for the care of other family members. Children live with their families until they marry, and they care for their aging parents. After the death of the oldest man within the family, the oldest son becomes head of the family.

Vietnamese Female Roles.   Women are raised more strictly and given less freedom than men (Ho, 1990). A woman is expected to obey her father when single and her husband after she is married. When she is widowed, she is expected to live with her eldest son and accept his authority.

The Vietnamese woman's marital status seems to have a significant bearing on her adjustment to U.S. life. Older Vietnamese women without spouses demonstrate more serious psychiatric and social problems than their married counterparts.

Cultural Values.   The differences between the Vietnamese culture and the mainstream U.S. culture have been points of confusion and clashes for immigrants. Most noticeable and strongly observed are the behaviors of "saving face" versus frank expression, interdependence versus independence, quiet reserve versus openness, and authoritarian male hierarchical control versus individual freedom and egalitarian choice. Children learn very early that candid communication with parents is not respectful. They also learn that communication is usually unidirectional from mothers to children or fathers to mothers (Morrow, 1989).

VIETNAMESE AMERICAN FAMILIES AND THE EDUCATIONAL SYSTEM

According to Dillard (1987), the major stressors for Vietnamese refugee youths are (1) moving to a different community and school, (2) having difficulty with the English language, and (3) communicating with teachers and peers in school and social settings. Most refugee youths are not prepared to function in American schools where students are expected to take an active role. A number of academic and behavioral problems have been noted among some of the undereducated, the unaccompanied minors, and the Amerasians. Amerasian girls generally fare better in school than male Amerasians. It has been reported that Amerasian girls view their new education as a true luxury.

Vietnamese youths face incredible challenges and obstacles as they adapt at home, at school, and in the community. Many youths are faced with loneliness and social isolation. Yet there are cases of Vietnamese students attaining valedictorian status in their high school classes and succeeding in college. Their drive and hard work pay off when they take advantage of opportunities offered. Their parents frequently expect high academic achievement from their children, but they are slow to give encouragements of praise or positive reinforcements. As one researcher states, achieving all A's on the report card is the baseline expectation for many Asian American children (Nagata, 1989).

Vietnamese parents often emphasize self-discipline rather than external controls. Children are expected to behave, to excel in school, and to be respectful of teachers and elders. They are socialized to internalize morality and will feel bad if they misbehave. Parents often remind them of their obligation to the family.

VIETNAMESE AMERICAN FAMILIES AND THE HEALTH CARE SYSTEM

Vietnamese refugees typically have serious health problems. Many carry infections such as tuberculosis, hepatitis, parasites, and other infections that result in chronic nutritional deficiencies. Many have suffered malnutrition and starvation, along with excessive stress, resulting in stunted growth, delayed puberty, and other syndromes (Carlin & Sokoloff, 1985). Some Amerasians develop psychological problems from coping with their mixed race. Identity problems seem to be more complex for Black Amerasians than others (Biagini, 1989).

Vietnamese woman employed in manufacturing jobs such as in the garment industry earn minimum hourly income. These women face the struggle of maintaining a traditional role as a mother and wife in a family and at the same time are employed full time outside the family. Conditions for women in these households can be very stressful and lead to severe depression. According to the Asian Task Force study (2005) on domestic violence, Vietnamese respondents were more tolerant of the use of force and more likely to justify the use of violence against a wife.

These data reveal the belief in male privilege or that some wives deserve beatings. In this study 72 percent of Vietnamese women experienced or witnessed abuse as a child, and 27 percent witnessed their fathers regularly hitting their mothers. It is believed that the magnitude of the problem is greater than studies indicate and that cultural, linguistic, socioeconomic, and political barriers prevent these women from seeking help.

Older people tend to acculturate more slowly than the younger generation; therefore, they tend to be more isolated from the mainstream of society as well as from their own family members. Most of the elderly Vietnamese are unable to speak English, cannot drive a car, and spend most of their time at home alone. The older they are, the more depressed they are. Some have experienced extreme forms of violence, but shame keeps the elderly from discussing the past. Symptoms of post-traumatic stress disorder (PTSD), such as avoidance, hyperactive startle reactions, emotional numbness, intrusive thoughts, and nightmares, have been noted in those who have sought psychiatric treatment (Carlin & Sokoloff, 1985). According to Kinzie and Leung (1993), approximately 50 percent of Southeast Asian refugees could be suffering from post-traumatic stress disorder.

As the more traditional or elderly Vietnamese experience conflict and misunderstanding with Western medicine, they seek links to traditional healers who may be miles away from their homes. There are three categories of healers that they may turn to, including traditional Western medicinal care as well as magic, which could be the source of illness or its cure. Ancestral spirits can also be protective or malevolent entities. For those who have little difficulty interfacing with Western medicine, they may still find certain procedures used by the health professional disturbing and fearful, such as taking blood. The belief is it takes a long time to replenish blood taken out of the human body (Devore & Schlesinger, 1999).

Many health beliefs and behavioral systems have ethnic, class, and cultural roots. How ethnic people respond to "sickness" gives professionals the clues to understanding the far-reaching influences of cultures. The problems of people must be viewed within the cultural context of their lives, the interplay between ethnically derived attitudes toward health and illness, and the influential consequences of biopsychosocial factors.

VIETNAMESE AMERICANS AND THE GOVERNMENTAL SYSTEM

The picture of Vietnamese refugees and their relationship to the U.S. government is still coming into focus. Vietnamese refugees were not sufficiently supported when U.S. programs and policies settled Vietnamese families throughout the United States, precluding their gaining emotional support from other Vietnamese families, like most immigrant groups. Researchers believe that social support networks are the single most important factor in the adequate adjustment of the Vietnamese to the United States. Also, the shifting of health and nutritional responsibilities from federal to state governments made services either inadequate or inaccessible.

THE ECOLOGY OF KOREAN AMERICAN FAMILIES

The first wave of Korean immigrants started in 1904 and continued until 1924. Most of the people migrated to Hawaii as plantation sugar workers, intending to stay temporarily. The second wave, from 1953 to 1967, were mainly made up of students and Korean wives of American servicemen, as well as war orphans who were being adopted. The third wave was the result of the Immigration and Naturalization Act of 1965, which opened the way for approximately 30,000 Koreans to immigrate yearly to the United States. Many of these newcomers were looking for better economic opportunity for themselves and educational opportunities for their children.

Unlike prior immigrants, the new Korean immigrants came with a good education and desirable employment skills. A high proportion of the Korean adult immigrants had four years of college or more and had previously held white-collar jobs in Korea, although problems arose mainly associated with the need to use the English language. This often created barriers to finding desirable employment, which led to the strategy for some families to open up small family-owned businesses (Devore & Schlesinger, 1999). Approximately 90 percent of the total population of 850,000 Korean Americans are new immigrants who came after 1965, with 59 percent in the labor force (U.S. Census Bureau, 2000).

Family Structure and Selected Family Values

Most Korean American adults are Korean born, and therefore, traditional family roles and values are central to family functioning. The traditional practice of patriarchy and patrilineal descent of preference for sons manifests itself in the father-to-son sequence of family inheritance. Oftentimes father-to-son relationships are considered more important than husband and wife relationships. The role of women, historically, was to be subservient to men, which translated into not making direct eye contact with outsiders, smiling at them, or touching their hands. Throughout history, Korean society has taught men to have authority over women, even to the point of condoning the use of physical force. Today, this vertical hierarchical power structure is being challenged as more wives seek outside employment.

Once comfortable traditional roles now encounter unfamiliar practices in this new socioeconomic environment. As Korean American women work outside the family to contribute to the family income, they do not always practice traditional roles, although their husbands may wish to hold on to traditional ways. In some cases, the women are the breadwinners if their husbands are ever unemployed or underemployed. In cases where men are not employed during the initial five years of establishing residency, there are often indications of very high levels of stress within families that can lead to incidences of domestic violence (Young, 1992). It is not uncommon to find that Korean women rarely discuss this issue with anyone because of cultural views of self-blame and shame. There exists sharp sex role segregation such that Korean women in the United States still do all the household chores and care for the children, even while employed full time outside the family. There are those who believe that working Korean women in the United States have gradually eroded the male dominant role of the traditional family.

As children are born and raised in the United States, strong traditional Korean family values have begun to weaken, leading to enormous frustration and miscommunication between the generations. These values include the following primary aspects: The family is seen as the central unit of society and not the individual, there is a strong emphasis on family interdependence rather than independence, and children are expected to be obedient to and responsible for their parents. Approximately 90 percent of those below age 30 are U.S. born. This younger generation often faces cultural conflicts as their parents try to impose traditional values on them, especially emphasizing docility and the conforming to parental wishes. Korean American children often believe that their parents do not wish them to express opinions that differ from their own and are afraid that parents are critical about their adopting Western ways, such as in dating and dressing. Conflicts often arise around individualism and self-assertion, considered such a negative trait in traditional Korean society. It is obvious that basic American cultural values conflict with traditional Korean values. However, the majority of Korean Americans value concepts of filial piety and status based on authority. The younger generation find that modesty and proper decorum in social relationships still remain important.

Korean Male Roles. The family is considered the foundation of society and it is believed that failure to have a son could mean the extinction of a family. Therefore, sons are preferentially treated and father–son relationships are more highly regarded than husband–wife relationships. Traditional sexual role socialization establishes the man as the ultimate authority and power in a family, and even the Korean language reflects this stratification and segregation of the sexes (Young, 1992).

Korean Female Roles. Traditional Korean society has socialized women to accept a subordinate position to men and for men to have authority over them. There are clear distinctions of roles that more traditional wives assume, such as cooking, babysitting, shopping, cleaning the house, doing the laundry, and other household tasks. Migrant Korean males have shared in certain tasks that require outside activities, such as buying a house, driving the car, paying bills, and buying groceries.

Stress of Immigration. Traditional Korean family roles are being challenged. The demands of adapting to a new culture where a woman's status is so different results in challenges and frustrations regarding established ethnic family roles. According to a Korean family legal counseling service in Los Angeles, wife abuse is the most serious of all domestic problems occurring in immigrant Korean families. Because families often reject outside professional help, culturally sensitive educational information written in Korean must be made available for men and women.

KOREAN AMERICAN FAMILIES AND THE EDUCATIONAL SYSTEM

The younger generation of Korean Americans experience cultural conflicts while attending American schools. These conflicts arise because of internalized values taught by their parents, such as being obedient to authority and being quiet and polite in social interactions such as those found in the classroom or with peers. These values are contrary to the expectations of American teachers and peers, which include demonstrating self-assertiveness and expressiveness. Misperceptions are formed and can be a serious problem in communication.

Education is highly valued as a means of achieving wealth and success. Parents make enormous sacrifices to give their children a good education. Mothers often are evaluated as being a successful parent according to their children's choice of college or career. This translates not only into a child's academic performance being viewed as very important for their future, but also for the status it brings to the family. Rarely is this message subtle, and it is more often clearly and frequently stated, to the point of demand.

There is a gender bias in terms of choice of career goals. It is expected that girls have more flexible educational goals in order to combine family with career, whereas Korean young men are expected to have professional career goals that can lead to family (as opposed to personal) wealth and prestige.

KOREAN AMERICAN ELDERLY AND THE HEALTH CARE SYSTEM

As with all immigrant groups, how health problems are dealt with often depends on the interaction between one's ethnic reality and the problem being experienced. For example, Korean immigrants describe *hwas-byung,* a folk illness label used to describe a number of physiological and psychological complaints. This is a cultural expression for experiencing major depression and related conditions (Devore & Schlesinger, 1999). Another example is the strong belief associated with dreams that may occur during sleep. Dreams hold an important message that could affect the listener as well as the dreamer, if they are shared during daytime hours. If the dreamer talks and shares their contents at night, it will not affect either the listener or the dreamer (Kavanaugh & Kennedy, 1992).

The health problems of the Korean elderly are of growing social concern. Eighty-six percent of Korean elderly perceive their health as fair to poor. The elderly prefer to be treated by Korean doctors, and only 8 percent seek out other American doctors. Approximately 52 percent have Medicare or Medicaid coverage, with 48 percent having no health insurance of any kind. Perceived racial discrimination is a major factor related to accessing the mental and physical health care system in the United States. In this study, 48 percent of the elderly had strong negative feelings about racism, 20 percent answered, "as anticipated," and 34 percent had "no opinion" or were hesitant to express an opinion (Kim & Kim, 1992).

Korean elderly not only face economic insecurity but have an enormous language barrier when interfacing with the health care system. Oftentimes their children have moved away and the parents are left living by themselves or with relatives or friends.

The elderly are affected in additional ways because of their limited ability to speak English. This language barrier often leads them to gravitate to where other Koreans are living, such as Korea Town in Los Angeles, Chicago, or New York. Isolated from family members, the Korean elderly are often left in fear and mistrust of "outsiders" who are not Koreans.

The Korean elderly also are very concerned about saving face, and therefore find it difficult to ask others for help, including other Koreans who are not their immediate family. Because of a competitive cultural style, their mutual support system within the family, as well as within the community, is weak.

KOREAN AMERICAN FAMILIES AND THE RELIGIOUS SYSTEM

Compared to other Asian Americans, Korean Americans are known as churchgoers. The number of Korean churches has grown faster than the population, from about 75 churches in 1970 to approximately 2,000 Korean churches in the United States, approximately 1 Korean church for every 350 individuals. It has been reported that 70 to 80 percent of the Koreans in Chicago and Los Angeles attend church at least once a week.

Possible reasons for this pervasive church participation include praying and seeking religious support, meeting friends and engaging in social activities, and seeking peace of mind. The church, in return, gives support and a helping hand to those who are psychologically distressed or experiencing other personal crises, such as family separation, physical illness, financial difficulties, immigrant status change, language problems, and underemployment. It is assumed that the churches play a significant role in promoting cultural assimilation of Koreans into U.S. society.

HELPFUL TECHNIQUES FOR SERVING ASIAN AMERICAN FAMILIES

Service professionals of many kinds often find themselves interacting with Asian Americans. Although more recent Asian Americans are highly educated, they still need assistance in gaining information about the availability of many government and community programs and activities. There are also Asian Americans whose use of English is limited and who need the assistance of interpreters. For the service professional, this will be a first priority. Also seeking in-depth information about how to overcome some of the cultural issues that make serving this community difficult will be another priority. Sometimes, in an effort to be friendly, individuals use joking and idiomatic phrases that are very culturally oriented with non-English-speaking or limited English-speaking Asian Americans. Unfortunately, many new immigrants or older individuals do not understand these language usages, so it is very important to avoid using them.

It is also important to keep in mind the importance of the family in place of the individual. Many Asian Americans have a symbiotic link with their families. The rights of, and responsibilities and obligations to, family members are often more important than individual needs, as clearly described in the previous three examples. The familial self predominates the individual self, which is quite foreign to the Western view of the individual self. Loyalty and cooperation are expected of family members (Roland, 1988).

Professionals who interface with Vietnamese, Hmong, Laotian, Meo, or Cambodian families should try to gain a realistic understanding of their unique issues (Burton, 1983). Women from these groups are often very reluctant to share their personal circumstances with perceived outsiders. Enabling women to use a form of their own oral history can often ease that uncomfortable relationship. Such historical perspective will allow you, as a professional, to gain insights into the cultural heritage of these women.

Probably one of the most important dimensions of communication, however, is to allow enough time to build trust in your relationship with Asian American families. As a caring professional, one of the most difficult aspects of relationships is to avoid misunderstandings that often lead to fear, resistance, and defensiveness. In many Asian groups, it is rude and impolite to say "no" directly to an authority figure, so the use of "yes" may actually mean "no."

Remember to allow the growth of mutual respect through such actions as limiting direct eye contact or extended gazing. This nonverbal gesture, if used, can lead an Asian American individual to experience a sense of "losing face." Another American gesture that is discouraged is to curl the index finger toward someone, to say "come here." This is considered an insult, implying that the person is a slave or domestic servant. Cross-cultural understanding and appropriate cultural assessment and decision making will help reduce anxiety and resistance. You will find subtle cultural variations that make each subgroup unique, and knowing the differences will help you bridge the gap in your role as a professional.

✦ CONCLUSIONS

On the surface, Asian Americans appear highly successful. The stereotype of the "model minority" disguises a complex community of controversies and a tug of war between traditional Asian practices and assimilation into the majority culture. In the Asian American community, family pride and loyalty, academic achievement, hard work, and pressure to succeed have high priorities. Asian Americans occupy a unique position in the United States. They are not considered a part of the majority, nor are they recognized as a minority in certain circumstances, but rather are considered a "monocultural" entity. This often hampers access to opportunities and services targeted for minorities, and not all Asian Americans fit the stereotype of a model minority.

A major problem among Asian American communities is the plight of the elderly, who are caught between the traditional role of being revered for their wisdom and their age-related status of respect within their families and communities, to a status where acculturation has eroded and diminished their active participation. Also, as the younger generation leave home, their elders are often left alone and isolated. In certain circumstances, they are taken advantage of financially and psychologically because of loneliness and frustration in communicating successfully with the outside world of lawyers, bankers, salespeople, and other service providers.

A review of demographic trends in the United States identifies acceleration toward diversity. Since 2004 approximately the same number of Asian American refugees, immigrants, and elderly are falling under the poverty line. Ethnic subgroups of young people, especially in the Midwest, are dropping out of the educational system while, at the same time, a generation of young Asian Americans have invested themselves in becoming educated and are reaching for the goal of American promise and success.

✦ STUDY QUESTIONS

1. List 10 countries that many Asian Americans call their ancestral homes.
2. Make a list of 10 historical facts about the early Asian American immigrants from their earliest days.
3. List the relative percentages of the U.S. population represented by Asian Americans. What do these data tell you?
4. Three distinct groups of Asian Americans were identified for extensive discussion. List these groups and their identifying characteristics.
5. Describe the typical family structures found in Asian countries that were discussed in the chapter.
6. What religions were listed as contributing to the cultural values of Asian Americans?
7. What is happening with respect to children of recent immigrants who enter American schools?
8. What data were offered to show Asian Americans' success in the educational system?
9. List in complete sentences the facts that show Asian Americans' participation in the economic system.
10. There are names for each generation of Japanese Americans living in the United States. List these names and give definitions.
11. What do you know about Korean Americans?

12. List 10 facts in complete sentences that show how Japanese Americans have been acculturated.
13. Write a short paragraph describing Amerasians.
14. List seven ways that a service professional might assist Vietnamese Americans.

✦ APPLICATIONS

1. By claiming that Asian Americans are a model minority, society can use them as an example to challenge other minority groups. Are Asian Americans a "model minority"? Write a two-page essay giving at least five reasons why you do or do not support this characterization. Who benefits from the perpetuation of this stereotype?
2. What are some of the holidays celebrated by Asian Americans? For example, are there various celebrations for the new year, for religious celebrations, for honoring important people, or for rites of passage?
3. Do you believe that Asian Americans are overrepresented in colleges in the United States? Research this idea further, and give your opinion in a two-page report.
4. In a two-page essay, discuss your opinion regarding the number of immigrants from Asia entering the United States.
5. Some feel that Asian Americans do not fully integrate into the majority culture as well as other immigrants because they are slow to adapt to the English language and they hold on to their cultural distinctions. How do you feel about this? Do some library research, and write a two-page essay on what you learn.
6. A large portion of elderly Asian people experience stress and anomie in the United States. What are some suggestions to alleviate these problems? Write a one- or two-page essay.
7. Like the English language, the food we eat is a mixture of different influences. Make a list of foods you have eaten that have an Asian origin. Make a list of Asian foods that you have heard of but never tried.
8. Go eat lunch at an Asian restaurant and order something different, such as sushi.
9. Some authorities treat cultural differences as though they do not exist. Others believe that putting differences squarely on the table is the best way to clear the air between individuals and groups. Write a one- or two-page essay defending one of the views.

✦ MEDIA RESOURCES

From a Different Shore. The Japanese-American Experience [Video, 50 minutes, color]. (Available from Films for the Humanities and Sciences, Box 2053, Princeton, NJ 08543-2053)

✦ KEY INTERNET RESOURCES

Marriage and Family Encyclopedia—Asian Americans
http://family.jrank.org/pages/108/Asian-American-Families.html

Asian American Children and Families
www.casanet.org/library/culture/communicate-asian.htm

Coalition for Asian American Children & Families (New York)
www.cacf.org/index.html

Asian American History and Demographics
www.asian-nation.org/model-minority.shtml

→ 7

Arab American Families

Key Concepts

- Islam
- Qur'an
- Patrilineal

Be proud of being an American, but also be proud that your fathers and mothers came from a land upon which God laid His precious hand and raised His messengers.
—Kahlil Gibran (1883–1931)

Most immigrants, although proud to be Americans, as Gibran suggests in the preceding passage, still fondly remember their homeland. This chapter introduces you to Arab Americans. It may come as a surprise to many that more than 4 million Arab Americans live in the United States. By 2010, the population is expected to be about 6 million. Since September 11, 2001, Arab Americans (who are mostly Muslim) have experienced harsh racial discrimination and treatment by other fellow citizens. Many have faced ugly targeted remarks such as, "You don't belong here. Why don't you go back to your own country?" Many Americans have only recently become aware of how little they know about Middle Eastern people. The Arab world has been grossly neglected in the education of most Americans. As helping professionals, you may have occasions to work with Arab American families.

WHO ARE THE ARAB AMERICANS?

Arab Americans have lived in the United States for over a century and a half, having immigrated from the Arab "homeland"—a vast region that comprises 72 percent of its territory in Africa and 28 percent in Asia. More specifically, it stretches 5,000 miles from the Atlantic coast of northern Africa in the west to the Arabian Sea in the east, and from the Mediterranean Sea in the north to Central Africa in the south. By comparison, the United States comprises 3.6 million square miles. Although representing different Arab countries and ecological regions, many Arabs see themselves as one nation. They formed the League of Arab States in 1945 representing 22 separate Arab nations (although the United States only recognizes 19 of them): Algeria, Bahrain, Comoro Islands, Djibouti, Egypt, Iraq, Jordan, Kuwait, Lebanon, Libya, Mauritania, Morocco, Oman, Palestine, Qatar, Saudi Arabia, Somalia, Sudan, Syria, Tunisia, United Arab Emirates, and Yemen.

Generally, Arabs prefer to be defined as members of the Arab nation who enjoy a common heritage, language, culture, and destiny, with the Islamic religion and the Arabic language constituting its two predominant cultural features. Interestingly, the source for both Islam and Arabic dates back to 622 A.D., when the Qur'an, the holy book of Islam, was revealed to the prophet Muhammad and, subsequently, recorded in Arabic.

Although Arabic is written and spoken by over 150 million inhabitants of the Arab world, it is also used by a seventh of the world's population. Millions of people in Africa and Asia write their languages in the Arabic alphabet. Farsi, the language of Iran, and Urdu, the language of Pakistan and some parts of India, are written in the Arabic script. The Turkish language employed Arabic characters until the 1920s. In addition, Arabic script is used today in Afghanistan, Indonesia, Malaysia, sections of China, and even in the Muslim areas of the Philippines and the former Soviet Union. Arabic developed over the centuries into a language of amazing richness and flexibility as it came into contact with other cultures, traditions, and religions.

Although Islam remains the dominant religion of this vast region, both Judaism and Christianity originated in this area. Islam, faith of the vast majority of Arabs, is more than just a religion; it is the focal point of Arab society for Muslims and non-Muslims alike, permeating their culture at every level—political, social, economic, as well as private. To appreciate the enormous force of Islam in the Arab world, one must understand the basic tenets of the faith and how it emerged and grew. Islam originated in the Arabian Peninsula—present-day Saudi Arabia—in 622 A.D. According to Islamic tradition, God (Allah) conveyed to Muhammad, a tradesman, a series of revelations that were to form the basis of the new faith. Islam means submission—submission to the will of God; a Muslim, in turn, is one who has submitted himself to Allah and who acknowledges Muhammad as his prophet.

Muslims consider Prophet Muhammad to be the last in a series of prophets, which included Abraham, Moses, and Jesus, to whom God revealed His divine message. Islamic tradition, in fact, takes into account the doctrines of both Judaism and Christianity, which preceded it. For example, Muslims believe, as do both Jews and Christians, in *one God* and in an afterlife. Islam also acknowledges Jews and Christians as the "people of the Book" (*ahl al-kitab*), "the Book" meaning the Bible, and has granted them privileged status from the early days of the Islamic empire into modern times. For this reason, religious minorities throughout the Arab world have survived and flourished during periods of severe cultural and religious repression elsewhere. The body of revelation that Allah delivered to Muhammad through the angel Gabriel is contained in the Qur'an, the holy book of Islam. The Qur'an, written in Arabic, the language of Allah's divine transmission, provides the Muslim believer with all he or she needs to know to lead a good and pious life. In addition to its obvious religious significance, the revelation of the Qur'an represents the crowning literary achievement of the Arabic language. It has been both an immeasurable influence on the development of Arabic literature and an inspiration for all branches of literature and scholarship. Islamic acts of devotion and worship are expressed in the Five Pillars of Islam. These involve not only profession of faith but also recognition of God in all aspects of human conduct. These are the Five Pillars:

1. Profession of faith, or *shahada* in Arabic, which requires the believer to profess *the unity of God and the mission of Muhammad.* This involves the repetition of the formula, "There is no God but Allah and Muhammad is the messenger of Allah." This assertion forms part of every prayer, and in a critical situation, one may repeat the first part to establish one's identity as a Muslim.

2. Prayer, *salatt,* which is required five times a day: at dawn, noon, midafternoon, sunset, and dusk. It must be performed in a state of ritual purity, and every word must be in Arabic. The worshipper has the choice of praying privately, in the open air or in a house, or with a group outdoors or in a mosque. Islam opposes the practice of withdrawing into ascetic life. For this reason, there is no priesthood, as is known in the West, only *'ulema,* learned men, who are well versed in Islamic law and tradition. Throughout the Muslim world, services are held at noon on Fridays in mosques. Muhammad did not explicitly designate Friday as a day of rest, only a part of which is devoted to a special religious service. Merchants are free to open their shops before and after the service.

3. Almsgiving, *zaka* or *zakat,* the third Pillar of Islam, embodies the principle of social responsibility. This precept teaches that what belongs to the believer also belongs to the community in the ultimate sense, and that only by donating a proportion of his or her wealth for public use does a person legitimize what he or she retains. The *zaka,* in addition to the other tenets of Islam, is a religious obligation, and believers are expected to treat it seriously.

4. Fasting, which is the fourth Pillar of Islam, is known as *saum.* To a Muslim, it means observing Ramadan, the month during which, it is written, God sent the Qur'an to the lowest heaven where Gabriel received it and revealed it in time to Muhammad. Fasting demands complete abstinence from food and drink from dawn to sunset every day during Ramadan.

5. Pilgrimmage to Mecca, *al-haij,* the last cherished Pillar of Islam where God's revelation was first disclosed to Muhammad. Believers worship publicly at the Holy Mosque, expressing the full equality among Muslims with a common objective—all performing the same actions, all seeking to gain the favor of God. All pilgrims, from various cultures and classes, wear identical white robes as they assemble around a single center, the *Ka'aba,* which inspires them with a strong sense of unity. Every Muslim is expected to make the pilgrimage at least once during his or her

lifetime. Attached to the experience of the pilgrimage is added status: After the individual returns home, he or she is addressed as "*al-Hajj*" or "*al-Hajjah*" (the pilgrim), a title that carries great prestige.

Although the Islamic community throughout the world is united by the two essential beliefs in (1) the oneness of God and (2) the divine mission of His prophet, there developed shortly after Muhammad's death a debate within the Islamic community over who should succeed the prophet as leader of the faithful. This debate split the community into *Sunni* and *Shi'ite* Muslims. It is important to remember, however, that on fundamental issues, Sunni and Shi'ite Muslims are in basic agreement because they both draw on the Qur'an and the Shari'ah, the body of Islamic law.

The early immigration of Arabs to the United States from about 1880 to 1940, and their rapid assimilation, is a complex and largely unfamiliar story. Thousands of young Arabs arrived in America shortly before World War I. The great majority came from villages in the Mount Lebanon area of the Ottoman Empire, now western Syria. Speaking Arabic dialects and holding Christian, Islamic, and Druze faiths, they quickly established family and trading networks across America. Like many immigrant groups from Europe and elsewhere, Arabs tended to congregate in urban areas of the United States, such as Detroit and New York City, and they sent their money back to their homes. In the Middle East, news of economic success in America spread quickly and brought other businessmen, skilled laborers, and craftsmen, many of whom also became economically successful and returned home prosperous (Naff, 1985). Success was a dream families had for their sons. It was customary for family resources to be pooled to help the young immigrant. Although economics has remained an important factor in recent Arab immigration, other social factors, such as political unrest, professional opportunities, and opportunities for their children and family, have often influenced today's Arabic people's decisions to leave their homelands and come to the United States.

The Syrians (who came during the 1950s and the 1960s), and the Palestinians, the second largest group of Arab immigrants who came between 1940 and 1948 (and then again in the 1970s), immigrated mostly for political reasons. A majority of the Palestinian people, who are of mixed religious orientation—including those who are Muslims, Protestants, and Catholics—immigrated to the United States during the upheaval caused by the founding of Israel. In the 1970s there was an influx of Arab immigrants, mostly Lebanese, Palestinians, and Iraqis, who came because of political upheavals in their regions. During 1997–1998, Algerian immigrants immigrated to the United States mainly because of civil war and unrest, which began in 1992 as a result of a fundamentalist movement to purge their country of nonbelievers.

Those who migrated mostly for professional opportunities for self and family include people from Bahrain, Kuwait, Omani, and Qatari, who are, for the most part, among the wealthiest groups of immigrants. They have come from stable nations with a good economy and good living conditions.

It is believed that by 2010, the Arab American community will surpass the Jewish American population. Given its growing population and influence, there is little acknowledgment or written recognition of the many contributions of the Arab American ethnic group to the history and social fabric of the United States. For example, American youth study algebra without any knowledge of its Arabic origin.

Today, there is a mingling of the "old" Arabic immigrant with that of the "new" Arabic immigrant living in the United States. There are many first-generation Arab immigrants learning Western ways for the first time while retaining many of the characteristics from their homeland. Others have been previously exposed to Western education and values and have an understanding of Western culture and language. About 4 million Arabic people count themselves a part of the Islamic community in the United States, and the discussion in this chapter only focuses on those who represent these Islamic communities.

According to Haddad and Lummis (1987), possibly five major worldviews are operating among Muslim immigrants in the United States. First, there are the *liberals,* who are probably the most acculturated of the Islamic community. Members of this group have no recognized religious leader, with many American born or highly westernized. Secondly, there are the *conservatives,* westernized Arab Americans who adhere to the minimum requirements of Islam, such as belief in personal piety, dietary restrictions, and prescribed practices. The third group is the *evangelical* group, which places great emphasis on scriptural foundations and the Prophet Muhammad. As isolationists, they tend to form small groups with other like-minded Muslims who take special care in following all prescriptions of Islam in their daily living. The fourth group is the *neonormative* one, similar to the third group but with the additional dimension of monitoring and enforcing compliance of Islamic public life. Their goal is to change society so that Islam may rule. The fifth group are the *Sufis,* who focus on the mystical aspects of Islam (Haddad & Lummis, 1987).

THE ECOLOGY OF ARAB AMERICAN FAMILIES

Given the regional and ethnic diversity in any one Arab nation, it is difficult to construct an Arab family profile. It is not uncommon to find negative stereotypes of Arab Americans as seen in movies or the news. Sadly, these images are the only information most people have of Arab Americans, which then influences their perceptions. Arab citizens are lumped into one generic group and have been targeted with hate crimes whenever the United States determines that certain Arab nations are "our enemy." Undoubtedly, there is a geopolitical relationship between how Arab Americans are perceived and treated and how the Arab world is viewed.

You must understand that although our description of Arab Americans represents a generalization and may not be characteristic of any one individual or family, certain cultural nuances and social knowledge can provide important information for building bridges between people. As suggested by Germain (1994), a more appropriate way to look into life experiences is to consider the development of an individual or family in relation to historical time, individual or family time, and social time. Just as the definition of an American may vary from individual to individual, there are factors such as religion, education, economic conditions, ethnic subgroups, and generational degrees of acculturation that affect individual and family values. The five types of worldviews underscore the importance of understanding the differences that exist within the Arab ethnic group. The first two groups are the most acculturated and, therefore, may represent most of the Arab American families presently studied and reported on.

Arab American Families and the Religious System

In Detroit, Michigan, there were approximately 200,000 Arab American residents in 1988 (Ahmed & Gray, 1988). Within this population, the four major nationality groups represented are the Lebanese/Syrian, Palestinian, Yemeni, and Iraqi-Chaldean. The typical religious affiliations of the Lebanese and Syrians are Greek or Syrian Orthodox, Maronite and Melkite Eastern Rite Catholic, or Sunni or Shia Muslim. The Palestinians are typically affiliated with Greek Orthodox, Roman Catholic, Protestant, or, more often, Sunni Muslim religions. The Yemeni Muslims are Shafei and Zeidi. Generally the Iraqi/Chaldean are Eastern Rite Catholics or Muslims. The first mosque was built in the United States in 1919, in Highland Park, Michigan. By 1959 it was estimated that only 1 Arab-American in 18 was Muslim (Kayal, 1983).

Some Arab Americans are Arab Christians whose roots lie with the heritage of Eastern Christianity and the culture of the Arabic Middle East. It is often difficult to understand the experience of this complicated group, specifically those with Syrian and Lebanese origins. They are divided into two major religious bodies, Catholic and Eastern Orthodox Christians, and two nationalities, Syrian and Lebanese. There is considerable cultural mixing because for generations marriage rates with partners outside the group have been very high, even exceeding 80 percent in the 1980s (Kayal, 1983). Intermarriage accelerates the process of acculturation and eases or erases the lines between groups.

Because of recent Arab–Israeli conflicts, contemporary Syrian Lebanese Americans have been forced to examine their history, their ethnic identity, and their relationship with other Arab Americans and the Arab world. It is left to each family to decide which Arab cultural features to retain and which features to accept from American culture.

Arab American Family Structure

The structure of the Arab family is usually described as patrilineal, patrilocal, patriarchal, and extended. In *patrilineal* families, descent is traced only through the male heirs, and loyalty of all family members is directed toward the father's family (see Figure 7.1). *Patrilocal* means that a newly married couple moves into the house or compound of the husband's family. *Patriarchal* refers to the father's complete authority over other family members. The Arab *extended* family refers to all male heirs and their families over the generations. In many ways, Arab Americans have kept this traditional view by having large families in which all aunts, uncles, cousins, and grandparents are considered part of the immediate family, even if there is only one breadwinner in the household.

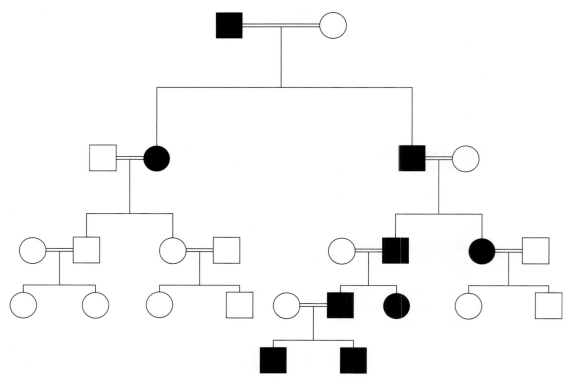

Although a child is related to both mother's and father's side of the family, the official family membership or family name is passed on only through the male descent (shaded).

Symbols represent:

☐   Male

◯   Female

⚌   Marriage

| Descent/offspring

Figure 7.1   The Patrilineal Family System

In the ancestral homelands of most Arab Americans, the traditional Arab family is patrilineal, thus shaping the structure of the extended family to include the father, grandfather, father's brother's families, and sisters, as well as grandparents on the father's side, his brothers and sisters, and his brothers' sons and daughters. Also, his sons and his sons' children, as well as his daughters, will be in his patrilineage (Aswad,

1988). This means certain individual rights are inherited only through a child's father. For example, a young man can be involved in sporting activities with his father or be a part of his father's professional life, whereas a daughter is restricted from participating in sporting activities or in public dating. If the father believes in traditional values that women should not work outside the home, the young woman will have to obey her father.

A child from birth belongs to the father's group, and this group never changes. The father's group is responsible to the child, and the child is answerable to them for all behavior. A woman will always be a part of her father's group from birth. However, her children will be a part of the husband's patrilineage. In traditional groups, the actual responsibility for life and death decisions of an individual belongs to the patrilineal group (Aswad, 1988). This is a powerful unit for political and economic success. Islamic tradition allows for a couple to divorce. However, the custody of children below the age of 7 for boys and 9 for girls is usually awarded to the mother until they reach such age, when they must go with their fathers. In the United States this practice has been altered, given the position taken in the United States that most young children should be with their mothers or in joint custody.

Female Roles and Responsibilities

Arab women also have rights and privileges. Clear Islamic teachings spell out the roles of women and their rights and duties in the patrilineage. When women marry, they retain their father's name and seldom adopt their husband's name. Father and brothers are expected to assume protection over girls and women. Close relationships are often formed between brothers and sisters. Under Islam, women may also inherit property; however, the majority of the holdings usually remain in the control of the patrilineage or male heirs.

Given these characteristics of Arab families, some of the problems that develop after immigrating into the United States might be related to role changes and reversals as individuals acculturate at different rates. However, we have to be careful not to overgeneralize these values and cultural practices for all Arab Americans. For example, Egyptian immigrants come from a country with the least restriction on women, especially if the family is from the upper class. It is not uncommon to find that their ascribed status holds considerable power in managing their households.

But for the most part, because of cultural differences in role expectations, female Arabs who come to the United States, or Arab American families who socialize daughters here, often confront many problems. The family's name and honor are very important in Arab families. In the structure of the Arab society, family honor is intricately woven with loyalty to religion, sect, and community. For more traditional Arab American females, the issues of coeducation in public schools, equal education, manner of dress, driving a car, voting in elections, opportunities for leadership roles, and working alongside males other than relatives can be interpreted as shaming the family honor. The fear of shame may tend to restrain the female from accepting the ways of the majority culture and from accepting new family values.

Living in a new culture places a difficult burden on Arab mothers, for it is primarily the duty of the mother to socialize children in ways that maintain the respect and honor of the family and the family's name. For example, because the honor or dishonor of an individual reflects on the entire extended family, it is important in the traditional patrilineal lineage that women remain virgins until marriage, with the breaking of the hymen being a test of virginity on the marriage bed. This practice is being seriously challenged by some Americanized Arab young women, as it is in some other groups. Therefore, to protect the family's name and honor, many traditional Arab American parents allow, even encourage, their daughters to marry at an early age, rather than risk pregnancy and the resulting shame and dishonor to the family. Early marriage, however, limits the young women's opportunities to pursue higher education. Challenges to the legal marriage age in many states may also follow.

Many Arab women in their native countries lived cloistered with extended family members behind compound walls, whereas in the United States, Arab American women generally live in single-family homes or apartment units. Arab women typically enjoy close ties with other women, creating networks for helping and visiting each other, assisting with child care, sharing food, and emotionally supporting each other. In their home countries, Arab women primarily functioned in the private or domestic sphere, and men dominated the public sphere (Aswad, 1988).

Stereotypes are found in many Western descriptions of the Arab woman, who often is not as powerless as suggested. It is not uncommon for a woman to support another married woman from another lineage or within the same family group. An Arab woman may resort to influencing her male kinsmen and/or spouse to exert pressure on another man if he mistreats his wife or daughter. There may be husbands who are tyrants, but the actual picture is usually of strong wives with authority and much to say in the running of the households (Ahmed, 1999).

Often overlooked are the Koran's (Qur'an) pronouncements on the subject of all women. The Qur'an is considered the holy book of Islam. In it, infanticide is prohibited; *monogamy* is prescribed as a rule, and *polygamy* only as an exception to be contracted in certain abnormal circumstances. The Qur'an outlines legal structures by which women could protest injustice and ill treatment, institute divorce in certain situations, and sue if their inheritance (half a man's share) was denied them. The Qur'an gave women the right to inherit property for the first time, granted them inalienable rights to their own inherited wealth, their personal jewelry, and their own earnings (Fernea & Bezirgan, 1977). Amiruddin (1939) emphasized that the prophet Muhammad raised women from the lowest social position to one of equality with men in most matters, and removed from women the stigma of responsibility for original sin and the fall of man, supporting legal and social reforms to improve the condition of women. However, there is a great variance between the protections for women commanded in the Qur'an and what is currently practiced in Muslim societies. Disregard of Islamic precepts is partly blamed for the low position of women in Muslim societies today.

Many modern Arab American women pursue a career. As more Arab American women become more acculturated in Western ways, more educated, and more interested in finding work outside the home, family change, family stress, and family struggles occur (Aswad, 1988). One of the most profound impacts on the Arab family today is the emancipation of women through education, and the growing freedom of women to move outside the home into the community (Berger, 1962).

Elders: Respect, Power, and Prestige

Prestige and power are attached to age, and especially to Arab grandparents. The grandfather is the undisputed head of the household or clan, and everyone submits to his authority. He passes on the oral traditions of the Arab culture, using parables for the moral guidance and character development of younger generations.

The grandmother is also very powerful in her role as mediator for the grandchildren. She often intercedes on behalf of her grandchildren when she views the child's father (her son) as being too harsh. Respect for the elderly is clearly demonstrated.

Many Arab American nuclear households have both husband and wife working full time. Without an extended family, the care for the elderly has become practically nonexistent. Some families can afford to hire a nurse to come into the home, but for many this is impossible. According to some Arab Americans, there is nothing in the Qur'an stating that the elders must be cared for by family members. Although this is desired, the importance lies in how well they are cared for rather than who cares for them (Haddads Lummis, 1987).

Children and Youths

Children are viewed as "the wealth of the Arabs." Therefore, the best marriages are those that produce many children. For most traditional Arabs, a son is preferred as the firstborn child. Arab women may be blamed when they give birth to girls, even though it is the male sperm that carries the chromosome for determining the sex of the fetus. However, female infants are also pampered and cherished, especially if they follow a male child. All infants and children are indulged. They are fed at the slightest sign of restlessness or hunger. An Arab child enjoys touch, play, security, and a sense of belonging to a group.

Children are always considered a part of the family. This value is displayed by the custom of addressing a child by a title that describes the child's relationship to the speaker rather than by a given name. The paternal uncles are of particular importance. For example, in the event of a father's death, the traditional practice is for the father's brother to assume all of the responsibilities in rearing his brother's children and supporting his widow.

Names are chosen from religious, historical, natural phenomenon, personality trait, or occupational categories only after much deliberation and consultation. Given names are often identified with the prophets or people in the holy books, the Qur'an and Bible. Children are not named after a parent or any living relative unless an aging grandparent or relative makes a request.

The father's role becomes increasingly important as children mature. Although the father is the final authority and chief disciplinarian of children, he is usually warm and tender toward his young children. However, parents are seldom viewed as children's friends (Shabbas, 1979). There is clear status and power distinction between the younger and older generations, and children are expected to show respect for all Arab elders.

As family values have been influenced by "American ways," some traditional practices have gone by the wayside. However, in some families, values related to childhood and the role of the child in the family are undergoing very slow change (Shabbas, 1979). Arab Americans feel it is important that all children learn a social code, or system, of the right etiquette. The code prescribes correct behavioral patterns expected of well-behaved children, including the following: Obey parents, respect elders, be polite in the presence of elders, and demonstrate generosity, cooperativeness, humility, and helpfulness toward others. Arab Americans expect the family to instill these values by interweaving them into their everyday life and interactions with family members, friends, peers, and people in authority.

As children mature, and with each successive generation, struggles between parents and youth concerning acculturation have become more prevalent. Many youths who defy traditional views are seen as trying to dominate their parents. More traditional parents feel that the American culture allows and promotes an excessive amount of freedom for youngsters, and they worry about the consequences for their children.

Arab families that arrived recently in the United States see younger third- or fourth-generation Arab Americans exhibiting new values and behaviors learned in the American culture. Many parents attribute this change to the educational system. Their fear is that these new values and mores will lead to less self-control and toward more criminal behaviors, drug and alcohol use, out-of-wedlock babies, family violence, decline of the work ethic, and less economic security in the younger generations.

However, accommodation and change are characteristic of adult Arabs, as well as the younger generations. Educated urban Arabs are moving away from the traditional patterns of raising their children exactly as they themselves were raised. Children from Arab countries are seeking to express their individuality, something unheard of in the past. Some Arab parents are beginning to relax their control. Daughters are allowed more freedom in their choice of a husband, and in certain subgroups, interethnic marriages are not viewed as a major crisis.

ARAB AMERICAN VALUES

Many proverbs taught in the Arab culture reproach those who lie, gossip, quarrel, or say unkind words to others. Other proverbs express values of proper behavior, including dignity and modesty, cooperation, hard work, and common sense. The family is the central institution. It is at the center of both the theology and the sociology that are primarily responsible for teaching religious and moral attributes (Ahmed, 2001). The most desired and cherished values of Arab Americans are communal cohesion, honor, endurance, and grace of words and fluency of expression.

Communal Cohesion

Communal cohesion exists at different levels of complexity and is fluid in its boundaries. Loyalty to the group is paramount, and disloyalty has, at times, led to the law of retribution ("an eye for an eye. . ."). For example, in the country of origin, if any member of the family is assaulted, there might be some form or attempt at retribution. The whole family becomes involved in the confrontation or crisis. The extent of the group's cohesiveness varies and can even reach across the patrilineage to encompass other Arab nations.

Honor

Honor and respect are interchangeable to the Arab. Honor is displayed in behavioral terms, particularly in one's attitudes toward others, whether old or young, male or female, weak or strong. To be honorable refers to that "which strengthens the group and serves its interests. Shameful behavior is that which tends to disrupt, endanger, impair or weaken the social aggregate" (Patai, 1983, p. 90). In an effort to avoid loss of face, Arabs often hide troubles from those close to them.

Endurance

Harsh ecological conditions of most Arab regions and the adaptation long ago to a nomadic lifestyle exacted stamina and strength of will from individuals. The virtues of forethought and self-control contribute to the sustaining principle of physical and moral endurance, resulting in the hard-work ethic of many immigrants.

Grace of Words and Fluency of Expression

A great appreciation of literary expression, spoken or written, is found among Arabic people. Portrayals of experiences and emotions are laced with grace and embellishments. What counts is not the logic of the argument but the grace of the words and the fluency of the expression (Abd al-Auhir al Jurjani, 1972).

Probably one of the most admired writers was Kahlil Gibran, an Arab American. Kahlil Gibran was admired for his grace of words and fluency of expression. His book *The Prophet,* published in 1923, is described as mystical and covering emotions such as love, joy, friendship, and sorrow. The essence of his many writings was the brotherhood of man and the healing power of supreme love. His fame endures, and over 7 million copies of his work have been sold (Ashabranner, 1991).

ARAB AMERICAN FAMILIES AND THE EDUCATIONAL SYSTEM

Arab American children are taught to respect teachers and to take advantage of the formal educational system. However, in some Arab communities, for example in the Detroit area of Michigan, Arab American organizations are concerned about the low educational standards of the local school system and the subsequent low educational attainment by Middle Eastern youths.

The public educational system reports that Arab youngsters encounter problems in school. The problems seem to result from a lack of proficiency in the English language. This lack impedes Arab American children in adapting to and succeeding in their new educational system. Consequently, many Arab Americans, disappointed with the public school system, have organized and financed private schools enrolling large numbers of their children.

A fact often overlooked is that most American educators have little or no personal experience or prior exposure to the regions of the Middle East, other than conflicts in these regions recounted daily on television news reports and in major U.S. newspapers, usually conveying a negative image of Arab Americans.

Often excluded from the textbooks used in the United States are many contributions of the Arab world. Here are some examples:

1. Arabic words that have become common in our culture, such as *ginger, coffee, sugar, syrup, sherbet, cotton, sesame, spinach, lemon, saffron, and oranges*
2. Sciences founded in the Middle East, such as astronomy, algebra, chemistry, and technology
3. Medical discoveries, such as anesthesia, disinfectants, and the vaccination for smallpox
4. The word *check,* introduced by American banks, which comes from the Arabic word *sakk*
5. Grafting and fertilizing, introduced in the agricultural industry

Stereotypes and discrimination encountered in the cohort culture contribute to the difficulties experienced by Arab American youths. Representations of Arabs in the media are often negative, and, as a result, Arab Americans may have difficulty establishing relationships with other American youth. These troubles are heightened during periods of conflict in the Middle East. Anti-Arab sentiments among some Americans create conditions that make life difficult for many younger Arab Americans. Fortunately, a large number of Arab American scholars are overcoming previous barriers, and highly educated immigrants are appearing on university campuses. Today, Arab Americans as a whole are more highly educated than many other ethnic groups, especially those whose families of origin came from cities. Their willingness to adjust to technological advances with a balanced view of modernization have contributed to their success story (http://fauclty,newe.edu/toconnor/soc/355lect14.htm). Their scholarship should help inform people of Arab Americans' needs, as well as provide positive models of Arab Americans to college students.

ARAB AMERICAN FAMILIES AND THE HEALTH CARE SYSTEM

According to Bernado (1981), St. Jude's Hospital in Memphis, Tennessee, famous for its treatment of leukemia-stricken children, was built by Danny Thomas, an Arab American actor and celebrity, to give thanks to America. ALSAC, previously known as the

American Lebanese Syrian Associated Club, and now an acronym for Aiding Leukemia Stricken American Children, is a nonprofit charitable organization devoted to fund-raising for the Memphis St. Jude's Hospital.

In case of mental health issues, it is important to realize that the Arab individual from birth is socialized to be a member of a group. Members of a group or extended family are responsible for each other and will assist in any intended intervention directed at an individual member of the group. It is unrealistic to expect Arab Americans to solve problems by themselves.

ARAB AMERICAN FAMILIES AND THE GOVERNMENTAL SYSTEM

Arab Americans have lived in the United States for over a century and a half. The Arab presence has been largely inconspicuous in American written history. Few schoolchildren learn anything at all about Arab Americans. The relatively small size of the Arabic immigration, and the scattering of immigrants across the country, as well as their political quiescence, may offer some explanations for omissions. Some Americans took note when the Arab states curtailed oil production and oil prices rose or when shipments of oil didn't reach the United States. Up until that point, many Americans perceived Arabs as picturesque, penniless nomads seeking water for their herds (Leuchtenburg, 1977). This image, particularly promoted by the film industry, included the nomad, the camel, the mosque, the desert, the palm tree, and the water hole. Today's media portray Arabs mostly as terrorists in countries like Iraq and Afghanistan and in the Middle East.

Whenever the U.S. government perceives an Arab country as an enemy or a threat, Arab Americans are targeted with hate crimes. The largest number of attacks occurred after events like the hostage crisis, The Gulf War, terrorist bombings, and the September 11 twin towers devastation. There is definitely a geopolitical link between perceptions of Arab Americans and the U.S. government. This reminds us of the old film *Guilty by Reason of Race,* a documentary about Japanese Americans during World War II and the propaganda that led to their internment experience.

Today, as the size of the Arab American populace expands and gains economic parity, the younger generation of Arab Americans has begun to take a more active and visible role in politics. For example, former Senate majority leader George Mitchell is a prominent Arab American, having been a federal judge before he was elected to the Senate. However, Arab Americans are more likely to win elected office in towns where their families have been prominent and where their ethnic origins play little or no part in their political success (Naff, 1983). Many Arab Americans feel that future generations should avoid assimilation to the extent of becoming invisible.

ARAB AMERICAN FAMILIES AND THE ECONOMIC SYSTEM

A standard stereotype of those from the Arab world is that they are sharp traders or businessmen. This view may arise simply because many emigrants from Arab lands have become people of commerce in many countries they emigrated to. Small businesses are often organized on a kin and ethnic basis (Zenner, 1982). It is not uncommon to find small grocery stores and liquor stores operated and owned by Arab Americans in U.S. inner cities. Because Arab Americans do not drink alcohol, it is not uncommon for others in the community to be resentful and feel exploited by their businesses. This controversy is felt more often by other ethnic minority groups who also live in the inner cities. Some Arab Americans are achieving their economic goals of a good life, but others are poor, sometimes extremely poor.

There is a generation gap between the established Arab Americans and the newcomers. Members of established Arab American communities are largely urban dwellers taking active roles in business and commerce. The newcomers experience problems of economic inactivity centered on their lack of necessary experiences, skills, and education. One of the greatest problems many newcomers face is difficulty in learning the English language. For some, language is the greatest obstacle to adapting to and succeeding in the new American culture.

HELPFUL TECHNIQUES FOR SERVING ARAB AMERICAN FAMILIES

Arab Americans are eager to participate actively in certain aspects of American life. Most want to learn English quickly. They accept assistance and guidance that lets them help themselves and reject social services intervening in their private family affairs. Many who enter the United States have family members here who are relied on for most of their support. However, if you are going to offer assistance, remember that, in many families, the Arab American male holds the dominant role in the family; it may be necessary to approach him to help a child or a woman. If the family is Egyptian in origin, the woman can usually be approached. In the United States, often the most appropriate nonverbal language is to shake hands when welcoming or introducing yourself to the other. However, you must be ethnically sensitive because there are certain taboos that may be practiced by the Arab American. Therefore, be aware that public touching of the opposite sex is forbidden. If one is of the same gender one may shake hands, look at the person's eyes, and stand close to the other, so the Arab American can read your eyes.

Both spoken and written Arabic are unknown to most Americans. Learning some key Arabic phrases may be useful in developing friendships and rapport. It is especially important to realize how many misconceptions arise because of language differences; therefore, you may need specialized language help to avoid conversational misunderstandings.

Here are a few tips to consider when conversing with an Arab American. Expressions of negative emotions are often carried out with hand gestures, and the use and choice of words are considered culturally very important. At all times, you must not insult or swear during a conversation, especially if you, as a professional, find it annoying when confronting what you perceive is not a believable statement. For an Arab American, if it is believed that a higher value is of importance and at stake, bending the truth is acceptable. There could be instances when not understanding the verbal and non-verbal meanings of symbols can create misunderstandings. For example, the nonverbal for yes is to nod your head left and right and to say no is to nod your head up and down, just the opposite of the majority culture. To say "go" is to wave the fingers toward the palm of your upright hand, which in U.S. culture would signify "come here." Understanding the meanings of these gestures may seem less important than the task at hand; however, if you are to communicate and facilitate the building of a relationship, it is important to know them.

✦ CONCLUSIONS

Although immigration records for Arab Americans are inadequate, an estimated 4 million Americans claim their heritage as coming from someplace in the Arab world. In recent times, the number of Arab Americans speaking Arabic, who consider themselves Muslims, has been on the rise.

Many Americans today maintain negative stereotypes of Arab Americans. Textbooks covering history, geography, and social sciences offer inadequate and biased information on Middle Eastern peoples and countries (Suleiman, 1988). Many teachers are unaware of the omissions and biases, and so a true picture of the culture is never conveyed.

According to the *Washington Report on Middle East Affairs,* years of educational outreach by American Arabs have recently been undermined by the terrorist actions of a few. A number of prominent political and law enforcement officials, including former President Clinton, former New York governor Mario Cuomo, and the director of the FBI, have recently stressed that the Muslim community, as a whole, should not be made a scapegoat in the wake of a few terrorist acts (Noakes, 1993).

Arab American organizations immediately condemned the 1993 attack on Manhattan's World Trade Center as well as the September 11, 2001, terrorist attack on the twin towers. In a plea to the general public to avoid blaming the entire Arab American community, the American Arab Anti-Discrimination Committee said, "It is a horrendous act; there is no place in America for this kind of senseless violence" (Willford, 1993). Just as all majority citizens are not blamed for a crime committed by a member of their racial group, Arab Americans as a group should not be blamed for such acts by professed Islamic terrorists, who look at the United States with undisguised revulsion.

There are many others who come to the United States seeking asylum and opportunity. This is reflected in the number of immigrants from Arab lands that are closely related to political unrest. War and bloodshed in their own countries compel many Arabs to emigrate elsewhere to seek a safer life for themselves and their families.

With the historic signing of the Palestine-Israeli Accords in September 1993, it was hoped that one of the world's hot spots had been defused. The Accords outlined a process for reconciling long-standing differences between the Israelis and Palestinians, getting each to acknowledge that both parties have a right to live in the region peacefully, productively, and with human dignity.

Watch closely as the future of this region of the world unfolds. Your work with families in your own Arab American community will be profoundly affected by progress or lack of progress toward more harmonious relations.

→ STUDY QUESTIONS

1. Write down the countries that Arab Americans consider their ancestral homes.
2. The approximate population of Arab Americans today is ___.
3. Name the organization that united the Arab states. When was it founded?
4. What religion was most typical of America's first Arab immigrants? Today's immigrants?
5. When and where was the first mosque built in the United States?
6. Define Qur'an, Islam, Allah, Muhammad, and mosque.
7. Define patrilineal, patrilocal, and patriarchal as related to the Arab family structure.
8. Describe male and female roles in Arab culture.
9. Discuss each of the four categories of Arab American values.
10. List contributions to American life that originated in the Arab world.

→ APPLICATIONS

1. Read background material on various Arab countries in an encyclopedia. List countries that are predominantly Arab, predominantly Muslim, and predominantly both Arab and Muslim. Which are considered Middle Eastern?
2. Review five articles in a daily newspaper or a newsmagazine depicting an event in the Middle East or an event about Arab Americans.
   a. Describe each article briefly and record the citation.
   b. State whether, from the Arab American viewpoint, you feel the coverage is fair. Discuss in a two-page essay.
3. Perform a word association using the word *Arabs*. Write down the stereotypes that come to mind. Discuss whether your words are positive, negative, or neutral. Decide whether they are words you would like to have said about yourself. Write a one-page report.
4. Interview two Arab Americans, and ask them about their family history. (Remember, some may have been here for generations.) Ask: How long they or their ancestors lived in the United States? What were the circumstances of their immigration? Did they know English when they came? How did they fare in their first months after immigration? Write a report of what you learn.
5. Check out these Internet Sites:
   a. American Arab Anti-Discrimination Committee (www.adc.org/)
   b. Arab World

c. CIA Map of the Middle East
d. Sample of Spoken Arabic.
6. Read Devore and Schlesinger, *Ethnic Sensitive Social Work Practice* (Needham Heights, MA: Allyn & Bacon), 1999. There are many excellent case studies and suggestions for intervention practices.

✣ KEY INTERNET RESOURCES

Arab American Institute
www.aaiusa.org/
American-Arab Anti Discrimination Committee
www.adc.org/index.php?278

→ 8

Native American Families

→ **Key Concepts**

- Native American
- Native Peoples
- Indigenous Peoples
- American Indian Citizenship Act
- Matriarchal and Patriarchal Tribes
- Relocation Act
- Acculturation
- Assimilation
- Powwow
- Pan-Indian

I am tired of talk that comes to nothing. It makes my heart sick when I remember all good words and all the broken promises. There has been too much talking by men who had no right to talk. If the White man wants to live in peace with the Native Americans he can live in peace. Treat all men alike. Give them all the same law. Give them all an even chance to live and grow.

—Chief Joseph, 1889, Nez Percé

T he preceding quote by Chief Joseph could easily serve as a statement today of Native American values. As a helping professional, you will more than likely be called on to serve or work with the very first peoples of the North American continent—the Native Americans. As a child, you may have studied Native American history in school, but you will need to learn much more about these indigenous people to serve them adequately. You may have seen the commercial on TV that shows a Native American man with tears rolling down his cheeks as he observes the disregard for the natural environment and the rapid degradation of his beloved mother earth. This portrait of a silent, contemplative, and emotionally controlled individual portrays a certain aspect of the traditional value of respect for the natural environment inherent in Native American culture, although much of it is probably an exaggerated stereotype of the stoic "Indian." After studying this chapter, however, you will gain a deeper understanding and appreciation of Native Americans and the values that typically influence their lives.

WHO ARE THE NATIVE AMERICANS?

The term *Native American* refers to all Native Americans, Alaska Natives, Aleuts, Eskimos, and Metis, or mixed bloods. Some controversy surrounds the names previously and often currently used to describe the indigenous peoples of North America: American Indians, Indians, AmerIndian, Amerinds, or Indigenous, Aboriginal, or Original Americans. In Canada, they are known as First Nations. Much of the controversy stems from a variety of reasons, one of them being the prior use of the term *Indian,* given to the various native tribes by European explorers, which led to resentment among native tribal peoples about being referred to by a collective name, and the presumed political implications of such a name. Although no name has found universal acceptance, the most politically acceptable title is that of Native American, which emphasizes the "First Nation" aspect of the indigenous peoples of North America. When referring to specific individuals or groups, however, tribal designations, such as Blackfeet, Cherokee, or Navajo, are used.

Native Americans are a nation of people who proudly claim that 36 percent of their population lives on identified native land, or reservations. These 314 reservations and trust land areas include recognized native reservations, tribal trust lands, Alaskan villages, and designated historic areas such as the Cherokee Village found in Oklahoma (U.S. Census Bureau, 2000). The Native American population in any area may range from one tribal

Will Hart/PhotoEdit Inc.

member living off the reservation, to approximately thousands living on the Navajo nation's reservation, which is the largest in the United States (Bureau of Indian Affairs, 1985, 2000).

Native Americans are made up of many different people. As of July 2005, 4.5 million people, or 1.5 percent of the total U.S. population, reported that they were Native Americans or Alaskan Natives (U.S. Census Bureau, 2005). Currently, there are 562 federally recognized Native American tribes and another 245 not recognized but that continue to submit paperwork to obtain recognition (Paige, 2006). A majority of the tribes are located west of the Mississippi River; only four states are east of the Mississippi: Michigan, Maine, Florida, and New York. California has the highest total population of Native Americans of any state followed by Oklahoma.

Two hundred distinct tribal languages are spoken today (Leap, 1981). However, most Native Americans report speaking mainly English at home, with the exception of the Navajo, Pueblo, and Eskimo people who most often speak a native language at home. The Navajo has the highest percentage who speak their own language at home, compared to 5.3 percent of the Inuit people of Alaska (U.S. Census Bureau, 2000). If we were to average the data out, approximately 25 percent of Native Americans and Alaska Natives 5 years and older speak a language other than English at home.

Each native tribe developed its own unique language, customs, and beliefs, and each had its own history of experiences that led to various strategies for dealing with the rapid changes in their traditional lifestyles. As indigenous peoples of the Americas, their origin stemmed from many different tribal groups, which resulted in a variety of adaptive strategies for cultural expressions. These differences among Native Americans were chronicled by explorers and historians during the early history of exploration and contact. As time passed and as each generation was forced into submission to the larger social order, it became clear that autonomous tribal groups could not change discriminatory practices and policies made at state and national levels aimed at assimilating Native American groups and keeping them politically helpless. As Native Americans confronted these issues, they realized that they needed to level the playing field where policies were being made that had an impact on them without their input. The Pan-Indian Movement was formed to serve as a unified identity, a Nation, to the outside world, although it was understood among the tribal groups that one's primary ethnic identity lay with tribal affiliation.

Historical Background

Native Americans of the North American continent are the descendants of the only ethnic group that did not immigrate into North America in the last 500 years. They were here long before settlers came from Europe and other parts of the world, but, ironically, they only became U.S. citizens under the American Indian Citizenship Act of Congress in 1924. Some groups, like the Iroquois, have argued that they are not citizens of the United States because their nation existed in America before the formation of the U.S. government. Rather, they are citizens of their own nations.

Compounding identification matters was the Wheeler-Howard Act of 1934, which set up tribal corporations on Native American lands. Political power conflicts between the U.S. government and tribal groups conveniently became the rationalization for the Reorganization Act of 1934, allowing Native Americans to self-govern and self-direct their nations. As legal and politically sovereign nations, they have expressed their self-determination in self-governance at least since the first treaties were signed. The act upholds the understanding that tribes are like states and local governments. Treaties promised Native Americans constitutional sovereignty. However, it was only in 1970, during President Nixon's term in office, that this sovereignty for Native American nations finally became a reality in legislating Native American affairs.

According to social policy specialists, it was President Nixon's message to Congress on July 8, 1970, that led to respect for Native American participation and control concerning policies and programs that affected Native American life. Nixon argued that a trust relationship between the government and Native Americans should be guided by egalitarian principles and the keeping of the treaties signed (Gross, 1989). Even today, debates on issues related to Native American sovereignty rage in the halls of Congress and in corporate offices across the country.

Congress and Native Americans still grapple over issues of self-determination and self-government. Many tribes are now demanding recognition of their rights, as guaranteed through treaties over time with the U.S. government. For example, some tribes are involved in legal battles over fishing and hunting rights, and some are seeking payment and restoration of stolen land. Some Native Americans are reestablishing traditional religious ceremonies as a source of strength and a way of life, and some are also forming their own schools to balance the knowledge of modern survival with the knowledge of Native American culture and philosophy (Reyhner, 1994).

Demographic Information

Today a majority of Native American families live on a median income that is about $33,627 based on a three-year average (2003–2005). For example, in 1986 the median income for families on reservations was only $9,942 (U.S. Census Bureau, 1987). In 1952 Congress passed the Relocation Act, which was designed to assimilate Native Americans into the mainstream population by promises of training and jobs if they moved to the cities. Given the high unemployment rates that were found on or near reservations, it was not surprising that more than 67,500 heads of households were relocated through a direct employment program (U.S. Census Bureau, 1970). Many Native American reservations have limited job opportunities for adolescents and for adults except for those reservations that are moving into the gaming business. Today, a majority of Native Americans are found in and around major urban cities, such as in Los Angeles, Long Beach, and Riverside, California.

As Native Americans increase their numbers, the birthrate has exceeded that of the general U.S. population and all minorities since 1955. For example, the birthrate in 1990 for all Native Americans was 28.0 per 1,000 persons as compared to 15.6 per 1,000 for all ethnic groups (U.S. Department of Health and Human Services, 1993). Between 1950 and 1990, sympathetic policies were enacted to improve health care services to Native Americans. The outcome has resulted in reduced infant mortality rates and increased life expectancy for adults. Also, in 2001 the Native American birthrate dropped to a low of 16.8 per 1,000 people. The decrease in birthrate and infant mortality and the increase in life expectancy have been attributed to improvement in health care services and to a surge in willingness to identify themselves as "Native American." Increased ethnic pride has resulted in enhanced self-identification as Native Americans consider themselves members of a tribe, rather than as individuals in a family or community. According to the census of 2000, the Native American tribes with 100,000 or more people were the Cherokee (729,533), Navajo (298,197), Choctaw, Sioux, and Chippewa, and they account for 42 percent of all those who responded to this census inquiry. The largest Alaska Native Tribal grouping in 2000 was the Eskimo (54,761) whose preschoolers make up 26 percent of the state's preschool children.

THE ECOLOGY OF NATIVE AMERICAN FAMILIES

The ecology of Native American families includes the people, the natural environments, and the sociocultural adaptations to the environment. There are as many variations of family ecological systems as there are Native American families. Different tribes have had unique cultural adaptations resulting in a variety of family forms. For example, the Hopi, a matrilineal society, live in the Southwest as do the Navajo, a patrilineal society. The many required roles of individuals differ among the many tribes that exist today. However, the importance of the family, its cultural heritage, and family tribal customs permeate the modern-day thinking of Native Americans.

Family Structures

Historically, there has been a wide diversity of family structures among Native Americans. However, through time, this diversity has diminished. Some tribes are structured

along matriarchal lines, such as the Navajo of the Southwest, where women control
the power in the family. Traditional Navajos practice *matrilineal* descent, where the lineage or descent is traced through the woman's line. They are *matrilocal,* with the bride
and groom moving in with the bride's mother's family. The typical Native American
woman sees her destiny as a reflection of her tribe and her people. Her role is as diverse as the tribal cultures. In some tribes she is devalued; in others she wields considerable power. In some tribes she is a familial clan adjunct; in others she is virtually as
autonomous as her psychological makeup and economic circumstances permit. A Native American woman has distinct personality traits that are unlike Western ideals or
roles for women. For example, statistics show that Native American women are more
likely to exit marriage through legal proceedings than through widowhood, as found
among Black or White women (Yellowbird & Snipp, 1988).

In *patriarchal* tribes, men are powerful and the primary decision makers. They exercise the governing roles in the family, as well as in the clan and the tribe. Evidence indicates that the traditional roles of men have been greatly changed. In matrilineal
tribes like the Hopi and the Seminole, fathers' roles disintegrated as families were influenced by the larger society. Men's roles have also been affected in patrilineal societies. Not being able to provide economically for his family affects the self-concept of
the patrilineal urban Sioux's authority and status within his family and community. In
patriarchal tribes, women's roles are related to the care of the children and to functioning at the core of the family. Today many Native American women work outside
the home to contribute to the economic survival of the family.

Family Practices

Native Americans have always had diverse family practices. Practices vary regarding
bride price, bride service, and dowry; arranged marriage, interfamily exchange marriage, and adoptive marriage; bride abduction and elopement; cross-cousin and parallel-
cousin marriage; monogamy, polygyny, and polyandry; patriarchy and matriarchy;
divorce, temporary marriage, and trial marriage; wife lending and spouse exchange;
and patrilineal, matrilineal, and bilateral inheritance and descent (John, 1988, p. 326).
Assimilation and acculturation have reduced the diversity that once existed in Native
American family structures and practices mimic more the life styles of the majority culture. This is especially true of urban families who are separated from the reservations.
If there is any common model of the Native American family, it is the extended family
model. The Native American extended family is generally highly valued, although they
do not universally practice this form.

In 1978 Red Horse, Lewis, Feit, and Decker offered a typology of three distinct
family patterns existing among Native Americans today. They were the traditional, bicultural, and pan-traditional patterns and were a continuum based on the degree of
acculturation felt and expressed by these families. In 1988 Red Horse suggested a six-
category continuum of family types based on preferred language (native or colonial),
religious beliefs (native, pan-Indian, or Christian), attitudes about the land (sacred or
utilitarian), family structure (extended, fictive, or nuclear), and health beliefs and behaviors. For example, a *traditional* type of Indian family speaks the original Indian language,

lives in an extended family, practices native religion, retains traditional health beliefs and practices, and holds the land as sacred. There is the *neotraditional* family, which is similar to the traditional families except for the inclusion of new healing rituals, remedies to deal with health problems, and converting of a new religion into their spiritual beliefs. The *transitional* family has moved to urban centers and away from its original base. Daily life is based on the world of the Anglo-American. Attempts are made to socialize the children with a native language and to keep connected to extended family, native homeland, and spiritual practices. The *bicultural* family type maintains a generic Indian identity but can straddle both cultures with ease. The *acculturated* family type is indistinguishable from the Anglo family in beliefs and practices. The *pan-renaissance* family type lost all vestiges of the old ways and is now trying to regain its lost Indian beliefs and practices, forming still a new hybrid form (Red Horse, 1988).

Acculturation refers to the degree of adaptation one group makes to the majority culture. Differences arise based on the language used in the household, religious practices, value systems, and the kind of recreational and cultural activities the family participates in and with whom. Despite these degrees of difference in acculturation, there remain some common bonds among the three groups—traditional, bicultural, and acculturated—regarding family structures, relational bonding, and preferences in recreational and cultural activities.

Extended Families

The complex ecological web of family relationships extends to the clan, the tribe, and the Native American society. The web also extends over time and between generations. There is a collective mutual support system, or intergenerational and intertribal interdependence, that provides and nurtures an atmosphere of strong kinship bonds and affection. The many forced relocations and outside threats from non–Native Americans over many generations have aided and contributed to the solidarity of the Native American people.

Members of the extended family network play important roles in facilitating the well-being of individuals within the community and the tribe. Extended family members are important teachers for transmitting traditional ways and values. Older generations of grandparents, great aunts, and great uncles are often as important as parents in serving as teachers and models for the children (Red Horse et al., 1978).

The extended family form varies in different ecological settings. Family structures are different in small reservation communities from those in urban areas, and in interstate extended families from those in large metropolitan areas (John, 1988). Under some circumstances, family structures include kin and nonkin. Approximately 55 percent of Native American households include a married couple, and another 23.4 percent live in single-parent, female-headed households. There are proportional differences among various tribes. For example, there are fewer single-female-headed Navajo families than Sioux families (Yellowbird & Snipp, 1998). According to Guillemin (1975, p. 142), an important dimension of who constitutes a Native American family includes the face-to-face interactions that are so important to such families. These families are made up of individuals who are blood related as well as non–blood related. It is considered a horizontal and vertical family—people who belong are those who are accepted as a family member. Interactions convey far more meaning than letters or phone calls (John, 1988, p. 330).

A high family value is that of interdependence among family members, which leads immediately to identification and sharing of resources, both human and material. A commonly held belief and practice among Native Americans is the value of "what is mine is also yours." Extended families have their own rules, norms, values, and traditions governing how they help and care for their members. Understanding the extended family requires an in-depth immersion into their cultural context and careful observations over a period of time.

Elders

A highly placed value in all Native American families is the interaction and integration of the young and the old. Native American elders are the safe keepers of tribal stories and songs and are held in the highest respect in tribal groups. Forming an indispensable part of the community, the elders share and pass on to each new generation the tribal oral traditions (Ryan, 1980). The tradition of passing information orally from one generation to the next is typical of all tribes.

Elders also defend the values of the family through deeds, as well as through words and thoughts. This, coupled with respect and integration of the young and the elderly, helps explain why Native Americans have withstood assaults from outside professionals or officials who, with their differing values, have often had little sensitivity toward Native American ways. Elders represent a pattern of family strength in the cultural fabric by assuming responsibilities and obligations to future generations to pass down orally their traditions and history—creating interpersonal bonding in the process. Interdependence of the elderly with their extended family keeps them in the mainstream of family life and not in retirement. Native Americans are taught that their life force carries the spirits of their ancestors and that this tradition is passed down through the generations by the elders (Red Horse, 1980).

Unfortunately, in more recent times, Native American elderly are undergoing role transitions that are limiting the responsibilities they once performed in their communities. Many are caught, in the acculturation process, in conflicting cultural values of their status and their place in society. Under tenuous economic conditions, many maintain social and cultural obligations to their families. According to data from NICA (National Indian Council on Aging), 26 percent of the elderly have taken charge of caring for at least one grandchild, and more than 60 percent live within 5 miles of family who depend on them for chores and other routine obligations (Yellowbird & Snipp, 1998).

Children and Youth

Children are universally viewed as beloved gifts of life. Native Americans believe that each child is born with unique characteristics that help determine his or her place in the tribe. Depending on the traditional structure of the family, the child's naming ceremony takes place shortly after birth, or in some tribes it may take months or even years after the child's birth, to ensure that a proper name is given at the naming ceremony. Respect for the individual's autonomy begins at birth. It is exemplified by the traditional practice of observing the newborn over a period of time to determine an appropriate given name for the child relative to the child's specific characteristics and surrounding circumstances. Names are meant to provide a cultural map or path. Spiritually, a name may provide sustenance and rest in the afterworld. Structurally, a name organizes an obligatory and supportive network for the child's family such as aunts, uncles, and grandparents who are often namesakes, and sometimes trusted nonkin is selected. Namesakes assume major child-rearing responsibilities, such as being a role model and being in contact with the child on a regular basis. This form of social insurance does not undermine parental roles.

From the time of birth, Native American infants are reared in a cultural milieu valuing aspects both of autonomy and interdependence. For example, a child is nurtured in a community where members exhibit community tolerance. Tolerance and respect for individuals are expected of the community. A cultural value of individual autonomy is practiced by rearing children in an environment where they are free to explore, to make decisions, and to make choices from a very young age. It is not unusual for Native American parents to ignore the inappropriate behaviors of children. It is commonly believed that children learn by experiencing the natural consequences of their decisions and choices. This is expressed as follows by a Pueblo grandmother of 11 boys and girls:

> When you go to our children,
> try to become a friendly tree that
> they will want to sit near.
> Enjoy them. Forget yourself.
> If we all could only forget ourselves
> a bit more—then our children
> would feel free to be a bit more themselves.
> Sometimes we get too close to our
> children; we scare them with—
> with ourselves. They can't become themselves.
> It is them we should try to know. (Coles, 1977)

The Native American style of parenting that values autonomy and interdependence is contrary to the non–Native American view of child rearing and has often resulted in civil litigation against the Native American family and community. This cultural misunderstanding has resulted in children becoming victims of power plays. Many non–Native American family service providers, because of a lack of cultural understanding and wrongful expectation, react callously to Native American child-rearing practices. It is important for every helping professional to learn to recognize and appreciate the special cultural strengths of the Native American child.

When there is a cultural match between Native American families and the surrounding community, children mature with a deep sense of cultural identity. In contrast, where families and the surrounding community lack the cohesive forces of cultural similarities, children experience psychological stresses that could impede their sociopsychological development as they move into other social systems outside their families. For example, Boyce and Boyce (1983) found a higher incidence of mental health clinic visits for Native American youth among those families who were poorly matched with the surrounding community.

Native American Values

Cultural values shape the Native American's way of thinking, perceiving, acting, and speaking. Traditional values are subject to change, and there are various expressions of cultural values or beliefs. Each person appropriates various values in an individualistic way. However, Figure 8.1 provides examples of contrasting values between Indian cultures and majority cultures. There have been many such tables of cultural contrast; this has been created to include those values most likely to cause misunderstanding between groups.

Native Americans judge things and people according to what is inside their being. They firmly believe in the importance of seeing inside things instead of looking at only outward appearances. In searching for a world invisible to others, Native Americans believe that a good person can give good advice that flows from courage and wisdom.

Native American Indian	Majority Society
Group emphasis/collectivism	Individualism
Process living	Goal oriented
Here-and-now orientation	Future orientation
Nonemphasis on time	Emphasis on time
Elders are revered	Youths are revered
Cooperation	Competition
Harmony with nature	Conquest and control of nature
Sharing/giving	Hoarding/saving
Nonaggressive	Aggressive
Silent or soft spoken	Noisy or brash
Respect for other's religion	Contempt for other's religion
Aestheticism	Materialism
Permissive/self choice	Coercive/other directed
Shame	Guilt
Natural resources belong to all	Natural resources belong to individuals
Egalitarian	Class conscious
Inner harmony	Outside appearance
Individuals serve others	Individuals serve self
Interdependent	Independent

Figure 8.1   Contrasting Cultural Values

In contrast, they feel the majority of people judge according to outward appearances, individual achievement, or through the possession of material things.

According to Native Americans, all things, inanimate and animate, are related and are holy or sacred, possessing power. Relatedness, unity, or oneness is often expressed by the circle, a symbol of wholeness. Being in harmony with nature and other people is important. Sensitivity to others and a desire to get along with others has often been misinterpreted as apathy or low self-esteem. In their desire to be in harmony with others, Native Americans believe it is important to share, especially that of which you have more. This means sharing resources such as material goods, money, information, emotional support, or time. Among Native Americans, time is related to the task or event at hand, which is more important than the actual time involved. Time is not used as a measuring tool (Paniagua, 1994).

The Native American way of life is detailed, practical, and concerned with the immediate. These traits are uniquely expressed in distinct family units of each of the tribes. Each family nourishes certain basic values that form distinct personalities, engendering generosity to other human beings and respect for individual rights. These characteristics are mediated through emotional restraint, tolerance, and even humorous relationships.

CULTURAL EXPRESSIONS OF VALUES

Native Americans have various ways of expressing their values, noted in the following four traits.

Self-Reliance. Native Americans are often hesitant to ask and receive help from non–Native Americans. Personal freedom is based on making personal decisions that are not imposed or coerced.

Noninterference. Many Native Americans consider interference in other people's lives a sign of disrespect, a threat, or an insult. There is a strong belief that people learn from their own mistakes and decisions. Native Americans do not interfere and do not want to be interfered with.

Nonconfrontation. Native American people prefer not to confront those with whom they disagree. If possible, they avoid people who are confrontational.

Respect for Elders. Traditionally, Native Americans have revered the elderly in their society. They often defer to an older majority person whom they trust, even though they disagree with the person.

Understanding these traits as you become involved in the dynamics of interpersonal relations is important. Many professionals and officials who interact with Native Americans don't recognize the importance of these cultural values and traits. Misunderstandings and frustrations are likely to occur as a result. It is important for a helping professional to learn about and to become sensitive to these traits.

NATIVE AMERICANS AND THE EDUCATIONAL SYSTEM

In 1812 a Cherokee named Sequoyah invented a phonetic syllabary, a notation system for the Cherokee language. This accomplishment was an extraordinary achievement and unprecedented in world history. Within three years all Cherokees could read and write their own language, and by 1828 the tribe had its own newspaper, a written constitution, and a code of laws (Parrillo, 1985). Parrillo emphasized the fact that the first public education for Native Americans was developed by themselves and not introduced by others.

In the early 1900s, most schooling for Native Americans took place within tribal communities. Later, the majority were in public boarding schools run by religious missions and the U.S. Bureau of Indian Affairs (BIA). The approach to education was in strict conformity to Anglo culture. Students were punished for speaking native languages, wearing native dress, or identifying with anything resembling the Native American culture. Public and private boarding schools were used by the federal government as a channel for forced assimilation and acculturation.

By 1970, according to the U.S. Census, approximately 141,000 Native American children were attending public schools; of those, 52,000 were in BIA schools and 11,000, in mission schools. During the 1970s both federal and state governments worked to improve high school graduation and college attendance rates of minority groups. These educational efforts dramatically increased high school graduation rates for all minority groups except for Native Americans (U.S. Census Bureau, 1995).

In 1980, 57 percent of Native American men and 54 percent of Native American women were high school graduates. School enrollments varied greatly among reservations, with the highest enrollments (95 percent) among the Pima and Papago reservations in Arizona (Feagin, 1989). From 1981 to 1992, progress in attaining undergraduate degrees or graduate/professional degrees for Native Americans has been less than 1 percent (U.S. Census Bureau, 1995).

According to the National Center for Educational Statistics (1989), Native American and Native Alaskan students have a dropout rate of 35.5 percent, approximately twice the national average and the highest dropout rate of any U.S. ethnic or racial group (Reyhner, 1994).

As Native American youth attend school with other Americans, difficulties often arise for many reasons. Some of the youth speak a native language as a first language; they practice a native religion with a loving respect for nature and have a sense of tribal spirituality (Hungry Wolf & Hungry Wolf, 1987). Strong cultural traditions often inhibit the Native American youngster from being direct, verbal, or assertive. These different cultural characteristics may result in a Native American child being misperceived and misunderstood at school and elsewhere.

Native American youths usually spend six or seven hours daily in an institutional setting of overtly different values and perplexingly subtle and ambiguous cultural expectations. Here they are expected to perform according to conventional majority culture and associated educational standards. One dilemma for Native American youth is how to balance the majority's cultural expectations of individual achievement and success with the Native American beliefs of cooperative interdependence, sharing, and working together. Often this becomes discouraging and results in a very uncomfortable existence for Native American young people.

Native American children's discomfort is recognized by those critical of Columbus Day celebrations in our schools and communities. From a Native American point of view, the following questions may arise concerning the arrival of Columbus to the Americas in 1492: If you stand in an Native American's shoes or moccasins, would you be happy to celebrate the European adventurer who started the invasion that killed your people, stole your land, and herded you off to reservations? Would you celebrate an event that led to the deaths of many of your people and still today leaves Native American survivors among the poorest economically in this land, with poor health and poor housing, and still portrayed as being obstacles to Western civilization and the westward expansion?

Every year Native American children are confronted with the Columbus Day celebration. The emotional support needed from others to circumvent the possible feelings of self-blame and anger may not be available in a typical school system, community, or family. Also, with an increased movement to urban areas, Native American families have become isolated from their extended families and communities, with the supportive network of the extended family thus disrupted. As a result, the psychological well-being of many youth often suffers. Many Native American parents remember having experienced similar school stresses. With the continuing pressures of discrimination and impoverishment throughout adulthood, many Native American parents have developed an attitude of overwhelming hopelessness (LaFromboise & Graff Low, 1989).

A study done in Oklahoma reported that successful Native American students attending college were those who were more likely to conform to the standards and style of the majority educational institutions. In other words, they had become totally acculturated or had learned to balance both cultural systems. However, another Oklahoma study found that suicide rates among young Native American men were increasing and were highest among those who were the most assimilated within the White culture (Feagin, 1989). In certain environments, Native American youths who succeed in school are berated by their native peers for acting like Whites and looking down on their own people. Research studies show that Native American students who come from the most traditional homes, speak their native language, and participate in traditional religious and social activities do not feel that the majority school curriculum is inappropriate for their studies (Ho, 1992). Perhaps a strong sense of cultural identity can be an advantage in school for some youths.

According to the 2000 census, 24.4 percent of the Native American population who were 25 years of age and older had a high school diploma, and 14 percent had at least a bachelor's degree. Instead of pursuing an associate's or bachelor's degree in the majority society, one can attend one of the 34 tribal Native American colleges in the United States. These colleges are often located on reservations, and most of the teachers are Native Americans. These institutions are trying to preserve Native American cultures, such as their languages, their traditional cultural practices, and their values.

Problems faced by Native American youth may be those of cultural discontinuity, as well as those associated with other ecological issues, such as large schools in urban areas, passive teaching methods, economic necessity of finding jobs, long-distance commutes to school from reservations, alcoholism, teen pregnancy, insensitive teachers, and boredom with the school curriculum.

NATIVE AMERICAN FAMILIES AND THE HEALTH CARE SYSTEM

The roots of Native American health care practitioners are as ancient as the ceremonies attached to their medical care and belief systems. Practitioners have been called by many names, such as shaman, healer, or the more Westernized medicine man. Armed with an extensive pharmacopoeia and faith, they have striven to maintain and promote the physical and mental well-being of individuals. These early successful Native American medicine men used over 200 drugs and medicines that were mostly derivatives of botanical sources and later included in official pharmaceutical manuals. However, other botanical supplements that Native Americans use have not yet been tested for safety concerns by scientific research regarding long-term use.

With the arrival of the Europeans, however, ancient Native American medical heritage and tradition were severely challenged (Vogel, 1972; Washburn, 1970). Contact with Europeans brought disaster to the Native American population. Direct and indirect introduction of viruses and bacteria caused diseases such as smallpox, measles, bubonic plague, cholera, typhoid, pleurisy, scarlet fever, diphtheria, mumps, whooping cough, colds, venereal disease, and probably typhus, which decimated the population (Dobyns, 1983). Catastrophes of epidemic and pandemic outbreaks ravaged the Native American communities that had not been exposed to these pathogens and had no immunity to ward them off.

To protect American soldiers in frontier military outposts from contracting these infectious diseases, the War Department became involved in the administration of medical services to Native Americans. Later, the responsibility for Native American health was transferred to the newly created Bureau of Indian Affairs under the Department of Interior. Then, in 1954, health care was transferred to the Department of Health, Education, and Welfare, under the direction of the surgeon general (Mail, 1978). Presently, the Department of Health and Human Services is responsible for monitoring Native American health concerns. With this emphasis on providing improved health care to Native Americans, there is still an alarming high of 30 percent lacking health insurance coverage (U.S. Census Bureau, 2006).

The Indian Health Services have maintained records of Native American medical problems occurring since 1955. The top-10 causes of death for Native Americans have been accidents, disease of the heart, malignant neoplasm, cirrhosis of the liver, cerebrovascular disease, influenza and pneumonia, diseases of infancy, diabetes mellitus, homicide, and suicide (U.S. Public Health Service, 1974). In recent years, however, chronic disease and mental health problems, including alcoholism, have become the major health problems among Native American people. During their lifetimes, Native Americans generally have higher death rates than White Americans. They are twice as likely to be victims of accidents or drowning, more likely to be victims of homicide, twice as likely to commit suicide, and almost three times as likely to die from heart disease (U.S. Department of Health and Human Services, 1993).

To alleviate the shortage of medical personnel in Native American areas, Native American paraprofessionals have been trained to provide a range of primary health care functions. These workers serve to alleviate the language gaps and help reach out to culturally distinct people, especially those living in remote areas of Native American reservations. Most urban Native American programs, many of which have their origins in volunteer services, are predominantly staffed by Native Americans. The urban programs attract the skilled Native American professionals away from the rural reservations, adding to the shortage of professionals on the reservations.

Increasingly, Native Americans are becoming trained and taking responsibility for the health care of their people. Modern medical knowledge and expectations are becoming more widespread, even as recognition of the value of some traditional Native American medical practices increases. Modern Native American students who are participating in the health care services are seeing value in both traditional and modern medicine and are providing better health care services to Native American people.

In areas of mental health, the individual's environment and social context must be incorporated. Each Native American tribal culture has its own definition of appropriate behaviors that must be taken into account. For example, Dell (1980) reported, "The Hopi feel that a child's repetitive negative or 'bad' behaviors have a cumulative effect and the accumulation of these behaviors leads to eventual change." A Hopi parent might therefore accept—even welcome—the repetition of negative behaviors as a sign of imminent change. A non-Hopi therapist might conclude that the parents appear to be reinforcing poor behavior with their continual optimism and refusal to intervene. A non-Hopi therapist's intervention aimed at eliminating these reinforcing behaviors would strike at the very core of Hopi philosophy (LaFromboise & Graff Low, 1989).

Some traditional interventions have been used effectively, such as the purification and prevention "sweat lodge" ceremonies. Participation consists of fasting, praying, and offerings throughout serial purification sessions, referred to as "rounds." Ceremonies last for hours while participants make offerings for health and balance in life (Manson, Walker, & Kivlahan, 1987). Tribal practices, such as "four circles" or the "talking circle," are reported to work well with Native American youngsters needing professional assistance. These are their versions of rap or discussion groups. Tribal healers are valued as the keepers of the tribe. Healers working with Native American therapy centers have helped in deciphering traditional values that come into conflict with the values of the dominant culture (Trimble, 1981).

Despite modernization and policies of assimilation, Native American cultural beliefs and practices continue. Today, native medicine has incorporated some traditional Native American beliefs and healing practices into conventional medical treatment. Systems serving the needs of Native Americans must become aware of the details of these various beliefs and practices. This is especially true for the elderly Native American, who rarely seeks help from mental health systems. Complaints often are of physical problems that are not easily identified as psychiatric, although the root cause may be threatening one's wellness and internal harmony (Neligh & Scully, 1990).

NATIVE AMERICAN FAMILIES AND THE GOVERNMENTAL SYSTEM

The Iroquois Nation, made up of the Cayuga, Mohawk, Oneida, Onondaga, and Seneca peoples, united in a League of Nations in 1570. A sixth tribe, the Tuscarora, was added in 1722. This league had a pronounced influence on the provisions of the Articles of Confederation, the forerunner to the U.S. Constitution, when Benjamin Franklin drafted the Federation of States. The league's democratic processes served as the model for the colonists to emulate and include in the constitutional practices of representational government (Farb, 1968, p. 128).

In 1830 the Indian Removal Bill passed Congress and became law. All Native Americans living east of the Mississippi were to be expelled from their homeland. The U.S. government embarked on a policy of containment as a means of controlling the Native Americans and encouraging settlers to move in.

One of the ugliest periods in American history began in October 1838 when army troops hunted, herded, and marched the Cherokee Native Americans westward to Oklahoman territory from South Carolina along what has since been named the Trail of Tears. Ten to 20 Native Americans died each day from exposure, hunger, illness, and other miseries. Over a third of the Cherokees died on the way to the Indian Territory, which is now Oklahoma.

Most of the approximately 300 existing Native American reservations were established between 1850 and 1880. These were areas set aside in various states to segregate the Native Americans. The results were devastating, with military force being used to constrain these proud and independent people. One method used to accomplish assimilation was to force the Native American to depend on the government for food, rations, and supplies.

In 1933, under President Franklin D. Roosevelt, the assimilation policy was shifted to one of pluralism. *Pluralism* meant that the Native Americans could maintain autonomy as an ethnic group and participate in the development of their culture.

To maintain strong self-governance and growing economic development, Native Americans have realized that they must forge a closer and stronger relationship with Congress. By employing strategic planning and effective lobbying, they have begun to actualize their pan-Indianism. By promoting an active pan-Indian organization, they are able to protest for their rights politically and legally. More than 170,000 Native Americans are veterans today for having served in the U.S. armed forces. This is a testament to their loyalty and dedication to the ideals of the United States, although many are from a sovereign Native American nation.

NATIVE AMERICAN FAMILIES AND THE ECONOMIC SYSTEM

Traditionally, in the Native American family, property of economic value was owned by the extended family and the tribe. Property and resources were shared in common. "The country was made without lines of demarcation, and it is no man's business to divide it," claimed Chief Joseph of the Nez Percé. No member went without necessities if the rest of the tribe had resources. However, sometimes individuals owned personal items like songs, crests, and ornaments. This was a value favoring a cooperative economy among tribal groups, rather than being involved in the competitive economics of today.

The world owes an economic and culinary debt to early Native Americans. Over half of the world's present food crops originally came from Native American agriculture (e.g., potatoes, corn, squash, beans, and pumpkins). In many tribes women contributed to the economy through activities such as growing and processing various agricultural products. In certain areas, fishing, hunting, and gathering food from wild plants were practiced by the tribes.

Jobs are linked to available resources, and adequate resources for productive employment were often lacking on Indian reservations. The problems of poverty and overpopulation on reservations were not examined seriously until 1952. At that time, the BIA offered some 40,000 individuals financial aid to relocate to urban areas. Most of the Native Americans who chose to relocate only found unskilled and semiskilled jobs, and the program was not particularly successful. More than a quarter of the people left the cities to return to the reservations, where there was still a severe lack of jobs. This program was abandoned after 1960.

Today 4 out of 10 Native Americans live in the West. Thirty-one percent live in the South, 17 percent live in the Midwest, and 9 percent live in the Northeast. The 10 states with the largest populations are California, Oklahoma, Arizona, Texas, New Mexico, New York, Washington, North Carolina, Michigan, and Alaska (U.S. Census Bureau, 2000).

Approximately 10 years ago, the economic picture looked like this. Native Americans were underrepresented in white-collar jobs and overrepresented in service occupations. These occupational distributions tended to be related to their patterns of residence. For example, if they lived on reservations, they were more likely to be employed in blue-collar jobs, and if they lived off reservations, they were more likely to be employed in white-collar occupations (Snipp, 1986). According to the 2000 census, 26 percent of Native Americans and Alaskan Natives work in management, professional, and related occupations. There are approximately 3,600 Native-owned firms with receipts of $1 million or more and a total of 201,187 businesses with total receipts of over $30 billion.

The three-year average poverty rate for Native Americans and Native Alaskans (24.3 percent) was not statistically different from the rate for Blacks and Hispanics. The poverty rate averages between 2002–2003 and 2003–2004 did not change for Native Americans, whereas the 1990 statistics showed that Native Americans had the lowest median income (65 percent of Whites) and the highest unemployment rate (Aguirre & Turner, 1998; Snipp, 1986). The economic picture for Native American families was much brighter in 2000, with a median income of $33,627 based on a three-year average from 2003 to 2005.

However, there are indications that the Native American Nation is experiencing a bifurcation of its economic growth, with some tribal groups increasing in monetary might while others are plummeting into despair. Unemployment on some reservations can range from 45 to 80 percent. This remains a serious problem for Native American families. Why is this the case when some reservations are so rich in natural resources? For example, the 53 million acres of 22 western tribes contain the nation's richest reserves of natural gas, oil, coal, and uranium (Parrillo, 1985). The difficulty arises from conflicting values between the corporate world and religious ideals. Native Americans generally hold a spiritual reverence for the land, creating a reluctance to exploit resources: these riches are part of Mother Earth. There is a history and a living legacy whereby corporations and governmental institutions have gained access to the natural resources of Native American land, sometimes victimizing and subordinating Native Americans and their cultural heritage.

Economic Development on Reservations

Much political controversy surrounds economic development on tribal reservations today. The following are examples of these economic developments.

Tribe	Industries
Eastern Band of Cherokees	Largest mirror company in the United States
White Mountain Apaches	One of the largest ski resorts
Navajos	Leased rights for mining uranium
Passamaquoddies of Maine	Cement company and blueberry farm
Ojibwa, Seminole, and others	Large-scale bingo, casinos, hotels, and resorts
Lummis	Fish-farming industry

Economic progress and development have exacted a price in eroding the cultural heritage of tribal nations. For many Native Americans, the more prosperous they become, the more difficult it is to preserve their Native American heritage. Some welcome many aspects of the cultural change; others struggle to retain many traditions of the Native American culture and still be a part of the larger U.S. society. Respect for individual preferences is essential as difficult choices are made.

With increased interest in expanding their ethnic identity in business, Native Americans have expanded their industries. In a report of the *U.S. Census Bureau News* (June 20, 2006), revenues for American Native American and Native Alaskan–owned businesses near $27 billion. In 2002 there were 201,387 American Native American and Alaska Native–owned businesses. In 1991 there were a total of 2,268 special trade contractors with earnings of $97 million, food stores with receipts of $54 million, automotive dealerships and service stations with receipts of $65 million, as well as ownership of other firms and businesses (Fost, 1991). In the 2006 report, industries with the most American Native American and Alaska Native–owned businesses include over 32,253 construction, 26,651 other services, 24,482 health care and social assistance, and 22,505 professional, scientific and technical services. The Survey of Business Owners defines American Native American and Alaska Native–owned businesses as firms in which they own 51 percent or more of the stock or equity of the business. States with the highest number of American Native American and Native Alaskan–owned firms include California, Oklahoma, Texas, New York, and Florida.

HELPFUL TECHNIQUES FOR SERVING NATIVE AMERICAN FAMILIES

Native Americans have been displaced from their land, cheated at almost every turn by such nations as Canada, England, France, and Spain, and by U.S. governmental bureaucracy and policies, by large-scale economic ventures, by small-scale business, and by ordinary people. All these forces have created an atmosphere of distrust and hesitation for any Native American entering a Eurocentric society. To establish a relationship of trust, it is necessary to become familiar with critical events and the impact of these events on Native Americans. These time periods, as referred to by Walker and LaDue (1986), include the Precontact period, prior to 1492, when many of the Native American rules, roles, values, and beliefs were developed. In the Manifest Destiny period, 1492 to 1890, there were epidemics and the development of racism and discrimination. It was during this period that the U.S. government created the reservations and boarding schools. During the Assimilation period, 1890 to 1970, racism and discrimination forced many Native Americans to accept the ways of the majority, a Eurocentric adaptation, or else end in misery and depression.

The last is the Self-Determination period, 1970 to the present, when Native Americans were given the right to self-govern and gain leadership roles in federal Indian programs. Four positive congressional acts were passed during this time period: the Indian Self-Determination Act (1975), the Indian Health Care Improvement Act (1976), the Indian Child Welfare Act (1978), and the Indian Religious Freedom Act (1978). Because Native American reservations are sovereign nations within the United States, the Native Americans govern themselves through tribal council leadership and by enacting tribal laws. They have their own police force and their own system of justice. The reservation is the spiritual and cultural home for all members, including those living far from the reservations.

We cannot overcome a history of discrimination, however, though there are ways to help build trusting relationships with Native Americans. It is important for helping professionals to act with humility and quiet respect. This is especially important when offering genuine help forged out of cultural understanding and knowledge, and not out of ignorance. Being honest with clear and forthright answers is a start. Remember that Native Americans value silence, and therefore "talking too much" should be avoided. Avoid asking too many personal questions or staring at people or their personal belongings. Expect to be treated like a new acquaintance and ask for their opinions. Develop the capacity to laugh at yourself and, if you are teased, it is a good sign of being included. Being flexible in thought and deed means capturing information and seeking out resources to help yourself, such as attending workshops and participating in ethnic events (i.e., a powwow, which today is a celebration that involves food, singing, dancing, and arts and crafts, rather than the traditional powwow, which was a gathering of medicine men and spiritual leaders in a curing ceremony). When you are invited to participate with Native Americans, remember that by participating actively in their culture, you will be able to recognize the differences between yourself and others and learn to respect the differences. At the same time, do not let these differences impact the quality of your service and respect.

⤗ CONCLUSIONS

Native American traditions provide some holistic, humanistic, and existential principles that can benefit our contemporary technological society. The democratic federal principles on which the United States was founded draw on the League of the Iroquois Confederacy. Strong relationships among tribal members have led to a resiliency that has helped them withstand assaults over the decades. As a result of strong feelings of identification with family, group, or tribe, their informal supportive family kinship networks provide for affection and support. This is exemplified by Alexarae Funmaker, who won the prize for the best essay in the 2005 Miss Indian World Pageant. In her essay she stated,

> Native people have always held close bonds with one another. Perhaps because no matter the tribe one belongs to there are many of the same threads, trials, and tribulations running though our hearts and those of our ancestors. The bond that holds our people together is that of family. To the Anishnabe, family means people who care for each other, share with each other, and accept each other. The importance of family relationships cannot be determined from what place they sit on the family tree. . . . It is not unusual for Anishnabe families to have more than one set of parents or grandparents, several brothers and sisters and [an] unlimited number of aunties, uncles, cousins, and most of the time none of them are related by blood other than the fact they are Native people belonging to one, two, or many of the over 500 tribes of North America. (Funmaker, 2005)

To care for each other, to share with each other, and to accept each other leads to many exchanges and contributions of practices and knowledge between Native Americans and the early settlers. If it were not for their knowledge and skills in agricultural practices, outdoor survival skills, and geography of the land, the early colonists may not have survived their first year in this New World. Their impact has been so immense that even today, many popular foods we consume are contributions of Native American agricultural know-how (Vogel, 1972). Native American contributions include native names of many states, cities, counties, lakes, rivers, and mountains; youth groups, such as the Boy Scouts, Girl Scouts, Campfire Girls, and YMCA Guides, which include in their programs many Native American practices and lore, arts and crafts, and outdoor living skills; a majority of roads and highways across the United States, which followed ancient Native American trails and maps, except for major expressways that were forged with modern machinery to create more direct routing of traffic; and finally, what many believe are English names for North American flora and fauna are really Native American derivatives.

Sadly, so little is taught in schools about the many contributions of Native Americans who promote, honor, and respect the traditional, spiritual, and physical relationship with the land, waters, and resources of this continent. Ecologists today are beginning to understand the importance of the Native American traditions of respecting nature and the circle of life. All power comes from the earth, the sky, and the water. Understanding and working with diverse peoples is crucial if we are to move toward fruitful strategies for leading the good life with all peoples on the planet Earth.

> They had an ancient, lost reverence for earth and its web of life. They had what the world has lost. The world must have it back. . . . lest it die. (Collier, 1947, p. 15)

✦ STUDY QUESTIONS

1. How many federally recognized Native American groups are there? How many languages?
2. America is over 200 years old. In what year were Native Americans officially made U.S. citizens?
3. President Nixon in 1970 changed the Native Americans' status by what principle?
4. Do Native Americans prefer to be considered as (1) individuals, (2) tribes, or (3) community?
5. Name and describe the typical Native American family structure. Use the special words that describe the type of structure.
6. Native Americans observe a number of family practices. Name five of them.
7. Tell what Native American elders do to maintain their contact with their family.
8. Describe the Native American philosophy of child rearing.
9. List at least 10 values of Native Americans and the contrasting values of the majority society.
10. List the different ways that Native American youngsters have been educated over the years. What are some typical educational problems of Native American children and youth?
11. Outline some of the health care issues that the Native Americans have been confronted with over time.
12. State at least five major federal government decisions that have affected Native Americans for years.
13. List the numerous ways that Native Americans have contributed to both the culinary and economic wealth of the world.

✦ APPLICATIONS

1. Make a list of things your early teachers taught you about Native Americans. Discuss these teachings, bringing up points you have learned in this chapter or elsewhere. Write a one- or two-page report.
2. Perform a word association task by listing the first 20 words that come to mind when someone mentions Native Americans. Write an essay on the facts and

fallacies included on your list. Then write a paragraph on how such stereotypes must feel to Native American youth your age.

3. Discuss with three people their childhood recollections about celebrating Columbus Day. What do they recall? What is the problem, if any, with Columbus Day celebrations? Write a one-page report.

4. Native Americans request that certain artifacts from museums be restored to the Native American territory they came from. Discuss your personal attitude toward this requirement in a one-page essay.

5. Write a thoughtful essay of one or two pages on what must be learned before serving Native Americans as a professional in your chosen career.

6. Attend a Native American powwow. You will witness men's and women's dance contests such as the women's jingle dance where participants wear dresses decorated with seven layers of metallic chimes that jingle; drumming, communal dancing, a variety of contests, storytelling, and, most importantly, you will enjoy the uniqueness of such Native American social gatherings.

✦ MEDIA RESOURCES

More Than Bows and Arrows. (1992). Color, 60 minutes (Available from Insight Media, 2162 Broadway, New York, NY 10024)

Native American Cultures. (1992). 60 minutes (Available from Insight Media, 2162 Broadway, New York, NY 10024)

Navajo Moon. Color, 28 minutes (Available from Films for the Humanities & Sciences, P.O. Box 2053, Princeton, NJ 08543-2053)

✦ KEY INTERNET RESOURCES

National Native American Families Together
www.nativefamilynetwork.com/

✦ FURTHER READING

Allen, P. G. (1987). *The sacred hoop: Recovering the feminine in American Indian traditions.* Boston: Beacon Press.

Caduto, M. J., & Bruchec, J. (1988). *Keepers of the earth: Native American stories and environmental activities for children.* Golden, CO: Fulcrum.

Deloria, V., Jr. (1988). *Custer died for your sins: An Indian manifesto.* Norman: University of Oklahoma Press.

De Genova, M. (1997). *Families in cultural context.* Mountain View, CA: Mayfield.

Farb, P. (1968). *Man's rise to civilization.* New York: E. P. Dutton.

Klein, B. T. (Ed.). (1992). *Reference encyclopedia of the American Indian* (6th ed.). West Nyack, NY: Todd.

Porter, F. W., III. (Ed.). (1983). *Nonrecognized American Indian tribes: An historical and legal perspective.* Paper of the McNickle Center for the Study of the American Indian, No. 7. Chicago: Newberry Library.

Red Horse, J. G. (1980). American Indian elders: Unifiers of Indian families. *Social Casework, 61*(8), 490–493.

Slapin, B., & Seale, D. (Eds.). (1991). *Through Indian eyes: The native experience in books for children.* Berkeley, CA: Oyate.

Vogel, V. (1970). *American Indian medicine.* Norman: University of Oklahoma Press.

9

Amish Families

→ Key Concepts

- The Plain People
- Ordnung
- Meidung

Dennis McDonald/PhotoEdit Inc.

Little children you should seek
Rather to be good than wise:
For the thoughts you do not speak
Shine out in your cheeks and eyes.
                    —Hostetler & Huntington (1971)

Religious minority groups cannot be divorced from concerns regarding the functions of their values and behaviors that differentiate them from the larger society and set them apart as a unique subgroup. It is for this reason that considerations of religious and ethnic groups are included in this study of ethnic minority families. Religion can be a major variable related to an ethnic minority's status. If you, as a professional researcher someday, have the opportunity to work with religious minority families, it will be very important to have a solid knowledge base about their religious and cultural values to be truly effective in your research. An excellent, and dramatic, example of such a minority group is the Amish because they maintain a distinctly separate way of life from all other societies.

WHO ARE THE AMISH?

The Amish are generally considered to be a very conservative Christian faith group, with an Anabaptist tradition (baptism occurs only as an adult, not as an infant). Since early colonial days, the Amish have lived in the United States and Canada, preserving their distinctive culture, dress, language, and religion in peace and prosperity. They wear plain clothing fastened with hooks and eyes, not buttons. Their men and boys wear broad-brimmed black hats and plain-cut trousers, and the women and girls wear bonnets and ankle-length dresses. They generally oppose automobiles, electricity, telephones, and higher education beyond eighth grade, believing that these will contribute to speeding up social change and separating their community in various ways.

Equal access to power is foreign to the Amish people's definition of self and community. They want only to have the right to practice their beliefs without persecution, and they have chosen and maintained a way of life that disregards notions of political power, as usually understood by the dominant American society. They are an example of an ecological subgroup that has maintained a semiclosed boundary between themselves and the majority culture, having very limited transactions with the larger society. The Amish will accept certain types of modernization but only those usually associated with meeting the needs of the living, such as modern medical services. Even this practice may vary from family to family. The compromises they make must maintain the Amish standards and not disrupt their social structure.

Unfortunately, what may appear to be a relatively protected ecological haven for the Amish was tragically breached in October 2006 when 10 girls were shot in an Amish school at Nickel Mines, Lancaster County, Pennsylvania, by a lone gunman. Charles Carl Roberts IV, 32, a milk delivery person from Bart Township, entered an Old Order Amish one-room school carrying a 9-mm handgun, a 12 gauge shotgun, a rifle, a bag of black powder, two knives, tools, a stun gun, 600 rounds of ammunition, a personal lubricant, wire, and plastic ties. Perhaps anticipating a long siege, he also brought a change of clothing. He ushered 15 boys, one pregnant woman, and three other women with infants from the school. He bound 11 students who remained, all girls, age 6 to 15, with plastic flex ties, and prepared to shoot them. Student Marian Fisher, 13, stepped forward and asked that he "shoot me first" in an apparent effort to buy time for the remaining students. Her younger sister, Barbie, allegedly asked Roberts to "shoot me second." Of the 10 girls who were shot, 3 died immediately, 2 others died in a hospital the next morning, and the sixth died later that week. Roberts committed suicide when the police stormed the school. Police believe that he did not have a grudge against the Amish community itself. Rather, he selected the school because of its lack of security and easy availability to young female students.

Astonishingly, out of this deep tragedy emerged a shining example of the true nature of the Amish faith: a resolute and absolute exhibition of Christian compassion and forgiveness. The Amish community reached out to the family of Carl Roberts in forgiveness and Christian love by embracing the family members, taking food to them, and inviting them to attend the funerals of the girls. Journalist Tom Shachtman, author of *Rumspringa: To Be or Not to Be Amish* (2006), said, "This is imitation of Christ at its most naked. If anybody is going to turn the other cheek in society, it's going to be the Amish. . . . I don't want to denigrate anybody else who says they're imitating Christ, but the Amish walk the walk as much as they talk the talk."

Historical Background

The Amish have been called "The Plain People" or "Old Order" Amish and originated in Switzerland about 1525, taking their name from an early Anabaptist, Jacob Amman.

Today no Amish are left in Europe. They migrated to the United States starting in the early eighteenth century, where they initially settled in Pennsylvania on land given to them by William Penn, who granted them a haven from religious persecution.

The land given to the Amish was an attractive inducement for their families and way of life. They could farm and live next to each other as neighbors and form their tight-knit religious community. The Amish and their descendants who remained in Europe in the eighteenth century either reunited with the main body of European Mennonites or gave up their Amish identity. Many suffered extreme religious persecution. Subsequently, all Amish settlements in Europe died out (Hostetler, 1968).

As pacifists, the Amish resisted military service, sharing doctrines of nonresistance, or pacifism, adult baptism, and separation from the world. Their chosen lifestyle of nonviolence and peace pervades every aspect of their lives, even when personally confronted by force and violence in a crisis situation (e.g., the tragedy described earlier). However, the degree of separateness of the Amish from the world is defined differently by each of the Plain People's religious groups. The strictest group is the Old Order Amish.

During the last half of the nineteenth century, the American Amish group again divided because of differences in religious views. The name Old Order Amish distinguished those retaining the old traditions from other Amish who became assimilated, by varying degrees, into the American mainstream. The more assimilated individuals often joined the Mennonite Church (Scott, 1988). Amish settlements differ on issues of conformity and on the norms of religious practice. The many variations of the Old Order Amish are based on the rules of the church, called the *Ordnung*. The Old Order Amish, currently found in more than 20 states, are at the conservative end of the continuum; the "Beachy" Amish, who own and drive automobiles and use electricity, tractors, and other labor-saving technologies, are at the progressive end. Many of the differences among Amish groups, however, are unnoticeable to outsiders.

Groups of like-minded Amish tend to live in a community or church district. Amish church districts that are in fellowship with one another are rather homogeneous in character. Each district fellowship interprets the Ordnung similarly. The Ordnung is the blueprint for their private, public, and ceremonial life. It serves to order their way of life by way of tradition rather than strict rules. It is an understood behavior that an Amish youth learns and is expected to live by. There are at least seven different Old Order Amish affiliations that are not in fellowship with one another. Therefore, one church district may belong to the conservative group while across the state another community of Amish may belong to the more progressive branch (Huntington, 1988).

Redfield's (1947) definition of a folk society includes the Amish, who formed small, isolated, traditional, simple, and homogeneous settlements. In these settlements, personal and emotional relationships and tradition and customs are highly valued, where practical experience and knowledge are more important than formal education, science, or abstractions. Every attempt is made to balance change, which is uncomfortable, and tradition, which promotes stability. The Amish have an attitude of "we-ness," or the gemeinschaft-like community overshadowing the concept of "I-ness."

Amish traditions and customs are patterned with symbolic meanings and ingrained in everyday behaviors. For example, at the dinner table, the Amish father sits at one end of the table with his sons on one side and daughters on the other side next to their mother. Another example is the avoidance of saying "thank you" after someone helps another with a task because the helping behavior is expected. Religion is diffused throughout everyday living, from playing and singing to harvesting and planting. All of life is an act of living out their Christian faith. Influences from outside the Amish community, like voting or television, are deplored and resisted.

Although surrounded by a rapidly changing American society, the Amish community has largely maintained its customs and has remained relatively unchanged. The practice of *meidung*, or shunning, pressures individuals and families to follow the Ordnung by banning an individual from ceremonial and social participation within the community; any interaction or transaction between the individual and others, including family members, for example through eating, sleeping, buying, or selling, is prohibited. Shunning is used to control the behavior of the erring members who seem to be moving toward the attractions of the outer society. According to Huntington (1988), shunning is used to help the erring members realize the gravity of their sins and return to the rules of the church and is not enforced as a means of harming or ruining an individual. In most cases, the shunned church member is welcomed back into the fellowship again. The practice has helped insulate the Amish culture from infusions and assaults by the larger society.

Demographic Information

The Amish group is a growing church with an increasing membership. In 1905 the Amish population numbered approximately 8,200; in 1980 there were approximately 92,000, and today, approximately 180,000 members (Milicia, 2005). They do not proselytize, but high birthrates (about seven children per family), as well as a determination to keep their grown children and families within the Amish community, help perpetuate this unique culture, which has been doubling about every 20 years. According to recent studies, the Amish have been able to retain their young people within the community at a rate of approximately 85 to 95 percent. As more Amish are working off the farm and are coming in contact with "outsiders" (those who live outside the community; really, the rest of the world), there is a fear that more rapid cultural change will occur. Those who do leave join either the Mennonite or Beachy Amish groups. The stability of the Amish community offers those remaining a more simple and self-sufficient lifestyle.

THE ECOLOGY OF OLD ORDER AMISH FAMILIES

Old Order Amish communities are mostly rural and known for their smallness, distinctiveness, homogeneity, and self-sufficiency. These small communities are scattered predominantly throughout the rural Midwest. Nearly 70 percent of the Amish population resides in Pennsylvania, Ohio, and Indiana; some of the other 22 states with Amish communities include Missouri, Wisconsin, Iowa, Illinois, Michigan, New York, Delaware, Tennessee,

Minnesota, Kentucky, Maryland, Mississippi, Kansas, Oklahoma, Virginia, and Florida (Huntington, 1988; Milicia, 2005). Amish communities are also found in Canada, Mexico, and Central and South America, with many settling in these countries to continue the farming occupations of their ancestors.

Agricultural Enterprises

Members of each Amish settlement usually include small businessmen, such as blacksmiths, harness makers, carpenters, buggy makers, and plumbers, who help form a self-sufficient community. These businessmen support the farmers, who are the backbone of the community and who may farm without the use of modern machinery. The family farm is the Amish man's kingdom. Some reports say they produce at least as much per acre as their non-Amish neighbors who use mechanized equipment (Ruth, 1985).

Prior to 1970, the Amish had been protected from the encroachment of technology and more modern ways of farming. Since then, however, more rapid changes have been taking place because of a growing population and the increasing cost of farming. A large investment is required for starting up a 100-acre farm, which costs approximately $1 million in areas like Lancaster County, Pennsylvania, where families have farmed for generations.

The Old Order Amish who prohibit the use of automobiles, telephones, and electricity also have strict dress codes and forbid rubber-tired tractors, central heating, and cameras (Huntington, 1988). Their lifestyle is a deliberate way of separating themselves from the world and maintaining self-sufficiency. Examples of this are the use of bottled gas to heat water, cook on a modern stove, and run a refrigerator, and using gas-pressured lanterns and lamps to light homes and barns. They believe that the use of electricity will accelerate the rate of outside influences through television and other forms of conveniences. However, as more Amish come in contact with the so-called outside world, many of the once-banned forms of technology are being slowly adopted, thus opening up their ecological boundaries. However, any changes must never compromise their faith and their belief in "the common good of the group/community."

Obedience to Amish Codes of Behavior

Amish clothing has changed little over the centuries. There are a number of subtle differences in dress among the groups, such as the width of the strings or ribbons on the women's caps, the use of pins rather than buttons, or the type of cloth used for clothing. To the Amish, clothing is a form of communication. There is disdain for the flashy and quick-changing fads of the outside society.

Differences in dress among Amish groups are usually not discernible to outsiders, and appear uniform and simple in style and color. For those within the community, however, differences are always noted, such as the width of the brim and the height and shape of the crown of a man's hat (which denotes the orthodoxy of the wearer, so that a wide brim, low crown, and narrow hatband denotes the oldest and most traditional style).

Horse carriages are the major source of transportation and offer another example of strict obedience among the various Amish groups. The carriages, or buggies, are painted different colors representing degrees of conservatism, with black for liberal, yellow for middle conservative, and white indicating the most conservative. Owners of white buggies reveal that they follow traditions of an earlier period when undyed cloth was considered most proper. Their practices, values, and beliefs include the strictest rules of behavior, which strongly emphasize the importance of the family and the cohesion of the Amish community. Because of the similarity of Amish carriages in a given area, members of a group can be identified by the buggies they drive. For example, in Lancaster, Pennsylvania, you may see a gray buggy driven by an Old Order Amish and a black buggy driven by an Old Order Mennonite.

Language

The Old Order Amish read the German Bible and exclusively speak in Amish High German when conducting worship services and formal ceremonies. A German dialect called Pennsylvania Dutch is the preferred language and used in the home and the community. The Amish can also speak, read, and write in English, which is taught in school out of necessity.

Pathway Publishers hires Old Order Amish writers and publishers for three publications written in Pennsylvania Dutch: the *Young Companion, Family Life*, and *Blackboard Bulletin*. There is also a weekly newspaper, the *Budget*, published in Ohio. Each Amish community has its own reporter, who informs the *Budget* of recent births, illnesses, deaths, and topics of interest to other Amish communities. These publications are produced with nonmodern means, such as hand-set printing presses (Wittmer, 1990). Those who have left the Old Order communities can be found reading newspapers and other sources of information coming from the communities.

Community Organization

An Amish settlement typically consists of a church district led by a bishop, two ministers, and a deacon, and it contains 25 to 35 nuclear families that join together with a network of communing church districts (Huntington, 1988). The size of the community is mainly determined by density. As worship services are held in homes or barns, when the community becomes too large, the district divides.

No single, visible boundary typically sets off the Amish community or district. However, the ideological boundary is formed by traditional believers who follow the Ordnung in each of the districts. Within these districts, people are "in fellowship" with each other, sharing a common identity and sense of community. A tradition such as reciting the unwritten Ordnung of their particular church district is an example of an oral tradition that helps keep the communities intact for generations.

Amish Family Structure

The family is the basic unit in Amish society, and rearing children is the most important family function. According to Amish beliefs, parents are accountable to God for their children's spiritual welfare. Fathers and mothers are always expected to be united in disciplining their children, and they are responsible and obligated to nurture their children by standing united in teaching, guiding, loving, and admonishing them. They constantly strive to be good role models for their children. Amish women have a long reproductive period, with no indications that contraceptives are used. Typically, families are large, with an average of seven children each.

The husband is the head of the household, but an Amish man's occupation is only important in providing the basic economic necessities of living; it is in no way given the same status or importance as jobs held by the larger community. The husband is expected to be considerate of his wife emotionally, physically, and spiritually. A wife's commitment is first to God and then to her husband. Despite the Amish being a patriarchal family, the wife's position in the Amish culture can best be explained by her position in the church, where she has an equal vote but not an equal voice (Huntington, 1988). A wife is expected to support her husband in all relationships with others, including the children, grandparents, and neighbors. Amish women do not work outside the home. In an economy where self-sufficiency is desired, however, women are responsible for home production. The Old Order Amish are monogamous, and divorce is prohibited.

Amish Life Stages

The home is the center of life where the Amish person passes through six stages from birth to death. In the home, each of these stages carries different responsibilities and obligations, such as hosting services for courtship, weddings, and funerals. Although these stage labels are typical of many cultural groups, they represent important and unique behavioral dimensions among the Amish.

Infancy.   This stage covers the period from birth until the child learns to walk. Infants are always welcomed by families and the community. The Amish believe that babies are without sin and can do no wrong. The first two years of life are filled with indulgence and love, whether the baby is a girl or a boy. No strict feeding schedule is followed. If the baby cries, caretakers believe the baby is in need of comfort or food, not discipline. Mothers, fathers, brothers, sisters, uncles, aunts, cousins, and members of the community all share in a similar style of permissive child rearing. Amish babies are rarely left alone. They are held during waking hours, bathed on their mother's lap, and sleep in the parents' bed. When Amish go on outings, babies are barely conspicuous because the Amish do not want outsiders to notice them, and they do not have outsiders caring for their children (Hostetler & Huntington, 1971).

Preschool Children.   This stage covers the period from walking until entrance into school. After the second year, discipline becomes important, and Amish children are taught to respect the authority of the parents. Parents are deeply concerned about their children and are responsible for teaching them the "right way." The right way translates into the Amish religious way, which includes learning to care for anyone younger and less able, and sharing and helping others. Parents insulate children by separating themselves and their children from the moral and physical dangers of the outside world.

During the preschool years, children learn that work is perceived as helping others and is a part of one's responsibility. Tasks are done without being thanked; a job well done is reward in and of itself. Both boys and girls accompany their father around the farm and help their mother with household chores. Young children are expected to be useful, but they are chastised for asking too many questions.

Schoolchildren.   This is the period when children attend public or Amish schools. They are often referred to as "scholars." Children attend Amish schools between the ages of 6 and 15. Although parents are primarily responsible for teaching attitudes and values to their children, teachers are from the Amish community and play an important supplemental role as socializing agents in their lives. Children are taught the importance of being concerned for other people, and they are rewarded for developing responsibility, appreciating work, and practicing the right attitudes of humility, forgiveness, admission of error, and sympathy.

Although most scholars help wherever they are needed, boys mostly work with their fathers and girls with their mothers. Scholars are taught to do things with their hands. For example, girls learn to cook, bake, sew, and make things for their playhouses. Boys build toys and birdhouses, as well as feed the livestock and poultry.

Young Adult.   This is the stage where those who have completed their eight years of schooling can now do a full day's work. They are often between 14 to 16 years of age and engaged in the social life of their peers. The young person is no longer in elementary school and is vulnerable to the influences of the outside world. Amish adolescents who attend a public high school often experience great anxiety because of conflicting cultural norms and values. Such anxieties may last for a lifetime. The Amish believe that schooling beyond the elementary years hampers successful integration into adult Amish roles and living in an Amish community; in states requiring education until age 16, the Amish school their youths at home.

The Amish also believe that the peer group is much more influential than the parents or church. Therefore, Amish parents strongly hope that the adolescent will have Amish peers for friends and not the "English," as they call those of the majority culture. They fear that if adolescents associate with the English, they will eventually leave the Amish community for the outside world. Yet, even if young persons break many of the rules and venture into the outside world, their belonging to Amish peer groups almost guarantees their return to the values of the Amish culture. Amish parents often ignore the minor transgressions of youth, such as owning a radio or attending a movie. The Amish adolescent is allowed a little more freedom at about age 16 to the mid-20s, to test the boundaries of the Amish cultural ecosystem. *Rumschpringes*, commonly called "time-out," is considered a prolonged joy ride, the last chance for having a good time in the "real world" before baptism as an adult.

However, the recent testing of the Amish community's boundaries by its young adults involved transgressions of society's legal system. What were once thought of as impenetrable boundaries for illegal acts are no longer firm. Amish young adults bought drugs from a motorcycle gang and distributed the drugs to Amish youth groups at weekend gatherings (Labi, 1998). Substance abuse is no longer a problem of the outside world, but now, as feared, is a part of the "inside." The old ways of allowing the young adult to test the boundaries of their community by parents ignoring minor transgressions no longer apply.

Most Amish teenagers grow safely into adulthood. For these young teenagers, being 16 years old means it's OK to go out courting. Informal Sunday evening singing get-togethers are common in the Amish community, with socializing and singing. Dates are arranged, however. Other social gatherings where young adults can meet include barn raisings, corn huskings, weddings, and other work-related activities. Secrecy pervades the entire courtship period. According to an interview of an elderly Amish man, today's Amish children are more completely socialized into an Amish world than their grandparents (Milicia, 2005).

Adulthood.   Baptism signifies religious adulthood; however, it is marriage and the birth of a baby that define social adulthood. Although marriage itself proclaims social adulthood, full adulthood is achieved with the birth of the first child (Huntington, 1988).

An Amish man or woman must marry another person of the Amish faith, someone either from the same district or from another affiliation that is in "fellowship." Should a young adult choose to marry someone from the majority culture, excommunication and shunning result. Most men marry between the ages of 22 and 24; women usually marry a few years younger.

The Amish wedding ceremony differs from settlement to settlement. For example, most Amish marriages in Lancaster, Pennsylvania, occur in November, December, January, and rarely in February. Farm work, religious beliefs, and traditions all help determine when a wedding will take place. The preferred day for weddings is Thursday, with Tuesday the second choice (Scott, 1988). In other Amish communities, weddings are held in almost any season except during the summer, when preservation of food at a wedding feast is a problem because of the lack of refrigeration.

The role of the bride's and groom's parents differs greatly from one Amish community to another. In Lancaster, for example, the parents of the bride have special privileges and are not responsible for planning any part of the wedding. In other communities, the parents of the bride are responsible for managing the food preparation for all guests. The customs and traditions of the wedding ceremony and those followed after the marriage usually differ from one Amish group to another (Scott, 1988). Weddings usually begin at 8:30 A.M. with no kisses, no rings, no photographs, no flowers, and no caterers.

First-cousin marriages are taboo, and, although second-cousin marriages are discouraged, they do occur. One must take into account that the Amish of early times recorded only surnames because they married only within their group for generations. Thus many of the people in communities today may remain closely related genetically.

The Amish adult is responsible for maintaining and transferring the Amish way of life to the next generation. Adults are guardians who protect and watch over the boundaries of their culture, preventing children from assimilation and acculturation into the outside world. To maintain their boundaries from intrusions, families try to remain economically self-sufficient. For instance, they do not participate in the Social Security system but rather help one another and accept no outside aid, welfare, or insurance. The Amish community takes care of its ill. They largely prefer not to take part in the political system by voting or serving on juries. However, if they feel threatened by systems that infringe on traditional Amish rights and beliefs, they will actively protest their case to the government. One instance was when the Amish fought to keep their traditional educational system for their youths.

The Elderly.   Amish socialization patterns provide for the individual throughout the natural stages of human life. The age for retirement in the dominant society holds no meaning within Amish communities. Retirement for men and women is voluntary and often influenced by the combination of their health and the need to relinquish farmland to their children, usually the youngest child, to earn a living. The Amish elderly generally retire after their youngest child has married and started a family, although they usually continue to help their married children on certain occasions or when they have specific needs.

The Amish elderly patriarch indicates his retirement by moving into the "grandfather house," which is usually an adjacent farm dwelling or one near the edge of the community. The elderly Amish live close to their children and grandchildren and do not enter homes for the aged. Grandfather continues to have his own horse and buggy, which still plays an important part in his life. The elderly still have many obligations, such as attending funerals and visiting the sick (Hostetler & Huntington, 1971). Freed from most of their normal farm and household tasks, they are able to do good deeds for relatives, neighbors, the community, and the world.

Prestige and respect accompany old age. The elderly serve as ties to the past and to the old ways of living. Knowledge of how things were done is transmitted by the older people, who readily give advice to the younger generation. Grandfather is an important source of information on farm management problems. Grandmother is an expert on children and helpful with child-rearing concerns. The elderly have a strong sense of belonging in a society that finds the elderly an important asset in maintaining traditional ways. According to Hostetler and Huntington (1971), the elderly Amish look back at their lives with satisfaction.

The elderly usually die with dignity at home, surrounded by friends and relatives. At the death of a family member, the family is relieved of all household tasks and farm chores. Members of the community take over all funeral arrangements, and the family members meditate and pray. Friends call to see their deceased friend and talk to the bereaved family sitting by the bier. Mourners stay up all night for a wake. Traditionally the dead are placed in simple wooden coffins devoid of fine fabric or ornate carvings. In some Amish communities both men and women wear white for burial, and there are no flowers or eulogies. Following the burial, mourners return to the house of the deceased to share a meal together. All roles and relationships return to normal with the sharing of a meal on the third day after the death. Age-old customs dictate the rituals to follow after a death (Hostetler & Huntington, 1971).

THE AMISH AND THE EDUCATIONAL SYSTEM

Historically, the relationship between the Amish and the public school system has been tumultuous. The Amish believe that the public school may be suitable for children who want to be a part of the world, but not for training their own children in humility and the simple way of life. The Amish have increasingly built and managed their own elementary schools. In 1925 the American Amish had one school; in 1950 there were 16 schools; in 1970, over 300 schools; and in 1990, many more. In the past, the strong Amish belief in remaining separate from the world has meant spending time in jail to support their conviction of separate schools for their children.

Amish elementary schools are integrated into the whole of the Amish agricultural community, including planting and harvesting. Teachers, who usually have only an eighth-grade education, support and reinforce the Amish family's values and way of life. A qualified Amish teacher is not a state-certified teacher, but one with "God-given" abilities to be a good role model and teacher. A person is approached by Amish parents to teach in their schools and not vice versa.

Children in school learn that cooperating is more important than competing with one another. Their willingness to help one another and to work together at difficult tasks is encouraged. Most knowledge is taught through traditional memorization and drill.

The Amish Vocational School

Formal education ends with eighth grade, which is then followed by vocational training for children ages 14 to 16. The teaching methods vary with the teacher and the children's age; however, the primary emphasis is on combining technical skills with a job role. The students and teachers meet at least once a week; most of the curriculum covers home projects. Usually young men help with chores on the farm or begin an apprenticeship as well; young Amish girls are usually taught housekeeping skills. This practice allows the young people to work with family members, as well as with others in the community. Amish young people obtain satisfaction from manual work.

Few Amish young people enter the public high school. Parents fear that if a young person goes to a high school outside the Amish community, it is almost certain he or she will not remain Amish. Amish children are socialized into the Amish world, and about 90 percent of youth remain with the church (Milicia, 2005).

THE AMISH AND THE RELIGIOUS SYSTEM

In America, the Amish people have maintained their unique fundamental Christian religion for over 250 years. At first glance, religion is thought to be the stronghold for maintaining their stability, with approximately 90 percent of Amish youth remaining with the church, which is the highest percentage since 1930 (Milicia, 2005). However, religion is also an area of vulnerability. Like a two-edged sword, religion is a realm in which other Christians have similar knowledge and background and, therefore, are able to communicate with the Amish. Communication with outsiders creates the possibility of a more permeable cultural boundary (Huntington, 1988).

Religious services are held every other Sunday in the home of one of the members. Neighbor women prepare food on Friday at the host family house. After the preaching service on Sunday, everyone shares a meal. Activities and behaviors are steeped in tradition and symbolism. For example, men and women are seated on opposite sides of the room in which the service is held. Everyone, including infants, attends.

The Amish practice only adult baptism (from which the name of their religious sect is derived: Anabaptist). Therefore, once a year, an adult baptism service is held for young adults who wish to join the Amish Christian faith. This baptism commits the adult to the responsibilities and obligations of keeping the Ordnung of the church community. Upon taking the vow, a youth becomes a complete adult in full fellowship, and, if called, is expected to be willing to serve as a minister in the church community. Only men become ministers, and they serve for life.

The maintenance and continuance of the Amish church community is structured by the Ordnung. Each district has its own Ordnung with its various rules and regulations. To maintain the Ordnung, shunning, or meidung, and excommunication, or banning, are practiced. Shunning is enforced on anyone who breaks the rules. The individual is considered an outcast and avoided economically, socially, physically, and religiously by the entire community. One cannot even eat at the same table with the shunned person until the individual repents publicly.

Excommunication is more severe than shunning. Members who have broken their vows and will not mend their ways are excommunicated from the church community. No further communication or transactions are allowed between the Amish and the excommunicated. For example, an Amish who marries a non-Amish, or "outsider," is excommunicated.

THE AMISH AND THE HEALTH CARE SYSTEM

Amish families have many children, and fortunately, they also have good medical care. They do seek and use professional services. This is attributed to their relatively high standard of living (Huntington, 1988). The Amish find nothing in the Bible that prohibits them from seeking modern medical care, immunizations, or blood transfusions.

Even if the Amish do not have hospitalization insurance, their bills are paid and, therefore, they are considered desirable patients. When families need help in paying medical expenses, the Amish band together to help pay for the expenses.

The Amish have a system of beliefs and practices that relate to health and illness. Most of these practices come from everyday experiences. When scientific concepts of health care conflict with their idea of traditional folk medicine, this creates stress for the individual or family. Illness that is not cured by professionals is treated with traditional folk remedies that are usually considered benign (Helman, 1990).

THE AMISH AND THE GOVERNMENTAL SYSTEM

The relationship between the Amish and the national, state, and local governments has not always been cordial. According to Locke (1992), the Amish have been forced into many legal battles with the U.S. government. For example, because of their strong pacifist beliefs, they have often been treated as traitors during times of war; they have fought against compulsory high school education for their adolescents; and they have fought against paying Social Security because they do not take any aid from the government. The Amish practice political separatism and have had to confront issues in the courts that conflict with their beliefs. However, rather than personally defending themselves in court, they are represented by a non-Amish group, the National Committee for Amish Religious Freedom.

Despite their separatist beliefs along sociopolitical lines, the Amish are a generous people. They are known for their charitable contributions at home, as well as their support of relief organizations throughout the world (Locke, 1992). The Amish also pay real estate, state, and federal income taxes. They also pay country taxes and sales taxes. However, the Old Order Amish do not pay Social Security tax or collect any benefits. There is a long history of "taking care of their own." In the case of Amish individuals employed by "outside" businesses, they pay into the Social Security system like the rest of U.S. citizens.

THE AMISH AND THE ECONOMIC SYSTEM

The Amish tend to be self-sufficient as an economic unit. They are mostly small farmers or small businessmen. More Amish are beginning to work off the farm, for example in factories and construction jobs, and once-banned technology is finding its way into their small businesses (Milicia, 2005). However, for the most part, the Old Order Amish live simply and cheaply by making most of their clothing; building most of their houses and barns; maintaining their own equipment; planting vegetable gardens; raising pigs, cows, chickens, and horses; gathering honey and maple syrup; and selling homemade quilts, bread, and other small items (Locke, 1992). Their own population growth, which has been doubling every 20 years, and the encroaching urban sprawl, however, have had a significant impact on their way of living. The result is that nearly 40 percent do not work at any farm-related jobs. It has become difficult for an Amish family to purchase and live on a small farm. The shift from farm to nonfarm employment is perhaps the biggest social change in the last century (Milicia, 2005).

HELPFUL TECHNIQUES FOR SERVING AMISH FAMILIES

As helping professionals, your interaction with the Old Order Amish will likely be limited, aside from a few encounters in offices, stores, or small businesses. However, changes in their workplace also mean a change in how the Amish interact with non-Amish. It will be important for you to learn some of the particular characteristics of the Amish community to give them the respect they deserve and appreciate the difficulties they face in interacting outside their home community. As the Amish young adults interact with the outside world, sensitive and supportive professionals can listen and guide people to safely negotiate the sometimes dangerous time-out. Your study of the Amish could be a model for studying any other religious group, helping you to be sensitive to their values, goals, and practices. We encourage you to make this kind of study of your own faith. Are you curious about what you might discover?

PROMOTING RESPECTFUL RELATIONSHIPS

The Amish are a humble people who believe in quiet and peaceful coexistence with their neighbors and communities. Although they may not express themselves to others about their distress when encountering outsiders, there are certain ways to show your respect of their religious ways. Here are a few helpful hints that can pave the way for better tolerance and understanding:

> Respect their privacy.
> Amish buggies have the same right of way as a moving car or truck. Never use a horn because it can upset the horse pulling the buggy. Only pass when the traffic allows you to do so.
> Do not take photographs of Amish men, women, and children.
> Modesty in dress is respectful when visiting Amish country.

✦ CONCLUSIONS

It is often difficult for the Amish to resist pressures from the majority community, especially if larger economic rewards are needed when families remain large and the youth do not leave home to make a living elsewhere. When businessmen of the church community, such as carpenters and plumbers, need specialized equipment, they often must communicate directly with outside institutions. Also, some Amish people, to make ends meet, work in small outside factories, and they are treated differently under the Ordnung. Allowing for differential treatment encourages outside influences that slowly erode the basic foundations of the church community.

A serious problem is the shortage of available farmland for the Amish children. Amish families expect their children to settle nearby and wish as parents to help raise their own grandchildren. Diversified family farming is followed to promote self-sufficiency and help ensure a good Amish life. The Amish belief in a simple life provides an experiment for a more sustainable agricultural system needed to help protect the global ecosystem and keep it free of pesticides and herbicides.

It is estimated that in another century the Amish population could be more than 5.7 million. As farmland in the United States has become scarce, some Amish families have already emigrated to other countries in areas such as South and Central America in search of agricultural land to survive economically. They have had to compromise and adapt to conditions in a rapidly changing society. The biggest struggle is the cost in investing in farmland for future generations, thus speeding up the process of cultural change.

Humans and environments are in a nexus of interactions. To sustain this ecological relationship and have a good quality of life and quality of environment, it is necessary to become good stewards of the earth's resources, which are finite. The resilient Amish have presented the human family with an alternative way to resolve issues of environmental injustice.

✣ STUDY QUESTIONS

1. List some names that refer to the Amish.
2. After reading about the Amish people's history, make a list of important facts. Where are Amish communities in the United States? Elsewhere?
3. Ordnung, meidung, and banning are names of three practices followed by the Amish. Define these terms.
4. Make a list of demographic characteristics of the Amish people.
5. Make a list of characteristics of the Amish farmers' operations.
6. Make a list of characteristics of the Amish home and family.
7. List characteristics of each life stage of the Amish.
8. Describe a typical Amish child in the educational system.
9. Describe how a typical Amish family practices its religion.
10. Describe health care for a typical Amish family.
11. Describe the typical Amish family's interaction with the governmental system.

✣ APPLICATIONS

1. Describe in a one-page essay any experience you have had with Amish people either directly or indirectly. List any questions you had following these experiences.
2. Consider your own or another religion; use the same headings from this chapter, and write a two-page essay describing the families of that religion. Describe how a helping professional might interact with those of the religion you are analyzing.
3. Visit the site www.holycrosslivonia.org/amish/index.htm
4. Write an essay on how you would prepare to be a professional in a community where you might encounter Amish people.

5. Trace your family lineage for as many generations as possible. Do this by creating a family genogram. How many generations can you go back? Can you trace your family back to the country or countries of origin?

6. Select two or three Amish values, and write a two-page essay on how your own values are alike or different from theirs.

7. Study the Amish child-rearing practices; then write a two-page essay on how the child-rearing practices of your home community are alike or different.

8. Write a one-page essay on how communication could be developed or maintained with Amish members of a community.

9. Perform a word association using the word Amish. Write down all the concepts that come to mind. Write an essay regarding these stereotypes, and discuss it with your classmates.

10. What are the strengths of the Amish community? How do you think these communities have managed to remain stable for so many years?

✦ MEDIA RESOURCES

Ruth, J. R. (Producer), & Hostetler, J. A. (Consultant). *The Amish: A People of preservation* [25- or 53- minute 16mm film]. (Available from Encyclopedia Britannica, 425 North Michigan Avenue, Chicago, IL 60611)

✦ ADDITIONAL RESOURCES

You may wish to visit these locations for more information about the Amish people:

Goshen College, Mennonite Historical Library, 2215 Millstream Road, Lancaster, PA 17602

Mennonite Historical Society of Canada, www.mhsc.ca

✦ KEY INTERNET RESOURCES

Working with the Amish
http://ohioline.osu.edu/hyg-fact/5000/5236.html

Article on Old Amish Education
http://findarticles.com/p/articles/mi_qa3673/is_199704/ai_n8759200

Amish Country News (Pennsylvania)
www.amishnews.com/amisharticles/traditionalfamily.htm

III

LIFESTYLE VARIATIONS AMONG U.S. FAMILIES

→ 10

Teenage Single-Parent Families

→ **Key Concepts**

- Cohabitation Households
- Feminization of Poverty
- Fecundity
- Never-Married Parents
- Temporary Assistance to Needy Families (TANF)

Krista Greco/Merrill

Unwed mothers, at that time, were a specific group; they fell somewhere between criminals and patients and, like criminals and patients, they were prescribed an exact and fortifying treatment; they were made to disappear.
—Rickie Solinger, 1992 (Description of maternity homes of 1958)

Single-parent families have existed throughout the history of the United States. These have included never-married single parents (whose circumstances have always been diverse), single parents who are divorced, and widows or widowers. It is clear from our social history that people hold different opinions and make value judgments about the appropriateness of single-parent families as environments in which to raise children. The interest and concern for this family form, the political targeting of this group for interventions, and the extent of the literature on this family form warrant an entire chapter on never-married teenage single parents. Chapter 11 focuses on divorced single-parent families.

SOCIETAL CONCERN AND DEBATE

Between 1970 and 1995, the number of single parents with children under 18 living in the home increased almost fivefold, from 3.8 million to 18.9 million (U.S. Census Bureau, 1997a). From 1995 to 2000, the birthrate to unmarried women declined back to the 1990 level, with the majority of change in rate accounted for by teenagers and women age 20 to 29 (Ventura & Bachrach, 2000). Societal feelings of responsibility toward the nurturance of children fueled a public debate about how children and families are endangered by the increasing number of single-parent families. In much of this debate, there was a controversy over our public and private interests and responsibilities. Because the socialization of children is an important function of families, much of the debate has centered around whether single-parent families can appropriately nurture and rear children to productive adulthood.

If we study the single-parent family, we notice that this category is not so simply described. Social class, race or ethnic background, and previous family history are all important influences on the structure, prevalence, and success of single-parent families. In actuality, when we categorize a family as a "single-parent family," the only thing we know about the family is that at least one child is present and there is no current legal marriage involving the child's biological custodial parent. Because 83 percent of children living in single-parent families live with their mothers, the discussion is usually about mothers and children (Fields & Casper, 2001).

Although the 2000 census revealed that 51.7 percent of all households held married couples, one out of every four households was a one-person household and 7.2 percent were female-headed households. Nationally there were three times as many married-couple households with children as female-headed family households with children, but compelling regional differences were noted. In the District of Columbia, there were *more* female-headed family households with children (25,000) than married-couple households with children (21,000). These regional differences require different planning for appropriate services from region to region (Fields & Casper, 2001).

As professionals, if we want to understand how to support teenage single-parent families, we need to learn about the circumstances of subgroups of these families and then look closely at individual families themselves. What we find are limited similarities; the structure of the family is a single parent with a child or children, but great diversity exists in resources and practices within these families (Brooks-Gunn & Furstenberg, 1986). These differences can be seen in the division of labor or responsibilities, in the relationships to other supportive resource systems, and in the specific parenting patterns.

NEVER-MARRIED PARENTS

Birthrates to unmarried women increased relative to married women from 1960 to 1999 (Ventura & Bachrach, 2000) (see Figure 10.1). Estimates from the 2002 current census population survey indicated that 1.1 million never-married women gave birth (Downs, 2003). In the latter part of the twentieth century, we saw an increase in two primary groups of never-married parents: The larger group is adolescents, and the smaller

Figure 10.1 Birthrates for Married and Unmarried Women: United States, 1960–1999

Source: Ventura, S. J., & Bachrach, C. A. (2000). Non-marital child-bearing in the United States, 1940–99. *National Vital Statistics Reports, 48*(16), 5. Washington, DC: U.S. Department of Health and Human Services, Centers for Disease Control and Prevention, National Center for Health Statistics.

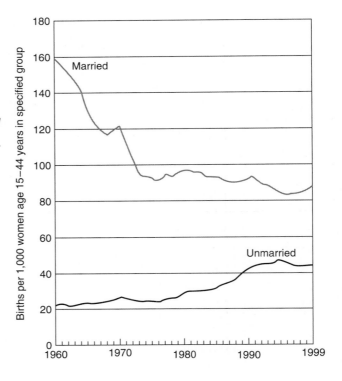

group includes older professional women nearing the end of their childbearing years who finally decide to fulfill a maternal desire. The two groups differ in many respects. By the mid-1990s, 70 percent of births to single women were to mothers in their 20s and 30s (Hetherington, 1997). In 2002 population surveys show that 89 percent of all births to teenagers were to single women: 50 percent of births to women in their early 20s were out of wedlock, and only 12 percent of women age 30 to 44 gave birth out of wedlock (Downs, 2003) (Table 10.1).

Discussion of never-married parents in the United States quickly focused on the young teenage parent because of the great increase in their numbers starting in the mid-1980s. There are strong feelings of concern for successful child outcomes in families headed by young never-married teenage mothers. Income, education, maturity, and support are in short supply for this type of family. Dramatic increases in the number of teenage pregnancies and changing patterns regarding marriage, abortion, and adoption have fueled discussion. As discussed in a previous chapter, in 1996 Congress passed the Personal Responsibility and Work Opportunity Reconciliation Act. Known as the "Welfare Reform Act," this legislation has important implications for teenage parents.

Table 10.1 Children in Single-Parent Families, by Marital Status of Parent, 1990–2000

Year	Parent Never Married	Parent Divorced	Widowed Parent
	Percentage of Children in Single-Parent Families		
1990	7.8	15.9	1.8
1991	8.8	16.1	1.4
1992	9.3	16.7	1.3
1993	9.8	16.8	1.2
1994	10	16.7	1.2
1995	9.8	17.2	1.2
1996	10.6	17.3	1.2
1997	11.1	16.9	1
1998	11.3	16.4	1.2
1999	11.2	16.6	1.2
2000	11	15.6	1.2

Note: Data on children are for related children, which means related to the head of the household through birth, marriage, or adoption.
Source: U.S. Census Bureau, (1997). How we are changing: Demographic state of the nation. *Current Population Reports*, series P23–193.

TRENDS IN NUMBERS

The largest number of births in the United States since 1962 occurred in 1991. From 1986 to 1991, there was a 24 percent increase in the birthrate to teenage mothers, largely related to the higher birthrates and earlier pregnancies of Hispanic and African American women. Prior to 1980, most teenagers giving birth were married, whereas in the late 1990s most teenage parents were unmarried. For age 15 to 17 years, the percentage of unmarried mothers changed from 23 percent in 1950 to 88 percent in 1998. Among 18- to 19-year-old mothers for the same period, the unmarried percentage changed from 9 to 74 percent (Ventura, Mosher, Abma, Curtin, & Henshaw, 2001). In 2002, 65 percent of total births to Black women were out of wedlock, compared to 36 percent for Hispanic women and 25 percent for White non-Hispanic women (Downs, 2003). From 1991 to 2000, there was a 22 percent drop in the birthrate to teenage mothers largely because of a decrease of 26 percent in birthrates to African American teenagers, although Hispanic and non-Hispanic White teenagers also showed birthrate declines of 13 and 19 percent, respectively (Ventura, Curtin, & Mathews, 1998). Births to young never-married mothers were not uniformly distributed across ethnic groups. In 1998 the birthrate for unmarried women under 20 was 85.4 per 1,000 for African American teenagers, 93.6 per 1,000 Hispanic teenagers, and 35.2 births per 1,000 for White non-Hispanic teenagers (Ventura, Martin, Curtin, & Mathews, 1998).

Increase in Adolescent Parents

Some particular details of these trends have caused concern. In almost 70 years, from 1917 to 1983, the birthrate for adolescent women declined slightly, but by the late 1950s, the post–World War II baby boom had increased the total population of teenagers. During this same period, older women reduced their birthrate, so that of those infants born during this postwar period, an increasingly larger percentage were born to teenage mothers (Solinger, 1992). Family life professionals were concerned that the largest rise in the birthrate in the late 1980s was occurring in the under-15 age group. Practically all of these births to very young adolescents were to African Americans (Williams, 1991). Researchers have substantiated that young adolescents who become sexually active wait an average of a year before using some form of birth control. Older teenagers are more likely to use birth control earlier and to use more effective birth control methods (Allen-Meares, 1989). Between 1988 and 1995, there was a 6 percent reduction in women who were not using some form of contraception. There was also a simultaneous increase in the use of more effective contraceptive methods (Ventura & Bachrach, 2000).

Increase in Fecundity

Historians note that one important reason for the rise in births to teenagers is the gradual increase in the general health and fecundity (capability of having children) of young women. Whereas in 1870 only 13 percent of 17-year-olds were fecund, by 1992, 94 percent of American 15-year-old girls were. Between 1940 and 1968 alone, the proportion of fecund 15-year-old girls in the United States increased by 31 percent (Coontz, 1992).

Differential Birthrates

Differential birthrates contributed to the increasing alarm about births to unmarried women. Non-Hispanic White women give birth to an average of 1.9 children in their lifetimes, and African American women average 2.5 children. Hispanic women's birthrates range from a low of 1.5 children for Cuban Americans to 3.2 for Mexican Americans. Asian birthrates range from 1.1 for Japanese Americans to 3.2 for Hawaiians. American Indians and Alaska Natives show a birthrate of 2.7 percent (Haub, 1993). Whereas in 1950 African Americans represented 75 percent of all minority groups in the United States, by 1990 they represented less than half (see Figure 10.2).

By 2025 minorities will account for almost half of all U.S. children. Because childbearing is differentiated across the ethnic groups and teenage births occur more frequently among Hawaiians, African Americans, Hispanics (except for Cubans), and Native Americans, the predictions of increased proportions of children born to young never-married women raise some concerns (Schorr, 1988).

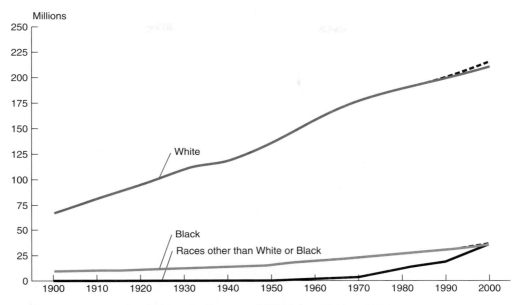

Figure 10.2   Total Population by Race and Ethnicity: 1900 to 2000

Note: For Census 2000, the lower value represents people reporting the specified race alone, while the higher value represents people reporting the specified race, whether or not they reported any other races.

Source: U.S. Census Bureau, decennial census of population, 1900 to 2000.

As shown in Figure 10.3, by 1995 the U.S. Hispanic population was younger in age than the general population. In 1995 almost one in five births in the United States were to Hispanic women (Ventura, Curtin, Martin, & Mathews, 1998). Some ethnic groups, such as Mexican Americans and other Hispanics, continue to give birth well into their late childbearing years; Black and Native American women tend to begin having children early but complete their families while relatively young. Figure 10.4 (see p. 215) presents data for birthrates for unmarried teenagers by race and ethnicity. These different birth patterns tend to predict different life courses and problems for a single mother whose first child is born during the mother's adolescence.

Changes in Marriage Patterns

The story of adolescent births in the United States is compelling because the unwed mother represents a contrast to the traditional model of two-parent families. It is generally acknowledged that following World War II, the United States promoted a return to the traditional pattern of a nuclear family, with one spouse working. Many women who had worked in the defense industry or in other jobs to

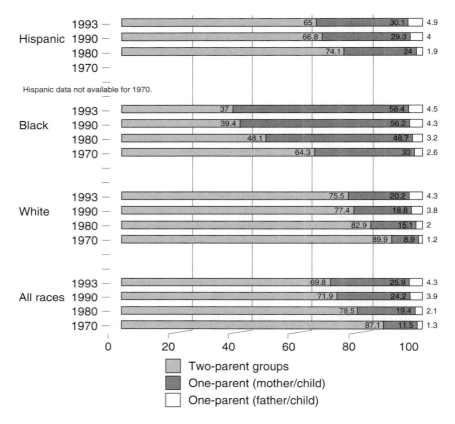

Figure 10.3   Composition of Family Groups with Children, by Race and Hispanic Origin: 1970–1993 (Hispanic may be of any race.)

Note: Family groups comprise family households and subfamilies.

Source: Rawlings, S. W. (1994). *Household Family Characteristics: March 1993* (P20-477). U.S. Census Bureau. Washington, DC: U.S. Government Printing Office.

support the military were encouraged to leave the workplace and return home. A patriarchal family model was emulated, and early marriages increased. By the late 1950s, almost 50 percent of all women were married by age 20 (Coontz, 1992; Wojtkiewicz, 1993).

The postwar early marriage rate produced a record number of births. Births rose to a high of 25.3 per 1,000 women of child-bearing age in 1957. The birthrate for the third child in a family doubled between 1940 and 1960, and for the fourth child, it tripled (Coontz, 1992). These baby boom children grew to adolescence in the late 1950s and early 1960s and had a remarkably visible influence on society. Simultaneously, the vigorous pursuit of civil rights legislation fueled a backlash of conservatism about the procreative practices of minorities. At the same time, many inner-city neighborhoods saw an

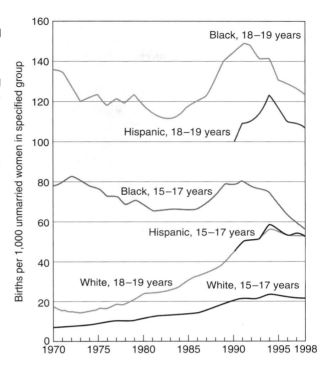

Figure 10.4   Birthrates for Unmarried Teenagers: United States, 1970–1998

Source: Ventura, S. J., & Bachrach, C. A. (2000). Non-marital child-bearing in the United States, 1940–99. *National Vital Statistics Reports, 48*(16), 8. Washington, DC: U.S. Department of Health and Human Services, Centers for Disease Control and Prevention, National Center for Health Statistics.

influx of ethnic minorities seeking urban employment in areas with inadequate infrastructure to sustain successful communities.

In the 1980s an increase in cohabitation, or "living together," began. By 1994, 39 percent of out-of-wedlock births were to cohabiting couples. Figure 10.5 shows that the percentage of mothers categorized as cohabiting almost doubled between 1984 and 1994. Concurrently since the 1960s, the proportion of women who married upon discovery of a premarital conception declined from 49 percent to 23 percent, almost entirely accounted for by the white population (Ventura & Bachrach, 2000). In the 1990s a small but statistically significant increase occurred in the marriage rate among 15- to 19-year-olds. The first increase since a high in 1950, the marriage rate in 2000 was 4.5 percent for this population (Fields & Casper, 2001).

The national trend in cohabiting households has been documented by the current population survey since 1995. In 2002, 11 percent of children living with a single mother lived in a household that included her unmarried partner. Children who were living with a single father were three times more likely to be sharing a household with his unmarried partner (33 percent). Therefore, 2.5 million children listed as residing with a single parent also lived with a second adult who undoubtedly contributed some resources to the child (Fields, 2003). These patterns differed markedly across racial, ethnic, and gender lines. For example, in 2002, 48 percent of all Black children

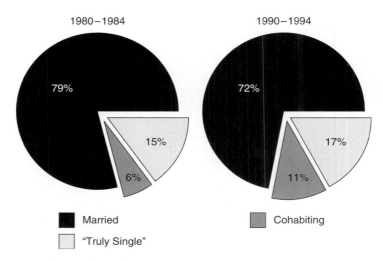

Figure 10.5   U.S. Births, by Mother's Living Situation, 1980–1984 and 1990–1994

Source: Ventura, S. J., & Bachrach, C. A. (2000). Non-marital child-bearing in the United States, 1940–99. *National Vital Statistics Reports, 48*(16), 5. Washington, DC: U.S. Department of Health and Human Services, Centers for Disease Control and Prevention, National Center for Health Statistics.

lived with a single mother, and 5 percent lived with a single father. However, only 6 percent of those who lived with a single mother also lived with her unmarried partner, whereas 30 percent of those who lived with a single father also lived with his unmarried partner. In the Hispanic community, the percentages were 12 percent and 46 percent for single mother/unmarried partner and single father/unmarried partner, respectively (Fields, 2003). These household data suggest great differences in available human resources through friend/kin support. Data on the number of children living with cohabiting adults present a need for careful interpretation. Scommegna (2002) summarized a number of research reports that document an increase from 6 percent in 1984 to 11 percent in 1994 of children born to parents who lived together but were not married. In fact, the large increase in unmarried childbearing from 1980 to 1995 appears to be mainly the result of an increase in births to cohabiting parents. About two out of five babies born out of wedlock actually went home to two biological parents (see Figure 10.6).

Researchers estimate that 40 percent of all children will spend some time in a cohabiting family before their 16th birthday. Reviewing the data in Figure 10.6, the amount of time children will spend with cohabiting parents as well as with married parents appear to show more available adult resources than a legal definition of family would suggest.

Changes in Adoption Practices

Another change that attracted concern related to the decisions of never-married mothers about keeping children or giving them up for adoption. In the 1950s and 1960s, 90

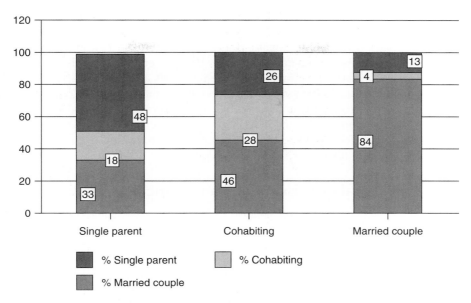

Figure 10.6   Expected Share of Childhood Years Spent in Various Household Types, by Household Type at Child's Birth, 1990–1994

Note: Share of childhood years, U.S. children age 0–16 (shares do not always equal 100 due to rounding).

Source: Ventura, S. J., & Bachrach, C. A. (2000). Non-marital child-bearing in the United States, 1990–99. *National Vital Statistics Reports, 48*(16), 5. Washington, DC: U.S. Department of Health and Human Services, Centers for Disease Control and Prevention, National Center for Health Statistics.

percent of all adoptions were of children born to unmarried mothers (Solinger, 1992). White pregnant adolescents in particular were encouraged to give their children up for adoption. Many of these pregnant adolescents were labeled mentally disturbed and described as angry at their fathers and seeking revenge against their parents. A psychological diagnosis that included a mental disturbance enabled a White adolescent with economic means to receive a therapeutic abortion. If this option was not possible or not desired by the family, a frequent pattern was to have the White adolescent "disappear" on a trip or on a scholarship for a period of time until the birth and adoption had been completed. Stories of black market baby mills and pressures to be "cleansed" or "retrained" in homes for unwed mothers are documented in a number of studies of this period (Solinger, 1992). The description that opens this chapter is part of that picture.

During this same time it was much less likely that Black adolescents sought abortions. With a tradition of strong independent women being forced by racism and social and economic circumstances to rear children alone, the African American community did not view adolescent pregnancy so negatively (Barnes, 1987). It was more likely that extended family members in the African American community would assist an adolescent parent, and they frequently played vital roles in the rearing of the children. During the 1970s economic restructuring in the United States brought severe job dislocation to many African

American men. Black median family income was only 56 percent of White median family income from 1979 through 1987 (U.S. Census Bureau, 1990). In 2001 the poverty rate for Blacks was 22.7 percent, for Hispanics 21.4 percent, for non-Hispanic Whites 7.8 percent, and for Asians and Pacific Islanders 10.2 percent (Proctor & Dalaker, 2002).

Because poverty reduces the resources available to establish independent households, Black adolescents were less apt to marry. In 1960, almost a third of all 18- to 19-year-old African American women were married. By 1984, less than 3 percent were married (Saluter, 1989). In 1950, 78 percent of Black family households consisted of married couples. By 2000, only 44 percent included married couples (Fields & Casper, 2001).

Political Criticism of African American Patterns

A particularly difficult period of social history was marked by the 1958 introduction of House Bill 479 by David H. Glass, a Mississippi state representative (Solinger, 1992). The purpose of this legislation was to pass regulations requiring the sterilization of African American women, particularly adolescent mothers. The legislation was not passed, but it illustrated an active struggle with racism in the march toward civil rights legislation.

In 1965 the landmark Moynihan Report on the family was published. The impact of this report has been described as eliminating a balanced scholarship about adolescent parenthood and African American families for at least 20 years. Moynihan was the assistant secretary of labor to President Lyndon Johnson (1963–1968), and his description of the African American family as a matriarchal system marked by poverty, joblessness, and illegitimacy in a tangle of pathology had sharp political overtones. The report suggested that the strains on the African American family were related largely to the inadequacy of the Black man to exhibit the necessary responsibility, discipline, and diligence to support a family. A strong theme of poverty was stressed, with an inadequate exploration of the real power of racism to limit opportunities for the African American family.

In response, governmental policymakers began an era of institutional racism by advocating work programs for African American women and aggressive child-support enforcement against Black men. In the resultant political debate between liberals and conservatives, a redemptive romanticized picture of African American families as resilient, creative, religious, and nurturant to all children was presented. Probably neither view contributed to balanced social and economic policies.

From 1980 to 1996, the focus of government policy was to reduce aid to dependent individuals and families and to urge self-control and the delay of sexual activity. Not until the publishing of the landmark work, *The Truly Disadvantaged: The Inner City, the Underclass, and Public Policy*, by W. J. Wilson (1987), did the debate begin to return to an understanding of the effects of poverty and social class on birthrates and family patterns. Wilson sounded an elegant alarm that the real problems of African American families were not cultural but economic. The modernization of the industrial sector had reduced the need for low-skilled jobs, and citizens with less access to education could not compete. The affluent and middle-class urban dwellers had all fled to the suburbs, and the remaining infrastructure was inadequate to inspire or recruit either low-income youths to stay in school or adult workers to enter retraining or vocational transition programs.

Wilson and other social scientists claimed that the social problems being blamed on the inadequate family structures of African Americans and other minorities were the results of the power of poverty and economic dislocation, and they were enough to ruin hope in any ethnic group. In addition, economists noted that a delay in marriage and in establishing independent households reflected insufficient incomes to cover the expenses involved.

One of the ironies of the alarm about minority single parents rests on the confusion generated by data. Whereas the birthrate for unmarried African American women fell by 12 percent between 1980 and 1989, the birthrate of married African American women fell by 38 percent, and the marriage rate of African American women fell by 50 percent. Thus the proportion of Black children born to single parents has grown. During the same period, the percentage of unmarried White women giving birth rose by 27 percent (Coontz, 1992). These trends continued into the 1990s. The birthrate for unmarried White women doubled between 1980 and 1994 and then remained stable. Since the mid-1990s, the birthrates for unmarried non-Hispanic White and Hispanic women have generally declined, but the proportion of unmarried women in society has remained high, and thus the percentages of children born to single parents has increased (Ventura & Bachrach, 2000).

SOCIOCULTURAL FOUNDATIONS

Responses to never-married single parents illustrate great conflicts in American society. Discussions about the never-married single-parent family often revolve around early sexual activity, responsible parenthood, healthy parent–child bonds, the father's role, and the economic and career possibilities for the mother and child. In the 1970s the link between marriage and sexual activity was severed, and pregnant adolescents did not see marriage as an imperative. Raising the child as a single mother or electing an abortion were options often replacing marriage. In 1995, 42 percent of pregnant White women, 43 percent of pregnant Black women, and 34 percent of pregnant Hispanic women ended their pregnancies by abortion (Ventura & Bachrach, 2000).

Adolescent mothers may see parenthood as a way to express maturity and become more responsible. These values of responsibility and affectionate relationships with children may also reflect a sense of despair or frustration in establishing nurturing relationships with a partner. For African American women, finding an eligible man who is employed and can be a responsible partner has been increasingly difficult. By 1987 women of marriageable age in the African American community had less than a 50 percent chance of finding a partner who was not in jail, on drugs, or unemployed (Wilson, 1987). Many critics of the welfare system claimed that single parenting and the African American custom of extended kinship and joint parenting have been facilitated by benefits from the Aid to Families with Dependent Children (AFDC) program. This concern was one of the motivations behind passage of the 1996 Welfare Reform Act, with specific provisions regarding education and employment for teenage parents.

Among all women, the influence of the women's movement and the tendency to redefine marriage as a companion relationship, rather than primarily a procreative relationship, have opened options and created alternative practices. If men and women see marriage as largely an arrangement to ensure the birth and nurturance of children, then a devotion to children may include the positive valuing of marriage. If marriage is viewed as a relationship that must be individually satisfying to both partners, a consequence may be greater marital instability among young people.

ECONOMIC STATUS

One of the most alarming characteristics of never-married parents is their economic vulnerability. However, the economic status of all young families became discouraging in the latter part of the twentieth century. The poverty rate of single-mother-headed families in 2001 was 26.1 percent, and the poverty rate of single male-headed families was 13.1 percent (Proctor & Dalaker, 2002). Nearly 75 percent of American children growing up in single-parent families experience poverty during their first 10 years, but, in contrast, 52 percent of total years of childhood poverty occur while the children are in two-parent homes (National Commission on Children, 1993). By 1992, 66 percent of America's poor children lived in two-parent families.

Many adolescent mothers live with their own mothers as subfamily groups. Prior to 1982 the U.S. Census did not identify these adolescent mothers as family heads. In 1997 about two thirds of mothers living in related subfamilies were never married (U.S. Census Bureau, 1998). When the paternity of their children was not declared and child support enforcement was lax in the late 1980s and early 1990s, only 20 percent of unmarried mothers were awarded child support (National Commission on Children, 1993). With the passage of the Welfare Reform Act of 1996, any parent who applies for Temporary Assistance to Needy Families (TANF) is required to file a petition for child support from the other parent (Golonk, Steisel, & Ryan, 1996).

The social status of unmarried mothers tends to be lower than that of mothers who are married, divorced, or widowed. However, ethnic and social class patterns around status vary. In some communities where there are few jobs and little hope for a career, one of the only ways for young women to acquire status is to become a mother. Murray (1997) describes the neighborhood environments of poor urban families as providing no motivating models of alternative life courses that could impress young men and women. This issue of role models and realistic employment goals is proving to be difficult for case managers implementing the federal TANF regulations. Under the new law, states that receive funding from the federal government must guarantee that they are meeting certain program requirements with their clientele. Most important is the regulation that, beginning July 1, 1997, an adult may only receive 60 months of TANF support over a lifetime, whether consecutive or not. Also, unmarried teenage parents who are under 18 must live with their parents, an adult relative or guardian, or seek an exception to the regulation. In addition, these young parents are required to attend high school or a General Equivalency Diploma (GED) or alternative approved education or training program.

These regulations affecting young parents reflect national concern that families headed by an unmarried teenager are economically vulnerable and may start a pattern of lifelong public assistance. Obviously, the educational requirement presents immediate child-care demands that not all states are prepared to answer. In the summer of 2002, the 60-month limitation of benefits was impacting many TANF recipients at a time when a significant economic downturn in the United States reduced the availability of entry-level employment. Earnings for the poorest 40 percent of families headed by women doubled from 1994 to 2000, when the recession eliminated much of those gains (Wolf, 2006).

In addition to the time limits, living requirements, and educational regulations imposed for TANF clients, an increasing percentage of recipients are required to engage in supervised volunteer work or employment over the duration of their TANF participation. By the year 2002, 50 percent of all families who participate in TANF must work or volunteer at least 30 hours per week. By 2006, a new Bush administration policy was implemented to encourage states to more vigorously require job training or community service from the 50 percent of welfare recipients who were not working. These work provisions have been reinforced by political and business leaders challenging both the public and private sector to actively recruit and train TANF recipients. This goal was severely compromised by the economic downturn following terrorist attacks in New York City on September 11, 2001. And, employers report varying degrees of success with employing TANF recipients. Most women who leave TANF to enter the workforce are stuck in low-paying, unskilled jobs, and those remaining unemployed often have multiple handicaps.

A state can be penalized by losing a percentage of its allocation from the federal government if it fails to comply with the provisions of the act. However, all states can apply for specific waivers that "set aside" the federal requirements and allow them to experiment with TANF practices that they feel are more appropriate to their circumstances. Forty-eight states have received such waivers, and these actions represent a great variety of experiments with changing "welfare as we know it."

For young teenage parents, the commitment of TANF case managers to complete an accurate assessment of their skills and circumstances is a critical process. Because a tremendous range of benefit levels and support programs are in place across the country, a teen parent could have very different experiences depending on the county and state of residence. Some states, such as Wisconsin, have been aggressive in instituting one-stop service centers to assist all TANF recipients in entering the workforce. Other states, such as Colorado, have let counties make the determination on specific programs to use in supporting clients. Although states are making different decisions about what young parents should be entitled to, there are many ways human development professionals can be involved in these developments. Where agency attitudes are punitive and isolationist, it is unlikely that teen parents will receive the comprehensive support they need to obtain education, child care, and life skills to enter appropriate employment. Examples of life stories of young women who report this effect are told by Williams in *Black Teenaged Mothers: Pregnancy and Childrearing from Their Perspective* (1991).

CHANGING ROLES OF WOMEN

Among single-parent families, the vast majority of unwed or never-married parents with custody of children are women, although the proportions are gradually changing (Bryson & Casper, 1998). In 2000, 82 percent of single-parent families were headed by females (Fields & Casper, 2001).

In the precarious world of poverty, it is frequently the mother-child system that provides the only stability or centeredness for a household. Frequently, grandmothers or aunts are important supports for teenage mothers and children, especially in the African American community (McAdoo & McAdoo, 1985). In 1996, 13 percent of African American children were living with grandparents, compared with 4 percent of White children and 7 percent of Hispanics (U.S. Census Bureau, 1998). Some adolescent parents report an enhancement of their status to that of a companion with their mother or grandmother once they have given birth. Adolescent mothers who rely heavily on their mothers and grandmothers for child care and support may resent the involvement of the older generations in the discipline and care of their children. Davis, Rhodes, and Hamilton-Leaks's (1997) study of African American teen parents showed the nesting of support in the community and the strong role played by both maternal grandmother and grandfather, even if they did not both reside with the young parent. The teens reported great support from their mothers but relationship issues with both mothers and fathers. In her intensive study of Black adolescent mothers, Williams (1991) reports the interest of some young mothers in moving away from their maternal home and establishing their own households to achieve independent power. This is a more difficult option since passage of the Welfare Reform Act.

CHANGING ROLES OF MEN

Young men who have fathered children in their adolescence or with a female adolescent frequently have precarious relationships with the mothers of their children. In Moynihan's 1965 report, African American men were compared with African American women and found to be worse off in education and employment. Opportunities for service jobs at minimum wage have been more often open to minority women than to men (Sorensen & Zibman, 2000). The inability to obtain employment and persist in educational pursuits has decreased the power of many adolescent fathers. Vulnerable in the areas of education and employment, many of these young men are not able to maintain stable relationships with mothers of their children. A University of Chicago study reported that in 1990, employed Black men in the inner city were 22 times more likely to marry the mother of their children than were unemployed fathers (Coontz,

1992). In a study of noncustodial African American fathers, Hamer (1997) found that the fathers' view of their role was largely based on a pattern of contrasting or refuting the behavior of their own fathers.

There were conflicts between the men's valuing of their contributions to their children's lives relative to that of a traditional Western paradigm of fatherhood used by agency professionals, a situation that may reflect the precariousness of their economic circumstances. These fathers felt strongly about spending time with and providing emotional support to their children. In addition, they wanted to provide discipline and gender-appropriate role models. Economic support was the least important function.

The Guttmacher Institute has claimed that 25 percent of young women who became mothers in adolescence were impregnated by men in their 20s whom the young mothers perceived as authority figures (McAdoo, 1980). Taylor, Tucker, Chatters, and Jayakody (1997) cite studies that show 42 percent of fathers of infants born to 15- to 17-years-olds were 4 to 7 years older than the mothers, and 7 percent of the men were 10 to 14 years older, making many professionals recognize the possibility of incest and rape.

In a dramatic 1986 television program, video journalist Bill Moyers showed young adolescent men whose only way to exhibit power was to father children for whom they showed little subsequent economic responsibility (Moyers, 1986). In contrast, a number of social service programs have observed that 80 percent of birth fathers visit their new children during the hospital stay of the mother and child. Studies by Hetherington (1997) showed only 12 percent of African American teenage fathers reported having no contact with their child, versus 30 percent for White fathers and 37 percent for Hispanic fathers. The Budget Reconciliation Act of 1993 requires all states to offer simple processes for in-hospital voluntary declaration of paternity around the time of the child's birth. Once paternity is established, support orders can be issued (Children's Defense Fund, 1993).

In her study of adolescent mothers, Williams (1991) reports the frequent phenomenon of failure to report the father's name because the public policy demands for child support payment are beyond the young man's ability to pay. Although she may withhold this official information, the young mother may still enjoy visits and a variety of services and goods purchased by the father. Family life educators who have organized programs for adolescent parents frequently comment on the frustration and despair of adolescent fathers who wish to be involved more actively and responsibly in their children's lives but cannot identify a legal public role without incriminating themselves. The Welfare Reform Act has resulted in more of these fathers being identified and more directly involved in supporting their children. However, many TANF benefits are designed for custodial working mothers and not for nonresident fathers who work (Sorensen & Zibman, 2000). One frequent pattern is involvement of the paternal grandparents in helping with child care or economic support. Coles (2001) reported on a survey of single black full-time fathers who identified strongly as both nurturers and providers for their children. They showed high behavioral expectations of children and identified their own mothers as a primary source of support and advice.

SOCIALIZATION OF CHILDREN

The 2001 census classified 35.2 percent of Black single-mother households as poor, compared with only 7.8 percent of Black married-parent households. This compares with 22.4 percent and 4.5 percent for comparable White families and 37.0 percent and 13.8 percent for similar Hispanic families (Proctor & Dalaker, 2002). Children of never-married parents are vulnerable to the effects of poverty and the low educational level of their parents. Children of single mothers are significantly more at risk for learning problems, for being left back a grade, and for dropping out of school. The literature on school dropouts and maternity rates indicates that young women who are one to two years behind grade level are at risk for early childbearing.

Of more direct concern for the children of young never-married women are parenting skills. Some studies have reported that adolescent parents are apt to provide for the physical care of their children without understanding their need for stimulation and individualized nurturance. Newberger (1977) developed a model of four levels of parental understanding based on Kohlberg's stages of moral development. Some family life professionals have used this model to observe adolescent parents. These levels are egotistical, conventional, subjective, and analytic. The egotistical parental understanding tends to be self-centered and fails to take the individual needs of the child into consideration. A parent with a conventional understanding of the role tends to see strict "good boy/bad boy," or normative, rules for correct behavior. With subjective, or individualistic, understanding, the parent tries to understand the child's point of view, and finally, an analytic level of understanding involves a mutual understanding of both the parent's and child's needs and some ability to negotiate the meeting of those individual needs.

In William's (1991) observation of 30 adolescent unmarried mothers, only two exhibited the more immature egotistical parenting style. The group ranged in age from 15 to 19 and exhibited all levels of parental understanding. Williams noted that adolescent mothers who showed an analytic understanding of parenting also were more independent and goal oriented about their own lives. Such mothers more frequently attended school or vocational programs, and they supported themselves and their children. This same interaction between the mothers' self-development and parenting skills was documented in early programs, such as the St. Paul (Minnesota) Mechanical Arts High School program, which indicated that the greatest development in parental skills was seen when the young women's own educational and vocational needs were supported (Schorr, 1988).

Pianta, Lopez-Hernandez, and Ferguson (1997) completed a three-year study of young children and their parents, contrasting adolescent mothers with those in their early 20s. Regardless of the age of the mother, the child outcomes were explained almost entirely by the educational level of the mother. This study shows the importance of programs that enable teen mothers to continue their own education and development.

DEMOGRAPHICS

The 2000 census reported that while the *number* of two-parent households remained relatively stable from 1970 to 2000, the *percentage* of married-couple households with children declined to 24 percent of all households, down from 40 percent in 1970. In the same period of time, the *percentage* of single-parent households grew from 11 to 16 percent of all households (Fields & Casper, 2001). Over this 30-year period, the number of single-mother families grew from 3 million to 10 million while the number of single-father families grew from 393,000 to 2 million. The *proportion* of single-parent families grew to 31 percent of *all* family households, up from 13 percent in 1970. The demographic shifts that account for much of this change are the delay of marriage with more years in single status, and the growth in divorce among couples with children.

There are reported differences in the frequency of unmarried parents by ethnic group. In 2000, White non-Hispanic single-mother families were more likely the result of divorce (50 percent) as compared with Black single mothers (17 percent). Thirty percent of White mothers had never married, as compared with 65 percent of Black mothers (Fields & Casper, 2001). Of teenage mothers, 79 percent produced children out of wedlock in 2000. The substantial progress in reducing teenage birthrates in the 1990s (20 percent) is especially promising because the largest reduction was in the 15- to 17-year age range (26 percent) in comparison to a 15 percent reduction for teenagers 18 to 19 years old (Ventura & Bachrach, 2000).

EDUCATION

There are negative consequences in education for both parents and children in the families of never-married parents. Early childbearing for a single woman frequently interferes with education. Indeed, until the 1960s, pregnant young women were expected to drop out of school. Early pregnancy is the single most important reason that young women leave high school before graduation. Finally, schools began making classes available for pregnant students and for young mothers, including classes on caring for infants.

Statistics from the National Commission on Children (1993) show that young adults from age 18 to 23 with basic educational skills in the bottom fifth of distribution in comparison to their peers are nine times as likely as those in the top half to bear a child before marriage.

In a study of adolescent mothers done by Furstenberg, Brooks-Gunn, and Morgan (1987), there was a high incidence of eventual return to education. For 80 percent of the group, the outcome for these adolescent mothers, 20 years after the birth of their first children, was fairly positive and independent. This successful group generally returned to school or obtained a GED and became self-supporting. However, in contrast to the mothers, the children of this sample tended to show difficulties with school achievement and educational goal setting. Children in single-parent families are twice as likely to drop out of school as children from two-parent families; they also score lower on standardized tests and receive lower grades in school (National Commission on Children, 1993). Being raised by a single parent is frequently cited as one of the risk factors for school failure. However, one risk alone does not determine outcome. The real concern for education of never-married parents and their children is that they are too often also poor, unemployed, underemployed, uninsured, and living in dangerous neighborhoods. The combination of these factors is seen most obviously in poor school performance or dropping out.

RELIGION

Within this population there are no clear unifying religious themes, but a variety of studies offer some insights on the influence of religion. Some young never-married women who become pregnant indicate that their religious values eliminate abortion as a viable option. Other young women report that religion enabled them to find ways to support their children without a partner and to bring structure and hope to their lives.

Particularly because of the romanticized image of the African American extended, resilient, religious family, which emerged in contrast to Moynihan's (1965) report, it is interesting to note a lack of an early assertive response from African American churches to support unmarried parents. Recent efforts to enhance the development of young urban men, and to include single parents in the church community, are viewed very positively in a variety of high-stress, low-income neighborhoods. One remarkable reflection in Williams's (1991) study of adolescent African American parents is the absence or irrelevance of the church community in their urban lives. For many of those young mothers, the neighborhood exhibited a striking lack of social or religious groups or activities to nurture them during adolescence or provide support for them in single parenthood. In Murray's (1997) study of 1,666 African American high school graduates, the majority reported being regular church attendees. In the recent political climate, changes in attitudes toward the faith community have meant that churches, particularly in inner-city neighborhoods, are becoming more active in providing a variety of educational and social services. President George Bush's appointment of the director of the Office of Faith-Based Initiatives has reinforced this action.

THE HEALTH CARE SYSTEM AND TEENAGERS

Professionals in the health care and medical systems are concerned about preteens, teenagers, and their sexual practices and pregnancies. Many programs have been designed to prevent preteen and teen pregnancies. Particularly in the Bush administration, a strong message of abstinence and responsible behavior appears to have encouraged more active use of contraceptives, particularly among Black women. Between 1988 and 1995, contraceptive failure among Black women fell from 31 to 21 percent (Fu, Darroch, Haas, & Ranjit, 1996). In 1998 Secretary of Health and Human Services Donna Shalala announced that a 1995 survey of family growth found that the percentage of teenagers who had sexual intercourse had declined for the first time in two decades (Lancashire & Smith, 1997). Earlier studies had shown teenage intercourse at 29 percent in 1970, 47 percent in 1982, and 55 percent in 1990. The increased use of injectable and implant contraceptives indicates more deliberate decision making among sexually active teens (Ventura, Curtin, & Mathews, 1990). In addition, the prolonged economic vigor of the 1990s provided opportunities for jobs and education that encouraged the postponement of early pregnancy. Even the economic downturn in 2001–2002 did not reverse this trend (Dye, 2005). Pregnancies have been reported at ages as young as 9, with the rate of pregnancies in preteens increasing. Professionals are finding evidence of incest and rape in some of these pregnancies. Some fathers of teenagers' infants are reported by the girls to be in their 50s. In addition, men are reported to be seeking younger girls for sex (prostitution), both here and abroad, in hopes of avoiding infection with acquired immune deficiency syndrome (AIDS). However, some infected men will transmit the virus to the girls. Such reports show that teen pregnancy is frequently not the result of a romantic interlude between two classmates, caught in a passionate moment without contraceptives.

Adequate education concerning reproductive health, family planning, abortion and adoption options, and prenatal health care needs to be part of health care programs for teenagers. In the 1995 National Survey just cited, 90 percent of women 18 and 19 years of age reported that they had received formal instruction on sexually transmitted diseases, safe sex, and how to say no to sex. It is common for teens to be unaware of where the nearest health services are located and how to access them, especially if parental knowledge of their pregnancy is a concern. Such conditions give substance to arguments for in-school clinics. Contraceptives must be understood by and be available to young girls who refuse to maintain their virginity. The archaic notion of protecting the girls from information on sexuality, birth control, and methods and supplies for family planning may actually lead to girls' pregnancy, illness, and death. Boys also need this information if they are going to fulfill their responsibility for preventing pregnancy, infection with the AIDS virus, and other sexually transmitted diseases.

A strong family-planning component for any preteen and teen parenting program is an imperative. Certainly, preventing a second pregnancy should be a required goal of parenting programs designed by teens, parents, and school authorities, if there is to be hope of responsible parenthood and a good life for mothers and infants. This would allow a teenager to pursue high school and gain employable skills.

Medical authorities are very concerned about girls with immature bodies giving birth. Giving birth at young ages contributes to high maternal mortality rates and high infant mortality rates, especially for low-birth-weight infants. Many experts, for a variety of reasons, strongly discourage girls from getting pregnant until they are beyond their teen years. Early prenatal care is a major concern for prevention of many serious problems for mothers and infants. Early measurements of the birth canal, proper nutrition for the mother, and regular monitoring can produce healthier infants and mothers.

Many teens are smokers, too, adding another negative factor in the prognosis for their infants. Compared to nonsmokers, mothers who smoke have more low-birth-weight infants. Low birth weights create significant problems for infants. Alcohol consumption can contribute to fetal alcohol syndrome (FAS), a form of mental retardation—a lifetime burden to the family and society. Drugs of many types can damage the fetus, with serious outcomes. These facts give school authorities compelling reasons to include complete health information in their school services and curricula.

Teachers and school health care workers are often unperceptive about a girl's pregnant condition. Some girls have played basketball into the later months; others have given birth in the rest room. The lack of any class that prepares adolescents for parenthood is commonplace. Although such classes are offered by some school systems, the classes are seldom selected by all students or even by those who are pregnant at the time and attending school.

The health of the never-married single-parent family depends on access to medical services (including insurance, Medicaid, and transportation), an understanding of the importance of preventive health measures, and the motivation to use them. Access to health care is reported as one of the factors that discourages marriage because medical benefits given to teen mothers by the Medicaid program are lost upon marriage. The new welfare reform legislation allows for 12 months of Medicaid transitional coverage by a family leaving TANF.

When the never-married parent is a young adolescent, health officials are generally concerned about the adequacy of American teenagers' diets during pregnancy. A frequent problem in the adolescent population is a diet low in calcium, iron, zinc, folate, fiber, vitamin E, and the B vitamins. In addition, the teenage propensity to snack on poor quality food, binge diet, skip meals, and eat foods too high in sodium, fat, and cholesterol creates risks for a pregnancy (Story, 1997). Because diet is one area where economics and personal values and goals play a major role, access to programs such as the Women, Infants and Children (WIC) program and the Food Stamp program of the Department of Agriculture can assist young mothers in balancing their diets. Women who give birth under 16 years of age are twice as likely to have low-birth-weight infants and three times more likely to have an infant who dies in the first month of life, in comparison to women who give birth after the age of 20.

All professionals and persons concerned about the pregnant and parenting adolescent need to be concerned about adolescents' attitudes toward diet and weight gain. Professionals who have worked with pregnant adolescents report heightened concern about loss of a slim figure and a dramatic change in self-image, along with ignorance about the importance of adequate weight gain (Story, 1997). Frequently, such young women try to reduce their food intake to slow down an inevitable physiological change.

Another reason for inadequate health care during pregnancy relates to the lack of emotional acceptance of the pregnancy and poor planning for a successful birth on the part of the young mother. Frequently, young women do not admit to pregnancy or seek assistance until some point in the second trimester. Because significant fetal development occurs in the first trimester, a compromise in the mother's diet and a delay in adequate prenatal care concerns health professionals. Only 26 percent of 15- to 19-year-old pregnant women seek health care in the first trimester, versus 84 percent of women age 25 to 29 (Story, 1997).

There is disagreement on the physiological stress on the body created by an early pregnancy for a healthy adolescent. Physiological principles of species survival suggest that the health of the pregnant mother will be compromised to ensure that nutrients for development are absorbed by the developing fetus. The adolescent mother may not feel as healthy or energetic as she would on a more adequate diet, and, therefore, her ability to plan and prepare for the birth may be compromised. Three high risk factors are known to account for two thirds of all low-birth-weight infants: smoking, below normal weight gain during pregnancy, and below-normal prepregnancy weight (Story, 1997). Smoking and weight gain can be topics of direct education for the pregnant teen.

The family size of a never-married single-parent family shows variation by social class and ethnic group. Frequently, because the young, never-married mother may be living in an extended family, the household size may include several adult relatives and their children. A public criticism of young unmarried mothers is that many of them initiated pregnancy and birth to enhance their own independence and create an income. Studies increasingly discount this argument as simplistic and inaccurate (Coontz, 1992), and the Welfare Reform Act has created limits to the independence of a teen parent while receiving benefits. Young unmarried women who have their first child before the age of 19 frequently show a motivation to limit the size of their own family, but their ability to act on this goal is strongly influenced by the size of their family of origin, their access to contraceptive information and contraceptives, and their own educational and vocational goals.

In a longitudinal study done by Furstenberg et al. (1987), the education of the adolescent's parents, the adolescent's educational goals, and an understanding of and access to effective family-planning techniques strongly influenced family life outcome. Most of the questions about access to health care are mediated directly by income. Inevitably, younger unmarried heads of households have access to Medicaid, which can enhance health care. It is more often the underemployed, minimum wage-earning unmarried parent who does not have access to health care for the family. Of the 37 million Americans who did not have insurance in 1992, 85 percent of them lived in families with at least one working adult (White House Domestic Policy Council, 1993). Young parents frequently find employment in part-time jobs that offer no benefits.

ECONOMIC FACTORS

The erosion of real income for all families is an American crisis; for families with young children, it is especially alarming (Edin & Lein, 1997). In 1991 the average income for a White family with two parents working was $46,629. If only the husband worked in a two-parent family, the family income was $33,961. If only the wife worked, the family income was $26,151. A single, White working mother's average income was only $13,012 (National Commission on Children, 1993). For the decade of the 1990s, real median family income increased gradually. After September 11, 2001, this pattern changed (DeNavas-Walt & Cleveland, 2002).

Forty-eight percent of all children living in female-headed households were poor in 2000; among African American female-led households, 50 percent were poor. This is five times the poverty of children living in married-couple families (Proctor & Dalaker, 2001). For the adolescent single-parent-headed household, the figures are even more dramatic. Starting a family before there has been adequate time to develop education or an employment record to enhance income creates risks for families.

From 1973 to 1990, young families with children lost significant economic ground. Adjusting for inflation, families with children and a head of household younger than age 30 lost 44 percent in real income. For young Black families with children, the loss was 70 percent, and median income decreased from $13,860 to $4,030 in real dollars. By 2001, 26.4 percent of female-headed households were classified as poor compared to 4.9 percent for married couple families (Proctor & Dalaker, 2002).

Looking at the economic resources of the never-married female-headed household, there are dramatic challenges to all systems in society to assist in nurturing both adults and children. In Dye's (2002) analysis of mothers who participated in AFDC, food stamps, WIC, and Medicaid, 59 percent of participants were unmarried at the birth of their first child, whereas of mothers who don't participate in government programs, 25 percent are unmarried at the birth of their first child.

HOUSING

Housing for the young unmarried family is frequently communal or three-generation housing including other adult family members or friends. Only since 1983 have these single-parent subfamilies living with their parents been reported as separate families by the U.S. Census Bureau. Prior to 1983 the mother was coded as a child, and her own child was coded as a relative of the household head. When the Census Bureau made this reporting change, the number of single-parent families approximately doubled in one year (Mulroy, 1988)! Communal living enhances the resource base for the nurturance of family members. In Dye's (2002) research, only 13 percent of teen mothers participating in government support programs lived with no adult age 18 or older, and 58 percent lived with one or more adult relatives (not a spouse).

In 2000, according to the U.S. Census Bureau, 3.7 percent of all households were multigenerational (Simmons & O'Neill, 2001). In 2000 a third of grandparents who were caring for their grandchildren lived in "skipped generation" households where neither parent of the grandchild was present (Fields, 2003).

The question of housing options cuts directly to the question of culturally preferred patterns for family life. American dominant culture patterns suggest that a nuclear family separate household is preferable for all families. A government policy that gave housing preference to individual family units illustrates that fact; in 1985 direct governmental support for low-income housing was $13.9 billion. The same year, federal support for home ownership was four times that amount, or $53.9 billion. In 1995 two thirds of children of single parents lived in rented homes (U.S. Census Bureau, 1997a). Although families with incomes of more than $50,000 represented only 20 percent of the households, they received 52.2 percent of the federal government's housing subsidies. Such subsidies include a variety of mortgage assistance programs not available to many young families (Mulroy, 1988).

According to the Department of Housing and Urban Development (HUD), female heads of households occupy over 49 percent of "problem-ridden" residences. Sixty-seven percent of female heads of household with minor children have housing problems. During the Reagan administration, affordable housing programs suffered a 75 percent cutback in public investment. Families headed by a single mother were the largest growing segment of the homeless population in the United States between 1985 and 1990. A national 29-city survey of homeless families in 1987 found that two thirds were headed by single parents (Mulroy, 1988).

Housing Designs

In a policy study, authors Strober and Dornbush (1988) point out a need for housing designs that more clearly support current family relationship patterns and structures. New housing designs might include more appropriately planned communal space, such as laundry facilities, gardens, parks, and recreational areas with small units for families to maintain some privacy. Especially needed is convertible space that might be used for a variety of family structures. As we have seen, a number of cultures prefer and plan for households that include more than two generations and a variety of extended-family relationships.

Currently, many single-parent families live in old housing, which is expensive because of high utility costs from inefficient energy use and presents health dangers such as lead-based paint, asbestos, inadequate ventilation, and degenerating structural features.

GOVERNMENTAL POLICIES AND AGENCIES

There is probably no type of family on which governmental policies have had such a dramatic impact as the never-married single-parent family. A confusion of aims and contrasts between punitive and supportive policies marked the period from World War II through 1996. A general concern for the vulnerability of the single-parent family led to the establishment of the AFDC program. In addition, the establishment of the Medicaid health care program was aimed particularly at vulnerable young families. A variety of other programs, such as federal food stamps, public or subsidized housing, WIC, and Head Start, also respond to the needs of the vulnerable young family frequently headed by a single parent.

Although the intent of a number of these policies was to provide support for young families, the policies were frequently flawed in implementation or in design. Thus separate application and authorization offices were frequently created for each separate governmental program. Young families frequently had to go to a number of different offices to apply for benefits, and regulations were frequently discouraging to family stability. In addition, from 1980 to 1992, decreases in funding made them unavailable for many families that were previously eligible.

Public schools often expelled unmarried high school students from attendance or provided them with a homebound special education service. This meant that the young mother was immediately cut off from active involvement with other young people pursuing education, and from the support and positive resources of many aspects of the educational system.

In 1993 the National Commission on Children charged the welfare system with discouraging employment, family formation, and stability. The AFDC program did not allow for cost-of-living adjustments, and states were permitted to establish their own award levels for eligible clients. The welfare reform legislation continues a pattern of state and local control of benefit levels and ancillary program models. The national impacts have been dramatic in the numbers of families receiving welfare. Between 1996 and 2005, the United States experienced a 57 percent decrease in the number of families receiving welfare. Yet simultaneously other parts of the "safety net" for families—notably Medicaid and food stamps—have increased by 50 percent (Wolf, 2006).

The policies of the 1980s and 1990s included a concerted effort to require young mothers to enter education or job training, which frequently led to minimum wage work. The goal was to give girls some goals, as well as skills, for their lives. The TANF program specifies that only 20 percent of a state's allocation can be to individuals in vocational training or to teen parents in high school or GED programs. A number of states have eliminated college education as an option for TANF recipients, thus placing a limit on the kind of employment a recipient may obtain. After a review of school-based programs for teen parents, Stephens, Wolf, and Batten (2003) concluded that services that are designed to be more comprehensive and provide broader visibility and access for young parents are necessary in order to improve parent and child outcomes. Additional support for young parents may be needed for self-sufficiency to be a realistic goal.

A special provision of the welfare reform legislation was an incentive for states to reduce illegitimacy rates. Twenty million dollars were set aside for five states that achieved the greatest reduction in births to single parents, without increased abortions. This policy was clearly initiated as "profamily" and represents a strong concern for single-parent dependent households. It also requires accurate data on pregnancies and abortions.

KINSHIP NETWORKS AND INTERACTIONS

Among strong and well-functioning never-married single-parent families, the importance of extended friends and families cannot be overestimated. Young mothers frequently report that they survived the adjustment to parenthood only because of grandparent and other extended family members' support.

A clear message of the celebration of parenthood is given by many of these young families. In fact, in Williams's (1991) interview study of young African American mothers, almost all of the subjects reported not wanting pregnancies but being delighted with birth and infants. They indicated a positive socialization toward parenthood and a delight in parent–child bonding. Many young unmarried mothers describe the importance of the affection received from their children and celebrate the joy of parenting.

This desire to receive affection from a child has historically been of concern to some social service professionals. In extreme, this relationship is labeled a "role reversal" in that a young parent may be seeking love, affection, and stability from a child. A family system that demands loyalty, affection, and stability from a child can jeopardize the stability and development of both child and mother, especially when the child is unable to fulfill these needs.

If we are concerned about the stability and development of the young single-parent family, we need to encourage the support and services provided to both children and adults by their kinship network. As Furstenberg et al. (1987) argue, the presence of extended-family support to adolescent parents enhances the development of their children in the preschool years. This support in the family environment probably has no public service substitute. Hetherington (1997) summarized a number of studies by stating that teenage parents show successful outcomes for themselves and their children based on key protective factors: social support from grandmothers and extended family, completion of education resulting in stable employment, and a stable relationship with a partner. This finding was reinforced by DeLeire and Kalil (2001), who found that teens living with their single mother and at least one grandparent had developmental outcomes as good as and often better than those living in married-couple families.

CHANGE AND ADAPTATION

The major societal concerns about never-married single-parent-headed families relate to the vulnerability of youth. The feminization of poverty is illustrated by the fact that a female-headed household is six times more likely to live below the poverty line than a two-parent family. Furthermore, of never-married mothers who received welfare benefits, almost 40 percent remained on public assistance for 10 years or longer. Among Whites, daughters of single parents are 53 percent more likely to marry as teenagers, 164 percent more likely to have a premarital birth, and 92 percent more likely to be divorced. Sixty percent of single White mothers and 80 percent of single Black mothers receive no support from fathers of their children, according to a study done in the late 1980s (Children's Defense Fund, 1987).

The Furstenberg et al. (1987) 20-year longitudinal study of mothers who became parents in adolescence makes several clear statements about the resiliency of the human spirit. Approximately two thirds of the mothers, 20 years later, were maintaining economic independence and had achieved a sense of economic stability that was comfortable. Through a variety of personal challenges, they had acquired education, limited their subsequent childbearing, and gained self-confidence. Two areas of long-term struggle and adaptation are noteworthy. The children born to these adolescent parents struggled for their own academic achievement and balance during their early years (Pianta, Lopez-Hernandez, & Ferguson, 1997). One interpretation would be that although adults can assimilate lessons and reverse the negative effects of earlier life events, their ability simultaneously to protect and guide their children may be compromised.

A second finding of the Furstenberg et al. (1987) study is that young women who became parents in adolescence had discouraging subsequent relationships with men. The majority of the women in the study had a series of conflictive and time-limited relationships with men who did not become sources of stability in their lives. One wonders how much their attitudes help shape the acceptance of male partners or their ability to negotiate a stable relationship. Williams's (1991) teenage mothers were generally not interested in marriage and preferred to be independent, even when men asked to be economic and legal partners.

In a life dominated by poverty and uncertain economic security, adults who are not able to bring successful employment to the marriage find it difficult to form enduring unions. Many family-life scholars have suggested that an appropriate adaptation to these circumstances is to strengthen parent–child bonds and increase the informal family networking that helps coparent children in the extended family network.

One particularly difficult issue in the adaptation of single-parent families is the supervision of the young adolescent and the repetition of the early single-parent pattern in the next generation. Youth workers frequently describe the lack of positive role models and social organizations within neighborhoods with high poverty and unemployment (Murray, 1997). Without significant and powerful bonded relationships with churches and youth-serving organizations, it is difficult to find adequate supervision and alternative activities to premature sexual experimentation. Williams's (1991) study of young teenage mothers reported almost universally a lack of attention or supervision from their parent generation during their late elementary and early junior high years. Half of them had working mothers who didn't arrive home until hours after public school was dismissed.

The Guttmacher Institute studies have reported that the most frequent environment in which a young adolescent becomes pregnant is in her own home with no adult supervision (McAdoo & McAdoo, 1985). The finding from the National Study of Family Growth (Lancashire & Smith, 1997) of an increased use of contraceptives is promising. However, human service workers need to be alert to the needs of the most vulnerable teenagers.

Teenage mothers frequently report their own parents' ambivalence upon discovering their daughters' pregnancy. Although many in the grandparent generation desire education and economic success for their children, they also wish to convey to their young people their delight in parenting and their commitment to rearing children. They tend to encourage their pregnant unmarried daughter to bear and keep the infant as a validation of the grandparents' own earlier choices. In a community with few avenues for declaring accomplishments and strengths, becoming pregnant, bearing a child, and accepting parental responsibilities are often among the few roles open to young women. Rhein et al.'s (1997) study of teen fathers reported the fathers as less interested in having the child but less likely than the mothers to consider abortion.

In contrast to a 1950s attitude of alarm and a deterministic elimination of options for the adolescent unmarried female, today's options are more numerous and seem to be initially supportive of parenthood. Some political analysts suggest that this amounts to a tacit approval of unmarried parenting and a removal of societal controls on personal, self-indulgent, destructive behaviors. The never-married single-parent family is most often headed by a woman in poverty and out of the mainstream of education. Whether or not the development of children and parents continues in a positive direction depends implicitly on the ability of professionals in many systems to support them and their informal networks with appropriate service (Mylod, Whitman, & Borkowski, 1997).

HELPFUL TECHNIQUES FOR SERVING TEENAGE SINGLE-PARENT FAMILIES

One vital consideration in serving the never-married single-parent family is to understand the social-class and ethnic-group variation represented by these families. In addition, it is extremely important to distinguish between the programs in support of child and youth development in these families and the programs to support the adults (Nelson & Landsmen, 1992). A number of programs contain elements that blame the children or discriminate against them in the provision of services, based on a moral judgment of their parents' behavior. Repeatedly, research has illustrated that the most successful programs in assisting single-parent families in further development of their own skills—and those of their children—rest on services that respect the needs of each generation. Research with single-parent families is now emphasizing the resiliency aspects of their strengths, a positive direction for helping professionals.

According to Lizabeth Schorr (1988), social scientists and service providers already know what elements make for positive programs in support of vulnerable young families. The needs are for funding, service organizations, and positive professional attitudes and roles. Schorr relates that programs responsive to these families have the following characteristics:

1. They are flexible. They have rules that can be adjusted or changed as necessitated by the need to serve families.
2. They are comprehensive. They provide services for education, employment, child care, health, and the like, all in one agency or in close proximity and in a cooperative framework.
3. They are respectful of individual family needs and they create trust and partnerships between families and professionals.
4. They are adaptable, resilient, and able to change services and create new linkages among new service providers.
5. They stress that children are nested in families and family preservation is a strong goal.

These five qualities are very similar to the principles for empowering families presented in Chapter 3. They demand that each of us use our own powers of observation and criticism to increase the effectiveness of programs with which we work. These qualities also mark the programs in progressive states, such as Oregon, where a creative number of options are available to TANF clients.

Furstenberg et al. (1987) make an important point about professionals who work with young never-married parents. Frequently these service relationships are time limited, such as prenatal health care or preschool services. Professionals in such settings do not benefit from the opportunity to see these young parents over time and observe their continued development. Biases and limited information about the strengths of these families may limit these professionals' effectiveness in offering appropriate services.

Family-life professionals encourage researchers and service providers to ask families directly about the meaning of events or resources in their lives. Frequently professionals view families from their own experience and fail to understand messages from families themselves. Scarr (1989) commented that each of us is "biased by the human tendency to seek facts which are congruent with our own previous beliefs." Dilworth-Anderson, Burton, and Turner (1993) comment that there is no value-free work, particularly with other human beings. Marital relationships, parenting relationships, and gender and family relationships are all viewed through our own perceptions of what we think is important, what we ask about, and what we are interested in.

First Meeting

When first meeting a single-parent family, all we know about that family is that there is a parent and a child and no current legal marriage. We do not know how many fictive kin are associated with this family and are providing ongoing service and support. *Fictive kin* are defined as nonblood kin who, in relationships, define themselves as part of the family. This is a very strong pattern in Native American cultures, and clear examples of this are seen in African American communities. Hetherington (1997) reports that cohabitation now accounts for a quarter of all births to single moms, and professionals need to recognize these relationships. In 2002, 4 percent of all children lived with a parent or parents who were cohabiting (Fields, 2003), and 33 percent of children living with single fathers and 11 percent living with single mothers also lived with their parent's partner.

With regard to a single mother and child, we do not know how many significant men are providing enduring and supportive models to the child. We do not know how many neighborhood acquaintances assist in providing transportation, clothing, and food as needed for this family. We do not know if the parent has an affectionate and ongoing relationship with the child's other biological parent. In short, we have much to learn!

Our basic goals should be to create an atmosphere of inclusiveness for other significant adults in the child's life and parent's life, and to assist the parent in acquiring resources to meet their needs. Depending on the professional role we play with this family, such as a teacher, social worker, health practitioner, or juvenile justice professional, we need to look carefully at our own biases toward this family type. We need to assume diversity within this family type and reinforce every possible strength.

Establishing Partnerships

If a family enters a program you supervise, you need to indicate the program's objectives, engage the family members in a discussion of their own objectives, and negotiate, where possible, for shared objectives. You should assume there are serious economic and time constraints on the part of the single parent, and make certain that your requests do not place such an undue burden on the parent as to drive that parent away. For the child or youth you are serving, you need to provide maximum stability, opportunities to bond with positive role models, and opportunities to participate in meaningful decisions about his or her activities or goals.

Professionals should find ways to encourage single parents to learn from each other and to provide supportive networks in group meetings, telephone trees, social activities, and informal meetings. The positive results of the Head Start Parent Advisory Councils are well known to professionals working in that program. The opportunity that Head Start parents have to participate in decision making for their children, to join in a community effort at supporting educational programs, and to learn skills as decision makers has provided many parents with an initiation into job training, education, and more economic independence.

Compassionate Observations

Observations of the child or youth and the single parent need to be made compassionately and with an understanding of the personality characteristics of the child and the parent. Evidence that a child or youth is extremely compliant and supportive to the parent may indicate that a great deal of meaning for that child is vested in being a partner and support to the parent. Within limits this is a positive strength for that child. The parent may need assistance and encouragement to engage in adult activities, to enhance strengths, and to find other adult relationships that are reinforcing and supportive.

In a balanced view, however, new adult relationships, such as a new romantic partner or new close friends, can limit the power of a child who was a strong partner to a single parent. Helping the child find friends and motivating experiences for his or her own development is an important part of our ability to serve this family effectively. A child or youth who has had major family responsibilities can be encouraged to relax and enjoy learning, and to take leadership positions in other appropriate group settings.

Seeking Information

In gathering information about the family, we should be clear about the reasons for needing that information and be respectful of the family's need to withhold information. Thus questions such as "How do you handle this in your family?" or "What do you want for your son or daughter?" enable you to obtain information to help you form a strong partnership with the parents.

Encouraging a single parent to bring friends, unmarried partners, and other family members to events in your agency or school is extremely family supportive. Many parents assume only the legal parents of the child can participate in a school or agency event. Encourage children and youth to talk about who is important to them, and encourage parents to bring these people who are part of the child's ongoing life. Setting up barriers between a school or agency and the family simply encourages a child to show family loyalty by rejecting an organization's activities or services.

Make certain that you can provide information on other opportunities, such as organizations that are supportive of single parents; churches, synagogues, and other religious groups that have single-parent activities or programs; cooperatives that share child care, clothing, or exchange services; transportation systems; and a variety of free public services. Professionals working with young single-parent families frequently indicate that the parents may not know about available parks, libraries, youth-serving agencies, or may not feel they are eligible to use these services. A supportive family activity can be to gather a group of parents and attend some activity in a community agency.

Including Legal and Biological Parents

When offering parenting classes or education, be certain to include both the biological parent or legal guardian and other significant members of the child's household. Stress the sharing and participation aspects of parent groups. Ask the parents what challenges they would like to discuss.

Young parents often need assistance in practicing such skills as how to read aloud to their child, how to engage a child in conversations about TV "realities," how to enjoy play with their child, and how to set appropriate limits. Professionals who work with homeless families observe that many parents cannot engage in cooperative play with their own children until they, as adults, have had a protected time to enjoy the toys or activities themselves before interacting with their children. Such observations reflect the more limited experiences and economic means of many young parents. Professionals serving these young families are in key positions to develop partnerships with parents. After parents gain experience and confidence from a relationship with you, they will be able to seek services from the various helping agencies.

✦ CONCLUSIONS

Professionals serving the never-married single-parent family need to learn about the variations among these families, understand their own personal biases, and institute changes in language, practices, and service that empower the parent and nurture the child. When these families are in the early stages of development, what they learn about the sensitivity and skills of professionals can influence relationships for many years.

Professionals can help increase their sensitivity by understanding that parents often lack time and money. Encouraging linkages between parents in similar circumstances helps develop supporting groups. Exchanging information about services and opportunities can assist development. Encouraging personnel in agencies or services to collaborate in providing information, joint training, or educational events would be helpful to families.

Including additional significant adults related to the family in conferences and celebrations around your agency's services is an important acknowledgment of the variety of relationships that nurture both children and adults. Any educational or social services plan for an individual child or family should develop partnerships between professionals, families, and other people parents describe as significant and meaningful to their development (Raisner, 1997).

It is important to be respectful of the anger and frustration of a single-parent family. Many societal messages are critical, and much public debate concentrates on "what to do" about single parents. In some states or counties, TANF regulations may be quite punitive or rigid. For children and adults in these families to make progress toward their goals, they must use their energy to appreciate their own uniqueness and obtain developmentally supportive services. Professionals who are respected and trusted can become helpful partners as these families work hard toward their goals. In many cases, these families feel that the mainstream social institutions have denied their need for attention, supervision, education, and support. In the twenty-first century, the problems facing this group of families must be solved.

✦ STUDY QUESTIONS

1. State societal trends that contribute to the numbers of teenage single-parent families.
2. Review the positions of political leaders on the matter of teen childbirth over the last 40 years.
3. As you study the chapter, notice the economic factors that appear to contribute to the stress in teenage families. Make a comprehensive list of the statements you find.
4. Review different attributes and roles taken by fathers of infants born to teenagers.
5. How does the ecological framework help explain both the stressors and the support available to teenage parents?
6. Describe the changes in public assistance to teenage parents, from welfare to temporary assistance.

✣ APPLICATIONS

1. Contact the local school district to learn if there is a special program for pregnant and /or parenting students. If so, arrange a visit and interview instructors and some students regarding the goals of the program, any special curriculum in use, services for fathers as well as mothers, child care, and so on.

2. Assign a class member or members to review advertisements in the local newspaper or the yellow pages to identify groups that offer programs for single parents. Call the organizers of the programs, and inquire about the age requirement for attendance, the cost, the objectives of the program, and any qualifying characteristics such as divorced, never married, and so on. Report to the class on the availability of these support groups and educational programs. Include an impression of whether the never-married parent is welcome and served well in your community.

3. Make an appointment to talk with the Medicaid prenatal clinic supervisor or health practitioner who provides the majority of care to unwed adolescent mothers in your community. Ask the clinic director about the need for additional services or volunteers. If possible, observe a clinic setting and interview a client about her satisfaction with services in the community.

4. Contact a local family and consumer science teacher, family life teacher, or family sociology teacher at a junior or senior high school. Inquire as to whether a family studies class or marriage class includes information on the unmarried parent. Volunteer to present a program for the class, including a presentation by a young unmarried parent. Contact the local Medicaid prenatal clinic, the WIC clinic, or high school guidance counselors for the name of an appropriate young mother who would be willing to talk with other students about her experiences.

5. Attend an organized meeting of a young mothers' support group, if permission is given by the group organizer or chairperson. Be respectful and observant, and indicate to the members that you would like to understand more about the ways they are supportive to each other and what some of their goals are for their children. Talk with the group's organizer about the variation and special qualities of members in the group.

6. Contact the children youth and family committee chair in your state legislature. Find out whether or not there is an ongoing review for legislative proposals that impact the young family. Follow a piece of legislation through the process of committee hearings to presentation, or interview members of the legislature about how current state legislation impacts young unmarried parents.

7. Interview a member of the state or county Health and Human Services Department or Social Services Department about the department's policy toward young unmarried parents. Inquire about the integration of services between their department and others, and ask for a list of the three most important needs of the young unmarried parent in your state.

8. Make an appointment with the principal or counselor in a local high school in your community to talk about services available to unmarried parents in your school district. Inquire about medical services, family-planning information, parenting education, self-study or alternative forms of education, GED classes, vocational training, child care, and transportation.
9. Make an appointment with the manager of a local public housing family site to talk about services available to unmarried parents. If possible, visit an apartment and tour the facility. Look for evidence of parent support groups, safe play areas for children, parent education opportunities, and ties with the wider community.

✦ MEDIA RESOURCES

Kids raising kids [Video, 45 minutes]. Charleston, WV: Cambridge Educational.

Moyers, W. (1986). *The vanishing family: Crisis in black America* [Television broadcast]. CBS Special Reports.

Teen parent TV news [28 minutes]. Los Angeles: Churchill Media. (1992). Available from Clearvue & SVE, www.clearvue.com/video/, 1-800-253-2788].

✦ KEY INTERNET RESOURCES

Adolescent Parent Network
www.moappp.org/projects/adolescentparentnetwork.asp

Care of Adolescent Parents and Their Children
www.aap.org/policy/re0020.html

Census Brief—Children with Single Parents
www./divorced/single/grandparents

Guttmacher Institute
www.agi-usa.org./pubs/fbteensex.html

National Center for Health Statistics
www.cdc.gov/nchswww/releases/98facts/98sheets/tnbrth96.html

Facts in Brief: Teen Sex and Pregnancy
www.agi-usa.org./pubs/fb teensex.html

TeenwithChild.com
www.teenwithchild.com

Young Moms
www.youngmoms.org

United States Department of Commerce. U.S. Census Bureau
www.census.gov/Press-Release/cb97-73.html

✤ ORGANIZATIONS

Single Parent Resource Center, 1165 Broadway, Room 504, New York, NY 10001, (212)
     951-7030, ext. 231.
Sisterhood of Black Single Mothers, 1360 Fulton Street, Suite 413, Brooklyn, NY 11216, (718)
     638-0413.

✤ FURTHER READING

Robinson, B., & Barrett, R. (1988). *Teenage fathers*. Lexington, MA: Lexington Books.

11

Divorced Single-Parent Families

⇥ Key Concepts

- Bifocal Family
- Binuclear Family
- Division of Property
- Grieving Period
- Joint Legal Custody
- Joint Physical Custody
- Legal Issues
- No-Fault Divorce

The time in my life when I felt most supported and had the strongest group of good friends was during the years in which I was a divorced parent.

—Remarried parent

Most of us have experienced one of our closest friends or neighbors announcing that she or he is getting a divorce if we ourselves have not had the experience. Like many, we may admit not realizing that our friend's problems were "that bad." With 50 percent of present-day marriages heading for the divorce courts, divorce is a phenomenon that occurs in many families. About two thirds of divorces involve children (U.S. Census Bureau, 1995). Thus divorce complicates life for many children and youth.

All newly single parents have many adjustments and decisions to make while carrying on with the business of rearing their children. These families, whose situation is different from those never-married single parents discussed in the previous chapter, frequently are seen by helping professionals.

Most Americans have an unrealistic understanding of the variation and incidence of divorced single-parent families. By definition, this group experiences major changes in household structure. These changes often attract attention from many family members and friends, especially during the initial adjustment period. Maccoby and Mnookin (1992) comment that four relationships must be changed in divorce—parental, spousal, economic, and legal. When a family social group changes, this movement ripples through many different relationships in the environment.

HISTORICAL BACKGROUND

The divorced single-parent family represents an alarming situation to many citizens for both relationship and economic reasons. In the earlier part of American history, the most frequent cause of family disruption was the death of a parent. In fact, not until 1900 were there even any legal grounds and procedures for divorce in the United States. As medical care and diagnostic services improved, fewer parents died during their children's early years. By 1974 divorce eclipsed death as the leading cause of disruption of family life. Divorce causes a relationship loss for which many people have only the model of death, or a complete separation, for guidance. As our experiences with divorce have accumulated, it is clear that the economic strength of the family is often dramatically changed after divorce, and relationships can become more complex and ambiguous.

NO-FAULT DIVORCE

In 1970 California led a reform of legislation with a new no-fault divorce statute that eliminated the necessity of blame and fault in the legal proceedings. This change has also had a profound impact on the financial settlements between the divorcing parties. Before 1970 the so-called victim or injured party in a divorce usually received compensation through a financial settlement. Once no-fault divorce, with its assumptions of rationality and partnership, became the norm, the couple's assets were often divided equally, with unanticipated consequences for both men and women.

PROPERTY SETTLEMENT

When family property is equally divided following divorce, one spouse may be disadvantaged. This occurs because of the way marital property may be defined and distributed, and because of differing standards for awarding alimony and child support. Some divorce scholars believe that if one spouse has not been employed outside the home, or has a much lower earning capacity than the other, then that person is entitled to some of the ex-spouse's earning power. This recommendation reflects the understanding that both partners have, in fact, invested in and created the family asset, that is, the earning capacity of one of the spouses. The 1984 child support amendments to the Social Services Act required each state to establish by October 1987 guidelines for judges to use in determining child support awards. The controversy since then illustrates our societal confusion over divorce and public versus private responsibilities to nurture children. After the federal reforms took effect, about a third of all states used a simple "percentage of income" model that leaves out any possibility of earning power calculations or recognition of actual need.

In the mid-1990s, the "Wisconsin Model" of child support became a centerpiece for national child support and welfare reform efforts. This model and the writings of

Robert Williams have driven many of the decisions in child support cases, both for welfare clients and others (Gay & Palumbo, 1998). The great weakness of the model is an inaccurate understanding of child support expenses by using only household spending data from the National Consumer Expenditure Surveys. In addition, there are no considerations given to the ability of either parent to pay and the unique situation of an individual child or family. Gay and Palumbo (1998) suggest that new detailed research data are needed to support award decisions. Furthermore, they suggest fundamental laws of child support should make these assumptions:

1. Child support is for the care and maintenance of children.
2. Both parents should contribute to support.
3. All relevant information may affect the size of the award.

Alimony is a protection for the divorced spouse who has not been employed in the marketplace and is still responsible for family assets and obligations under no-fault divorce law. However, divorce awards since 1970 have tended to reduce or eliminate alimony awards from most settlements or dramatically decrease them to short-term "transitional" awards. This is a particularly difficult situation for an older woman coming out of a long traditional marriage and possessing minimal skills for employment.

CHILDREN'S EXPERIENCE IN DIVORCE

Child support has generally not been awarded at adequate levels to maintain child care, housing, food, and clothing. The Children's Defense Fund reported in 1992 that none of the 50 states provided a high enough allotment in Aid to Families with Dependent Children (AFDC) payments to keep families out of poverty. In 1999, 58.7 percent of divorcing parents had child support agreement, but only 46.2 percent of those received the full amounts ordered. This was, however, an increase from only 36.9 percent in 1993 who received the full amount. Of the 41 percent of divorcing parents in 1999 with no child support agreements, reasons most often cited were that they felt no need to make legal arrangements, they felt the other would not pay, or they felt the other parent was providing all he or she could. As a result of these transitions, many children in divorced-parent households enter the ranks of poverty (Table 11.1). As a group, women's income drops 30 percent following divorce, and 40 percent of divorcing women lose more than half of their family incomes. The poverty rate for parents receiving all their child support was 15.5 percent in 1999. Those receiving partial payment had a poverty rate of 25 percent, and those who received none of the amount due them had a poverty rate of 30 percent, as did parents with no support awards (Grall, 2002). Men, in general, experience an average income *increase* of 15 percent partially because they provide less support to their children (Maccoby & Mnookin, 1992).

Table 11.1   Economic Status of Children Under 15 Years Old, Four Months Before and Four Months After Parental Separation

Measurement of well-being	Before	After
Average monthly per capita income	$ 549	$ 436
Average monthly family income*	$2,435	$1,543
Average monthly household income*	$2,461	$1,546
Income/needs ratio*	2.4	1.8
Percentage whose mother worked full time, all weeks	33	41
Percentage whose mother did not work at all	43	31
Percentage reporting weekly hours worked	60	72
Average weekly hours of those with hours	34	37
Percentage in poverty	19	36
Percentage receiving child support	16	44
Percentage receiving AFDC	9	18
Percentage receiving food stamps	10	27

* The income-to-needs ratio is a ratio of family income to the poverty threshold. An income-to-needs ratio below 1.0 denotes a standard of living below the poverty level. Household income aggregates income of all persons residing with the child in a given month. Family income excludes income from persons unrelated to the child.

Source: Adapted from U.S. Census Bureau, *The economics of family disruption 1998* (SB 91-10). Washington, DC: U.S. Government Printing Office.

During the 1950s only 11 percent of all children reaching age 18 had experienced the divorce of their parents. Beginning in the mid-1960s, a rapid increase in the divorce rate culminated in the highest rate of 23 divorces per 1,000 marriages in 1979. In 1991 there were 21 divorces per 1,000 marriages. During the 1990s in most states the marriage and divorce statistics narrowed so the number of marriages per year is practically equal to the number of divorces per year.

Differences in ethnic group experiences with divorce are obvious from the data. The number of African American children who cope with divorce is lower than for Hispanic or White children because the African American marriage rate is lower. Black women are less likely to marry by age 30, less likely to move from cohabitation to marriage, and more likely to have cohabitation disrupted than other women (Bramlet & Mosher, 2002). In the 1990s the typical single African American mother was never married; the typical single White mother was a divorcee. Because divorce is more often experienced in the White community, and because children are more likely to be born into marriages in the White community, most divorced mothers are White. Since 1960 about two thirds of the increase in White single-parent households was due to divorce. By 1991, 70 percent of White children residing with a single parent lived with a divorced or separated single parent (National Commission on Children, 1993).

As the demographics of the United States change with immigration and differential birthrates, the number of children among ethnic minorities is climbing rapidly. Only since 1990 has the National Center for Health Statistics recorded births based on the mother's race and ethnicity. Prior to that time, there was confusion in the reporting of the child's ethnic group, depending on the mother's choice or on information filled out on different records. Of the 3.9 million children born in the United States in 2000, 63 percent were non-Hispanic White, approximately 11 percent were non-Hispanic Black, 19 percent were Hispanic, and 3 percent were Asian or Pacific Islander (Bachu & O'Connell, 2001). These statistics point to differences in the percentage of ethnic and racial minorities today in the United States as compared to a decade ago. In a 1994 paper, McLanahan reported on the differential effects of divorce on child outcomes in non-White populations. She reported that school failure is increased with family disruption by 24 percentage points among Hispanics, 17 percentage points among Whites, and 13 percentage points among Blacks. Family disruption also raised the risk of school dropout by 150 percent for White children, 100 percent for Hispanic children, and 76 percent for Black children.

SOCIOCULTURAL FOUNDATIONS

When parents divorce, the resulting separate households often experience great contrasts in resources and support from social systems. One of the most visible public debates about divorce is the assessment of whether a divorce enhances the development of any of the family members (see Ingrassia, 1993). Critics of divorce argue on moral, religious, and developmental grounds that children deserve and need sustained relationships in a unit that socializes them consistently throughout their childhood. In addition, they argue that the transitions into divorce and the likelihood of remarriage or cohabitation of the parents mean that different values are communicated to children at different times in their development. Most child developmentalists agree that consistency and security of structure are important foundations for healthy development. Although 20 percent of divorces occur because of spousal violence or extreme marital conflict, an increasing number are related to dissatisfaction with the economic and relationship aspects of marriage (Fine, 1993). Obtaining accurate data on the amount of physical and emotional abuse that often precedes divorce is very difficult. A number of partners separate but never divorce because of religious or cultural values surrounding divorce or limited access to economic resources, in spite of emotional abuse. In 1995 data showed that the probability a separation would move through legal divorce within three years was significantly influenced by income, education, and parenting status of the individuals as well as poverty rate and unemployment rate in communities (Bramlett & Mosher, 2002).

Research (Stewart, 1998) with 160 Boston families who were undergoing divorce showed a very direct relationship between a child's well-being and the psychological well-being of their parents. When divorce put an end to a highly conflictual marriage and increased the stability and balance of their parents, children benefited. But children younger than 9 years of age and those drawn into their parents' hostility were highly stressed.

Divorce has been made more feasible by the increasing economic opportunities for women, the encouragement of personal evaluation of the companion values of the marriage relationship, and the availability of birth control measures. Although 15 percent of divorces are initiated when one of the partners pursues another relationship, many divorces occur because of disengagement and dissatisfaction in the emotional exchange of marriage (Gigy & Kelly, 1992). The desire to have a marriage partner fulfill companion, friend, and sexual roles, as well as economic and reproductive ones, has caused more adults to feel dissatisfied with marriage and thus leave more readily.

With the prevalence of divorce in the United States, many parents are in the process of evaluating the merits of continuing or dissolving a marriage. As Whitehead (1993) comments, frequently the advantages for adults in the family may be in contrast to or in conflict with the advantages to the children. Overall, those values that encourage divorce are usually values of independence, self-actualization, and reduction of conflict. In addition, a number of men's rights groups comment on the American bias against the importance of men in their children's lives (Leving & Dachman, 1997), which also tends to encourage divorce.

Status

In general, the status of divorced parents has strong economic and moral interpretations. Among some elements of society, divorce represents a failed relationship, and a divorced person's status is lowered immediately. In other situations, a divorced person's status is directly related to the economic and employment status of each of the partners. At the personal level, divorced persons often comment about the loss of social support and stature. Much conflict surrounds the selection of enduring adult relationships after a divorce. Fear that divorce could happen to them as well often arises among friends of the divorced. Rands reported that approximately 40 percent of an individual's social support system disappears after a separation or divorce (Buehler & Legg, 1993).

Gender Differences

One important influence on changes in status reported by divorced persons involves gender. Because approximately 90 percent of divorced people who retain physical custody of the children are women, and only 10 percent are men, there are important differences among divorced parents' custody experiences (DeMaris & Greif, 1992). Many of these differences relate specifically to the role and status that women, in contrast to men, have in this society. One study showed that women with custody experience a 73 percent drop in their standard of living in the year following a divorce. In contrast, the same study found men showing a 42 percent increase in their standard of living a year after a divorce (Gottleib, Gottleib, & Slavin, 1988). Because the standard of living has clear status implications, men and women often find themselves with very different levels of status after divorce. In 2001 married-couple households had a median income of $60,471, female-headed households with no spouse present had a median income of $28,142, and male-headed households had a median income of $40,715 (DeNavas-Walt & Cleveland, 2002).

Racial Differences

There are also important status differences by race after divorce. Zinn (1992) reports that much poverty is the result of already poor two-parent households breaking up with inadequate resources to create two households.

Three quarters of Whites who become poor after divorce were not in that category prior to divorce. In contrast, of the African Americans who were poor after a divorce transition, two thirds had been poor before. These data are important to keep in mind because divorce scholars are concerned that policymakers believe divorce and single-parent households are to blame for poverty, rather than understanding the influence of social class and race in determining economic status for all families.

Increased Choices in Families

Most people understand that part of the rise in the divorce rate is related to increasing freedom and choice available to women in the United States. Availability of contraceptives; smaller families; influence of the women's movement; examples of friends, siblings, and parents who have divorced; and the increasing employment of women create more independence, freedom, and choice. Moreover, as we saw in the previous section, the economic realities of many communities have often deterred women from entering or remaining in a marriage that offers little economic security. Researchers document that the higher a woman's income, the more apt she is to seek divorce as a solution to an unsatisfactory marriage (Applewhite, 1997).

These choices may be reflected in the data that show 11 percent of children living with a single mother and 33 percent of children living with a single father were also sharing the household with the parent's unmarried partner (Fields & Casper, 2002). Undoubtedly, some of these single parents are divorced, and for a variety of reasons, both economic and social, they are choosing not to remarry.

Impact of Divorce on Daughters

The divorce literature is also very clear about the differential impact of divorce on girls, in contrast to boys. Because most children are in the custody of their mothers, and family research often describes the complementary role that mothers and fathers play in family interaction, it should be no surprise that children who live in the custody of their mothers react somewhat differently by gender.

Research findings first suggested that children living with the same-sex parent were happier and more socially competent than those living with the opposite-sex parent (Powell & Downey, 1995). Girls living with divorced mothers tended to see their mother as a model of greater independence and self-determination (Arendell, 1997). However, an age-related "sleeper effect" in the adjustment of girls and boys emerged in later research. Both boys and girls of divorce showed some increase in problems during adolescence (Furstenberg & Teitler, 1994). In a study of the impact of parental participation in welfare reform programs, findings were particularly problematic for adolescents. Whereas preschoolers appeared to be unaffected by their parental participation in welfare reform mandatory programs, school-age children showed higher measure of well-being and achievement in school *if* their parents were able to increase the family income from their program participation. However, adolescents were negatively impacted by parental participation in welfare programs even if family income increased (Schaefer, 2002).

Some studies indicate that preadolescent girls seem to adapt fairly well to divorce, but during adolescence they show higher levels of struggle in relationships with the opposite sex and anger toward fathers. Given the frequent decrease in the economic means of mothers, many daughters observe specific ways their mothers respond to this challenge. Some mothers are able to sustain their standard of living by substituting activities at lower cost, and by bargaining and exchanging goods and services with their friends. These mothers are seen by their daughters as creative and independent. Mothers who feel more victimized and less able to cope with the loss of income give their children a different message.

Women, more than men, are often described as the "kin keepers," responsible for maintaining supportive ties with extended-family members. Women, therefore, are sometimes more able than men to maintain helpful relationships with grandparents or with former in-laws because they were responsible for maintaining these relationships during the marriage (Duran-Aydintug, 1993). In 2000, 3.9 million American family households were multigenerational, most frequently a householder with a child or children and grandchildren. Often the adults in such families are grandmothers with their single daughter and her child or children (Simmons & O'Neill, 2001).

Another gender effect in divorce relates to the fact that 75 percent of divorces are initiated by women (Wallerstein & Kelly, 1980). Because an important part of postdivorce adjustment relates to whether or not the individual was the "surprised spouse," it is likely that fewer women suffer from anger and confusion over why the divorce occurred. However, one of the clearest gender differences after divorce remains the differential level of economic resources.

In a no-fault divorce, a woman may request custody of the children and leave the material objects to the husband. When a division of property is difficult because of joint ownership in a home, a family business, or a farm, the maintenance of the family resources sometimes depends on keeping the property together. Most often the husband is in charge of property, and property judgments have frequently favored men. However, settlements that consider both spouses' investment in the man's career or the employment skills of the woman are frequently more equitable, with the woman receiving enough of a settlement to maintain the family.

Increased Choices for Males

Changing roles for boys, men, husbands, and fathers are emerging also. In the postdivorce single-parent family, the father is usually the parent who lives apart from the children. Although joint custody actions have increased, a great deal of this custody is not physical joint custody. In other words, the divorce decree names both parents as equally responsible for decisions regarding the children, but the residence of the children is basically with only one parent. In their review of divorce judgments, Donnelly and Finkelhor (1993) report that a range of 2 to 16 percent of divorces includes some kind of joint custody. Most children still remain in the custody of their mothers following divorce. In 2000 single-mother families were 26 percent of all families, and single-father families were 5 percent of all families (Fields & Casper, 2002). As income and education level of the divorcing partners increase, joint custody levels also increase.

Fathers are most often in the position of paying some form of child support and of arranging a visitation schedule with their children. Fathers frequently report their distress and confusion about arranging activities for these visits. A feeling of being irrelevant to their child's life or only providing recreation and meals out in restaurants is distressing to men who wish to play a more fully involved parenting role. More than women, men often have to develop new parenting skills. They indicate great distress over access to their children and the need to form new patterns (Dudley, 1996).

The literature suggests that fathers who were involved in all aspects of parenting before the divorce are more apt to have sole or joint custody of the children and are more apt to share or cooperate more fully with the ex-spouse in raising the children. When divorced parents view each other as equal partners, they can create a parenting partnership with communication and decision making that is respectful of each other and their children. Fathers who visit their children on a consistent schedule and are involved in decisions about their lives are more apt to be paying child support regularly (Koball & Principe, 2002).

Early studies suggested that children who rarely saw their fathers exhibited psychological patterns that were neither healthy nor helpful for optimal development. Subsequent research did not support these findings (Bolgar, Sweig-Frank, & Paris, 1995).

Much of the research completed prior to 1975 on the effects of divorce on children was flawed by the assumption that the absence of the father was the most important characteristic of a divorced family with children in the custody of the mother. This is a simplistic interpretation of complex family changes. Many children whose mothers are not married or remarried have ongoing close relationships with friends, uncles, grandfathers, and other significant men. In addition, social-class considerations, particularly income and education, play profound roles in how the family prospers and develops. In most cases, race, education, family processes, and social class are more powerful determinants in predicting outcomes for children than the presence or absence of a man in the home. The quality of the relationship with the custodial parent and the mental health and competence of that parent appear to be the most powerful influences on child outcome (McFarlane, Bellissimo, & Norman, 1995). In data from the national Survey of American Families and Households, it was family process variables rather than specific family structures (single parent, adoptive, stepparent, two-parent, etc.) that predicted positive child and relationship outcomes (Lansford, Ceballo, Abbey, & Stewart, 2001).

Impact of Divorce on Sons

The early divorce literature showed that divorce had a different impact on boys than on girls. This appeared logical, considering that boys were most apt to be in the custody of their mothers. Although sons appeared to be more vulnerable than daughters to the family disruption, this seems to occur only immediately following the divorce. Initially, divorced mothers reported that their sons were more argumentative, angry, and exhibited acting-out behaviors. These boys may have been demanding that their mothers exert more authority and create structures that were previously established and maintained by the father in the home, or they may simply have been showing distress in the dominant social pattern allowed to them as males. Family-life scholars believe that children and youth learn their gender roles from a family that includes both mothers and fathers. This theory of social roles suggests that, without a father in the household, the male child may become disorganized and potentially angry. A girl in a home without a mother may respond with disorganization and rebellion, albeit of a female style.

In Wallerstein and Kelly's (1980) well-known study of divorce, the 15-year follow-up study showed that two thirds of the children had not heard from or seen their fathers in the previous year. Only one in three divorced fathers sees his children once a week or more (Seltzer, 1991), and noncustodial fathers' involvement with their children tends to decline over time (Arendell, 1997). In a study of single mothers who remarried or began cohabiting, both children and mothers reported a decrease in harsh discipline techniques and an improvement in the parent–child relationship (Thomson, Mosley, Hanson, & McLanahan, 2001).

SOCIALIZATION OF CHILDREN

The postdivorce family moves through a process of adjustment to the changing circumstances of their family life. Estimates vary, but some scholars indicate that a fourth to a third of divorced American parents exhibit a high degree of hostility, conflict, and often unsolvable legal disputes over details of custody, child support, visitation, and so forth (Kramer & Washo, 1993). For about a tenth of all divorcing couples, the animosity lasts throughout the growing-up years of all their children (Johnston & Roseby, 1997). During this process, the goals of socialization for the children may be less important than confrontational goals for adults (Brenner, 1993). Donnelly and Finkelhor (1993) report that many joint custody awards are actually bitter agreements following a prolonged or anticipated battle over custody. If joint custody is awarded in a highly conflicted situation, it very rarely works. Joint custody demands more time, negotiation, and discussion between parents than sole custody. Parents with a high degree of conflict are known to negotiate inadequately and exhibit behaviors that cause fear and anxiety among their children (Johnston & Roseby, 1997).

When there are dramatic pre- and postdivorce differences in life circumstances of the children and the parent with custody, socialization goals for everyone must include stability and comfort in the new situation. Children's positive adjustment to divorce is closely related to the lack of conflict in their parents' negotiations and to the stability of their current family life. If they remain in the same home, school, or neighborhood, with access to familiar friends, teachers, and extended-family members, children's adjustment is more positive. If parental conflict is high, the children change residences, dramatic differences in economic support occur, and the custodial parent is highly distressed, then children will logically display behavior that represents their own conflict, anger, and fear.

The research of Hetherington, Cox, and Cox (1985) and Wallerstein and Kelly (1980) documents a developmental process of adjustment to a divorce that takes approximately 24 to 36 months before some stability and resolution of the major life changes and conflicts are likely to occur. In a process that surprises both divorcing partners and friends, there is often a period of some stability 1 year after divorce and then increasing conflict and distress at about 18 months after divorce. This process may reflect an initial ability to handle or cope with crisis, followed by the gradual realization that dramatic grief processes must be completed as the family struggles for a new definition of functioning.

These grief processes include the loss of the idealized harmonious marriage, the change in available resources, the disruption of familiar patterns, and the loneliness of changing social roles with friends and other adults. Many divorced persons deal competently with the immediate demands of finding new housing or creating new family schedules, only later to find themselves overwhelmed with anger at their losses and filled with guilt over failures. This guilt and anger are frequently increased by society's criticism of the divorced family.

Two-Family Model

Ahrons and Rogers (1987) suggest that one of the most positive ways to view the divorced family is as a *bifocal family,* or *binuclear family.* These terms suggest that the child now has two homes, and the family consists of two major centers, whereas previously the family was described as nuclear, or having only one center, or nucleus.

One of the crucial tasks of this bifocal family is to decide whether it is an adult-centered or a child-centered group. Although neither extreme is appropriate for long-term functioning, a number of divorce experts have suggested that much of the law surrounding divorce is linked to the property and legal rights of parents and is not in the best interests of the child.

"Best Interests of the Child" Doctrine

The courts claim to use a doctrine of "best interests of the child," in relation to divorce judgments. There is sharp disagreement between mental health professionals and legal professionals on the meaning of the best interests of the child. Some argue that the best interests doctrine is still used to protect the interests of the father, who is defined as the head of the family and is more often responsible for family property and resources. In addition, some judges have deliberately awarded child custody to fathers with the rationale that this would keep more children off public welfare. Because fathers typically have higher incomes, they are given custody to reduce the need for public tax dollars to support a new single-parent family. However, a more frequent custody pattern is the preference for mothers, as illustrated by Stamps, Kunen, and Rock-Faucheux's (1997) study of judges' beliefs about custody.

A number of states have instituted joint, or shared, custody arrangements, and research is beginning to accumulate on joint legal and physical custody outcomes. Kuhn and Guidubaldi (1997) analyzed the incidence of divorce in states with joint custody awards and concluded that the overall divorce rate was declining in those states where a high number (over 30 percent) of custody awards were joint. Ehrenberg (1996) reviewed studies of custody arrangements and concluded that much research is flawed by considering only the legal definitions of custody and by gathering data from only one parent. In a study of cooperating ex-spouses, Ehrenberg (1996) found that couples had a variety of legal arrangements that did not account for their actual practical arrangements and parenting.

A great deal of support from helping professionals may be needed for fathers seeking to establish sole custody or significant ongoing coparenting responsibility for their children. Scholars who have studied custody and visitation arrangements report that children have a more realistic understanding of their parents' lives when given longer periods of time with the noncustodial parent, instead of just weekends.

When visits with the noncustodial parent are long enough, the parent and child settle into the normal events of that parent's life. If the child stays during vacation for an entire month or a summer, the child is more apt to understand life beyond an entertainment focus. Most child development and family-life specialists agree that longer periods offer a more realistic model for life roles and family behaviors. However, research studies show that less than a third of children of divorce who see their fathers have extended periods of time with them. Noncustodial mothers have more frequent and sustained contact with their children than noncustodial fathers do (Maccoby & Mnookin, 1992).

Role of Grandparents and Others

In the divorced family, the grandparents, uncles, aunts, and former in-laws are important connections for the stability and adjustment of family members. Grandparents in particular have traditionally represented ancestry and unconditional love and support for children. Since 1986, every state in the United States has passed a statute enabling grandparents to petition the courts for the right to visit their grandchildren. These petitions are frequently brought when there is a conflictive divorce and the grandparents are denied access to their grandchildren. The courts use certain guides related to ongoing stability and family relationships prior to divorce in responding to these petitions. Thus, if the grandparents have established significant relationships with the children, or even provided a household for the children during the divorce process, the court is more likely to award them visitation rights (Parnell & Bagbee, 1993). The U.S. Supreme Court ruled on grandparent visitation laws in *Troxel et vir. v. Granville* in 2000. Although the court struck down the Washington State Code that permits visitation of "any person," it cited "duties of a parental nature" and the beneficial nature of grandchild and grandparent relationships and refused to invalidate all grandparent visitation statues (Egan, 2000). In a National Education study of teens and their positive development across different family structures, those living with a single mother and at least one grandparent were developing as well as—and sometimes more positively than—those teens living in married-couple families (DeLeire & Kalil, 2001).

Some researchers have documented that informal relationships within postdivorce families often include regular time spent with former in-laws. It is interesting to note that many divorced parents report that they are often urged by friends and the general public to make a "clean break" or disconnect themselves from all relatives of an ex-spouse. It appears that individual parents use their own personal values and experience as a guide. Those who have had positive relationships with their ex-spouse's relatives often continue to maintain them.

In an interesting study of grandparents and relationships after divorce, Schutter, Scherman and Carroll (1997) found that most grandparents in their study were concerned about inappropriate intrusions into their children's and grandchildren's lives. Most grandparents waited to be asked for assistance and then were very helpful and positive influences in their grandchildren's lives.

Friendly Communications

Johnson (1988) reports that in a sample of middle-class divorced parents, a third of the spouses maintained positive ongoing relationships with ex-relatives. Divorced spouses who maintain an amicable relationship over their parenting responsibilities find that their children are more positive and better adjusted. This is a particularly challenging task for divorced families.

Communication between parents concerning responsibilities for the children needs to take priority over all other family topics. In most families, many things are discussed simultaneously. Discussions about the children's relationships often include references to adult relationships. Keeping such conversations effective and positive for the children's interests is a significant challenge.

Communicating effectively is a learning process for parents involved in divorce. Frequently, grandparents or extended-family members can help with this process by maintaining their relationships with the children and by reassuring them about the connections of the ongoing family traditions.

ECOLOGICAL FACTORS

The environment of the divorced parent changes quite radically following separation and divorce.

Demographics

American families have experienced a dramatic increase in the divorce rate in recent decades. In 2000, there were 12 million one-parent families out of a total of 37 million family groups. Whereas the number of children living with divorced single parents is still greater than with never-married parents, the proportion of children living with never-married parents has increased dramatically. In 2000 the percentage of single-parent families who were never-married householders was 42 percent, 54 percent were divorced or separated single parents, and 0.4 percent were widowed parents (Fields & Casper, 2002). During the 1980s only four states, Connecticut, Nebraska, New Hampshire, and Rhode Island, saw a decline in the percentage of children living in single-parent families. In 2002 only 69 percent of children living in the United States were living with two parents. Twenty-three percent were living with only their mothers, 5 percent lived with only their fathers, and 4 percent were living with neither parent (Fields & Casper, 2002).

One of the reasons for concern about the impact of the divorce experience on children is that we are experiencing a lower percentage of children as a part of the total U.S. population. Every child's optimal development is important to the country as a whole. In 1970 children constituted 34.3 percent of the entire U.S. population. In 2000 they were only 26 percent of the total population and are projected to be 25 percent of the population in 2020. In contrast, citizens over 65 constituted 8 percent of the population in 1950, 13 percent in 2000, and are projected to be 17 percent in 2020 (Fields & Casper, 2002).

In the 1950s, for every person of retirement age who was receiving Social Security benefits, 16 people were employed in the workforce contributing to the system. By 1990 there were only three employed workers for every person in his or her retirement years. Figure 11.1 shows the dramatic difference in the support ratio of children and the elderly projected from 1980 to 2050.

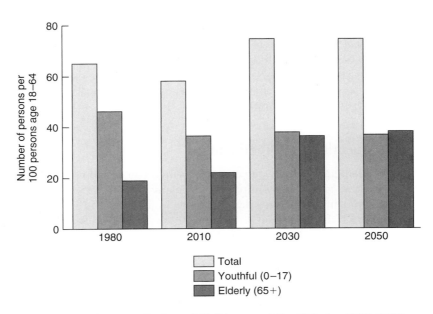

Figure 11.1   Support Ratios of Children and the Elderly: 1980–2050

Source: U.S. Census Bureau, *Age structure of the U.S. population in the 21st century* (SB 1-86). Washington, DC: U.S. Government Printing Office.

Experts predict that 40 to 60 percent of all marriages and 60 percent of all remarriages in the 1990s will end in divorce. Before they turn 18, half of all children living in stepfamilies will see their parents divorce again, and 80 percent will see their divorced fathers remarry. On average, divorced women who remarry spend approximately five years as single parents (Coontz, 1992). When these changes in family structure limit opportunities for optimal development of children and parents, our national human capital resource declines (Mulroy, 1988).

Aesthetics

For years, divorce was not talked about, even in families where it occurred. Thus literature and music about divorce are relatively new phenomena. Most of the literature or music that relates to divorce is autobiographical and portrays divorce as a crisis or life transition. The country and western song popular in the 1970s, "D-I-V-O-R-C-E," is an example of a folk cultural portrayal of an experience that is increasingly common. As talk-show hosts and comedians have included references to divorce in their routines, the increasing universal experience with divorce has been emphasized. There are whole new categories of self-help literature for both women and men following divorce.

In addition, there are now excellent books for children that give a child's view of divorce, from preschool through adolescence. Some outstanding examples of these books include those written exclusively by children. The *Kids' Book About Divorce* (Rofes, 1982) was written by students in a Boston private school classroom, and the author of the videotape *Tender Places* is a 13-year-old boy who experienced divorce (see References and Media Resources at the end of the chapter). One of the important functions of these personal stories is to help people deal with the cognitive and emotional transitions of the divorce process. For many people, the tasks associated with divorce are new and stressful. The arts provide universal ideas and perspectives that can be particularly supportive.

Education and Reeducation

The interaction between education and divorce is complex. Reentering the educational process is extremely important for many women experiencing dependency and economic limitation after divorce. Choices for men and women have been dramatically impacted by the Welfare Reform Act of 1996. The Personal Responsibility and Work Opportunity Reconciliation Act of 1996 (P. L. 104–193) changed the available public safety net for needy families. Where once eligibility was based on income and family size, with a combination of state and federal supports, after July 1, 1997, families faced a time limit to their federal benefits and a much stronger emphasis on creating a plan to move toward self-sufficiency. The new Temporary Assistance to Needy Families (TANF) program, discussed in Chapter 10, was intended to provide parents with job preparation, work, and support services to enable them to enter the workforce in their community. The lifetime limit of 60 months of benefits for any adult in the family began on July 1, 1997.

Although states may exempt 20 percent of their recipient families from the work requirements and the five-year time limit, such states will receive cuts in their federal block grant allocation if they fail to comply with the overall federal limits. The most important change that affects young postdivorced families is that TANF is no longer a government guarantee. It is now temporary assistance to help in job preparation, transportation, and child care according to eligibility criteria enacted by the states. All clients must receive a work skills, work history, and employability analysis, and by 2002, 50 percent of all families and 90 percent of two-parent recipient families had to work 30 to 35 hours per week in each state that is receiving federal support. But federal TANF requirement of work participation after two years of benefits, and community service after two months, is not enforced by penalties.

Of special interest to divorced families is the TANF requirement that child-support enforcement is linked to TANF benefits. Parents who receive cash assistance must participate in the state's program of collecting child-support awards. Noncooperation can result in reduction or termination of all assistance to the family. The federal legislation presumes a "recovery program" for TANF cash awards paid to a single parent where there is a child-support award in place.

States have a great deal of latitude to create their own plans in response to the federal law. Forty-six states have applied for at least one waiver to experiment with benefits. States are able to offer more generous benefits by using their own funds. Therefore, the actual experience of the low-income postdivorce family can be very different from state to state. If a newly divorced custodial parent has few work skills, an immediate effort to plan for education and child care for minor children will be necessary. In contrast to earlier benefit programs, federal money can no longer be used to finance college degrees. States will need to provide their own funds if they wish to encourage recipients' education at that level. In fact, one of the strongest criticisms of the federal legislation is that its intent is employment, no matter how low paying. In other words, TANF aims to reduce welfare rather than poverty. The actual impact on families, particularly those in the transition through divorces, is not yet known. Between 1993 and 2000, the proportion of custodial mothers receiving TANF benefits fell by more than half from 26.5 to 10.5 percent. During the same period of time, the number of custodial parents requesting child-support enforcement assistance fell from 5.8 to 5.2 million. From 2001 to 2002, a recession created hardship for many families, and researchers are concerned that the hardest hit are the "nearly poor," or those families with an income just 125 percent of federal poverty guidelines.

How Divorce Impacts Children's Education

The impact of divorce on children's educational goals and achievements is even more complex. There are clear variations depending on income and parent education level. Children in middle- and upper-class families are more likely to continue their education. Researchers have documented a concern on the part of teachers that family disorganization results in children being less successful in school. Children typically have less access to parents' support in completing homework assignments or their encouragement of academic excellence. Earlier studies associated these negative effects with the absence of a father in the home (Brown & Fox, 1979; Hepworth, Ryder, & Dreyer, 1984).

More recent studies on the impact of divorce have shown that the child's ability, the academic aspirations of the child and the family, and the ethnic group membership are more powerful than family structure in influencing academic achievement. In a statewide study of all sixth through twelfth graders in Rhode Island, the most powerful predictor of academic success was the student's perception of high parental academic expectations, regardless of family structure (Shim, Fellner, & Shim, 2000). Because children spend a great deal of their waking hours in school and are observed by a variety of people in that environment, it is likely that their fears and insecurities concerning the divorce may be exhibited in behavior in the school setting.

In Wallerstein and Kelly's (1980) 10-year follow-up work with children of divorce, two thirds of the original sample of 161 children continued to be successful in academic achievement. In addition, half of the children who originally reacted negatively to the divorce process (a third of the whole sample) had achieved some new sense of balance and academic success. The authors indicate, however, that a number of these originally distressed children were not fulfilling their academic abilities or promise. In addition, funding for higher education for children with divorced parents was problematic, even though this group of families was from middle- and upper-middle social classes.

Educational opportunity for young people is increasingly related to access to economic resources. In states where divorced parents are obligated to pay child support only through age 18, often no arrangements have been made for college costs. Many parents are finding it difficult to bear the costs associated with college attendance. For families who are extremely impoverished following divorce, concerns for minimum income and shelter often take priority over spending for education or health.

The structure and schedules of schools make cooperation difficult for parents without custody who want to stay involved in parenting their children. Notices about meetings or conferences are frequently sent to only one parent, who must then convey invitations to the noncustodial parent.

Preschool and school officials sometimes find themselves conferring with parents separately, especially when divorce processes have been marred by conflict. Divorced parents may be struggling to agree on basic issues relating to their child's development and cannot concentrate on school achievement.

Impact of Religion

Like never-married single parents, many divorced parents find support rather than adverse judgments of their actions in religion. Many pastors, priests, and rabbis are called on to provide support and counseling to parents considering divorce. A number of these professionals, through schooling, have enhanced their own skills at understanding and facilitating decision making around a potential divorce. Religious organizations that have provided support groups for single parents experiencing divorce find that these groups effectively have led to gains for both adults and children. For many divorced people, religion highlights deep conflicts arising from a perceived failure of their own personal choices in demonstrating the ideals of their faith.

Health Care Impacts

Family-planning information is available to divorced parents if they have the knowledge and economic resources to take advantage of this service. Fifty percent of divorced individuals say that a new sexual partner in the first six months following divorce was significant in healing the relationship wounds of the divorce. This finding suggests that many divorced persons are sexually active, and family planning can be an important resource for them.

A serious health problem for divorced parents is access to medical insurance and services for the children and the custodial parent. Although divorce decrees often include the requirement that medical insurance coverage be provided to the children on an ongoing basis, the custodial parent sometimes is left vulnerable. In 1992 about 4 in 10 parents with child-support awards had health insurance benefits included in the award, but about a third of the noncustodial parents required to provide these benefits did not do so (Scoon-Rogers & Lester, 1997). Thus only about 28 percent of parents with child-support awards actually received health benefits. Access to routine preventive health care is particularly a problem for many women who have not worked previously and whose income is sharply reduced following divorce. The 1993 Budget Reconciliation Act required procedures to be established in all states by April 1, 1994, to remove barriers preventing children from obtaining health insurance coverage through their noncustodial parents' insurance (Children's Defense Fund, 1993). After the passage of TANF and more rigorous child-support enforcement efforts, the number of health insurance awards increased. In 2000, 55.8 percent of parents with child-support awards had some health care provisions for their children (Grall, 2002).

The mental health literature documents that major transitions like divorce do impact a person's physical and mental health. Typically, an increase in stomach and digestive ailments, headaches, a susceptibility to upper respiratory infections and intestinal infections, lowered energy, and depression are all physical manifestations of the interaction of life events and health. Both adults and children may be exposed to new health risks, particularly if families change their residence. Studies report that 38 percent of children and their divorced mothers change their residence within the first year following divorce (Booth & Amato, 1992).

Economic Impacts

A husband's level of income and stability at work are among the strongest variables associated with higher marriage stability. This suggests that economic stability lessens the likelihood of divorce. Women who are divorced are particularly vulnerable to lowered economic resources. The proportion of female-headed families in poverty has remained stable at 45 percent for the past 20 years. In contrast, poverty among two-parent families has varied with changes in the economy (National Commission on Children, 1993).

The tremendous variation in the awarding and collecting of child support following divorce has created confusion and inequity in the economic condition of the divorced family unit (Scoon-Rogers & Lester, 1995). A national trend has been to require the recording of the Social Security number of a divorced partner with child-support obligations. Such record keeping would facilitate an integrated nationwide regulatory system of enforcement.

The Family Support Act of 1988 (P. L. 100-485) required states to begin wage withholding for all child-support orders issued after January 1, 1994. States may use the state child-support enforcement agency for collecting and distributing payments, even if the family would not otherwise be served by that agency. States are also permitted to establish a separate mechanism for wage withholding.

Many professionals believed the introduction of joint custody in no-fault divorce processes was one possible way to enhance the legal obligation and ongoing relationship between the parents and children, so that economic support would continue. However, given the level of conflict surrounding many divorces, and the skill needed to negotiate decisions between people living in different houses, joint custody has not proved to be as beneficial as once thought. In fact, some professionals have relabeled "no-fault divorce" laws as "no-responsibility" laws (Coontz, 1992).

Laws to Reduce Economic Impact

P.L. 9838-387, passed in 1984, required that all states establish standards to determine support awards for divorced spouses and children. Sixty-one percent of noncustodial fathers are ordered to pay support, but there is great variation in the enforcement of that support (Fine & Fine, 1992). The Family Support Act of 1988 required that the parents' Social Security numbers be listed on birth certificates of all children whenever this information was available, to enhance the ability of states to collect child-support payments. Child-support enforcement units in state departments of social services have the responsibility to collect awarded support for families who are receiving TANF, but there is great variation in their resources to complete this task.

Strong advocacy for a federal law to provide the mechanism for the Internal Revenue Service to collect child-support payments that are in arrears influenced language in the 1993 budget reconciliation bill. At the present time, the jurisdiction for child-support awards still resides with the court in the state that awarded the divorce. Parents frequently relocate after divorce, and obtaining legal assistance to enforce child-support payments from another jurisdiction becomes too costly for most families to consider. Because 80 percent of divorced fathers remarry, there are also competing demands on the remarried father's income and resources.

Family law specialists are in conflict about whether priority should be given to supporting the children of the previous or the present marriage. Some are disdainful of men who create family after family without supporting them. Numerous studies indicate that noncustodial parents often provide economic resources for their stepchildren with whom they reside before providing economic resources to their biological children not in their custody. These decisions obviously reflect current relationship pressures in new marriages. The topic of child support and the economic viability of divorced parents illustrate the male-oriented bias of many courts. Legal precedents that were designed largely to protect adult property rights are often inappropriate for making decisions related to dependent children and adults in divorced families (see Beld, 2003). The National Congress for Fathers and Children has developed a series of policy suggestions to encourage the involvement of both mothers and fathers and their extended families in the ongoing emotional and financial support of the children (Ballard, 1995). Included in these recommendations are statements to encourage access of both parents, restrict minor children from being moved out of state by one parent, and require accounting of how public TANF benefits are spent to support children. These recommendations clearly reflect the areas of conflict in postdivorce families and the specific frustrations felt by noncustodial fathers.

Housing Impacts

Following a divorce, the father typically leaves the family home and establishes a new place of residence. Many mothers who retain ownership of homes after the divorce process find the expenses and upkeep unrealistic on their current income. This often results in family homes being sold and the mother and children moving to a smaller residence. This process takes considerable time, during which the psychological sense of loss for children and mothers has to be dealt with.

The disposition of the family home is probably second only to custody questions in raising conflict around divorce. For the children, a house often means continuity and stability in their lives. This is one area where the rights and interests of the adults can be in sharp conflict with those of the children. For the divorcing partners, the house may represent conflict and old memories they wish to leave behind.

When there has been extreme conflict in the marriage and home, the home might represent the visual stage for these memories also. Many families do not own a home, and the divorce process leaves them dependent on public funding. Public housing sites include many mothers and children of divorce.

Another social phenomenon is the number of divorced families that have returned to their own families of origin. Middle-age parents are finding their children returning home with grandchildren. These arrangements can be successful, but they require skilled negotiation about property rights, boundary issues between the generations, and the amount of economic and supervision assistance the grandparents can provide. Grandparents frequently are asked to provide vital resources for the young family's survival at the same time when they may be dealing with their distress and grief over their children's divorce. In cultures in which extended-family patterns are frequent and valued by the community, this transition may be easier. In never-married single-parent families, the pattern frequently consists of the young parent giving birth and parenting while continuing to reside in the parental home.

Governmental Policies and Agencies

All divorced families have experienced interaction with the courts. Indeed, because of the rise in divorce and other family-related matters, currently 50 percent of all court cases relate to some aspect of family law (Fine, 1993). The fact that courts have historically been adversarial environments has led many states to institute enhanced responsibility for family courts or to encourage the processes of family mediation to maintain the marriage or to provide help with the divorce process (Wallerstein, 1998).

Many divorced families are also involved with the Department of Social Services through a variety of assistance programs, particularly the TANF program. As an outgrowth of these services, families interact with the Child Support Enforcement Division and with Medicaid personnel. With the passage of the TANF legislation, many states are attempting to create integrated one-stop service arrangements for TANF clients. These services are dramatically different across state, and often county, borders, and a variety of regulations are being implemented. Some such practices are very child centered; others appear punitive and unrealistic in providing a bridge to family stability.

Grandparents who raise their grandchildren because of divorce, death, or instability on the part of the child's parents frequently have a difficult time receiving any public assistance because the children are not in their legal custody. Miller (1993) comments that policies affecting adoption, custody, and the provision of benefits to children should be judged by their power to reduce the damaging effects of poverty on healthy child development. The income in such programs is often so low that parents cannot save money or acquire resources to help move them beyond the poverty level (Children's Defense Fund, 1993).

The Welfare Reform Act allowed states to establish their own reimbursement formulas for public assistance programs. Research on how different programs affect young divorced families could help improve futures for both these children and their parents.

KINSHIP NETWORKS AND INTERACTIONS

Kinship networks are extremely important to all families and to the divorced family in particular (Compher, 1989). Divorced parents often return to live with their own parents, at least for a period of time. Because of economic impacts, the young divorced family members are particularly dependent on the support of their friends and kin networks. In addition, as shown in Figure 11.2, two-parent families that are poor are more than twice as likely to divorce as families who have not experienced poverty.

In 1990, 66 percent of single mothers were reported in the workforce, with one in eight employed mothers working more than 40 hours a week. Many of the children of these mothers are cared for by friends and family while the mothers work. In 1990, 7 million children under the age of 13 were cared for by a relative other than a parent (U.S. Census Bureau, 1992). Many of these arrangements for care are relatively informal and vulnerable to the demands of competing influences on relatives' lives. The ability of a network of friends and family to exchange services and provide emotional and material support is extremely vital.

Family interactions around the celebration of holidays often become conflictual. When divorce has divided a household, it is often the extended family that has a difficult time adjusting to the reduced access to children in the family. The extended family will often not change its patterns to adjust to the reality of one divorced couple in the

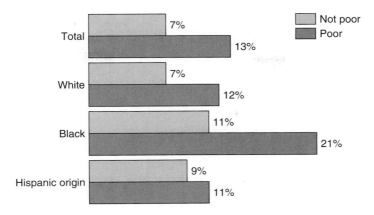

Figure 11.2   Percentage of Two-Parent Families That Discontinued Marriage Within Two Years: Mid-1980s

Note: Persons of Hispanic origin may be of any race. Poverty status refers to the beginning of two-year periods.

Source: U.S. Census Bureau, (1992, October). *When families break up* (SB 92-12). Washington, DC: U.S. Government Printing Office.

family network. This means that divorced parents often feel conflict and a lack of support around the times of the year when their earlier family memories may have been very positive and cohesive.

Stages of Divorce

Those who provide support activities and education concerning divorce recognize four stages of divorce, described as follows (Kuhn & Guidubaldi, 1997):

1. *A psychological/emotional divorce.* This stage is often initiated by one party and may be felt for an extended period of time before it is verbalized and acted on. In the United States, 80 percent of divorces are initiated unilaterally by one spouse.
2. *A physical divorce, or separation.* This stage may be linked to the availability of economic resources and usually means that one parent moves out of the family's home.
3. *A legal divorce.* This stage is often prolonged until the parties have the economic resources or the will to complete a legal divorce. In addition, there may be a legal separation document that precedes an actual divorce.
4. *A social divorce.* In this final stage, people declare that ties to certain social groups or friends are changed or severed, and new social relationships are established.

A person can obtain a legal divorce and a physical divorce and never complete the psychological/emotional or the social divorces. Some people accomplish the stages in a different order, some may never work through all stages, and some may need professional assistance in completing the processes.

Parenting Alliances

The literature on parenting through the divorce process includes many examples of parents struggling to assert a parenting alliance that allows the divorced parents to co-operate in decisions relating to their children. Whether or not they hold joint custody, both parents usually have an enduring interest in the development of their children.

When there is a high amount of conflict, a great deal of adult energy may go into maintaining the adult conflict rather than establishing new and stable regimes for themselves and the children in separate households (Johnston & Roseby, 1997). Some of these struggles result essentially in parallel parenting, that is, two separate households that deal with the child in separate ways with little negotiation or sharing of information between them.

Children can usually learn to adjust to new situations. They do adjust to differences between home and school, or between their parents' household and other extended family members' households. However, we can ask, what "adjustment" is appropriate or ideal for optimal development? Some agreement on values and reinforcement of achievement goals for children would seem appropriate for divorced parents. Children can grow to understand that both parents have the children's interests in mind and are cooperating for their good.

New Patterns

Single parents, who typically must become more assertive in disciplining their children, may find the discipline task challenging. Some research suggests that both divorced fathers and mothers find it difficult to put adequate resources into stable discipline. Depressed or exhausted by the divorce process, parents sometimes do not exert enough energy and resources to creating new stable patterns for the children. For divorced parents with custody, learning how to manage on a reduced level of resources with increased demands on their time and energy is extremely important.

Establishing new adult relationships is critical, yet single mothers often have fewer adult relationships just when they need them the most. Research on emotional stress suggests that social support is extremely important to buffer the effects of stress. With few new friends, a divorced mother often seeks social support from her immediate family. A role reversal situation, when a parent relies too heavily on the children for emotional and social support, is sometimes a result of this period of stress.

As divorced parents initiate their own social relationships, they must develop new roles. The divorce literature suggests that only 15 percent of divorced adults marry a person with whom they had a predivorce extramarital relationship. Many of these new postdivorce adult relationships will be with new partners. Balancing the need for adult exploration of relationships with the children's need for stability is an important function for all family members. Most divorced parents remarry, but statistics show that rates of divorce in a second marriage are a bit higher than in a first marriage. Given these realities, children who have experienced one divorce are likely to experience additional relationship beginnings and endings in the future.

HELPFUL TECHNIQUES FOR SERVING DIVORCED SINGLE-PARENT FAMILIES

Professionals serving these families should be aware that divorce, as a process of transition, continues over a number of months. The process involves loss, grief, anger, endings, and new patterns. These are processes that the American culture has often not dealt with comfortably. Frequently our work with these families requires assisting them in separating child needs from adult needs. Divorce-transition adults frequently tell their divorce stories to anyone who will listen, to gain clarification for themselves or to seek alliances. When meeting with parents and discussing issues relating to their children, the focus should be on the child's development and how to maintain the child's safety, stability, and optimal development. Professionals working with such families should try to meet with both divorced parents together, if that is reasonable. When it is not possible, professionals must set separate times to work with each of the parents, assuming that the noncustodial parent is available locally.

In consideration of children's needs, ground rules are needed, such as not allowing one parent to talk disparagingly about the other parent in front of the child. Also, the child needs to be encouraged to talk freely about and maintain psychological and emotional connections with both parents.

In schools and youth-serving agencies, literature and media resources should be available that talk about the process of divorce and describe people with a variety of family structures. Children whose parents have experienced divorce need to be kept in as stable a classroom situation as possible and close to staff members who can be empathetic and supportive. Reducing the number of changes children have to cope with is key, although often not possible.

Allowing children an opportunity to discuss questions or frustrations is extremely important. School-based groups for children and youth who have experienced divorce provide helpful outlets for children. Showing unexpected insight, children frequently indicate that their parents are so absorbed in grief and transition processes that the fears and anxieties of children are ignored. Children who are quiet, helpful, and positive during the divorce process can be feeling just as stressed and grief-stricken as those who are acting out and confronting authority. Kurkowski, Gordon, and Arbuthnot (1993) found that a technique as simple as having high school students complete a questionnaire about their feelings of being caught "in the middle" between two parents and sharing the group results in a letter to all households produced significant improvements in parent–youth communication. For children of all ages, the availability of a number of Websites that deal with divorce transitions can be very helpful. See the resource list at the end of the chapter for some of these addresses. It is particularly helpful for adults to review these sites and encourage youths to use them interactively or in a small support group.

Serving these families should always take into account reduced income and reduced time for family members to participate in education, leisure, or social events. Ideas for low-cost activities to participate in with children, combining several objectives in one family activity, can promote family effectiveness and economy.

Professionals need to understand their own attitudes when working with families of divorce and be careful not to convey unhelpful attitudes to families (Gray & Coleman, 1985). Referring to a family as broken, separated, unsuccessful, or "in trouble" reinforces negative images and expectations concerning this difficult transition. Children can be expected to feel distressed and to show some changes in their behavior while they adjust. Arranging a school or social setting where children feel comfortable will enable them to speak about and stabilize their behavior. Professionals serving such children should expect changes, be supportive, and give the child assurances and structure rather than confront the parent with the child's anxieties. Two to three years may be required for new sound relationships to become stabilized within a family. For young children particularly, three years can be a very long time, and they need positive and supportive educational and social environments.

Staff Training

All staff working with families need high-quality in-service education on current family demographics and the process of the entire divorce transition. Such education should include an opportunity for staff to discuss the variations in their own family experiences, particularly reflecting on support needed for transitions involving grief and loss. The divorce process can be facilitated by informed and supportive professionals who can assist in the restructuring of family relationships. Finding ways to understand the normal transitions of divorce, and becoming aware of how to be supportive, are important professional skills. Developing a good list of resources for use by staff and parents is helpful. Referring children or parents to agencies that have individuals skilled in divorce transitions and counseling can be another positive act. Parents who have had earlier experiences with divorce can be a helpful resource. You can encourage newly divorced parents to seek out single-parent support groups, as well as support groups for children. Introducing parents to others who might be sources of support and friendship is another helpful step.

Independence and isolation of the nuclear family form in America is still alive and well. Coontz (1992) comments that a general Anglo-American notion that dependence is immature and weak interferes with the social support and interdependence that is so helpful in divorce transitions. Understanding the importance of sharing resources and needs with other families can be an important professional goal as you work with many families of divorce. As a professional, you need to help families of divorce understand the importance of networking and cooperating with other families or groups.

When families come from an ethnic group or culture that is supportive, there will be good support for the divorce adjustment process. However, some religious and ethnic groups are not supportive of the divorce process, even though they are supportive of extended-family relationships. Because of their personal choices, divorced parents then may feel an acute loss of approval and bondedness within the religious and ethnic setting. Finding other people who can be supportive and linking them with divorced families is certainly a needed service you can provide.

New Celebrations

Encouraging divorced families to establish new rituals, festivals, and celebrations is another important aspect of your professional work. Because extended-family networks often compete for attention during traditional holiday times, divorced families may need to initiate other events that become special to their family. For example, if children visit the noncustodial parent on weekends, a Sunday night homecoming ritual or a Monday evening family time may assist children in starting new patterns that will work well within the new family structure.

✦ CONCLUSIONS

Families experiencing divorce need professional support during this important period of transition. The specific circumstances of individual families will be different, but there are important supportive actions you can take concerning divorced and separated families. You need to be sensitive to the loss of economic resources and the complexities of establishing new households. Children need stability, reassurance, and permission to communicate their concerns. Adults need supportive connections with other families and assistance in creating appropriate new patterns in a two-household family.

✦ STUDY QUESTIONS

1. Define the terms *alimony* and *no-fault divorce*.
2. Review the statistics and explain which U.S. group has the greatest number of divorces.
3. Describe gender differences with regard to economic outcome for each parent following divorce.
4. What do studies show as recent factors contributing to more divorces among families with children?
5. Define the terms *joint custody, legal joint custody,* and *physical joint custody.* Discuss what conditions would encourage each choice.
6. State what studies show to be the impact of divorce on sons.
7. State what studies show to be the impact of divorce on daughters.
8. What is a typical time requirement for the divorce process to be completed and stability to come in a family?
9. What is the "best interests of the child" doctrine?
10. Why do we see dramatically different individual outcomes among a group of children who have experienced divorce?

✦ APPLICATIONS

1. Compare and contrast a child-centered family with a parent-centered family.
2. Discuss why father-absence research is inadequate in understanding the divorce process.
3. Compare and contrast parallel parenting with parenting alliances.
4. Study and describe the positive and negative aspects of children residing, after divorce, in the custody of their mother. What does it affect, and how?
5. What systems are most significant in impacting the feelings and success of divorced families?
6. Make a list of guidelines for helping professionals to use in working with divorced parents.
7. Write a three-page essay giving advice to a friend of your own gender about how to proceed once a decision is made to divorce.

✦ MEDIA RESOURCES

Dad's house, Mom's house. (1986). (33-minute video). (Available from National Film Board of Canada, Norman-McLaren Building, 3155 Côte-de-Liesse Road, St. Laurent, Quebec, Canada)

Dear distant Dad. (23 minutes). Worcester, PA: Vision Video, Inc.

A kid's guide to family changes. (40 minutes). Englewood, CO: Learning Tree Publishing.

Do children also divorce? (1988). (28 minutes). New York: Filmmaker's Library.

Tender places. (1988). (25 minutes). MTI Film and Video. Deerfield, IL: Group W Television Sales.

✦ ORGANIZATIONS

American Coalition for Fathers and Children. 1718 M. St. N.W. #187, Washington, DC 20036 (800)978-3237

The Joint Custody Association, 10606 Wilkins Avenue, Los Angeles, CA 90024, (213)475-5352

Grandparents Rights Organization, 100 W. Long Lake Road, Suite 250, Bloomfield Hills, MI 48304, (248)646-7191

National Council on Family Relations. 1910 West Country Road B, Suite 147, St. Paul, MN 55113, (612)633-6933

PACE (Parents and Children's Equality), 1816 Florida Avenue, Palm Harbor, FL 34683, (813)787-3875

Parents Without Partners, Inc., 8807 Colesville Road, Silver Spring, MD 20910, (800)638-8071

✤ KEY INTERNET RESOURCES

American Coalition for Fathers and Children
www.acfc.org/site/PageServer

Divorce Online
www.divorce-online.com/articles/f156919.html

**National Center for Disease Control and Prevention, National Center for Health
Statistics**
www.cdc.gov/nchswww/fastats/divorce.html

Children's Rights Council
www.vix.com/crc/sp/spcrc97.html

✤ FURTHER READING

Bieninfeld, F. (1987). *Helping your child succeed after divorce.* Claremont, CA: Hente
House.

Colbert, J. (1999). *Divorce common sense handbook.* Crofton, MD: Tuff Turtle Publishing.

Covington, J. (1982). *Confessions of a single father.* New York: Pilgrim Press.

Kamerman, S. B., & Kohn, A. J. (1988). *Mothers alone: Strategies for a time of change.* Dover,
MA: Auburn House.

Nelson, J., Erwin, C., & Delzer, C. (1999). *Positive discipline for single parents.* Rocklin, CA:
Prima Publishing.

Pruett, K. (1987). *The nurturing father: Journey toward the complete man.* New York: Warner
Books.

Thorndike, J. (1996). *Another way home: A single father's story.* New York: Crown.

Ware, C. (1982). *Sharing parenthood after divorce: An enlightened custody guide for mother,
father and the kids.* New York: Viking Press.

Wayman, A. (1981). *Successful single parenting: A practical guide.* Meadowbrook: Simon &
Schuster.

✤ FURTHER READINGS FOR CHILDREN COPING WITH DIVORCE

Danziger, P. (2007). *The divorce express.* London: Penguin Books.

Dolmetsch, P., & Shih, A. (Eds.). *The kids' book about single-parent families.* Garden City, NY:
Doubleday.

Fleming, A. M. (1985). *Welcome to Grossville.* New York: Charles Scribner's Sons.

Girard, L. W. (1987). *At Daddy's on Saturdays.* Niles, IL: Albert Whitman.

Marquardt, E. (2006). *Between two worlds: The inner lives of children of divorce.* New York: Crown.

Rogers, F. (2002). *Let's talk about divorce.* London: Puffin Press.

Watson, J. W., Swetzer, R. E., & Hirschberg, J. C. (1988). *Sometimes a family has to split up: A read-aloud book for parents and children.* New York: Crown.

Worthen, T. (Ed.). (2001). *Broken hearts. . . healing: Young poets speak out on divorce.* Logan, UT: Poet Tree Press.

→ 12

Stepfamilies

→ Key Concepts

- Binuclear Families
- Blended Family
- Cohabiting Stepparents
- Custodial Parent
- In Loco Parentis
- Nonresident Stepparent
- Remarried Family
- Residence Order
- TANF

Today's stepfamily consists of you, me, your kids, my kids, our kids, your ex'es, my ex'es, even our ex'es new mates, and all the kin of these various folks. Stepfamilies give a new meaning to the concept of complex family relationships.

—Delia Ephron (1986)

As helping professionals, it is important to understand the reality of life in stepfamilies, which can include as many as 26 different family types, according to Vurgoyne and Clark (1982). Scholars report that stepfamilies that fare well see this new and distinct family form as a challenge for each member (Ganong & Coleman, 2004). To succeed in meeting the challenge, these successful stepfamilies recognize that behaviors carried over from earlier marriages must often be revised, new forms of communication must be planned, and outside support from kin, friends, and professionals must be utilized (Ganong & Coleman, 2004). In spite of the organizational complexity, research shows that, on the average, a higher level of satisfaction occurs between second-marriage partners than between first-marriage partners.

COMPLEX STRUCTURE OF STEPFAMILIES

A stepfamily is a complex form of social organization with tremendous variation in structure. Stepfamilies may appear to many to be like traditional two-parent families. However, by creating a genogram, a detailed organizational relational chart, we can see the complexity of significant relationships that predate the current remarriage. Such complexity is not always recognized as a new cognitive frame or model of the family (Widmer, 1999). Glick (1989) defines a remarried family as consisting of a husband, wife, and children and at least one or both of the spouses being in their second or subsequent marriage. Further, a stepfamily is created when one remarried spouse has at least one biological child under age 18 who was born during a prior marriage or relationship. Stepfamilies may include divorced and widowed parents, gay or lesbian couples, and parents who were previously cohabitating with another partner. This chapter focuses primarily on stepfamilies formed following divorce.

Members of stepfamilies are sensitive to judgments of the wider culture, and therefore they have often been reluctant to participate in research. Some simply deny that they are any different than first-marriage families, and this myth often gets in the way of solving some of the problems they face. Over the years, America has experienced a public debate about the strength and stability of families. Because so many negative myths surround stepfamilies, their reluctance to reveal their innermost workings is understandable. Stepfamilies are newly committed to marriage; however, partners may carry feelings of failure from their first marriages and worry about their ability to develop better relationships in their new family. In addition, early research and discussion of parenting in stepfamilies often assumed negative child outcomes and family dysfunction with an emphasis on the *structure* of a stepfamily and little regard for family dynamics (Arendell, 1997; Coleman, Ganong, & Fine, 2000).

As helping professionals, we must understand the complex reality of life in stepfamilies. Scholars report that most conflicts in stepfamilies result from the inappropriate application of traditional parent–child roles in the new circumstances. Specifically, research by Grizzle (1999) suggested that serious conflicts in stepfamilies result from expectations over appropriate parental roles. Grizzle reported that American society is generally clear about parental expectations in first marriages, but there is widespread disagreement over expectations and, therefore, appropriate roles of parents in remarriages following divorce. With knowledge, professionals can facilitate the planning of realistic services to give stepfamilies the support they need.

A number of researchers and clinicians have provided guidance by describing stages of stepfamily development. Patricia Pappernow (1988) has suggested that successful stepfamilies must navigate through these seven stages of developmental adjustment:

1. Fantasy
2. Assimilation
3. Awareness
4. Mobilization
5. Action
6. Contact
7. Resolution

Smith (2000) gathered data that suggested five distinct stages: the honeymoon, hostility, ambivalence, transition, and resolution. Helping professionals can be more effective in assisting families through stages if they educate themselves on the unique challenges presented along the way.

HISTORICAL BACKGROUND

Stepfamilies emerge from a combination of out-of-wedlock births, a high divorce rate, and a commitment to marriage. A 1999 survey showed the changing patterns of parental marital status in the United States (Table 12.1). The increasing number of children born

Table 12.1   Living Arrangements of Children Under 18 Years, by Race and Ethnicity: Fall 1996 (numbers in thousands)

Living Arrangements	All Races	White	White non-Hispanic	Black	American Indian and Alaska Native	Asian and Pacific Islander	Hispanic[1]
Children	71,494	56,212	46,657	11,631	1,073	2,578	10,428
Living with two parents[2]	50,685	43,466	36,837	4,397	667	2,156	7,112
Both married to each other	49,186	42,333	36,110	4,126	605	2,123	6,627
In a traditional nuclear family[3]	39,746	34,859	30,132	2,985	395	1,507	5,024
One parent	18,165	11,131	8,632	6,320	345	369	2,870
Mother only	16,340	9,599	7,274	6,088	320	333	2,689
Father only	1,825	1,533	1,358	232	25	36	181
Neither parent	2,644	1,615	1,188	915	62	54	445
Grandparents only	1,266	637	501	571	34	24	143
Other relatives only	688	447	272	199	19	22	183
Nonrelatives only	622	622	383	122	9	8	105
Other arrangements	69	46	32	22	—	1	14
At least 1 stepparent	4,902	4,066	3,556	649	94	93	563
At least 1 foster parent	313	224	153	86	2	2	75

—Represents zero or rounds to zero.
[1] People of Hispanic origin may be of any race.
[2] In the Survey of Income and Program Participation (SIPP) data, children identify both of their parents regardless of their marital status. This means that both married and unmarried parents are included in this category in this table. This represents a difference from the Current Population Survey (CPS), because only married parents are recorded in two-parent households. Correspondingly, there are more children in two-parent households in the SIPP, and more in single-parent households in the CPS.
[3] Children in a traditional nuclear family live with both biological parents and, if siblings are present, with full brothers and sisters. No other household members are present.
Source: Fields, J. (2001). *Living arrangements of children.* Household Economic Studies. Washington, DC: U.S. Census Bureau.

out of wedlock means that stepfamilies may include parents for whom the marriage is the first legally sanctioned union. Two thirds of separated or divorced women and three fourths of separated and divorced men eventually remarry (Arendell, 1997). Data show that half of divorced individuals who remarry after a divorce do so within three years (Creider & Fields, 2002). White women are most likely to remarry and Black women are least (Bramlett & Mosier, 2002). Some social scientists think it may be unrealistic for adults in our culture to sustain one marriage throughout their lives with a person they chose in the early years of their adult development. An increase in life expectancy means that adults have more years to spend in their husband–wife relationships. Learning brings different opportunities to people. Life events affect individuals differently, and the women's movement has helped redefine a satisfactory marriage as one that involves much more of a balance of power between partners. Of women who married in 1945 to 1949, 90 percent reached their 10th anniversary. In contrast, only 73 percent of those who married from 1980 to 1984 reached their 10th anniversary. In the late 1990s, first marriages that ended in divorce lasted seven to eight years on average (Creider & Fields, 2002). Second marriages that ended in divorce showed a mean duration of seven years.

In 1992, 1 in 10 children lived with a biological parent and a stepparent, and about 15 percent of all children lived in blended families—homes that included at least one stepparent, stepsibling, or half sibling (Furukawa, 1994). By the late 1980s, 1,300 stepfamilies were being formed every day, but the trend in the 1990s slowed somewhat (Arendell, 1997). As shown in Table 12.2, there are differences in stepfamily numbers across racial and ethnic groups. While only about 3 to 7 percent of Asian and Pacific Islanders live with stepparents, in Black families 14 percent live with a biological parent and a stepparent. Coleman and colleagues (2001) describe conflicts in stepfamilies as most often related to a renegotiation of family boundaries shown in resource disagreements, loyalty conflicts, "guard and protest" ideology challenges, and conflicts with extended-family members.

Table 12.2   Children Living with Two Parents by Their Biological, Step, and Adoptive Status by Race and Ethnicity: Fall 1996

Characteristics of Parents	All Races	White, non-Hispanic	Black	Hispanic Origin[1]	Asian and Pacific Islander	American Indian or Alaska Native
Children living with two parents[2]	50,685	36,837	4,397	7,112	2,156	667
Biological mother and father	44,708	32,496	3,656	6,476	1976	538
Biological mother and stepfather	3,723	2693	505	435	61	58
Biological father and stepmother	1,004	761	105	113	19	26
Adoptive mother and father	702	496	45	38	88	35
Other	548	389	86	51	12	10

[1] Persons of Hispanic origin may be of any race.

[2] Includes mothers and fathers not currently married to each other.

Source: Fields, J. (2001). *Living arrangements of children*. Household Economic Studies. Washington, DC: U.S. Census Bureau.

Impacts on Children

A stepmother's first meeting with the children of her new spouse is often difficult. Her positive, skilled, and loving overtures may not be reciprocated by the children. As Spanier (1988) comments, "where but in stepfamilies do we find children and adults, once strangers, becoming relatives without the customary trappings of human development?" (p. ix). At a time in which the two newly married adults are positive about entering into a new relationship, they are also simultaneously faced with the tasks of assisting children with grieving the loss of the previous marriage and helping them move into new relationships (Einstein & Albert, 1982). Women often are responsible for managing the parallel and conflicting emotions of these two developmental tasks in the family.

The area of greatest conflict for stepfamilies is dealing with children residing with the current marriage partners. Hetherington (1999) commented that the higher divorce rates found in remarriages with stepchildren suggests the importance of resident children to marital instability. Cherlin and Furstenberg (1994) summarized stepparenting literature and concluded that the best predictor of the character of the stepparent–stepchild relationship is the quality of the effort made by the stepparent to create a kinlike relationship.

The second most common area of conflict concerns financial matters. Peterson and Nord (1990) report that when women remarry, there is a reduction in child support from the former husband. Evidently, the ex-husband feels some loss of responsibility and access to his children, and he begins to provide child support less consistently. This phenomenon may contribute to the fact that in 2000, only 36 percent of female-headed households reported receiving child support or alimony (Annie B. Casey Foundation, 2003). Mason (1998) reports that in a group of residential stepfathers, a quarter had minor children from a former relationship living elsewhere, and two thirds of these men reported paying child support. This confounds their ability to contribute to their current household's expenses. Although it is difficult to know all of the reasons for child support being reduced under these circumstances, it is probable that the mother is then put in the position of having to negotiate, protest, and seek child support from her ex-spouse to demonstrate her loyalty and commitment to her new spouse and their economic plans. Creating a positive relationship with an ex-spouse, to handle negotiation about child rearing and economic support, may be a very difficult task for some women, particularly if there was intense conflict in the previous relationship (Donnelly & Finkelhor, 1993).

Sex-Role Ambiguities and Abuse

Family crisis literature presents increasing evidence of rape and other forms of abuse and sexual harassment in stepfamily settings (Giles-Sims & Finkelhor, 1984). Brewer and Paulsen's (1999) analysis of two homicide studies revealed that in 48 to 50 percent of all wife killings, the victim was a woman who had minor children from previous partners. Family-life professionals warn about the potential for coercive sexual relations when adults and youth enter a new stepfamily without a history of well-defined nurturing relationships. Counselors and therapists working with stepfamilies need to be alert to the potential of abusive relationships because remarriage creates family intimacy and ambiguously defined new roles. Vogt's (1999) study of young adults who had spent childhood time in a stepfamily reported higher incidents of physical abuse than other respondents. Because most states mandate the reporting of sexual and physical abuse, families working with a reputable professional sign an initial release indicating they understand this obligation. Other professionals serving stepfamilies may need information to alert them to this potential for abuse and to the reporting obligation.

For both children and adults in stepfamilies, new relationships create some ambiguity in roles. Cherlin (1992) suggests that the need to create new role relationships in stepfamilies is a new challenge. Visher and Visher (1980) comment that one of the challenges for the new stepfamily is the lessening of taboos against sexual relationships among people who are not blood relatives, such as between new stepsiblings, or between a stepparent and child. Stepmarriages are more often formed between parents with children in late elementary and junior and senior high school, so issues that involve sexual development and sexual behavior are a normal part of the developmental stage. The literature on sexual abuse suggests that wife and child battering more often occurs in families with inadequate income and marked by "constant competition over who will be taken care of" (Kempe, 1980). The task of establishing new relationships and allocating scarce resources between competing needs can generate frustration and anger in stepfamilies. In addition, incestuous fathers and stepfathers tend to be socially isolated and have an overly private approach to the family (Rush, 1980). The demand for flexibility and responsiveness to a wide circle of relationships required in forming new stepfamilies may be unsettling for some men, and successful negotiation of positive sexual roles may be difficult.

Historically, one of the important functions of marriage and family life has been to define and provide support for socially sanctioned sexual relationships. Thus stepfamilies create new threats to the social order. It is not unusual for one stepparent to be significantly older than the other, or for the two spouses to have children of greatly differing ages. For example, a mother with preschool children may find it disconcerting or threatening to become the stepparent of a teenager. Children and youth in stepfamilies may be vulnerable to inappropriate sexual advances from new stepsiblings or a stepparent. The fact that both family members and professionals are often naive about the potential for sexual assault or abuse is evidence that many Americans are not yet able to foresee realistically the potential problems of new family forms (Johnson, 1980).

Over the past three decades, alarming data on physical abuse and homicides involving stepchildren have emerged. Daly and Wilson (1996) relate that early data on the higher rate of abuse of stepchildren have now been explored for motives. Young children have a sevenfold higher rate of abuse and a hundredfold higher rate of homicide in stepparent plus biological parent homes, in comparison to homes with two biological parents. Furthermore, whereas biological parents more often kill children while in depressed or suicidal states, stepparents appear to perform more assaultive angry homicides without depressive mental health patterns. Daly and Wilson (1996) suggest that researchers and practitioners need to work smart with the realization that stepparents do not typically have the same love and commitment, or receive the same rewards, as biological parents. The risk of physical abuse can be one outcome of the frustrating contrast.

Changing Roles for Females

High-quality studies on stepfamily functioning and patterns are emerging. Maglin and Schneidewind (1989) suggested that the shortage of guidelines has resulted in women and girls in stepfamilies feeling very isolated and without guidance for creating satisfying roles within stepfamilies. Our culture's view of the stepmother still tends to be dominated by the fairy tale stereotype of the wicked stepmother. Nielsen's (1999) review of the stepfamily clinical and research literature identified our "society's attitudes about mothers and motherhood" as one of four major explanations for stepmothers experiencing more stress than stepfathers. Nevertheless, many family scholars recommend that stepfamily as a title acknowledges the complicated rich structures of families. They recommend against using the term *blended,* which, like the concept of America as a melting pot, suggests the disappearance of individual differences and the erasing of previous family history.

A stepmother who parents her spouse's children is often haunted by the image of the absent, perfect, biological mother, in contrast to the image of a wicked stepmother (Ceglian & Gardner, 2000). Cherlin and Furstenberg (1994) and White (1994) comment that studies show the stepmother role is more difficult than the stepfather role. Karsky's (1999) study of stepmothers showed that the best predictor of a stepmother's emotional well-being was her own self-esteem and role acceptance. In Orchard and Solberg's (1999) study of successful stepmothers' role expectations, subjects revealed that they did not consider themselves primarily responsible for household duties, were not expecting a parental-like love relationship with stepchildren, and were adamant about not replacing the child's biological mother. If this less traditional mother role is acceptable to a woman, there may be more freedom and independence in the stepparent role than the biological mother role. It is clear, however, that not all women come to a stepfamily with these understandings. Church's (1999) study of stepmother expectations revealed the assumptions that made stepfamily functioning more difficult: 1) Nuclear families are best; all others are deficient; (2) there is agreement (without discussion) on how stepfamilies function; (3) stepmothers basically draw from their "natural" skills as mothers; and (4) extended-family members know how a stepfamily should operate. A subsample of this study was more realistic and had a "wait-and-see" flexible attitude. They often had personal experience as a child or adult in a stepfamily; they saw a variety of extended-family roles as possible and a healthy couple relationship as primary to stepfamily health. This acknowledgment of the importance of the marital relationship is often identified by researchers (Greene & Anderson, 1999; White, 1999).

Children may be less accepting of a new mother figure than a new father figure, and cultural norms about gender roles in families can confound this conflict. A study (Watson, 1995) of Greek and Roman social history illustrates the endurance of stereotypes of the stepmother as both treacherous and seductive. Women tend to have strong impulses to protect the mother–child bond. Thus stepmothers are often in the awkward position of forging new bonds with a stepchild while trying to help the child maintain bonds with that perfect biological mother. Research shows that stepmothers and biological mothers often have a rivalrous relationship, which creates more conflict than does the stepfather–biological father relationship (Hetherington & Henderson, 1997). As a result, noncustodial stepmothers find themselves often stressed and resentful over stepchildren visits.

The role of the new wife may be distressing to other women in the husband's life (such as the ex-wife) and may likely create complications among women in extended stepfamilies. Stepmothers acknowledge that their relationship with an ex-husband's new wife is often marked by conflicting emotions, which are natural given that the new wife may be doing most of the parenting of the former couple's children.

An additional complication of this task is that while the newly married mother with custody of her children wants to protect the bond and intimacy she has with her children, at the same time she must create a new bond with her spouse. This conflict appears stronger for women than for men placed in similar situations. Sevier (2000) found that stepmothers were most successful when they began making choices to support their own happiness and not just the happiness of others in the family. The essays in Maglin and Schneidewind (1989) give eloquent voice to women's pain when they try to make the stepfamily operate as a first-marriage family.

Changing Roles for Males

Studies show that fathers who receive custody of their children upon divorce have typically taken active parenting roles before the divorce. In 20 percent of stepfamilies, the father's biological children reside with the father; the mother's children reside in the new stepfamily in 80 percent of cases (DeMaris & Greif, 1992). The perception of satisfaction with a marriage varies according to which spouse's children are residing in the stepfamily's home. The biological parent of the residential children is more apt to see the marriage and family as satisfying and intimate than is the stepparent in that same household.

Researchers have noted that all children react to the remarriage of their custodial parents. Studies suggest that boys have a more difficult adjustment when living in single-mother families than girls do. Thus the entry of a stepfather into their family system appears to facilitate adolescent male development and stability. However, the literature also contains many stories of the stepfather's struggle to find an appropriate role to play with his stepchildren. Ganong, Coleman, Fine, and Martin (1999) reported that in families where step relationships were poor, there was generally competition from a nonresidential parent, the stepparents had "take-charge" personalities, and the stepchildren did not recognize the stepparent's affinity-seeking efforts. In contrast, successful relationships occurred when stepparents initiated a friendship with the children and continued those efforts after they shared a residence.

Replacing a biological father or imitating a biological parent is usually an inappropriate role. Research studies show that stepfathers and stepchildren generally report lower levels of warmth than biological pairs (White, 1999). New stepfathers should be sensitive to their ambiguous or precarious authority over stepchildren (Newman, Skopin, & McKerry, 1993). Because men and women often view males as heavy disci-pliners, it is tempting to encourage stepfathers to take on a strong authoritarian role. In most stepfamilies, the children are more accepting of discipline from their biological parent, even though this may change traditional gender-role patterns. A stepfather can often be most effective by supporting the mother's discipline efforts and gradually gaining the trust of stepchildren (Hetherington & Henderson, 1997). Stump's (1999) advice on how to be a successful stepfather includes recommendations that combine lower expectations for attention and power with sensitivity to the realities of this new family form.

Most successful stepfathers find that playing a role like an uncle provides clear structure and an affectionate relationship without trying to replicate or replace the bio-logical father. In Arendell's (1997) research with noncustodial fathers, she notes that 80 percent of the men took a fairly rigid transitional view of parenting and had diffi-culty adjusting to new access and relationship challenges with their children. Those fathers who were adjusting successfully were engaged in a child-centered process of innovation and creativity to develop new parenting strategies for changed circum-stances. Such men need to be encouraged to mentor or guide other fathers who are finding such transitions difficult. Erera-Weatherley's (1996) research with stepparenting types suggests that a friendship style was most successful for both children and adults in the new stepfamily. The other roles—biological parent, super good stepmother, detached, and uncertain—were less successful.

CHANGES AS CHILDREN AGE

Stepfamilies continuously adjust to new relationships over time; thus physical cus-tody arrangements are often different from legal custody arrangements. Ganong and Coleman (1993a) have shown that some children in stepfamilies change their physi-cal living arrangements without changing their legal status. Changing residence with-out changing legal status is particularly common in adolescence. When relationships with adolescent males have been full of conflict in a stepfamily, the son often moves out of the biological mother-stepfather household and back to his biological father's residence. In a longitudinal study of stepfamilies, Jones (2001) found that females in adolescence reported greater family happiness and males reported a reduction in step-family happiness over time. Adolescents in stepfather families reported more anxiety than those residing in stepmother families. Hetherington (1999) noted in her research that stepfathers frequently were rebuffed in their initial attempt to become involved with their stepchildren in a positive way. Without sustained, positive attempts and strong support from their spouse, stepfathers tended to retreat and disengage themselves from their stepchildren's lives. This finding suggests the tremendous commitment and creativity needed to forge new skills for parenting roles in the stepfamily, as well as the lack of social supports available for enhancing parenting skills among men.

Although stepparents and biological parents should spend some time with the children as an entire family, each parent also needs to spend some time with each child individually. A number of men in stepfamilies report that they felt independence and pride in forging their own individual relationships with children. In first-marriage families, wives often mediate the relationships between husbands and children because fathers may be inexperienced in interacting with children. If men have more private relationships with their children and stepchildren, then a greater range of expressiveness for fathers can develop.

SOCIALIZATION OF CHILDREN

Realistic socialization goals in a stepfamily involve the establishment of new relationships between children and family members: their stepsiblings, their new stepparents, and their biological parents.

Children may now have less access to their biological parent and more conflict over the new adult-determined relationships. Particularly in stepfamilies, it is very apparent to children that much of their world is determined by adult decisions, and they often feel angry and resentful about these new realities (Cherlin, 1999). Socialization skills for children in a stepfamily often need to include conflict resolution or negotiation skills for situations in which competing loyalties cause stress for the child. Children in stepfamilies are very clear about their anger over being put into positions in which they are disappointing one parent or another.

Children's adjustments are facilitated when stepfamilies can create friendly parenting alliances with biological parents (see White & Gilbreth, 2001). When the new stepfamily is formed fairly soon after a divorce, children's adjustment is more complex. Many issues may still remain that are not resolved from the previous marriage, and children need time to adjust to the reality of new and different roles (Anderson, 1999). Frequently the choices or loyalties of children are different from those of the parents. Conflicts often surround momentous events for children, such as high school graduation or a marriage ceremony—especially issues like who should be present and what roles extended members should play. If possible, a wise family facilitates the children's choices at these times. In Vogt's (1999) study of young adults, respondents who had spent any of their childhood in a stepfamily had more cynical views of marriage and family.

Positive adjustment to stepparents occurs when there is protected time for relationship building or maintenance for each child, with both the biological parents and the stepparents. The maintenance of an appropriate visitation schedule with the biological noncustodial parent can reassure the child, sustain those relationships, and provide the new stepparents the time alone for enhancing the new marital relationship.

ROLES OF GRANDPARENTS AND OTHERS

The role of grandparents and additional extended-family members in stepfamilies can be similar to the support role played in divorced families (see Chapter 11). Positive relationships can facilitate the transition to the stepfamily and soothe conflicts and fears on the part of both generations. Thompson (1999) described the enduring significance of grandparents' support with a sample of adult stepchildren in England. Family counselors and family-life practitioners often comment on the need for the grandparent generation to have education and support as they assimilate new roles, facilitate relationships, and deal with their own feelings of loss. Haberstroh, Hayslip, and Wohl (2001) found that grandparents can be the initiators of an enhanced relationship with stepgrandchildren by visiting more often and communicating more actively. Kennedy and Kennedy (1993) report that those who most valued grandparent relationships in their research study were young adults from stepfamilies. Kennedy and Kennedy believe that grandparents maintain a sense of family heritage and history that is comforting to young adults who need roots from which to explore their own development and growth.

ECOLOGICAL FACTORS

A number of systems affect stepfamilies and they, in turn, affect the systems with which they interact.

Demographics

The number of stepfamilies in the United States is difficult to determine accurately because the data are not all routinely reported. Stewart (2001) suggests that data accuracy is confounded by the practice in America of defining stepfamilies as "married adults with resident stepchildren." This traditional definition describes approximately half of the stepparents because "nonresident" stepparents are not included. Although it is believed that approximately 40 million stepfamilies existed in the United States in 1990, these data do not include unmarried couples living together and same-sex couples who define themselves as stepfamilies. Scommegna (2002) reported that the increase in cohabiting households from 1980 to 1995 show a greater number of families who could be classified as stepfamilies. In addition, children born into a cohabiting household experience more family instability over time and therefore a greater number of divorce-like and stepfamily experiences that are not represented in the national statistics. Table 12.3 presents data from 1996 to 2002 that show an increasing number of children under 18 years of age living with a parent and a person of the opposite sex sharing living quarters (POSSLQ). Because of the lower marriage rate among African Americans, the percentage of divorces among African Americans is lower, as is the

Table 12.3 Unmarried-Couple[1] Households, by Presence of Children: 1996–Present

(Numbers in thousands. Data based on *Current Population Survey* [CPS] unless otherwise specified.)

Year	POSSLQ[2]	Total Unmarried Partners	Without Children Under 18 Years	With Children Under 18 Years
2002	4,898	4,193	2,475	1,718
2001	4,893	4,101	2,435	1,665
2000	4,736	3,822	2,259	1,563
1999	4,486	3,380	2,048	1,331
1998	4,236	3,139	1,844	1,295
1997	4,130	3,087	1,787	1,300
1996	3,958	2,858	1,623	1,236

[1] These estimates of unmarried couples include households that have two unmarried adults of the opposite sex. They may or may not have identified themselves as householder and unmarried partner.

[2] POSSLQ, person of the opposite sex sharing living quarters.

Source: U.S. Census Bureau. Children's living arrangements and characteristics: March 2002. June 2003. Annual Demographic Supplement to the March 2002 Current Population Survey, *Current Population Reports* (Series P20-547).

percentage of remarriages. Crosbie-Burnett and Lewis (1993) compared White middle-class stepparents struggling with new kinship relationships to the complex relationships in the African American community. Permeability of family boundaries, parallel-parenting households, or parenting alliances that cross over biological or legal role definitions are some of the strengths of the African American families that can be instructive to many stepfamilies.

Aesthetics

Much of our popular culture creates a romanticized myth of stepfamilies through such portrayals as *The Brady Bunch*, a popular television program of the 1970s and 1980s; the 1970s movie, *Yours, Mine and Ours;* and television programs such as *My Two Dads, Full House, Getting By, Step by Step*, and *Hearts Afire*. These examples provide an overly optimistic view of stepfamilies (Ganong & Coleman, 1986). Calling the stepfamily "reconstituted" or "blended" suggests that marital history can be ignored and a new family form can emerge in some different blend. A stellar exception to unrealistic portrayals is the 1999 film *Stepmom*, in which complex and realistic family relationships were given an honest viewing. Such pictures belie the distinct subsystems and conflicts in the reality of step-families.

Many transitions in a society are first portrayed in the humor and personal litera-ture of the culture. This is certainly true for stepfamilies. The film *Mrs. Doubtfire* casts the comedian Robin Williams as a divorcing father who masquerades as a nanny in order to spend time his children at his wife's house. Maglin's (1989) review of step-family fiction reveals that stories of stepfamilies often exonerate men and place heavy responsibility for a stepfamily's success on women. Maglin and Schneidewind's *Women and Stepfamilies: Voices of Anger and Love* (1989) portrays with intense emo-tion, humor, and celebration the personal literature of stepmothers. These authors sug-gest that democratic and cooperative relationships can make a special contribution to life in stepfamilies. The two authors advise that this success rests on women giving up an overly responsible "good mother" myth and replacing it with a picture of a mature adult woman who develops effective interactions with both women and men in the extended stepfamily.

In movies from the 1990s that portray stepfamilies, the issues of forming new rela-tionships were explored. *Stepmom* (mentioned previously) portrays a battle for chil-dren's affection and a final compromise between mother and stepmother. In *Crazy Beautiful* the stepmother's fear of her husband's crazy child impacts the father–daughter relationship. In the musical review *Breaking Up When the Cookie Crumbles: You Can Still Pick Up the Pieces,* children are led through a number of vignettes whose purpose is to help them face reality without assuming guilt. Such productions can prompt important discussions of tough issues in stepfamily relationship building.

Education

In general, stepfamilies show a higher level of education than do first-marriage families or single-parent families. This is partly because stepfamilies are often formed later in adults' lives, after more education has been acquired. The other contributing variable is that social class is generally correlated with a higher frequency of marriages. The di-vorce and remarriage rates, therefore, are somewhat higher among more highly edu-cated persons.

One specific economic challenge in stepfamilies is the high cost of education for the children. Because only one in four divorced women receives the full court-ordered support for her children, and divorce decrees often do not include the costs of college education, many stepfamilies find their children's educational costs a heavy burden on the family. In addition to the lack of child-support enforcement, there are problems that surround the legal responsibility of the stepparents to their stepchildren. The find-ing that divorced mothers receive lower child support in a new stepfamily may relate to the pattern of fathers paying for the expenses of the children in their own new mar-riage. When a divorce and remarriage involve extreme conflict between the biological parents, consistent economic support for many child expenses, including postsec-ondary education, has often been problematic. Funds for college should be a point of negotiation in divorce settlements.

Religion

Many religious communities welcome stepfamilies. Indeed, a number of congregations have created special marriage ceremonies for stepfamilies, ceremonies that both honor their family history and provide a role for the children in the wedding ceremony. Particularly because of the commitment involved in a religious remarriage ceremony, congregations are glad to assist in the stabilization of this family form.

For the stepfamily, marriage in a religious community may be both positive and negative. The positive effects confirm family members' faith and place the new family within a supportive religious community. However, the newly married stepfamily may believe that using the symbols of the first-marriage religious community erases the real differences in the stepfamily. One can easily light a symbolic candle in a marriage ceremony, but establishing new rules for discipline, forging a widening array of new relationships, and accessing and distributing resources in a stepfamily are far more complex. The need for ongoing support, faith, and creativity in the new stepfamily cannot be overemphasized.

Health Care

Access to health care and family planning in stepfamilies is correlated strongly with income, social class, and residence. Although many children are born into existing stepfamilies, those data are not readily available. Couples need to be especially clear about their decision to have more children, and ages of both spouses can be a significant factor. The decision to have more children may be different if one parent has no previous children than if both are already parents. The total number of family members the two parents can support, both emotionally and financially, are considerations. At any rate, birth control should be used until relationships are clarified, just as in early marriages.

The most difficult issues around health may involve who should provide ongoing health care benefits for the children of previous marriages. Here the ambiguous legal status of stepparents clouds the issue. Some attempts to clarify this status in regard to economic support and the provision of health care benefits are underway (Mason, 1998). Both program administrators and family lawyers are reviewing options, some of which can be characterized as seeing the stepparent as a "stranger" or as an "in loco parentis." A stranger would have no financial or legal obligation; *in loco parentis* means a stepparent would "stand in place" of the biological parent, with all rights and obligations assigned.

Economic Factors

Stepfamilies typically have both spouses in the workforce, with both parents often having independently headed their households before the marriage and having invested in careers. In addition, the dual-career family status probably relates to the high cost of raising children, to the possibility that one of the spouses has to maintain economic support for children from a previous marriage, and to long-range economic security.

That is, once a spouse has experienced a marriage breakup or the death of a spouse, any economic independence achieved is very difficult to give up.

Housing is one of the important economic and relationship decisions for the stepfamily. It is usually not a good idea for the family to live in a residence that was formerly the residence of one of the marriage partners. This can cause territorial feelings for those people who resided in the house previously, or it can cause them to be protective of their space and to resent change and intrusion. Literature on children's transition through divorce and remarriage, however, stresses the importance of maintaining continuity and relationships for the children in neighborhoods and schools. Sometimes these two objectives can conflict, and the family must make tough decisions about how to establish a new home that is fair to everyone involved and gives all a chance for new interpersonal relationships. Whatever decisions are made, stepfamily members must then be sensitive to transitions and the need for support and clarification of rights and responsibilities.

When economic realities or market conditions suggest the need to remain in one of the adults' current residences, remodeling, redecorating, or reassigning space to facilitate the new relationships needs to be considered. It is particularly important that children of late elementary and junior and senior high school age have private space away from the parents' space. Such designs are sometimes difficult to find except in higher-priced housing.

When a divorced or widowed woman with dependent children remarries, her financial status typically improves. However, a divorced man who remarries typically assumes more financial responsibility and often feels torn between the financial demands of the two families. Stepfamilies bring their financial history from earlier marriages into the new relationship. The new marriage has more complex relationships and, perhaps, more sources of income, so new patterns of handling money may be needed. Aside from spousal employment, support payments (and their inconsistency) and money and gifts from noncustodial parents and relatives are additional sources of income. The pattern of pooling some sources of income seems to increase the stability of the new marriage. However, it may be necessary to keep separate records of how money for child support is spent. Spouses may wish for a measure of financial independence, too, symbolized by maintaining separate accounts.

Governmental Policies and Agencies

Stepfamilies have dealt with the court responsible for granting divorces, and many have dealt with the Department of Social Services enforcement division for child support or with Temporary Assistance for Needy Families (TANF). The lack of legal standing for a stepparent, with regard to the stepchildren, can cause concern (Mason & Mauldon, 1996). Stepparents who are strongly committed to their new family frequently voice frustration and confusion over their legal responsibility for their stepchildren in matters of health care. Legal guardianship usually remains with the biological parents until they die or give up legal responsibility for their children. In England, a new mode of parenting was introduced in the Children Act of 1989 (Mason, 1998). In this model, an individual who has been a stepparent for at least two years may petition for a *residence order* for his or her spouse's child. The order provides the petitioner parental responsibility toward the child until the age of 16 but does not extinguish the biological parents' rights.

In situations where the biological noncustodial parent agrees, stepparents can legally adopt their stepchildren. When a single never-married parent marries, there are ambiguous interpretations of statutes surrounding the parental rights of the noncustodial biological parent. When a single person without children marries a person with children, the new stepparent may have especially favorable feelings toward adopting the stepchildren. These new family relationships point out the need to revise policies that are now inadequate. Because new technologies have created more complex methods of conception and parenthood, this debate regarding stepparent adoptions is not likely to be easily resolved.

Children report that when their parent and stepparent divorced, after establishing a caring relationship with a stepparent, they found no legal protection for that relationship. In addition, if a custodial biological parent should die prematurely, the children may be placed in the custody of the surviving noncustodial biological parent, even though they have been living happily with and were being nurtured by a stepparent who desires to continue that role. Grandparent relationships also are often severed by death or divorce in stepfamilies.

FAMILY INTERACTIONS AND KINSHIP NETWORKS

Extended-family interactions in divorce and remarriage can be either supportive or harmful. Stepfamilies create an increasing number of relationships, and there must be negotiations about the intensity of involvement, the scheduling, and decision-making power in extended-family relationships. A new stepfamily needs to establish its own practices but also honor the connections to meaningful relationships that were established prior to the marriage.

Patience and creativity on the part of the new family members are needed. Honesty and clear negotiation with extended-family members are also important. Stepparents frequently report that the extended-family members provide helpful respite care for children or continuity of relationships while the newly married pair establish their own patterns and take time for nurturing their relationship (Duran-Aydintug, 1993).

Strength and satisfaction in the marital relationship are strong predictors of satisfaction and endurance in the first marriage, according to most family literature. However, within stepfamilies, the satisfaction with—or the lack of conflict in—stepparent and stepchildren relations is the most powerful determinant of family satisfaction and endurance (Kheshgi-Genovese & Genovese, 1997). Therefore, it is important for extended-family members to help stabilize and encourage positive stepparent–stepchild relationships and to provide support and nurturance for the new family. Understanding and flexibility can help maintain realistic and caring connections with the new stepfamily.

CHANGE AND ADAPTATION

The stepfamily that arises after divorce is a relatively new reality in American society, and many of our social and educational systems are not yet sensitive to the needs of this family type. Because of negative societal attitudes and inadequate information, many stepfamilies struggle alone with very complex challenges. The adaptations required in a stepfamily often challenge ideas about how resources should be shared, how children should be raised, and how families should function. Many adults entering stepfamilies have not had informed professional support in making their decision and planning for this new family form. Men in particular have been socialized to a more rigid role, allowing less flexibility in the family. A stepfather needs to create a new role with stepchildren and with other extended-family members. Professionals working with stepfamilies find that over time the rules and relationships often change (Pappernow, 1980). Stepfamilies need to remain flexible and responsive to members' needs.

Just as divorce studies suggested that a period of 18 to 24 months following a divorce is necessary to reintegrate and balance the new family structure, stepfamilies also report a need to adjust and change over time. Stepfamilies with adolescent children seem to be particularly stressed by divided loyalties, challenges to family decisions, and the competing activities of peer groups. Noncustodial parents, trying to maintain healthy relationships with their adolescents, find that individual time with their children is increasingly difficult to arrange. Noncustodial parents usually find it necessary to travel to the community where their children reside in order to participate in school and community activities during their children's adolescent years. Similarly, stepfamilies find that attendance at school and community events quickly makes them confront the challenge of maintaining positive communication with ex-spouses—the children's biological parents.

Over time, many children in stepfamilies may change their residence as conflict increases or as the need for different resources becomes apparent. Adolescents nearing college age may move to the community of their other biological parent to qualify for residential status near an institution of higher education. Other young people may change their residence to be in a job market that provides more employment opportunities for a young person who is saving for college or other goals. Parents may find that much of their relationship has to be maintained by phone, e-mail, or letters.

New stepfamilies often find that extended-family members are usually immediately positive and initiate invitations for the new family to join in. Following this initial enthusiasm, a realistic pattern of inclusion and support must evolve. As children in stepfamilies mature, maintaining relationships with a variety of extended-family members can be very positive (Sanders & Trygstad, 1989). When conflicts may emerge between a stepparent and child, a supportive grandparent, aunt, or uncle may facilitate the maintenance of family bonds (Bray & Berger, 1990). Children benefit from the richness of all the relationships that support positive development, resulting in a stepfamily that works well together.

One of the most difficult periods of time for all stepfamilies comes when the family members recognize that life is complicated and that active negotiation skills are needed. The fantasized myths portrayed in literature, or imagined by two adults during the courting period, must be laid to rest before positive, realistic family patterns can be accepted. When harmony and effectiveness are not achieved automatically, a stepfamily can become discouraged at this lack of success. Professionals and other stepfamilies can be key supporters, providing humor, support, and realistic family plans.

HELPFUL TECHNIQUES FOR SERVING STEPFAMILIES

Research and clinical literature give a number of helpful guidelines for professionals serving and supporting stepfamilies. You may find that one of the most helpful activities for you as a professional is to read diaries, autobiographies, and Websites where stepfamilies speak with their own voices. Given the rate of divorce and remarriage, most adults know some stepfamilies who may be willing to provide informal unique education about their realities. You can then begin to see the world through different eyes and perform your own analysis of how systems can become more supportive to stepfamilies.

In recent years, research literature has provided more realistic guidance to helping professionals who service stepfamilies. Researchers such as Ludwig (2001) have begun to describe the importance of looking at stepfamily functioning and suggest that stepfamilies often show a lower level of cohesion than is typically associated with a well-functioning family. Numerous clinicians and researchers (e.g., Gerrard, 2001, 2002) comment that a stepfamily is always born out of grief whether divorce or death. Although the variables such as timing, culture, economics, and personality mark each stepfamily's journey as unique, many stepfamilies have not fully dealt with the grief and anger associated with losses even as they are concentrating on new beginnings.

Inadequacy of Agency Forms

The forms used by educational and human service agencies frequently do not provide adequate spaces or correct titles to account for all members of the household or family. Enrollment forms frequently only ask for parent names. Stepfamilies are then confused about whether they should list custodial parents, stepparents, or biological parents, or, for reasons of insurance or emergencies, for instance, only the person with the health care policy. These examples illustrate the need to modernize our processes and procedures for gaining accurate information about families in order to serve them well. A simpler form that asks for the names of persons in a household or family and each person's relationship to the children, as well as their status for health care, would aid educational discussions as well as decision-making sessions with professionals.

Support Groups

As children and youth enter stepfamilies, remember that their attitudes are likely to be different from those of the adults. It is vital to acknowledge and celebrate changes with children, in their school, neighborhood, youth group, social setting, church, mosque, or synagogue, but it is also important to be sensitive to the children's feelings about these changes. A public announcement about a new stepfamily may need to be preceded by special private time with a professional in which the child or youth has a chance to express confusion, fears, and concerns about the new family form. Professionals serving these families should acknowledge children's feelings, helping them deal with these significant transitions. Encouraging children to provide drawings or photographs of everyone in their family and to talk about the new relationships are important parts of this process. Support groups for children and youth, led by professionals skilled in identifying the expected struggles of children in transition, are also helpful.

Children and youth are often not certain whether their new family form is acceptable in the wider community. Professionals supportive of children can initiate positive introductions and interactions among the group of parents and extended-family members (Austin, 1993). Family conferences in which decisions about children are made should include, where possible, all relevant adults involved with the children. Family nights or intergenerational programs should make families feel welcome to bring both the biological parents and stepparents to celebrate with the child.

Ask the legal guardians directly about who the young child can be released to and what information can be shared with other significant adults. School evaluation sessions, report cards, and news about neighborhood youth events can then be shared with more than one household.

The goal of your relationships with stepfamilies, as a professional, is to facilitate good family relationships and the child's growth and development in the new family. Literature and media pieces that include references to stepfamilies and information sources for stepfamilies will provide help and make this family form more visible and supported in the wider environment. Because approximately a quarter of divorced and remarried families show high levels of conflict and anger (Johnston & Roseby, 1997), joint conferences might be impossible. Ask the parents directly for their advice and desires about including noncustodial parents, grandparents, stepparents, and others in planning.

Encouraging children and youth to invent new names and special rituals with new relatives will also help in their adjustment. New rules need to be developed for the specifics of each particular stepfamily. When a young person has been living with a single parent, the inclusion of the new stepparent in personal decisions or in household work discussions can be frustrating and awkward. Helping a stepparent and stepchild negotiate new rules with a third party can be an important function for a sensitive professional. Examples might include helping a child learn how to introduce a stepparent, or to know which family matters need to be discussed by both parents before a decision is made.

Attempts to make the stepfamily like a family from another era or structure are inappropriate. Organization in this new family requires intelligence, good humor, and creativity on everyone's part. Professionals can sometimes play key roles in providing new perspectives, approval, and acceptance of new family rituals and relationships. When children's entrance into a stepfamily results in a move to a new neighborhood away from friends, professionals can help with this transition. Youth organizations, for example, sometimes have farewell celebrations for the child. Providing photographs for the children to take with them and some ways the children can keep in contact, either by phone or by letters and e-mail, are important transition supports for a new life structure.

Many stepfamilies are not supported by a national or local group for stepfamilies. The Stepfamily Association of America, formed in the 1980s by Emily and John Visha, worked for 20 years providing a newsletter, local chapter support, an annual conference for professionals, and numerous other resources. In 2006, they turned all their resources over to the National Stepfamily Resource Center maintained at Auburn University. The Stepfamily Foundation has educational and advocacy information for members and the public. Consult the names and addresses at the end of this chapter for information. All professionals in regular contact with families should also be members of these organizations, in order to receive their materials. The latest accurate and positive information can then be shared with coworkers and clients.

✢ CONCLUSIONS

Both the number and the complexity of stepfamilies are increasing in the United States. Although there are some social-class differences in the numbers of stepfamilies, they increasingly involve people from all ethnic and cultural groups in the United States. Cohabiting heterosexual adults or homosexual partners with their children often function as stepfamilies but are not always counted as such (Baum, 2000; Christensen, 2000). A number of separated adults do not divorce or remarry because of religious, legal, or economic considerations. When public assistance, child support, or alimony would terminate upon a parent's remarriage, some parents make the decision to forgo legal marriage to maintain economic security. Such personal decisions reflect the inadequacy of family law, public policies, and society in dealing with new family forms.

A stepfamily involves relationships that are more complex than first marriages, even though many stepfamilies pretend they are just like first-marriage families. The U.S. legal system has largely neglected stepfamilies, and our social systems are just beginning to understand and support these relationships.

For stepfamilies to succeed, they must understand the diversity and complexity of their new structures. Dealing honestly and openly with the differences in each of the family members' perspectives and needs is important. Although the divorce rate is somewhat higher among stepfamilies than first-marriage families, adults seem generally satisfied with their second choices. Relationships with the children in stepfamilies is a significant key to the success and stability of the marriage, and the successful marriage provides family strength even when stepchildren are not close to a new parent. Professionals who provide transition groups for stepchildren, and for children and parents together, are delivering an important service to these families.

Finally, stepfamilies provide opportunities to understand and recognize the joys and complexities of diverse families. Ceglian and Oscarson (2000) found that women who had received education and support for the new family challenges before marriage were more successful and realistic in the stepmother role. Positive supportive messages from you, as a helping professional, will go a long way toward helping these families deal realistically with challenges. The myths of the wicked stepmother and the blended family group should disappear with recognition that successful stepfamilies can be flexible, complex, and resilient family forms.

✦ STUDY QUESTIONS

1. What are the negative implications of the terms *blended families* or *reconstituted families?*
2. Currently, how many first marriages in the United States end in divorce? How many remarriages end in divorce?
3. What major trends have increased the number of stepfamilies in the United States?
4. Why do some stepfamilies deny the parental remarried status?
5. What are the most important predictors of a strong, enduring stepfamily?
6. Why is it recommended that a stepfamily move into a new home rather than remain in the present house of one of the partners?
7. Describe ideal roles for a stepfather and a stepmother.
8. List the positive and negative aspects for children in a stepfamily.
9. List ways the extended-family members can show support for stepfamily members.
10. Why are some professionals concerned about incest or sexual abuse in stepfamilies?
11. Describe the typical stepfamily, relative to custody and residence of children.
12. How do the tasks for children entering a new stepfamily differ from the tasks of their parents?
13. How does the media view of stepfamilies interfere with positive stepfamily adjustments?
14. Describe the problems of stepparents' and grandparents' legal rights with their stepchildren.

✦ APPLICATIONS

1. Investigate whether there are Stepfamily Association affiliate groups in your local community, and attend a meeting of this group. Report on the issues raised and on the various family forms represented.
2. Interview stepfamilies who are willing to talk about their current family structure. Make certain to complete a genogram of the family, which includes a chart of all the significant biological, legal, and fictive kin relationships.

3. Obtain copies of the Stepfamily Association of America newsletter, and report on the central themes of articles.
4. Watch a popular current television show that portrays a stepfamily. Make up a list of the myths and facts illustrated to discuss in class.
5. Reflect on the power and psychological implications of stepparents having no legal right or responsibilities toward their stepchildren. Interview a stepparent on this topic, and write a one-page summary of his or her experiences and recommendations.
6. Design a family bonding ritual for a new stepmother with two biological children and for a stepfather with a biological son. Consider topics that should be included and activities to bond the new family form.
7. Design a family schedule for vacations and holidays for a stepfamily of five, including two children in custody of the father and one child from the wife's previous marriage, not in her custody.
8. Write a two-page essay on the implications of a new stepfamily being formed before the social and psychological divorces from the previous marriages are completed.
9. Create a set of rules for establishing a family budget in a new stepfamily comprised of one child from each of two previous marriages and two working parents.
10. Write a one-page essay on the advantages of viewing a stepfamily from a binuclear view.
11. Obtain the school enrollment and the emergency forms from a local school district. Write a brief summary of whether they are appropriate for the relationships in a new stepfamily.

✦ ORGANIZATIONS

Stepfamily Foundation, Inc., 333 West End Avenue, New York, NY 10023
www.stepfamily.org/

✦ KEY INTERNET RESOURCES

American Coalition for Fathers and Children
www.acfc.org/site/PageServer

APA Stepfamily Resources
www.helping.apa.org/step.html

The Stepfamily Foundation, Inc
www.stepfamily.org/content.html

Rainbows
www.rainbows.org/rainbows.html

National Stepfamily Resource Center
www.stepfamilies.info/

The Stepfamily Life
www.thestepfamilylife.com

✦ FURTHER READING

Burns, C. (1985). *Stepmotherhood: How to survive without feeling frustrated, left out or abused.* New York: Harper & Row.

Chedekel, D. S., & O'Connell, K. (2002). *The blended family sourcebook.* Chicago: Contemporary Books.

Clapp, G. (2000). *Divorce and new beginnings: A complete guide to recovery, co-parenting, solo parenting, and stepfamilies* (2nd ed.). New York: Wiley and Sons.

Cohn, R. (2003). *The steps.* New York: Simon & Schuster.

Demo, D. H., Allen, K. R., & Fine, M. A. (2000). *Handbook of family diversity.* New York: Oxford University Press.

Leman, K. (1994). *Living in a stepfamily without getting stepped on.* Nashville, TN: Thomas Nelson.

Thayer, N. (1981). *Stepping.* London: Sphere Books.

Visher, E., & Visher, S. S. (1988). *Old loyalties, new ties.* New York: Brunner Nagel.

Wallerstein, J. S., Lewis, J., & Blakeslee, S. (2000). *The unexpected legacy of divorce: A twenty-five year landmark study.* New York: Hyperion.

Whitehead, B. D. (1993, April 4). Dan Quayle was right. *The Atlantic Monthly,* p. 271.

Wolkoff, J. (1982). *Happily ever after . . . almost.* New York: Dell.

Zinn, M. B. (1992). Family, race and poverty in the eighties. In B. Thorne (Ed.), *Rethinking the family* (pp. 71–90). Boston: Northeastern University Press.

→ 13

Families with Children with Special Needs

→ Key Concepts

- Americans with Disabilities Act (ADA)
- Early Intervention Program
- Individualized Education Program (IEP)
- Individualized Family Service Plan (IFSP)
- Individuals with Disabilities Education Act (IDEA)
- Least Restrictive Environment
- No Child Left Behind
- Whole School Plan

George Dodson/PH College

Kids often stare and ask what's wrong with her. I don't mind because I tell them how being different makes her special. But when she's older, will she have any friends? Will other kids' curiosity turn into taunting?

It really hits me at the playground that Laura will never be normal. All the other kids are running and climbing and she needs my help. The oddity is that she has a great time while I get depressed.

—Father of a child with special needs

Families with members who are physically, socially, emotionally, or cognitively challenged are a population that needs focused, responsive educational and social service systems. The group of handicapping conditions includes those termed *disabilities*, which are technically problems in seeing, hearing, walking, talking, climbing or lifting (functional activities) or the self-care tasks referred to as activities of daily living (ADLs). These families as a group do not represent a specific structure, social class, or ethnicity. Rather, members with special needs are found in families of single parents, stepparents, communal cohabiting, homosexual partners, and across all ethnic groups. Obviously both children and adults can have special challenges, but this chapter focuses on families with children with special needs. Successful nurturing of a challenged child places unique demands on the family, regardless of its structure. Many parents of children with special needs talk about the dramatic change in their lives after the diagnosis of a disability or handicapping condition in their child.

PARTNERING WITH PARENTS

Parents need the partnering with professionals that is embodied in the new concept of service for families with a special needs member. According to Hudgens, Hobfall, and

Lerman (1989), chronic illness and disabling conditions are "powerful forces that often control the structure, actions, and reactions of family members. They can affect sweeping changes in family roles, realign subsystems within the family, and isolate family members from each other and outside influences" (p. 68). Many professionals comment that this group "does not discriminate. You can join at any time." Disabilities can develop from accidents resulting from the actions of someone else, creating a lifelong challenge.

Many service providers, educators, and researchers have described the powerful influence that a child with special needs can have on the family system. The family members have to cope with problems that usually don't exist for other children. There are questions about appropriate child care, finances for special services, and practical problems of relationship building and family care roles. There are also fundamental questions about how much independence a child can achieve, what kind of support these children will need to cope with certain challenges, and what the future holds.

Families face a lifetime of concern for a child with special needs. As noted in the opening vignette, parents may have strong reactions of grief, depression, and fear as they struggle with meeting their child's needs. Dramatic changes in laws and in the models of services for persons with disabilities and special needs have opened up many possibilities for children and their families (Gilbert, 1998). However, many children with special needs live in communities, neighborhoods, and families that may not know about the availability of or fully take advantage of benefits from recently enhanced services. As professionals serving families, you need to know how to partner with these families, and how to make certain that they receive information about all services for which they are eligible. This information must be provided in ways that enable the family to participate fully in decision making about services to their child.

The new model of an Individualized Family Service Plan (IFSP), provided for in the Education of the Handicapped Act Amendments of 1986 (P. L. 99–457), is a clear statement of a service philosophy for children with special needs and their families. However, at the same time that this new philosophy encourages partnerships between systems for the provision of services, economic strains and political conservatism in the United States have caused resentment and conflict over the cost and appropriateness of a variety of services. The 1997 amendments to the Individuals with Disabilities Education Act (IDEA) make a strong case for the need to raise expectations for all children with disabilities and focus more aggressive efforts to enhance partnerships between parents, service agencies, and educators. Professionals who serve families with children with special needs need skills in understanding advocacy, in interpreting public laws, and in coping with the realities of public opinion and public criticism of special services for children. Helping those with special needs become independent and economically self-sufficient are important goals for the country. Professionals working in this area need to learn about systems available to assist families with education, health services, care and respite services, and vocational training/employment services. In most of these areas, there are federal, state, and local programs that require specialized knowledge of eligibility and access.

HISTORICAL BACKGROUND

Significant progress in advocacy and legislation for persons with disabilities was achieved in the United States during the 1970s, 1980s, and 1990s. There are now clear statements in public law reinforcing the commitment to inclusiveness in education and social services, involving families as partners in creating appropriate services for their family members, and reinforcing goals of employment and independence. It is important to recognize that this new method of working with families is a departure from earlier periods in our history. If you review models of services for persons with disabilities in the late 1800s and early 1900s, treatment could be labeled as benign neglect. In other words, families were left to take care of their own members. If the child or young person did not readily fit into services or education provided to other children and youth, the family was expected to create needed services on their own. For persons with extreme disabilities, there were references to abandonment or to accidents that appeared deliberate or the result of neglect. Public institutions were at best custodial, and, at worst, physically and psychologically abusive.

Segregation

Families struggled alone with challenged members well into the twentieth century. Change came slowly as a result of aggressive actions on the part of a few social reformers and the publication of works such as Ward's (1946) *The Snake Pit*. As part of these reform efforts, family members and their advocates began increasingly to understand that the provision of services for persons with disabilities would not be made available unless family members themselves, who were most knowledgeable about the realities, became aggressive and eloquent spokespersons. Advocates' actions resulted in an increasing number of special services that would be labeled "segregated service," always separated from other children and youth who were receiving public education and community support. There was little thought that these children could become economically self-sufficient or included in the whole community.

Mainstreaming

As families and advocates continued to protest and educate the broader public and the policymakers, significant federal legislation introduced an era of integrated services, bringing with it the term *mainstreaming*. In 1975 the Education for All Handicapped Children Act (P.L. 94–142) was passed, mandating that all states must provide a free and appropriate education for all children. Prior to the Education for All Handicapped Children Act, more than half of all children in the United States with disabilities did not receive appropriate education and a million of them were excluded entirely from the public school system. A key provision of the new law was the development of an Individualized Educational Program (IEP) for each child and a commitment to serve the child in the "least restrictive environment." Under this philosophy of service, children were placed with their peers in so-called mainstream educational services. For example, children who were "learning disabled" spent time in a resource room with a specially trained teacher only for those subjects most directly impacted by the learning disability. At other times they participated in classes and social interaction with their age peers.

This era of mainstreaming, or integrated services, has had both positive and negative results. In a positive sense, on one hand, more children were allowed access to a variety of services and experiences in their education. Their lives were enhanced by these opportunities and they became more visible in the community. On the other hand, the federal law, which mandates these services, creates an imperative for school districts to provide appropriate services for children with special needs even when they are financially strapped in doing so. Some children with disabilities require extensive and sophisticated teaching and support in mainstream environments. When teachers have not been adequately prepared in preservice or in-service training, they cannot provide appropriate education for children with special needs and at the same time adequately teach all students in the classroom. P. L. 94–142 had great implications for teacher education. Colleges and universities are still enhancing their curricula to respond to these demands. Teachers who were trained before the curriculum prepared them for students with special needs required in-service opportunities and ongoing consultation. In the 1990s an emphasis on whole school plans or full inclusion with most children with special needs served in general classrooms presented serious demands on staff (see Kavale & Forness, 2000; D'Amato & Rothlisberg, 1997).

Partnerships

The current era of service models for children with special needs could be labeled a partnership; that is, a family-based model for education and services, linking the entire family and the professional. Although P. L. 94–142 of 1975 required parents to be present at the Individualized Educational Plan (IEP) meetings and sign off on plans, there was still strong emphasis on the parent as a recipient of professional recommendations. Subsequently, three relevant public laws have been passed that have changed these relationships.

Federal Legislation

The first was P. L. 99–457 of 1986. Part H of this act added to the Education of the Handicapped Act. This new act, known as the "Early Intervention Act," requires states to establish comprehensive multidisciplinary systems for early intervention services to infants and toddlers. With this act, schools became responsible for providing appropriate educational services for challenged children and youth from birth through age 25, placing special emphasis on the prekindergarten years.

In 1991 P. L. 102–52 gave states the option of taking two additional years to develop a system for serving all eligible children in their state. In October 1991 P. L. 102–119 reauthorized the early intervention part of the Education of the Handicapped Act and strengthened its family partnership provisions. These last three laws are known as IDEA, or the Individuals with Disabilities Education Act. The purposes of these laws are as follows:

1. To enhance the development of infants and toddlers and minimize potential developmental delay.

2. To reduce the need for special education classes once these infants and toddlers reach school age.
3. To increase the likelihood that individuals with disabilities will lead productive lives.
4. To enhance the capacity of families to meet their infants' and toddlers' needs.
5. To increase agencies' and service providers' capacity to identify, evaluate, and meet the needs of minority, low-income, inner-city, rural, and other underrepresented populations with special services.

Interagency Councils

To meet these goals, each state is responsible for developing comprehensive, coordinated, multidisciplinary, interagency programs for infants, toddlers, and their families. In addition, they are to coordinate the payment for these services from federal, state, local, and private sources of funding, and to improve and enhance existing services for intervention. An important requirement is that the State Interagency Coordinating Council, which oversees Early Intervention Services, must include a state education representative with enough authority to engage in policy planning and implementation. This protects children and families from having to advocate individually for the implementation of the plan agreed on in the interagency, interdisciplinary team meeting.

Family Participation

Legislation protecting family interests and mandating early intervention with regard to infants and toddlers exemplifies a new understanding of the importance of early development and partnerships with parents. One of the most important requirements of P. L. 102–119 is that of informed parental consent. Before any services are provided, the child and the family must receive an explanation of the recommendations. The family does not have to accept all services offered, but only those agreed to as appropriate by the family. In the new law, the Individualized Educational Plan was changed to the Individualized Family Service Plan (IFSP). The IFSP is the state's legally binding commitment to provide services to the family. Another important part of P. L. 102–119 is the requirement that states plan a smooth transition for the child from the Early Intervention Program into a preschool program for children with disabilities by age 3. The emphasis on early intervention is based on an understanding of the critical role that the preschool years play in establishing developmental paths for children. Yet this early emphasis on intervention may have created unrealistic expectations among some people that dramatically fewer special services would be needed in the K–12 years.

National Negotiations

From 1975 to 1997, the number of students classified as disabled increased to 12.4 percent of the school population with 70 percent of them taught in regular classes. The costs for special education of these students total $32 billion, with only $4 billion contributed from the federal government. In 1995 the Republican-led legislature was concerned about the costs of the programs and attempted to change the provisions of IDEA. School personnel wanted the flexibility to punish students with special needs even if that meant segregating or excluding them. Advocates refused to agree, and the IDEA legislation was deadlocked for two years. It was finally passed after tough negotiations and signed into law by President Bill Clinton in June 1997. It increases parents' and regular classroom teachers' involvement in IEP development, reduces incentives for segregated placements, increases federal funding, and provides more flexibility to states. In addition, it confirms the importance of classroom discipline while protecting the right to an education and enhances funding for infant, toddler, and preschool programs.

The No Child Left Behind Act of 2002 further impacted the administration of special education programs in public schools. The purpose of No Child Left Behind is to assure that every child makes "adequate yearly progress" in math, reading, and science proficiency. The various provisions of the bill stipulate results-based accountability, curriculum and teaching techniques based on scientific research, more options for parents, and increased local control to allow flexibility. The accountability component requires that districts test all students' reading and math skills, annually for students in grades 3 through 8, and at least once in grades 10 through 12. Special education students are not exempted from the adequate yearly progress provision. According to No Child Left Behind guidelines issued in 2003, school districts and states are allowed to use alternative standards to determine adequate yearly progress for some students—up to 1 percent of the student population. The guidelines indicate that only students with "significant" cognitive disabilities are to be included in the 1 percent. Other students who cannot meet the proficiency standards must be counted in the "nonproficient" category. State and local education agencies can request a waiver of the 1 percent cap if data can be presented to support the request (Applequist, 2005).

Involving parents in more of the decision-making processes regarding their child's education means that educators have an opportunity to encourage support and reinforcement of educational programs and activities throughout the daily and yearly cycle of their students' lives. When parents agree with the curriculum and teaching techniques, students may receive reinforcement for their demonstration of knowledge, skills, and for their efforts both inside and outside the classroom. In an age of instant access information (sometimes with low credibility, such as Internet sources), competing curricula, and multiple teaching techniques for a single learning exigence such as autism, parents may present an adversarial face to the educational team. Various provisions in the educational mandates (IDEA and No Child Left Behind) may encourage parents to bring litigation against the school district or other agencies to require use of a specific teaching technique or curriculum (Applequist, 2005). For example, there are lawsuits in at least two states where the parents of students with autism are requesting tuition reimbursement from the home school district so that their student can attend a private school; in both cases teaching techniques used at the private school are preferable, in the parents' judgement, to that offered by the home school district.

Bills to amend IDEA and/or No Child Left Behind are proposed every legislative session. Some are designed to prescribe relationships and responsibilities, and some are designed to procribe practices and opportunities.

In all these legislative efforts, a fundamental societal tension often emerges. Our public education system has been under attack for its quality and effectiveness for some time—especially as it responds to the talents and needs of special students. In the political transition of the early twenty-first century, in which many public functions are being divested from the federal level to state responsibilities, the guarantees of educational quality are being debated. Universal public education has long been an American value, but the economic and political support for high-quality education, particularly for any students with special needs, has been eroding. In a time when the United States is involved in a costly war and the economy is transitioning from pre-9/11 structures, state and local funding for No Child Left Behind requirements has been controversial. Educational and other service professionals who support families of these students have a responsibility to engage in discussions about the need for appropriate educational planning with families. However, it must be acknowledged that with budget constraints, many decisions may unfortunately end up in the judicial system, rather than in the ecosystems closest to the child and family. This can create adversarial relationships among parties charged with providing service to families.

SOCIOCULTURAL FOUNDATIONS

Children with special needs exist across all social classes and racial and cultural groups. Because there are so many different types of challenges, and so many individuals with multiple disabilities, describing these families as one group is not appropriate. As professionals serving these families, you need to understand how individual children with special challenges place demands on families and how the families organize themselves to respond.

Public litigation to protect the rights of and services to persons with disabilities over the last quarter of the twentieth century reflects a general compassion toward vulnerable children and families. Also reflected is a sense of justice and the recognition that public education and social and health services should be more universally available. Indeed, some claim the true test of a humane culture is the effectiveness of services to its most vulnerable citizens.

Providing appropriate nurturance and challenge to children with special needs represents a value placed on individual development, diversity, and independence. However, these values, which reflect a respect for individual lives and a shared responsibility for development, conflict with economic concerns about limited resources and the need to prioritize where resources are spent. Many families with children who have special needs talk about the constant demand to care for their children to the best of their ability, while being effective and aggressive advocates for appropriate services from school districts, health professionals, social service agencies, and other community systems.

Although the dual roles of caretaker and advocate are not unique to families with children who have special needs, a number of researchers and service providers describe the intense sense of stress, grief, and anger that these families experience (Mullins, 1987; Singer & Irvin, 1989). Beavers (1989) wrote about the need for families to grieve over the loss of the "perfect" child and to learn to deal realistically with the challenges their child presents. This parental task is not unique to parents of children with disabilities because most parents reveal the struggle to accept their child's individual characteristics as different from the child they imagined before birth or adoption. Yet parents who have a child with special needs may have to give up certain goals for their child. Grief and frustration are attached to the loss of companionship, vigorous athletic achievements, and economic and social success that they imagined for their child.

Delayed and Ambiguous Diagnoses

There are special struggles for families with children whose special needs are not recognized immediately at birth. Disabilities that are apparent only gradually, or occur after a later trauma or accident, present different challenges to families. A slow process of questioning, fear, and anxiety can be destructive to a parent's sense of pride and competence. In addition, limitations believed to be caused by parental behaviors, such as fetal alcohol syndrome (FAS), present a different struggle for families and society, ranging from compassion for the child to anger against the parent.

Helping professionals, service providers, and policymakers are often uncomfortable with the amount of ambiguity that surrounds the etiology of disabilities. About half of children with special needs show disabilities with unknown causes. In a society that values the scientific pursuit of knowledge, this lack of information frustrates and angers some people.

Appropriate Environment

In Connor's 1997 study, families with children with special needs described their conflicts regarding the appropriate learning environments for their children. If their children are given segregated education and services, they may be with like peers and have the protection and support of specially trained professionals. However, their world and stimulation are more limited. If these children are included by society in all their activities, then more children and adults are educated about the realistic range of human development. However, individual children with disabilities may be discriminated against, misunderstood, abused, or not provided with optimal services. In the 1990s the emphasis on "whole school" approaches embodied in the 1997 amendments to IDEA created even more need for effective education of all teachers and greater partnering with parents. Rather than provide children with special needs with "resource rooms" for individualized teaching and mainstream them in general classrooms in their highest functioning skill areas, children with special needs are included in regular classrooms with consultation for their teachers in order to adapt curriculum appropriately. Thus the "whole school" is responsible for understanding and adapting to these special needs.

These decisions about appropriate environments for education and care are complex because of the interaction of physical, cognitive, and socioemotional abilities and the political/economic stances of service providers. Because inclusive environments provide less protection and more stimulation, a critical evaluation of a child's socioemotional strengths should be made before any service is implemented. Every team that is developing an IEP or IFSP should consider the specific characteristics of the child, the family, and the potential placement environments. Many parents express a simple wish for their child to be accepted. However, ample evidence from research indicates that merely including a child with disabilities in an environment with other children does not guarantee acceptance and a positive outcome. In fact, according to Derman-Sparks and the ABC Task Force (1989), "Contact by itself does not necessarily reduce non-disabled children's misconceptions or fears. It may even intensify them unless adults take active steps to promote children's learning about each other."

Bern and Smith's (1998) in-depth research with six mainstream teachers illustrated the power of teacher attitudes and antipathy toward students with special needs. Bennett, De Luca, & Bruns (1997) describe the system complexity demanded by inclusion models for children with autism. Many parents of children with disabilities relate that their most difficult struggle with values is assisting their child with independence, appropriate to his or her situation. This is particularly an issue in adolescence, with questions about appropriate living environments, economic independence, and the possibility of procreation or sexual relationships with partners.

Status

Because of prejudice and the lack of experience in the wider culture, an individual with a disability is often seen as less valuable in an economic and social sense. A child with special needs represents new service demands on the family and the community.

Among families and professionals serving children with special needs, debates continue about the value of diagnostic labels. Categorical labels, such as "learning disabled," access state and federal special services. However, these labels can create lifelong categories of difference, and increased vulnerability to prejudice and misunderstanding.

Most families with children with special needs report that they often educate others who have no experience in responding to or appropriately interacting with children who have disabilities. This interaction stress can result in the sense of "marginalization" described by Greenspan (1998) in her description of mothers with children with special needs who feel invisible.

Changing Roles of Females

Typically, a family that includes a child with special needs creates a care challenge for the mother, who often is most responsible for the caretaking and interaction with professionals. May (1991) reports that one result of these practices is that fathers are frequently excluded and professionals have little experience dealing with the total family. Most often mothers are put in the position of interpreting information to their spouses or other family members when they may understand it inadequately themselves and/or are deeply distressed over its meaning for their family.

It is often mothers who have been instrumental in creating parent support groups and in reaching out to other parents of children with special needs. Early advocacy for persons with mental retardation was largely initiated by mothers. Many women reported personal gains in their self-confidence after advocating aggressively for the needs of their children. Sisters of children with disabilities are in a unique position in most families. Females are usually encouraged toward nurturing tasks. Sisters of persons with disabilities report a great deal of responsibility and involvement with their siblings with special needs. For some females, this can be a positive, growth-enhancing process. For others, it can cause anger and interfere with their own need for individualized parenting and nurturance. Because approximately two thirds of children with disabilities are male, a societal pattern of females caring for males is reinforced.

Changing Roles of Males

A number of researchers (Brotherson & Dollahite, 1997; Lamb & Billings, 1997; Murray & McDonald, 1996) have begun advocating strongly for fathers to be more actively involved in planning for their challenged children. They urge educators and social agencies to hold planning conferences in the early morning or late afternoon hours to facilitate participation by all family members without conflicting with work schedules. In addition, they encourage phone conferences or evening or weekend conferences, so that fathers might be more involved. Brotherson and Dollahite (1997) report ongoing work with fathers of young children with special needs to enhance the "generative ingenuity" in these men. Lamb and Billings (1997) and Murray and McDonald (1996) summarized the paucity of knowledge about how programs can better serve fathers and advocated stronger partnerships between professionals and fathers. Professionals who have led groups for fathers of children with disabilities note very positive support and sharing occurring between the men (Pruett, 1989). Professionals working with fathers often relate that it is difficult to help them express their feelings about their children with disabilities and to communicate effectively with their spouses. With support from professionals, fathers can gain more control over their lives by coming to terms with their grief, finding emotional support from other men, and learning appropriate father–child interaction patterns.

Family-life research suggests that men play the parenting role differently than women. Therefore, men need a chance to talk with other fathers about appropriate patterns and activities. Professionals find that discussion groups with fathers are most successful if leadership is shared by fathers, if time is provided for emotional sharing and support, and if time is provided for active skill development in which fathers and their children interact together. Having special father and child potluck suppers or outings with their children can reinforce skills and feelings of competence among fathers.

The higher proportion of males among persons with disabilities means that fathers more often grieve about the loss in potential development for sons instead of daughters. Increasing evidence indicates that fathers who are more fully engaged with their children are happier with themselves, show fewer signs of stress-related illnesses, and have wives who are more satisfied with their marriage. There is also evidence that fathers tend to set a tone for the whole family's attitudes toward children with disabilities (Frye, Greenburg, & Fewell, 1989). Therefore, understanding the father's perspective and role in the family is crucial to gaining successful help in support of a child's development.

Research comparing mothers and fathers of all children shows that mothers often become more skilled than fathers at parenting because they assume the caretaker responsibility more actively and accumulate more experience in interpreting their children's needs. This difference is heightened among parents of children with special needs. A man who already feels somewhat intimidated about his parenting skills may feel extremely sensitive about his inability to participate fully in parenting a child who is specially challenged.

Socialization Goals for Children

Family members need to talk about the amount and variety of resources available to provide for a child with special needs. With the advent of IFSPs under the federal law, more families are provided with respite care, or day care, that facilitates their own involvement in the workforce or in a wider social community. The parent of a child with special needs can become extremely hesitant about seeking assistance from friends, families, or professionals. Federal laws have provided dramatic changes for families. Now a quiet weekend for two or a break from caretaking for the rest of the family is not only possible but actively supported.

Family-life literature substantiates that the divorce rate is higher among couples who have children with disabilities. Because any stress in a family can affect the strength and viability of a marriage, this outcome is not unexpected. However, recent research has also suggested that divorce is more likely to occur if the disability is extremely severe and if it occurs relatively early in the couple's life ("Couples with Ill Children," 1993). Many professionals comment that a family that has successfully parented a child without disabilities has more confidence and strength when dealing with a child with special needs born later. Maturity and experience contribute to parenting skills and provide a better understanding of children.

The Role of Grandparents and Others

Families with children who have special needs often experience demands on time and caretaking beyond the demands other families experience. Grandparents may be important partners in dealing with these demands if they live nearby and are able to be supportive. Some parents report that grandparents exhibit more patience with the special learning challenges of their grandchildren. Of course, grandparents who are frail or lack concentration may have a difficult time with the physical care demands of some children. Most grandparents can probably learn to be supportive of the children's parents by encouraging them to seek information and take time for themselves.

A special note should be made of the grandparents' role in supporting their adult children's choices after learning the results of genetic diagnostic tests such as *amniocentesis* and *chorionic villi sampling.* As America has seen an increase in childbearing among older women, physicians usually recommend that these families take advantage of diagnostic tests. The possibility of birth defects and genetic anomalies increases with the age of the parents, especially the mother. More families are informed about potential risks and seek the additional information available through medical technology. Families opting for abortion following diagnostic results often do so without the knowledge of other people to avoid value-laden judgments.

Grandparents often report that one of the most difficult realities to deal with is their grief concerning the limitations on accomplishments of grandchildren who are seriously disabled. Grandparents who discuss these concerns with others are better able to come to terms with the realities of the support the family needs. The support and approval of the grandparenting generation are important to the stability and strength of families with children with special needs.

Grandparents as Substitute Parents

Of the 6 percent of all children in the United States reported to be living with their grandparents in 1996, 35 percent had neither parent present in the household (Casper & Bryson, 1998). Their parents were often unavailable because of incarceration, desertion, death, or problems with substance abuse. For parenting grandparents, the conflict between supporting the grandchildren and reconciling the disappearance or failure of their own adult children is a major task. Luckily, a number of support groups for these grandparents are being developed, and the media increasingly provides information about these new family challenges.

Substance abuse by the parents may have impacted the children. They may exhibit challenges caused by such abuse during their gestation. These challenges require interdisciplinary IFSPs that bring many service systems of the community together. At the same time, special consideration must be given to possible limitations on economic and legal resources of the family system. Grandparents involved in these systems need special support and strength.

In 1998 the Supreme Court ruled that HIV is within the broad scope of the Americans with Disabilities Act protection from discrimination. Because 95 percent of HIV-positive women are of childbearing age, we have seen an increases in HIV-positive infants who may have special needs. Although data (Isbell, 1992) show that the likelihood of mother-to-child infection is not as high as once thought, this is a unique group of children with special needs.

DEMOGRAPHICS

Both genetic and environmental events cause special needs. A number of diseases or disorders can be detected by genetic tests done before conception. Although the medical community is increasing its sophistication in diagnosis and genetic counseling, many of the rare, genetically inherited traits that cause disabilities occur at such an infrequent rate that most families are not prepared for the birth of a child with a genetic disability. Approximately 50 percent of disabilities that cause mental retardation are of unknown cause. Furthermore, we are increasingly becoming aware of disabilities that result from the complex interaction of genetics with the environment.

It is clear that the incidence of poor children of color in the ranks of children with special needs is higher than would be predicted from their percentage in the general population. Poor African American children are 2.3 times more likely to be identified as mentally retarded than poor White children. The increasing disparity between percentages of minority group children and minority group teachers (33 percent versus 13 percent) may increase the likelihood that a child from a minority group may not have an appropriate education.

As our nation ages, the number of citizens with specific disabilities will increase. In 1995, 1 in 5 Americans, or 54 million, reported some level of disability and 1 in 10 described their disability as severe (U.S. Census Bureau, 1997). As a nation, we will have personal and professional challenges in dealing with such trends.

Incidence of Special Needs in Children

The total incidence of special needs in the U.S. student population is generally quoted as 12.7 percent, depending on the definition of disabilities. When additional categories, such as culturally disadvantaged, are added to this group, then percentages up to 50 percent are sometimes quoted.

The most conservative estimate of the percentage of children with special needs in the United States is reflected in Table 13.1 (National Information Center for Children and Youth with Disabilities, 1991) with categories in descending order of incidence. One interesting phenomenon is our increased sophistication at differential diagnosis. Learning disabilities became understood as a separate category from mental retardation just 20 years ago. Only in the 1990s have we identified attention-deficit/hyperactivity disorder (ADHD) as separate and distinct from learning disabilities. This greater

Table 13.1   Estimated Percentages of Disabilities in Children Age 5–18

Disability	Percentage
Learning	4.73
Speech and language	2.5–4.0
Mental retardation	1.7
Visual impairment	1.2
Emotional impairment	0.8
Physical or health impairment	0.5
Severe emotional impairment	0.14
Autism	0.05–0.15
Total	11.62–13.22

Source: National Information Center for Children and Youth with Disabilities, (1991). Washington, DC: Author.

differentiation of special needs can result in more appropriate planning for children, but it also demands more sophisticated training and adaptation by teachers in whole school education models.

Impacts on Families

Different types of special needs can impact families in different ways, depending on how they affect the child's development. Disabilities that are visually apparent to the public, such as Down syndrome, blindness, hyperactivity, and those involving mobility, give an immediate message to onlookers. Many parents comment on how weary they become of the stares and insensitive questions from strangers when they appear with their children in public. Other parents have adjusted to these questions and see them as opportunities for public education and for making a statement about the rights and capabilities of children with special needs.

Other diagnostic categories, such as learning disabilities or emotional disturbances, are not so visually evident. Parents of these children might not get immediate questions or curious looks. However, when their children exhibit the behaviors associated with a disability, people are surprised and sometimes alarmed. Parents of children with mental retardation often comment that because their child may look physically normal, people expect them to act similar to their age peers. An "inappropriate" behavior is met with impatience, surprise, and sometimes even anger.

One of the most difficult realities for families with children with special needs is that many parenting tasks demand deliberate thought and planning (Snell & Rosen, 1997). In most families, parenting is interwoven with daily life events and reflects total values, experiences, and skills of the parents. Special needs demand a deliberate team effort in analyzing how to teach certain skills or how to encourage optimal development. A parenting role that requires deliberate teaching sessions or engineered activities with specific rewards for behavior that is considered difficult for children to learn is a new and demanding role for parents, requiring education as well as support.

A child's ability to learn impacts school achievement and lifelong potential. Impairment in communication and in social-emotional skills exacts a heavy toll on the family. Parenting is a demanding and complex task, and many parents comment on the love and affection they receive from their children as a primary motivator and support for this role. When children are depressed, extremely disturbed, or unable to express positive emotions, parents find it difficult to maintain the energy needed to provide loving, supportive learning environments for their children.

A DEFICIT MODEL

Parents of children with special needs sometimes feel all their time is spent emphasizing the deficits of their children instead of their strengths. That is, a parent may forget that a blind child can run, play, sing, talk, and laugh—all strengths parents enjoy. Parents of children with special needs interact frequently with diagnosticians who may only focus on a child's needs. These professionals become extremely skilled at making suggestions concerning the deficits rather than the child's strengths.

Our entire service system is built on defining a child's deficit by etiology or behavior (review Table 13.1), which draws attention to what the child cannot do. Parents and family members would like to see a greater concentration on the child's learning and relationship strengths and more time spent reinforcing those qualities. Parents need to see the positive strengths of the child in order to have the fortitude to deal with the child's special needs every day.

Family members also must cope with the stress of the unknown with their challenged children. Besides dealing with a stranger who does not understand why a child is behaving differently, projecting how a new medication might influence a child, or wondering what a child might achieve in the way of independence and economic self-sufficiency, there are many additional areas of ambiguity and uncertainty for parents of children with special needs.

Studies on stress substantiate the fact that individuals who feel they have little control over their environment and their future become emotionally stressed. Knowing this, many diagnosticians attempt to give families very clear diagnostic projections or specific goals for their children. The deficit approach can help families become realistic, but it also can be negative, concentrating on limitations and discouraging a family from trying unique and creative ways to enhance the future for their child. Helping professionals can assist both families and children in finding their strengths and emphasizing them.

AESTHETICS

Most parents of children with disabilities admit that it is difficult for their friends and relatives in the wider community to appreciate and love their children because they do not look as attractive or act as vigorous as other children. As a society, the United States has a deep love affair with physical beauty and perfection. Learning to appreciate and understand the inner beauty and small increments of growth of children with special needs is a constant struggle for their families. Many parents indicate that their children have taught them beautiful lessons about caring, patience, and nurturance.

The parents of children with special needs talk about their own strengths and the emergence of new humane traits in themselves through the experience of their parenting. The most eloquent statements about the special feelings and memories in parenting children with special needs are found in books written by parents themselves, such as Greenfield's *A Child Called Noah* (1970), and Simons's *After the Tears* (1987). The reader sees a clear picture of the impact children with special needs can have on families and the coping strengths that emerge.

EDUCATION

The education of children with special needs has been supported by federal legislation since 1975. It was increasingly apparent to both families and educators that teachers were ill equipped to teach children with special needs in regular classrooms. Consequently, teacher preparation institutions developed new specialized training for teachers who would have children with special needs in their classroom settings.

For families, the power of the most recent special educational legislation has been to support their role as decision makers on the team that creates the IEP. If an educational plan is to be successful, parents must understand and agree on its objectives and have information on how their family activities may be supportive of school activities and vice versa. This education service philosophy can be an extremely positive one for parents and other family members.

As research on the causes of various disabilities has proceeded, more accurate information is available to share with parents. In some cases, this is a welcome change from an era of "blame the parents" to an era of "partner with the parents." The case of autism is a very eloquent example.

Autistic behaviors include repetitive movements, alarm and concern about changes, avoidance of normal social interaction, and poor communication patterns. During the 1950s and 1960s, the reigning explanation for the cause of autism was a psychoanalytic model. A cold and rejecting parenting style was blamed for the disability. Subsequent research clarified the predictable traits of this syndrome and revealed that the cause is more likely neurological. In P. L. 101–476, the Individuals with Disabilities Education Act, autism was included as a separate disability category because of its complexity and the need for specialized training for effective intervention.

Inclusive Environments/Whole Schools

The inclusion of children with special needs in wider environments means that they will gain greater opportunities for stimulation and more normal experiences. For some children, this stimulation can be disorganizing and frustrating, and careful individual plans need to be made. Special education research has helped reveal how complex human learning is and how frequently children learn unexpected lessons from environments in which they participate. Although direct and targeted training of certain educational skills can be planned in the classroom, a great deal of incidental learning occurs informally around communication, support and interaction, inclusion or rejection at play, and social problem solving. Observations of inclusive educational settings often reveal a much richer educational environment than educators normally describe. These environments can be both positive and negative, and a team including parents, educators, and diagnosticians must make placement decisions appropriate for each individual child.

In the latter part of the twentieth century, educators in the United States were profoundly impacted by civil rights legislation and concerns about discrimination toward students needing special education. This discrimination was also seen in basic diagnostic assessments. During the 1970s it was documented that children from middle- or upper-class families were more likely to be diagnosed as learning disabled rather than mentally retarded in comparison with lower-class students. Although this judgment may represent diagnostic bias on the part of professionals, it also reflects the complex interaction of genetics and environment in the development of any child. A child being raised in a highly stressed community with few resources may fail to develop as fully as a child with similar genetic potential, but with an enhanced family and community resource base.

RELIGION

Many families claim that their religious faith sustains them through difficult times of stress. Children with special needs present special challenges to religious communities. Many religious communities provide religious education for children, such as Sunday schools, but they do not have specialized professionals who can appropriately support the inclusion of children with special needs. Finding compassionate and skilled adults who are able to be inclusive can provide special support for a family. Members of a religious community may have the organizational structure to help recruit and train child-care providers for families who need respite care from time to time.

Religious groups vary greatly in theology and in the formality of their structures. When theology suggests a deterministic view of human development, which states that a child with special needs may represent a judgment against the family, parents may feel a strong sense of shame and guilt, or martyrdom in relation to the care of their child. If the religious community helps parents build hope and positive goals for themselves and their children, then their religious faith imparts strength. Pastors, priests, rabbis, and other religious leaders can be powerful assistants in counseling and providing compassionate support as families make key decisions about the care and education of their special children. A religious leader may know of other families who have struggled with similar decisions and can bring families together to talk and share support.

In the informal social environment of a religious community, children may have more choices of what activities they participate in and what groups they can join. If their religious community has inclusiveness as a strong value, then families with children with special needs can have more creative and positive opportunities.

HEALTH CARE SYSTEM

Children with special needs often have special health requirements as well. If a child has a sensory impairment, such as blindness or deafness, or a specific mobility limitation or is confined to a wheelchair, costs are often associated with additional equipment and assistive devices to encourage learning and independence. Some disabilities have long been recognized, with special funding and services made available to the children and their families. Examples of these are the multiple services to the blind and services available through the Easter Seal Society.

Certain disabilities are likely to carry special health risks, such as Down syndrome. Children with Down syndrome are more susceptible to upper respiratory problems. This means that families must have access to regular preventive medical care, and all care providers must be sensitive to practices that enhance health.

The Americans with Disabilities Act of 1990 requires that all public institutions and places of employment make reasonable accommodations to include persons with disabilities in their environments. Adaptive aids and equipment, such as computers, head sticks, clamps, modified cups and eating utensils, and communication boards, are all now included in equipment and adaptive technologies available to persons with special needs. Specific health challenges requiring medication and careful monitoring of behavior, such as epilepsy, demand positive and open communication between parents, schools, and physicians to manage behavior successfully.

One special area for decision-making support from educators and the health community is family planning. Some parents limit the size of their families once they learn they have a child with special needs. Particularly when there is a genetic component to the disability, families may make use of genetics counseling. Some families report that they make decisions about future children based on clinical genetic information.

Many syndromes are rare and recessive, so the probability of another child similarly affected may be very low. A number of families have reported feelings of guilt and despair after receiving specific information from genetics clinics. The feelings of helplessness and self-blame after bearing a child with a genetic disability can be extremely stressful. Sensitive and compassionate support of parents is important at these times.

As children with special needs grow to maturity, their parents and health care professionals may assist with decisions about their active sexuality. An informed society must understand that all persons need and deserve a positive expression of their sexual selves. When persons with special needs consider an active sexual life, the nature, severity, and cause of their disability need to be considered. Some people with special needs have elected to refrain from becoming biological parents even when they are able because of the specific characteristics of their disability. Others have made a choice to be biological parents, to parent others' children as a teacher or aide, or to adopt or provide foster care to children who need a family. Various options can be considered when realistic and compassionate discussion takes place between family members and health professionals.

ECONOMIC FACTORS

Since the passing of federal legislation providing free and appropriate education to children with special needs, families have been continually advocating for assistance in respite care and other services to help their children with a variety of opportunities. The Vocational Rehabilitation Act and the Americans with Disabilities Act mandate the availability of devices and equipment necessary for the productive functioning of people with disabilities. Organizations like the National Rehabilitation Information Center provide information on parents' and families' rights, sources of funding, and information on how to obtain needed services and equipment. Many families need assistance in application procedures to obtain necessary equipment and resources for their children.

Throughout a family's life, the economic demands of having a child with special needs can vary. Initial needs for special equipment to position or support a child with limited mobility will change as the child grows. The Americans with Disabilities Act of 1992 is a landmark piece of legislation creating opportunities for education and employment to persons with disabilities. The act requires employers to make a "reasonable accommodation in their environment" for the employment of or the service to persons with specific disabilities. Although this legislation has alarmed many small businesses, there are reasonable ways to provide accommodations so the contributions and skills of persons with special needs can be optimally used.

Families of persons with lifelong special needs and limitations in income need to plan for lifelong support. The increasing availability of new technologies, group independent care situations, personal assistants, and home care services makes it possible for more independent living options. However, such options need careful planning, including the source of ongoing financial support. The Social Security Administration provides benefits through seven different programs including one for blind and disabled children. The Supplemental Security Program, or SSI as it is known, is important for a number of low-income families needing help with their children with special needs.

The 1996 Welfare Reform Act included a provision that alarmed advocates of children with special needs and created vigorous public debate. In 1990 a Supreme Court decision ordered the Social Security Administration to create an Individualized Functional Assessment (IFA) as part of the determination process for SSI benefits to children with special needs. Between 1990 and 1996, the number of children receiving SSI benefits grew from 350,000 to almost 1 million.

In the 1996 Welfare Reform debate, members of Congress became concerned that large numbers of children were receiving SSI benefits when they were not really disabled. The Welfare Reform Bill subsequently eliminated the IFA in favor of a listing of 100 disabilities and declared that only disabilities that caused "marked and severe limitations" created SSI eligibility. The Social Security Administration estimated that cases of approximately 300,000 children would need review and projected that 135,000 would be declared ineligible. Because these SSI recipients often represented low-income families with few care and supervision options for their children, child protection advocates mounted a vigorous protest. The American Bar Association created the "Children's SSI Project" with a toll-free 800 number for free legal advice in almost every state. This regulation, along with the more restrictive policies regarding food stamp eligibility, were seen as some of the most punitive aspects of the Welfare Reform Act. By December 1997 the Social Security Administration announced a review of 45,000 cases that had been declared ineligible for SSI and a vigorous educational campaign about parents' appeal rights. The commissioner of Social Security was particularly concerned about the variations in case processing and the fact that 50 percent of the people with mental retardation were declared ineligible.

The flurry over this aspect of the Welfare Reform Act probably represents a confounding of vulnerable traits that incited outrage among child and family advocates. When low-income families with children with special needs appeared to be discriminated against, it seemed to be mean-spirited national policy.

A provocative column in the *Wall Street Journal* ("Special Ed's Special Costs," 1993) described the increasing effectiveness of advocacy for students with special needs and declared that this effectiveness had resulted in mandated programs that are increasingly expensive. In school districts where budgets have remained stable or are decreasing, the increasing costs of mandated special education programs create economic conflicts. In an era of economic difficulties, there are increasing conflicts over programs for populations with special needs. Are the disabled "entitled" to these programs, paid entirely by public monies, or should family resources also be used? One suggestion is that parents who have children with special needs, who are financially able, should be required to pay a portion of the costs incurred in educating their children. However, a large proportion of students with special education needs comes from low-income families, so requiring family payments will not dramatically affect the educational budgets at the local level.

One lesson learned from economic shortfalls is that creative partnerships between schools and parents may help keep costs down. For example, if educators help parents understand that the schools do not have certain resources to provide optimal services for their children, parents might volunteer to help in special education programs or generate money through fund-raising and in-kind contributions. When there is a need for additional personnel to support the education of some children with special needs, families, neighborhoods, or religious communities might help organize a system of volunteers to help recruit the needed human resources. Increased attention to children's needs is a positive result of creating more inclusiveness.

Housing

Families with children who have disabilities often have special housing needs, which vary according to the needs of the child. They often include special concerns about supervision, safety of the neighborhood, and convenience for the use of wheelchairs or other helping devices. For a child with limited mobility, living quarters that are not safe and accessible on one floor can cause tremendous physical strain on family members from lifting the child, as well as the psychological strain of isolation for the child.

Sometimes the home can be made more appropriate for the child and family with some adaptations. These might include ramps into the house, the widening of doorways, or the construction of a wall or a higher fence to provide a protected play area. Many of these adaptations could be provided by volunteer labor in a community in response to needs that specialists or parents identify. Housing problems are especially acute for a low-income family needing to find affordable housing. In many cases, it may be important for educators and other health and educational service providers to advocate for families and assist in locating or adapting appropriate housing.

Government Policies and Agencies

Since the middle of the twentieth century, the federal government, and specifically public education, have assumed increasing responsibility for the education of children and youth with special needs. Throughout this time, it has become clear that educators must be a strong partner with health professionals and employers sectors in providing appropriate lifelong education, care, and jobs for persons with disabilities.

All professionals who serve families with children with special needs should be aware of regulations that need changing to facilitate coordination and communication. Each state department of education is responsible for creating a state plan that complies with federal mandates for serving children and youth with special needs. Most state departments designate intermediate or local school districts as their representatives in working directly with families and children to create services. Because the school districts must both provide services and find the clients who need them, departments of education may be somewhat reluctant to be strong advocates for children with special needs and their families.

Increasingly, volunteer agencies or organizations play an important role in helping educate families about rights for their child and in helping with Child Find, a national program using mass communication to find children who need special services. Those who wish to learn more about services available in their area or wish to advocate for a particular child or family can obtain a copy of their state's plan to implement special education services from their state department of education in their state's capital. The plan should include conditions for the involvement of parents, a description of parents' rights, and a process whereby parents can appeal decisions of the team providing services for their family member.

FAMILY INTERACTIONS AND KINSHIP NETWORKS

Families who are able to purchase additional services in the form of child care, respite care, household assistance, and/or special transportation and equipment have an advantage over families with fewer economic resources. For these families, the ability to activate support from their extended family, neighborhood, and community is an important asset. Families with strong and supportive circles of relatives and friends who provide wisdom and an assertive management style are able to activate many resources for themselves and their children.

Families with children with special needs relate that support groups that include other families with children with special needs help them in making plans for pleasure and respite. Sometimes exchanging child care and supervision is possible; however, this is not realistic for some children with complex care needs. Highly specialized care may require a contracted respite care service.

One special point is that families of children with special needs frequently need respite care and do not always adequately receive it. Caretakers need time away from their charges to remain strong and energetic. Strong feelings of martyrdom and guilt on the part of mothers can make it difficult for couples to have time alone to nurture their own relationship.

Single parents of children with special needs can be particularly vulnerable to burnout and stress. McNurlen (1996) found that other supports and relationships could take the place of a spouse or partner in single-parent families and provide resiliency to those families. Finding a group of friends that can be supportive can be especially helpful to single parents. The more severe the health risks and/or the caretaking demands of a challenged person, the more difficult it is to obtain assistance in respite care. Parents who have become very skilled at providing health services and care for their child may have a difficult time learning to trust and leave their child with other caretakers. For this reason, it is important to encourage relationships with two or more respite care environments and encourage parent participation in local advocacy and support groups.

A particularly difficult topic for families with children who have special needs is the issue of a family vacation. If families have the means to go on a vacation, they must face the question about whether they should leave their children with special needs in respite care or take them along. For more freedom and independent action, respite care would be best. However, taking children with special needs on family vacations can be a wonderful opportunity. Balancing competing goals is needed. Parents may need supportive professionals to assist with realistic information and problem solving concerning this decision.

CHANGES AND ADAPTATIONS

The most significant change and adaptation for families with children with special needs is the movement from a position of powerlessness to one of an active problem-solving and partnering role. This often involves a change from accepting professional diagnostic advice carte blanche to seeking information and participating more fully in decisions about their children. A movement toward assertive involvement can be encouraged by recruiting other experienced parents to serve as mentors or advocates (see Dawson, 1997) and by attending diagnostic sessions and planning sessions with experienced parents. Parents gradually learn to understand the limits of the system and the means for obtaining services and information from a variety of sources.

The second major challenge is to learn to adapt to the children's accomplishments and development over time. Caring for a child who has breathing difficulties as an infant is a much different proposition than handling the social frustration of a teenager with a learning disability. As families learn, they generally develop ways to cope with parenting challenges. The amount of power and control they may wish to have over each child's life can affect the role they play with their child with special needs. Most parents report that as their children approach adolescence and young adulthood, they face important changes for themselves as they support their youngster's greater independence.

Disabilities exist along a continuum ranging from minimal impact, such as a well-controlled seizure disorder or a stuttering pattern, to a lifelong limitation of cognitive skill or mobility. Family development must depend on the hopes and resources, not only of the person with special needs, but also that of the community. All of us need to understand that with increasing age comes the greater likelihood of having a disability. In 1992 the U.S. Census Bureau reported that 49 million noninstitutionalized Americans age 15 and older had a disability. As shown in Figure 13.1, the older the individual, the greater the incidence of both disabilities and those disabilities being defined as severe.

Table 13.2 shows that the causes of disabilities in older people are different from those of youth. For youth under age 15, these later life disabilities may be added to earlier diagnoses.

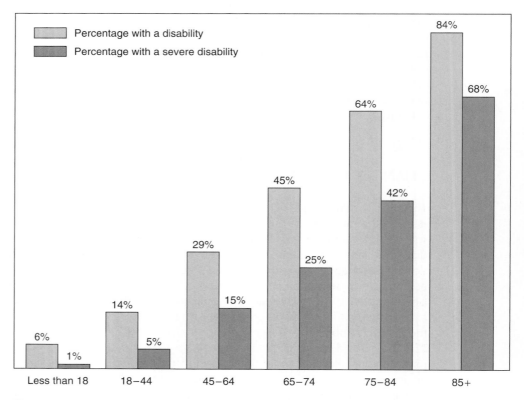

Figure 13.1   Percentages of Persons with a Disability and with a Severe Disability, by Age Group: 1991–1992

Source: U.S. Census Bureau. (1997). *One in 10 Americans reported a severe disability in 1991–92.* Washington, DC: U.S. Government Printing Office.

Table 13.2   Physical Conditions That Cause Disabilities

Condition	Number with Condition (millions)
Arthritis or rheumatism	7.2
Back or spine problems	5.7
Heart trouble	4.6
Lung or respiratory trouble	2.8
High blood pressure	2.2
Stiffness or deformity of extremity	2.0
Diabetes	1.6
Blindness or vision problems	1.5

Source: U.S. Census Bureau, (1994). *Americans with disabilities* (SB 94-1). Washington, DC: U.S. Government Printing Office.

HELPFUL TECHNIQUES FOR SERVING FAMILIES WITH CHALLENGED MEMBERS

Specialized educators are essential for serving families with children who have special needs. In addition, many other teachers, health care workers, religious leaders, youth workers, and family service providers will interact with these families. Your professional service may be in one of these key agencies.

Learn Relevant Laws

All professionals must understand the federal laws that outline services mandated for children and their families. These laws include specific requirements for education, access to services, vocational training, and independent living. Professionals need to obtain accurate information on the state plans and the agencies responsible for services in their area. For a professional expecting to work in this area, it is important to build trusting relationships with colleagues who can serve as consultants or provide information. There is an increasing emphasis on the importance of early intervention programs for children with special needs. The inclusion of children in mainstream environments goes a long way toward enhancing children's independence. Also, the opportunities for understanding and growth of all children are enhanced.

Seek Specific Information

Many professionals have not had extensive experience in dealing with children who have special needs. They need in-service training to learn more about specific diagnoses. Persons with special needs often state how important it is for others to be honest with them. Learn how to ask for information in a respectful and open manner. You might say, "I have never had an experience with someone who is blind. I will need information about how to be supportive and appropriate in my actions. Can we make an appointment to visit?"

Your goal is to become an informed partner with parents. If you are a teacher who is including a child with special needs in your class, try to see this new student in as many different settings as possible. Make a home visit. Go with the family on an outing so you can see the practices the parents have developed to enhance their child's opportunities. Once you have seen the child in a variety of environments, you can be more creative in adapting your own environment to suit the child and family. You can help ensure that family rights are respected and you are providing appropriate and accurate information for the other professionals in your service environment. Environments that include all children are richer in learning and creative opportunities than environments that provide only segregated services, but they place unique learning demands on staff.

Clarify Professional Recommendations

As a professional working with a family, talk with parents about their many interactions with a variety of professionals. Some interactions may be highly charged with tension, fear, and frustration. Helping a family continue to relate positively to professionals is an important part of your role. As you meet initially with families, give them an opportunity to talk about their relationships with other professionals to better understand developments that occurred before you began working with the child.

Families frequently share their frustration, confusion, or hostility about information provided by another group. Help parents articulate their questions so they may better understand information shared with them. To be supportive, you may need to accompany them to future appointments with specialists. However, avoid assuming responsibility for the family. Respectfully convey to other professionals when the family has been unable to use certain information and when it needs to be clarified.

Individualize Family Interaction

Ask family members what kinds of information or interactions have been most positive and supportive of their family goals. When you need to share information, you may find that a particular family prefers brief phone conversations about their child, whereas another family may need longer face-to-face visits. If you have difficulty contacting a parent, you might ask permission to communicate through letters. Sometimes at their request another trusted friend or extended-family member becomes an information gatherer for them. In all of these communications, convey that you hope to develop an effective information network that can respond immediately to the questions or concerns of anyone in the service group.

Many professionals that families talk to have their own specific limited agenda because of their professional responsibility, experience, or training. For example, the mobility specialist talks to a family about devices to assist with mobility. After a number of these conferences, a family may feel that no one has asked them specifically about their family goals for their child. These goals may not be immediately accomplished in your environment, but, knowing the family's interests, you can adapt conditions in your environment and assist parents in finding other resources to accomplish these objectives. An important style for these interactions is to ask periodically, "How are we doing with your son or daughter?" This will enable the family to feel free to talk with you about things that are going well and things they might wish to change.

Stress Human Values

One of the most important things you can convey when working with all families is that you see the child as a whole person. This means you recognize the child's temperament, personality, abilities, and the special unique characteristics that are beyond a special need. Every parent wants his or her child to be accepted in a compassionate, individualized way. Many of the interactions between professionals and families of children with special needs focus only on the challenges. In a comprehensive IFSP meeting, the planning group should first consider the child's needs as a human being. The specific detailed goals for skill development, say speech, should be discussed only after comprehensive goals are stated. Think about both the short-term goals as well as the long-term goals to demonstrate your commitment to your responsibilities.

Parents will feel comfortable in your environment if you develop a sustained relationship with them over time. If you have very limited interaction with a family, be clear about welcoming them, asking specific questions to discover their needs, goals, and values. Then develop a plan that is responsive to their goals. Sustained interaction over time will allow you to visit from time to time and inquire about the entire balance of the family's life. You can learn whether they are taking time for total family enjoyment. Do the parents have time as a couple? As a single parent, does she or he have some time away from family responsibilities? In this ongoing relationship you can encourage parents' right to lead a balanced life with supports and enrichments for their own growth, which usually helps the child. Parental burnout must be prevented for the child's good.

Grief and Sorrow

Grief is expected when a family member is born disabled or becomes disabled. This grief process has received much attention from specialists. There are references to the importance of family acceptance and adjustment to the reality of a child's disability. However, this is very different from the resolution of grief after a death. The anger, frustration, and denial concerning the special needs can provide the energy that families need from time to time for advocacy or assertiveness with professionals.

As professionals serving families, you need to learn to accept their intense emotions. There may be anger about missed opportunities for their child or inappropriate diagnoses or suggestions from professionals. Grief and frustration can be expected as parents realize that their dreams for their child's future may not be fulfilled.

As a professional, you'll gain experience in being compassionate and quiet at times. Other times you'll learn to be forcefully articulate in helping parents identify a specific incident that triggered their anger. Helping parents express their pain and frustration takes skilled responsiveness on the part of professionals. You'll train for years to develop this skill. You need to feel comfortable saying things like "You are really angry right now, and I know it will not be very productive for us to try to plan this today. Let's make an appointment for another time to deal with service plans."

Many parents of children with special needs indicate that they find it very useful to talk about their needs with other families and with members of community organizations. Community members and service club leaders often help change policies or provide new services for families whose needs have not been recognized. Encouraging parents to join parent support organizations, such as the Association for Retarded Citizens of the United States (now known as The ARC), or the Learning Disabilities Association of America (LDA), can give them opportunities to help advocate for their family members. Organizations can help families practice language and strategies for effective community and societal changes. Studies of parents (Lamb & Billings, 1997; Warfield & Hausen-Cram, 1996; Wyche & Lobato, 1996) relate how important support groups can be for enhancing their sense of community and effectiveness in nurturing their children with special needs. In a study of adoptive families with children with special needs, George (1997) found that contact with other special needs adoptive families was more helpful than therapy or counseling services. As professionals supporting family strengths, we can play a key role in introducing families to each other, encouraging support/discussion groups, and creatively encouraging informal family-to-family connections.

In addition, become acquainted with the many resources for parents available on the Internet. Particularly if care and supervision demands require that parents remain at home for much of their discretionary time, the Internet can provide social connections that provide both information and support. Mickelson's (1997) study comparing parents seeking support through the Internet and from face-to-face interactions showed that strangers can provide useful support throughout the Internet. See the list at the end of the chapter for ideas.

Given the stresses that some children with special needs place on a family and a marriage, the increase in the divorce rate is understandable. You may be in a position to counsel or support parents on the verge of a breakup or those going through a divorce. Finding ways to continue the appropriate care and joint decision making for the child with special needs is important.

Some divorced parents report that one of the most positive things about the divorce is having some time alone and being relieved of the responsibility of the children when an ex-spouse takes care of them. Your goal, if possible, is to help both parents deal with necessary decisions regarding their child with special needs. Distraught parents have been known to disappear completely from the family.

Families may feel unable to cope with the multiple appointments and numerous professionals. Your role in helping parents clarify their own values, their goals for their children, and their most comfortable way of interacting with professionals can help them make wiser use of available resources. For example, a highly specialized pediatric neurologist can probably spend very little time with a family. However, if you assist the family in writing out questions, and help them in the interview, they will find the consultation with the specialist more meaningful and supportive of their family goals and values.

A final important goal in dealing with all families is to reinforce a sense of inclusiveness and a sense of justice. To deny any of us the opportunity to see a full range of human characteristics is to render all of us less flexible, less creative, and less compassionate. Our work with families who have children with special needs can provide us many opportunities for including them and others in a richer and more varied community.

✦ CONCLUSIONS

Persons with special needs, first of all, are human beings. Anyone can join this category at any time, through accident or illness. Compassion and creativity are needed by everyone so that all children have a chance to give and receive from persons with a variety of characteristics. Long-term goals of self-sufficiency and economic independence can be achieved for many individuals.

Many people have never interacted with children with special needs and may be frightened by the prospect. Your role will often be to facilitate positive, clear information and to help achieve creative problem solving. All persons attending public schools ideally will soon have learned important and specific lessons about valuing and facilitating the development of children with special needs.

✦ STUDY QUESTIONS

1. Define the terms *disability, challenged,* and *handicapped.*
2. Write a paragraph describing what is meant by "least restrictive environment." Give examples of a 2-year-old and a 16-year-old in such an environment.
3. Define segregated services and contrast them with mainstream and whole school services in a one-page essay.
4. Define Individualized Educational Plan. What legislation requires this IEP?
5. Define Individual Family Service Plan. What legislation requires this?
6. Describe four special education eras: privatization, segregation, mainstreaming, and partnerships.
7. Define ambiguity and uncertainty around etiology.
8. Contrast the typical role of mothers of children with special needs with the role of fathers of children with special needs.
9. What is the total percentage of children with special needs in the American population? What is the most common disability?
10. How will the percentages of individuals with special needs change in the United States over the next 25 years?

✦ APPLICATIONS

1. Make an appointment with a special education administrator in a local school district. Discuss the district's current policy on inclusion and support to mainstream teachers for including persons with special needs. If possible, obtain a copy of the

policy, find out whether the district offers workshops for teachers, and arrange to observe an in-service meeting or workshop.

2. Call or visit your local Special Education office, and ask for a parent information packet. Review the forms that are provided to parents when an IEP meeting is held. Look over the parent approval forms and the outline for the educational plan. Evaluate the level of reading and education a parent needs to understand these forms and processes.

3. Attend a local chapter meeting of a Special Education Parent Support group. Listen to their program or interaction, and if possible, interview a couple of parents about the role this group plays in their lives and how valuable it is.

4. Interview a child/youth librarian at a local library on any books about children with special needs. Ask to see resources on understanding children with disabilities, and other resources that may simply include pictures of children with special needs as part of their illustrations. Write an evaluation of the lessons provided to children by these examples.

5. Make an appointment with the chair of the Curriculum and Instruction Department at your university or college. Discuss how teachers are prepared for the inclusion of children with special needs in the classroom. Ask how much of the program is devoted to children with special needs, and what part of a preservice, internship, or student teaching assignment includes such children. Ask them about their long-term plan for increasing commitment and involvement.

6. Find out if a local lawyer handles cases relating to advocacy and rights of children with disabilities. Make an appointment to discuss usual cases brought to his or her attention. Discuss whether they represent omissions in the law or in public communication and education.

7. Interview five students on campus about their personal experience with children and youth with special needs. Develop a set of questions about the students' knowledge, impressions, attitudes, and experience with students with special needs. What can you conclude about the value of these experiences?

8. Arrange with the administrators of the local special education program to observe children in both an inclusive or mainstreamed setting and in a segregated or specialized setting. Describe the activities you observe as well as the advantages to the students, the teacher, and the other students in the classroom. Describe the disadvantages for the same groups.

9. Call local special education administrators for information regarding respite care services. Where are they available? Call or visit an administrator of such a service. Describe the services provided, costs, and family experiences from the viewpoint of the agency.

10. Obtain the name of a family that has used a respite care service at least three times. Interview a member of the family by phone or in person. Why did the family decide to use this service? What are the advantages of this service to the family? What are the challenges?

11. Interview seniors in teacher education programs about their experiences with students with special needs. Summarize the courses each has had, and the

internship or placement experiences with challenged students. Discuss whether they feel prepared to include students with special needs in their classroom.

12. Locate the office at your college or university that handles information and support services for university students with special needs. Interview a member of that office about the recruitment and advocacy services for the institution.

✦ MEDIA RESOURCES

Drugs, alcohol and pregnancy: What you should know. (28 minutes). (Available from Human Relations Media, 175 Tompkins Avenue, Pleasantville, NY 10570). www.hrmvideo.com.

Special kids, special dads. (Available from www.fathersnetwork.org, or Washington State Fathers Network, Kindering Center, 16120 N.E. Eighth Street, Bellevue, WA 98008, (425) 747-4004, ext. 4286.

✦ ORGANIZATIONS

American Speech-Language-Hearing Association (ASHA), 10801 Rockville Pike, Rockville, MD 20852, (800) 638-8255.

Professional association for communication disability areas.

The ARC (formerly the Association for Retarded Citizens of the United States), 500 East Border Street, Suite 300, Arlington, TX 76010, (817) 261-6003.

The oldest and largest organization for advocacy and education about disabilities including mental retardation.

The Council for Exceptional Children (CEC), 1930 Association Drive, Reston, VA 22091-1589, (703) 620-3660.

Umbrella organization of professionals with subgroups for each area of disabilities.

Learning Disabilities Association of America (LDA), 4156 Library Road, Pittsburgh, PA 15234, (412) 341-1515.

LDA provides general information on learning disabilities as well as advocacy.

National Clearinghouse on Family Support and Children's Mental Health, Portland State University, P. O. Box 751, Portland, OR 97207-0751, (800) 628-1696.

Has directory of services for parents of children with behavioral and emotional disabilities.

National Information Center for Children and Youth with Disabilities (NICHCY), P. O. Box 1492, Washington, DC 20013, (800) 999-5599.

Has information and resources on all disability areas, legislation, and advocacy.

Technical Assistance for Parent Programs (TAPP), Federation for Children With Special Needs, 312 Stuart Street, Suite B 2-11, Boston, MA 02116, (617) 482-2915.

National project that works to improve services to underserved and underrepresented groups of parents of children with disabilities.

✣ KEY INTERNET RESOURCES

Social Security Administration
www.ssa.gov/

U.S. Department of Education, IDEA '97
www.ed.gov/offices/OSERS/IDEA

Human Rights Campaign, AIDS Update
www.htc.org/

No Child Left Behind
www.ed.gov/nclb/landing.jhtml

The Personal Responsibility and Work Opportunity Reconciliation Act of 1996
www.ssa.gov/welfare/legis_bu.html

✣ FURTHER READING

Greenspohn, S. I., Wieder, S., & Simmons, R. (1998). *The child with special needs: Encouraging intellectual and emotional growth.* Reading, MA: Addison-Wesley.

Johnson, B. H., McConigel, M. J., & Kaufman, R. K. (Eds.). (1989). *Guidelines and recommended practices for the individualized family service plan.* Chapel Hill, NC: National Early Childhood Technical Assistance Systems.

Meyer, D. (Ed.). (1997). *Views from our shoes: Growing up with a brother or sister with special needs.* Bethesda, MD: Woodbine House.

Meyer, D. J., & Vadasy, P. F. (1985). *Grandparent workshops: How to organize workshops for grandparents of children with handicaps.* Seattle: University of Washington Press.

Meyer, D. J., & Vadasy, P. F. (1986). *Grandparent workshops: How to organize workshops for grandparents of children with handicaps.* Seattle: University of Washington Press.

Meyer, D. J., Vadasy, P. F., & Fewell, R. R. (1985). *Sibshops: A handbook for implementing workshops for siblings of children with special needs.* Seattle: University of Washington Press.

Paley, V. G. (1992). *You can't say you can't play.* Cambridge, MA: Harvard University Press.

Pardeck, J. T., & Pardeck, J. A. (1997). Recommended books for helping young children deal with social and development problems. *Early Child Development and Care, 136,* 57–63.

Park, C. (1981). *The seige.* Boston: Little, Brown.

Randall-Davis, Z. (1989). *Strategies for working with culturally diverse communities and their clients.* Bethesda, MD: Association for the Care of Children's Health.

Shelton, T., Jeppson, E., & Johnson, B. H. (1987). *Family-centered care for children with special health needs.* Washington, DC: Association for the Care of Children's Health.

Simons, R. (1987). *After the tears: Parents talk about raising a child with disabilities.* New York: Harcourt Brace Jovanovich.

Sweeney, W. K. (1998). *The special needs reading list: An annotated guide to the best publications for parents and professionals.* Bethesda, MD: Woodbine House.

→14

Gay and Lesbian Families

→ **Key Concepts**

- Bisexual
- Conversion Therapy
- Defense of Marriage Act (DOMA)
- Domestic Partnerships
- GLBT
- Homophobia
- Second-Parent Adoption
- Sodomy
- Transsexual

We are the people who consider all the various traditions and customs and question them. . . . We have a great responsibility here. The human race depends on us to do this. . . . We question . . . we bring changes.

—S. Sherman (1992)

The various chapters of this book have shown just how truly diverse people and family structures can be. The quotation from Sherman reinforces the idea of questioning and looking rationally at every aspect of families. You have read, thought about, and discussed various family formats. One goal of this book is to give you skills for your role as a helping professional working with diverse families. Every family structure may have positive and negative aspects. You will make decisions about your own personal family choice based on all the insights you accumulate and with rights to your own privacy.

The twenty-first century will likely witness improved health conditions that result in greater longevity for the world's people. The importance of spousal partnership in families will deepen with increased life expectancy. The commitment of a spouse, partner, or companion who reciprocates with mutual and sustained support and affection over time takes on added meaning in the context of longevity. Loneliness for some humans is the worst of all existences. For many, living with cherished persons is the ideal happiness.

FAMILY DEFINITION REVISITED

As you have studied the diverse families highlighted in this book, you now appreciate more our early definition of a family—a group of persons who share common resources and a commitment to each other over time. This definition helps prevent a premature rush to judgment about any one kind of family. Although understanding different families requires objectivity, it does not require you to personally adopt or promote any lifestyle. As helping professionals, you will succeed if you reserve judgment and allow others to make sense of the human ecological system in which they reside and that serves their own needs ("The 21st Century Family," 1990).

In recent decades, two or more young professional single parents sometimes pool property and incomes to create a household and a supportive unit for rearing children. Several generations of adults may move into a joint household where they share space and other resources and responsibilities. In these households, the emphasis is on sharing economic resources and creating supportive social environments. Intimate relationships, or paired relationships, may or may not be included. What these households represent is a practical response to the reality of reduced family income in the United States. According to the 2000 census, there were 33.6 million American households defined as nonfamily. Eighty-one percent of these were persons living alone; the remaining 19 percent probably represent a variety of homosexual couples, several single parents and their children living together, or unmarried adults living together. In 2000 there were 5,475,768 "unmarried partner" households reported, which include both heterosexual and homosexual couples (U.S. Census Bureau, 2002).

Michael Newman/PhotoEdit Inc.

GAY AND LESBIAN FAMILIES

American views toward sexuality and family have undergone changes over the last few decades (Seligman, 1993). Controversy over appropriate definitions of families and their right to resources and benefits through the employment system or governmental policies has fueled extensive public debate. Different motivations for creating a family reflect the variation in human society. Part of society's debate and struggle to understand and support variation in families rests on people's comfort level with variation and inclusiveness, and with national struggles with problems of economics and morality relating to gender relationships. In many ways, these discussions concern public and private rights and responsibilities. Many discussions have reflected the rising influence of conservative community leaders concerned about moral implications of gay and lesbian lifestyles.

Increasing advocacy for gay and lesbian initiatives that seek legal protection and inclusive regulations have fueled emotional debates regarding access to resources. Although still a small minority, gay and lesbian family experiences are influenced by current struggles with gender roles and inclusiveness.

HISTORICAL BACKGROUND

There have probably been gay and lesbian families throughout the history of the United States. In general, though, this family form did not reach public discourse and debate until the 1970s and 1980s. In fact, it was not until 1869 that the term *homosexuality* came into existence (McWhirter & Mattison, 1984). When the 1948 Kinsey Report reported that about 4 percent of males and 3 percent of females were exclusively homosexual, the information was greeted with both surprise and discomfort by some observers of American family life. In the 1950s the McCarthy era of aggressive oppression of nonconformity coincided with witch hunts for and discrimination against homosexuals. A so-called normal family life became the first line of defense against treason. The FBI and other agencies launched unprecedented intrusions into private lives under the guise of investigating traitors. Gay baiting became almost as widespread as red baiting (Boyer, 1985). In 1969 the "Stonewall riot" occurred when New York City policemen, as many city police departments across the United States did periodically, raided a neighborhood gay bar, resulting in the injury and jailing of a number of patrons. On this night in June, a transgendered woman, Sylvia Rivera, resisted arrest, which touched off three nights of rioting. For many gays and lesbians, this event marked the beginning of a more public visible struggle for rights and recognition. Today some of our most prominent and respected citizens are openly homosexual, but in 1969 this information was still largely secret. During the 1950s and 1960s, a pioneering lesbian organization, the Daughters of Bilitus, supported efforts to provide community and identity for lesbians. Gradually, radical feminist theories dominated the organization, and the Daughters of Bilitus lost membership and influence. In these early days of organizing, a particularly vitriolic schism occurred between lesbians and male-to-female transgendered individuals who wished to be included in the lesbian community. Such divisions in the broad community are a common occurrence when minority groups ostracized by a dominant culture try to forge identity and power. In 1971 the Gay Activist Alliance (GAA) introduced an antidiscrimination bill to the New York City Council to protect homosexual people. In October 1979, 75,000 gays held a rally in Washington, D.C. Less than a decade later, in 1987, a gay rally in Washington attracted 600,000 participants. This time the event included militant AIDS protests, a public showing of the AIDS Memorial quilt, and a mass wedding of same-sex couples. Yet Osborn (1996, p. 25) commented that there was so little media coverage of the 1987 rally "that most of the world never heard about the largest, most energetic civil rights demonstration in American history."

In the 1980s the White House Conference on the Family featured a prolonged debate about an acceptable definition of family. In fact, this debate was so divisive that the 1990 Conference on the Family was canceled. By the 1992 national election, the rights and contributions of gays had become a controversial theme in party platforms. Gays became a visible and organized political force, drawing attention to discrimination in employment, health care, and family benefits. After his election, President Bill Clinton attempted to integrate the armed services by reducing barriers to homosexuals, an effort that resulted in a damaging and difficult political fight early in his presidency. Media reports of the debate, subsequent decisions, and initial court challenges repeatedly showed the public's fears about how homosexual behavior might affect the military. Within a traditionally male-dominated organization with the responsibility of aggressive military defense, a dialogue about homosexual rights and behavior was very difficult. It was clear that the most moving testimonies in the debate were from fathers or commanding officers and friends of homosexuals who had been deeply influenced by their positive personal experiences with professionals who had declared themselves homosexual. Clinton's 1996 signing of the Federal Defense of Marriage Act, clearly a political survival move, disappointed and confused the gay community. The act defined marriage and spouse as follows:

> In determining the meaning of any Act of Congress or any ruling, regulation, or interpretation of the various administrative bureaus and agencies of the United States, the word "marriage" means only a legal union between one man and one woman as husband and wife, and the word "spouse" refers only to a person of the opposite sex who is a husband or wife. (Defense of Marriage Act, H.R. 3396)

Thus no federal benefits could be allocated to a same-sex spouse.

Documenting exclusive homosexual behavior and bisexual behavior is difficult because of the negative sanctions of such admissions. The gay rights movement and advocacy actions of the 1960s and 1970s led to a gradual increase in acceptance by the general American public of gay and lesbian lifestyles. Briggs (1994) reported that between 1979 and 1993, the percentage of Americans that preferred not to have a homosexual as a friend declined from 54 percent to 41 percent. In general, those respondents who were female, more highly educated, or resided in major metropolitan areas were more liberal in their attitudes toward homosexuals. Blue-collar workers were the only demographic group that showed a decrease in tolerance, a trend documented in studies reported from 1988 through 1993. Butler (2000) used representative data from the General Social Surveys of 1989 to 1998 to document an increase in same-gender sexual partnering and a decrease among women in maintaining exclusive male sexual partnering. For men, the percentage reporting partnering with other males changed from 1.7 percent to 4.1 percent. For women, the change over the decade was from 0.2 percent to 2.8 percent. These findings were more significant for younger men and women and for residents of metropolitan areas. There were not significant differences for race or ethnicity.

In 1970 a half million Americans reported that they were cohabitating with an adult of the same sex. By 1988 there were 2.6 million persons cohabitating with someone of the same sex. It is likely that a significant portion of those couples had a homosexual relationship (Hare & Richards, 1993).

Because a homosexual lifestyle sometimes follows a period of heterosexual experience, approximately a third of homosexual households contain the biological children of one partner from a previous heterosexual relationship (Moses & Hawkins, 1982). Lambda Legal, the national advocacy group for homosexuals, reported in 2002 that 31 percent of lesbians and 23 percent of gay men have children under age 18 living at home (Lambda Legal, 2002a). An estimated 20 percent of gay men have been married (Harry, 1989), and 20 to 50 percent of all gay men who have been married have one or more biological children (Miller, 1979). For lesbians who were formerly in a heterosexual marriage, it is estimated that 50 to 75 percent have one or more biological children (Rila & Reed, 1980). Hoeffer (1981) estimated that there were 1.5 to 3 million lesbian mothers with 1.25 children per household in the United States. In addition, up to 10,000 lesbians have borne children through sperm donations or other procedures, and many gays and lesbians have sought the right to serve as foster parents or to adopt children. On July 4, 1990, an article in the *New York Times* declared there were 2 million gay mothers and fathers in America. Other estimates suggest that between

6 and 14 million children in America have at least one gay parent (Collins & Coltrane, 1991). The 2000 census reported 5.5 million "unmarried partner households," of which a half million reported a gay or lesbian partnership (U.S. Census Bureau, 2002). Because of the statistical requirements of the Defense of Family Act, direct comparisons between the 1990 and 2000 census data regarding households formed by homosexual persons are not possible.

Part of the reality of living as a homosexual in American society is facing the tremendous negative implications of the lifestyle. Many men and women report years of denial or hiding of their homosexual orientation while engaging in a heterosexual lifestyle. Researchers have reported that adolescent homosexuals are six times more likely to attempt suicide than heterosexual adolescents (Mercer & Berger, 1989). The actual number of people who successfully live a bisexual lifestyle, with both homosexual and heterosexual periods, is not known.

SOCIOCULTURAL FOUNDATIONS

Probably no other family lifestyle variation has caused as much debate and negative publicity as gay and lesbian families. Long-standing prejudice, secrecy, and misunderstanding have prevented an accurate perception of these families and denied them positive support from society. Nevertheless, a gay and lesbian advocacy movement emerged out of the political and sexual revolution in America during the 1960s. From the early efforts, much of this advocacy concerned a desire to create families and to be accepted by their families of origin. In 1972 Jeanne Manford marched beside her gay son in a New York City gay pride parade. Overwhelmed by the positive reactions from participants and observers, she went on to launch "Parents, Families and Friends of Lesbians and Gays" (PFLAG). PFLAG now has more than 400 chapters and 70,000 members (PFLAG, 1998). The National Gay and Lesbian Task Force (NGLTF) was formed in 1973 as a progressive civil rights organization. At the 1979 National March on Washington for gay and lesbian rights, a group of gay fathers formed an international network of gay fathers, which eventually became the Gay and Lesbian Parents Coalition International (GLPCI). A desire to be honest and to explore variation and individual freedom has been part of this movement, which has more recently moved into the court system to seek recognition and protection. The Lambda Legal Defense and Education Fund, a national organization committed to achieving full recognition of the civil rights of lesbians, gay men, and people with HIV/AIDS, and the American Civil Liberties Union Lesbian and Gay Rights Project identified the following topics for attention:

Antigay violence
Civil rights law
Domestic partnerships
Housing discrimination
Job discrimination

Marriage
Military
Parenting
Youth, students, and schools (ACLU, 1997)

There is evidence of differences in gay and lesbian lifestyles. A number of studies have found that lesbians tend to enter a sustained lover relationship after meeting as friends (Tanner, 1978). In fact, 75 percent of lesbian couples live together and tend to have more stable relationships than do gay lovers (Westin, 1992). Gay partners more often report entering the relationship because of sexual attraction and then building a friendship and a sustaining affection. Only a little over 50 percent of gay lovers reside together, and there tends to be a greater disparity in their ages than among lesbian or heterosexual couples (Westin, 1992).

Within the homosexual community is a great diversity of values and political commitments. Nowhere is this illustrated more clearly than in the adoption of public celebrations or marriage ceremonies for gay and lesbian partners. Particularly for homosexuals with affiliations in a religious community, a ceremony that offers spiritual support for their union can be very important. Other homosexuals view marriage ceremonies as public property declarations and, therefore, too reflective of traditional heterosexual dominance-submission practices to be appropriate. Contrasting arguments on this point are eloquently made in Suzanne Sherman's (1992) book, *Lesbian and Gay Marriage: Private Commitments, Public Ceremonies*.

One clear theme in these discussions is the struggle of homosexual people to decide whether to adopt practices associated with a heterosexual lifestyle for their own personal meanings and purposes or to view all practices of the heterosexual community as inappropriate for their use (Wolfson, 1996b). Like many minority groups, homosexual people search for practices that may increase their acceptance without compromising their identity and values.

Although the homosexual couple has a minority sexual orientation in American society, most practicing homosexual people resent society's extreme focus on their sexual behavior. Some observers see this as indicative of Americans' fascination with human sexuality in general, but it may also represent the presence of homophobia, or fear of one's own and others' homosexual tendencies (Buxton, 1991). A strong message regarding labels illustrates this conflict. The term *homosexual* has been used widely in the United States as a noun rather than an adjective. Homosexual persons protest that the noun usage implies that sexual orientation is the most fundamental and public identity assigned in our culture. To say "homosexual person" implies that there may be other significant attributes of that individual beyond his or her homosexuality label. In 1996 the FBI's collection of hate crimes showed that antigay hate crimes account for 11.6 percent of all hate crimes, up from 8.9 percent in 1991. The largest number of hate crimes were still reported in the racial category (61.6 percent), but the second most common, those in the religious category, were only about 4 percent more frequent than hate crimes related to perceived sexual orientation (Human Rights Campaign, 1998). According to a review of FBI statistics by the Southern Poverty Law Center (1998), individual homosexual people are six times as likely to be physically attacked as Jews or Hispanics and twice as likely as African Americans.

The values present in a homosexual household are a combination of values, like other family types, with a clear decision to act on one's sexual orientation in an intimate and honest way. Coupled with these commitments and values is an interest in personal freedom or right to express individualism and uniqueness. Many homosexual people also place a high value on social criticism, or activism, and standards of justice and equity. The gay rights movement has built on societal concern for democratic principles of equality, justice, and equal protection. The contrast of their sexual orientation with the dominant culture's patterns encourages values clarification and discussion. Osborn (1996, p. 248) comments that the lesbian and gay community has the following ideas to teach America:

1. A community ethic of caring
2. An affirmation of diversity
3. Moving beyond either/or thinking
4. Diversity in spirituality
5. Yin/yang balance of ideas

Status

The status of homosexual families in the United States reflects sexual, economic, legal, and social definitions. In Briggs's (1994) study of homosexual people, the demographics of the gay and lesbian sample mirrored the heterosexual population's distribution by age, gender, and ethnicity. The gay-lesbian sample reported significantly higher levels of education than the heterosexual sample, but this did not translate into expected higher levels of income. The gay-lesbian sample reported slightly lower incomes than the heterosexual population, driven largely by the lower income of gay men in comparison to heterosexual men. Butler's (2000) analysis suggested that the increased reports of homosexual partnering reflected an increase in economic stability and independence for women as well as a more liberal set of societal responses to homosexual persons. These responses include a movement by some states to prohibit employment discrimination based on sexual orientation, an increase in "sexual orientation" in civil rights codes, a greater number of employers providing domestic partner benefits and an increase in gay/lesbian foster parenting and adoption.

Reasons for Homosexuality

According to traditional definitions of the family by blood or legal ties, the homosexual family is viewed as deviant and less valued. Some of this negative definition relates to a general misunderstanding of homosexuality and the reasons people are homosexual. A variety of theories have been used to explain the cause of homosexuality (Downing, 1991). It has been suggested that homosexual individuals are products of disturbed or inappropriate relationships with domineering mothers or weak fathers. Other explanations include experimentation with same-sex relationships in childhood and becoming obsessed with their attractiveness, a psychological disturbance that makes heterosexual relationships unsuccessful, or a genetic predisposition toward homosexuality.

Recent research has suggested there is not one primary reason an individual becomes a homosexual, but there are a number of contributing factors. Some evidence indicates that a small portion of homosexual people are genetically predisposed toward homosexuality, from development as early as during gestation. Prenatal hormonal conditions have a powerful influence on the emergence of sexual characteristics. All fertilized eggs begin life as nonsexual organisms in which the presence of the XX or XY chromosome pair does not influence development until during the second to fifth month of gestation. Given the complexities of interaction in development, it is logical that some homosexual individuals are responding to basic physiological events in their own development (Ellis & Ames, 1987). In Hall's (2000) study of female monozygotic twins, pairs who were discordant in sexual orientation (i.e., one twin was heterosexual and the other was homosexual in orientation) had significant differences in finger ridge counts, reflecting prenatal environmental differences. This suggests that the intrauterine environment may be a significant variable in establishing homosexual orientation of some individuals.

Although there is inadequate research to pinpoint the exact causes of homosexuality, scientists are becoming increasingly clear about what does not cause homosexuality. For example, children raised by gay or lesbian parents seem no more likely to become homosexuals in adulthood than children raised by heterosexual parents (Gottman, 1989). The theory of a weak father and a dominant mother leading to homosexuality has not been confirmed. Likewise, the idea that females become homosexuals by choosing male role models has not been substantiated through research (Kirkpatrick, 1987).

Some researchers do believe that adolescent behaviors play a significant role in lifelong sexual patterns. Some findings have indicated that participation in homosexual behavior during adolescence—and intense and compelling relationships during this period—can encourage an adult homosexual orientation.

What we may be seeing, however, is adolescents recognizing their sexual orientation at an earlier age in a culture that has allowed more public discussion of this issue. One finding from research is that both researchers and clinicians have found it very difficult to change someone's sexual orientation, even when the individual has been motivated to do so (Harry, 1989; Millic & Crowne, 1986; Whitam & Zendt, 1984). These findings would suggest both powerful reinforcing satisfactions with a homosexual orientation and the presence of physiological determinants of homosexuality.

In the 1990s a number of organized attempts were made at reparative therapy, or helping homosexual people change their sexual orientation. Ads in major print media and appearances on a variety of talk shows brought attention to these efforts ("Variations on a Theme," *Newsweek,* 1993). With negative mainstream messages about homosexuality, it is logical that a number of gays would be motivated to try this method. But since the 1960s, when both the American Psychiatric and Psychological Associations declared that homosexuality was not a disorder, mainstream therapists have not supported "sexual conversion." However, in the popular culture, homosexuality has polarized some political groups to the extent that national mainstream political parties are taking positions on homosexual rights in the twenty-first century.

Legal Status

Although a number of scholars declare that "there is little social affirmation for homosexuality in our society" (Bigner, 2002, p. 525), specific campaigns to obtain legal rights related to parenting, marriage, and employment have made some progress. The legal area where progress is striking is the U.S. Supreme Court's refutation of the Texas "homosexual conduct" law in June 2003. The case *Lawrence v. Texas* was brought by a gay couple who were arrested for sodomy when police raided their home. The Supreme Court ruled that the Texas law, and by implication, sodomy laws in 13 other states, violated the U.S. Constitution's guarantee of privacy (Lambda Legal, 2003). Defined as "sexual acts between individuals of the same gender," sodomy was outlawed by state laws passed largely in the late 1800s and early 1900s. Beginning in 1962 in Illinois, 27 state legislatures repealed their sodomy laws, with Arizona acting as recently as 2001. In 11 additional states, the sodomy laws were invalidated by state courts (Lambda Legal, 2002a). For homosexual couples, the definition of their chosen relationships as criminal in such recent history is a powerful message that demanded social, political, and legal advocacy. This legal activism has resulted in efforts to legalize marriage or civil unions, to obtain domestic partner benefits, and to obtain legal parenting rights.

In the 1996 *Baehr v. Mike* decision, a circuit judge in Hawaii ruled that the state had shown no compelling reason to deny gay and lesbian couples the right to marry. The decision was immediately appealed to the Hawaii Supreme Court. In the meantime, in 1996 the U.S. Congress passed the Defense of Marriage Act (DOMA), which declares that from the federal government's view, marriage is defined as only occurring between a man and a woman. Presumably federal programs such as Social Security or veterans' benefits would use this definition.

Subsequently, approximately half the states introduced measures to declare their intention of not recognizing marriages legalized in another state. In the interim, a measure was introduced in Hawaii and placed on the 1998 November general election ballot to amend the state constitution to permit marriages to be restricted to opposite-sex couples. Advocates who campaigned against the ballot initiative commented that since 60 percent of all marriages in Hawaii are multiracial, the passage of a law discriminating against certain groups who wished to marry would deny the strong inclusive values of Hawaii. The ballot initiative was passed. In 2001 the state of Vermont passed a "civil union law" providing same-sex partners all the benefits given by the state to married couples (Lambda Legal, 2006). In 2003 the Massachusetts State Court ruled in behalf of seven same-sex couples who wished to marry, declaring that they could find no compelling reason why they should be denied a civil marriage. In the aftermath of the Massachusetts decision, several members of Congress introduced legislation that would amend the U.S. Constitution to ban recognition of same-sex marriages (Lambda Legal, 2003). Committed homosexual couples generally make wills that name each other as heir and write health care powers of attorney so they may take appropriate action for their partner in a health crisis or at death. National media attention about this concern was evident after the 9/11 tragedy when a number of homosexual individuals lost their committed partner and were denied access to family survivor funds. A New York state law was eventually passed that guaranteed spousal benefits from insurance companies specifically to approximately 20 gay and lesbian survivors whose partners died in the World Trade Center (Lambda Legal, 2002).

Beginning with the *Village Voice* newspaper in New York, a number of communities, businesses, and cooperatives have defined homosexual couples as domestic partnerships and have initiated policies that allow for insurance benefits and beneficiary status among homosexual couples. Wisenkale and Heckart (1993) comment that it is in more individualized environments, like communities and neighborhoods, that an understanding of homosexual families leads to the initiation of local regulations in support of their rights.

Among members of the gay community, there are strong differences of opinion about the advantages of domestic partnerships as a classification. Some activists view domestic partnership legislation as a breakthrough in policy definition of family. They appreciate the protection of property and the support for inheritance that domestic partnership statutes may provide. Other homosexual people resent domestic partnership legislation as an unnecessary intrusion into their private lives. It is interesting that in Wisenkale and Heckart's (1993) study of communities with early domestic partnership policies, six of these communities were in California, five were towns that contain major universities, and three were in coastal metropolitan areas. These areas probably support more liberal values toward regulation and contain a greater variation in household composition.

By 2002, eight states and the District of Columbia, numerous cities and counties, over 2,000 private companies, approximately 100 academic institutions, and more than 30 unions publicly reported their granting of domestic partner benefits (Lambda Legal, 2001). Recent rising health costs and the need for services surrounding the AIDS epidemic have prompted a number of court cases that provide some precedents for changing the definition of family. In the *Braschi v. Stahl Association Company* (1989) case in New York, the survivor of a gay couple who owned a home jointly was able to inherit the home. A clear statement about the financial struggles of homosexual households was made by the selection of the IRS building in Washington as the setting for a public marriage ceremony for approximately 10,000 gay and lesbian partners during the 1987 March on Washington for Gay and Lesbian Rights (Sherman, 1992). Benkov (1994) summarized significant legal conflicts beginning in the early 1970s as homosexual partners sought protection of rights for each other and their children. The landmark case in California, *Marvin v. Marvin* (557 P.2d 106, Cal. 1976), established a precedence of financial obligation to an unmarried partner at the breakup of a committed relationship. Although the Marvin case involved a heterosexual couple, it served to benefit gay and lesbian couples because of its recognition of the court's role in preventing exploitation by recognizing property-based agreements of an unmarried couple.

Public Disclosure

For committed homosexual couples, the issues of inheritance, benefits from the workplace, child support, parenting, costs of child care, and legal standing after entering into contracts are all troublesome. Those partners who are able to solve their legal questions and problems often still have to struggle with status in relation to friendships and families of origin. During the 1970s gay rights movement, a great deal of publicity was given to the process of "coming out" to one's family of origin. Osborn (1996) characterized these early actions as "come out and run" events, in which young people revealing their sexual orientation to their families absolutely abandoned the family. Many parents reacted with intense grief and "rushed right in to the closet their children left" (p. 36). Bigner (2002) describes disclosure as a stressor event that most likely produces a crisis reaction as members reconcile their knowledge and attitudes toward homosexuality with their relationship with their family member.

Health reasons compelled a number of homosexual people to return to their families of origin to seek assistance and support in dealing with sexually transmitted diseases, especially AIDS. After an initial shock, many of these families created supportive environments for their homosexual sons and daughters. Osborn (1996) reports anecdotal evidence that 75 percent of parents of gays and lesbians do achieve full or substantial acceptance of their gay children in three to five years, regardless of economic, educational, or cultural background (p. 33). These families have also reported their struggles with the wider community's prejudice against homosexual persons, and the family's need to seek strength and support from new relationships (Griffin, Wirth, & Wirth, 1996). Working for AIDS information networks, becoming active in one of PFLAG's 400 local chapters, and seeking help from a variety of counseling and support services have enabled some of these families to express their caring and to work in a supportive and positive environment for their family members (Sherman, 1992). Fields (2001) studied a group of parents who were members of the local chapter of a national advocacy group to learn how they processed and accepted their son's or daughter's disclosure of their homosexual orientation. Significant conflicts that emerged were questions regarding the causes of homosexuality and the parent's own contributions to their children's status as well as the roles they assumed in supporting their children's lives. Fields commented that many parents insisted that homosexual persons were "not unlike heterosexual persons" rather than choosing to help enlarge others' understanding of diversity in relationships as reflected in their own family experience.

Gay and lesbian persons frequently comment on the power of their family's responses to their sexual orientation to influence their happiness and balance in a homosexual family. Many gays and lesbians struggle to share honestly with coworkers and bring their partners to work-related events. They find that many of their interactions with the wider community involve an ongoing balance between risk taking and education. Some couples write "married" on enrollment forms and others write "single." Both responses are often coupled with feelings of frustration or anger and may include notes in the margin in an attempt to educate the bureaucracy represented (Sherman, 1992).

Support Groups

Like most minority groups that experience prejudice, homosexual families have created support groups and communities in which they can feel comfortable. In some larger urban areas, child-care cooperatives or centers run by homosexual families have provided a place of nurturance and support for these parents and their children. See the organization resource list at the end of the chapter for names and addresses of major national support groups.

As with any minority rights movement, some members of the homosexual community are uncomfortable with the extremism of some of the leaders' actions. Some homosexual leaders have criticized gays and lesbians for creating a family lifestyle that resembles a heterosexual lifestyle and have suggested that kinship should be emphasized only within the broader homosexual community. Consequently, bonded intimate relationships that resemble a heterosexual couple family are discouraged by these leaders.

A number of national support groups, advocacy campaigns, national information databases, and local affiliate groups are now available, often listed under a broader term "GLBT," or "gay, lesbian, bisexual and transgendered" individuals (see list at end of chapter under Organizations). Most American college and university campuses include gay and lesbian activist groups and publications. As with any minority advocacy group, a range of political positions may be represented in these groups. When an extreme position is taken by the leadership, some members of the community may not feel welcome or may need to initiate an open discussion of policies and positions. Because these groups operate in very different environments of acceptance and support, this ongoing discussion or process of education is important to all of us.

Feminist scholars have been particularly critical of the nuclear family as an environment in which power relationships discriminate against women, and they have recommended more permeable boundaries for all homosexual families. Radical feminists have tended to discount lesbians who advocate or practice a more conservative lifestyle. In addition, feminists have pointed out that gay men are more often victims of the AIDS epidemic. When gay and lesbian advocacy groups first formed to promote homosexual rights, it was often the rights of men that took precedence. Osborn (1996) reflects that early gay and lesbian movements were often quite separate and could be characterized as "gays seeking sex" and "lesbians seeking relationships" (p. 112). Particularly after the disappointment of President Clinton's actions in their behalf, gay and lesbian leaders acknowledged their need to do their own work. By 1996 there were more than 75 gay and lesbian service centers in the United States, as well as support for the importance of jointly crafting an advocacy movement.

CHANGING ROLES OF FEMALES

A lesbian family clearly represents a changing role for females in the creation of family form. In research by Koepke, Hare, and Moran (1992), lesbian couples with children scored significantly higher in relationship satisfaction and sexual relationship satisfaction than lesbian couples without children. There were no differences in satisfaction between child-free lesbian couples and lesbian couples with children based on the longevity of the relationship, or whether or not they had disclosed their sexual relationship to others. This issue of disclosure causes less pressure among lesbians than among gay men.

These couples did not show the depression in satisfaction scores because of the presence of children that is often found in the heterosexual community. Koepke et al. (1992) suggest that, because women are often the relationship builders or kinkeepers, lesbian couples engaged in joint parenting may find more relationship satisfaction than do lesbian couples without children. In contrast, though, the authors also point out that the lesbian partners risk substantial consequences to form their relationships. Rejection by their children or an attempt by ex-spouses to change custody relationships were listed as fears. Their parenting roles were viewed as stable and deeply committed in an environment that could be threatening to less mature partners. Lesbian couples, for obvious reasons, more often consider becoming parents in their relationships. Artificial insemination, private arrangements with an acquaintance, or adoption are all choices made by lesbians. Sometimes the choice of which woman in a couple should become pregnant is obvious; sometimes both women wish to become pregnant at different times and raise both children together. Sherman (1992) illustrates this decision faced by a number of lesbian couples.

An interesting finding in a study by Hare and Richards (1993) is that lesbian parents had more positive relationships with male friends and more concern for good male models than did women in heterosexual families. The lesbian mothers spent more time and were more comfortable in their interactions with their male friends. These friendships may provide positive role models for the children of lesbians by showing male and female friendships without the struggles that exist in sexual relationships. Thorne's (1993) description of social relationships between male and female children at school illustrates the number of ways in which society emphasizes differences and keeps the two sexes separated. In addition, Thorne documents a number of ways in which gender is a powerful divider, unless adults intervene and establish other ways for persons to relate. Children viewing the friendships between lesbian women and their male acquaintances may see a more comfortable friendship role that is part of an evolving understanding of male–female relationships.

CHANGING ROLES OF MALES

There are fewer gay families than lesbian families, and there are fewer gay families with custody of children. However, a quarter of gay men have been previously married, and there are an increasing number of gay men who are noncustodial parents or who seek to adopt or provide foster care for children. Studies of gay fathers show little evidence that men had originally married and procreated as a means to hide their homosexuality. Rather, they had genuine affection for their wives and children and only gradually realized the power of their homosexuality. For homosexual men who have not previously parented, decisions about how to become parents, how their children may develop, and what supports are available present complex challenges (Patterson, 1994). A number of gay couples have become foster parents, an increasingly available option because of a dramatic increase in the numbers of children needing out-of-home care and the decreasing pool of prospective adoptive parents (Brooks & Goldberg,

2001). Having proven themselves to be competent bonded parents, gay foster parents have then applied for adoption. In a number of states where single adults can adopt, one member of a gay couple may initially adopt and later a "second parent" adoption is initiated for the other partner. In a landmark New Jersey social service adoption suit, a male gay couple was granted the right legally to adopt the foster child they had cared for since he was 3 months old (ACLU, 1997). With this decision, New Jersey became the first state to declare that adoption can be denied to any unmarried couple based only on the same "considerations which also apply to married couples" (ACLU, 1997). Gay families have welcomed the New Jersey decision as representing precedence for the two members of a homosexual couple to have equal parenting rights. In 2002 Florida, Utah, and Mississippi were the only states whose laws expressly denied adoption to homosexual persons. Other states, in practice, have varying degrees of tolerance for homosexual couples adopting. One impressive demonstration of the commitment and skill in parenting can be seen in the examples of gay men adopting HIV-positive infants or young children and nurturing them to health. Brooks and Goldberg (2001) suggest that both a subtle homophobia and a respect for the strengths of gay and lesbian families to handle challenges has held to the placement of children with special needs with homosexual couples. Some gay and lesbian families felt unable to qualify to have normally developing children placed in their care.

Gay men have been most dramatically impacted by the health risks surrounding AIDS in the gay community. Because multiple partners have traditionally been more associated with the gay lifestyle rather than the lesbian lifestyle, and drug use has been historically higher among men than women, gay men have been particularly vulnerable to the AIDS epidemic. In many large urban areas, a third to a half of gay men have been directly affected by the death of someone in their intimate-friend circle.

In the *Braschi v. Stahl Association Company* (1989) case referred to earlier, in which a gay couple's home was awarded to the surviving gay member of the long-term couple, the court set four standards for the definition of a family:

1. Exclusivity and longevity of a relationship
2. The level of emotional and financial commitment of the partners
3. How the couple conducted their everyday lives in society
4. The couple's reliance on each other for daily services (Wisenkale & Heckart, 1993)

This definition of family was made after a judge's careful consideration of the gay couple's relationship and resources after one member died from AIDS. The state of California created a task force that settled on a functional definition of family that includes the following:

1. Maintaining physical health and safety
2. Shaping a belief system and values and goals
3. Teaching social skills
4. Creating a haven or recuperation from stress in the wider system (Wisenkale & Heckart, 1993)

These definitions reflect a change in the meaning of family, with a stronger appreciation for the social and psychological comforts of the family.

For gay men who are fathering children, the comfort and regenerative functions of the family are particularly important (Bozette, 1988). Gay fathers have reported that revealing their homosexuality outside the family causes negative consequences for their children, but not revealing it deprives them of the support of the homosexual community (Crosbie-Burnett & Helmbrecht, 1993). Osborn (1996) summarizes the responses of gays to coming out as "always worth it, no matter what the consequences." Although repeatedly gays reveal that the greatest fear about coming out is the loss of loved ones, a quote from a gay who was brutally beaten in his neighborhood echoes many "post-coming-out" feelings: "I'll heal this physical pain, but I couldn't heal the self-hatred inside with anything but being out" (p. 26).

SOCIALIZATION OF CHILDREN

Homosexual couples report the same goals for children as do heterosexual couples, except for heightened interest in the child's right to choose (Allen & Burrell, 1996). Because gay and lesbian adults create families by choosing certain relationships, they want to be very clear about the rights of their children to do likewise (Patterson, 1994). Most homosexual couples deliberately arrange for their children to know and interact with both male and female friends. In fact, some research suggests that the children of homosexual couples experience both males and females as significant-other adults in their lives more so than children of heterosexual couples. Benkov (1994), Bozette (1989), and Golombok, Tasker, and Murray (1997) describe the rich variety of supportive friendships and family structures that homosexual couples have created to help with their socialization goals for their children. This is probably a reflection of the permeability of family boundaries in a homosexual family with supportive friendships, or the more extended nature of some homosexual families. Children raised in homosexual families may learn more about the variation and freedom for both men and women to engage in instrumental and expressive roles.

Active researchers of homosexual families report that the children deal with their parents' homosexuality in a variety of ways: by boundary control, or attempts to control their parents' behavior; by nondisclosure; or by selective disclosure to trusted friends (Benkov, 1994; Bozette, 1998; Sears, 1994). The younger the children are when they learn of their parents' sexual orientation, the more comfortable they are with this information.

As mentioned earlier, homosexual people do not believe that their sexual orientation should be the dominant variable in how they are treated by the wider society. In fact, for both gay and lesbian couples who are rearing children either in their own custody or in the custody of former partners, the model is appropriately a stepparent model. Yet homosexual couples are rarely included in stepfamily meetings, and only recently are referred to in the literature as stepparents (Guggenheim, Lowe, & Curtis, 1996). In the 1990s counselors began to initiate training in how to support homosexual couples and stepparents living as homosexual couples.

THE ROLE OF GRANDPARENTS AND OTHERS

Most gay and lesbian families are characterized by the intentionality of their relationships, which includes *choosing kin,* managing disclosure, building community,
and ritualizing and legalizing (Duran-Aydintug & Causey, 1996; Oswald, 2002).
Westin's (1991) study of 80 racially and ethnically diverse gay and lesbian relationships showed the rich and varied complex of friendships and support that homosexual families created. Sharing meals, money, child care, holidays, and other resources
supports the strength and continuity of relationships. Oswald's (2002) study showed
that homosexual couples managed their relationships with heterosexual families and
coworkers by increased closeness to those who were accepting of homosexuality
and distance from those who were rejecting. Patterson, Hunt, and Mason (1998)
found that children of lesbian mothers had monthly contacts with at least six other
adult friends and relatives who did not reside in the household. In McWhirter and
Mattison's (1984) classic late 1970s study of 156 male homosexual couples who had
lived together a range of one to two years, only a small number reported experiencing open or covert rejection by parents or other family members. More recent evidence (Osborn, 1996) suggests this level of family acceptance continues even in
times of more controversial discourse on homosexuality. Contact with the family of
origin is common during a health crisis. In lesbian families, there have been some
reports of extended-family members being key sources of energy in the process of
birth and parenting. Most discussion of extended-family members involves the conflict and struggle by the parent generation to accept their children and grandchildren's family structure. Professionals can play a key role in helping with fears and
supportive relationships once these families have been confronted with their offspring's
homosexual lifestyle.

The importance of political activism and advocacy among grandparents and
extended-family members cannot be overestimated. The support and education made
available through the chapters of PFLAG and the National Federation of Parents and
Friends of Gays have assisted extended-family members with information to support
their private and public actions. Addresses of these organizations are given at the end
of the chapter.

ECOLOGICAL CONSIDERATIONS

Many of the most important ecological factors surrounding homosexual families relate
to the environment created by social relationships and belief systems. Where these
environments are supportive, sharing is possible for homosexual families. Where environments are extremely critical, or the homosexual partners feel their professional and
economic position does not allow them to reveal their family definition, then families can
feel quite isolated and stressed. Every homosexual family has significant developmental
tasks in defining and maintaining their relationship in a way that is satisfying for both
partners and the children involved. The fact that an unknown number of "homosexual"

individuals are bisexual or have had different periods of heterosexual lifestyle during their own development emphasizes the complexity of these decisions.

Like other minorities, homosexual families often resent the wider society's focus on one variable in their lives. In the 1990s there were repeated references to homosexual persons receiving more numerous physical and psychological attacks than racial minorities. The Gay and Lesbian Task Force completed a national study revealing that more than a third of individuals surveyed had suffered direct violence because of their sexual identities (Elia, 1993). Herek and Berrill (1992) reported that teenagers surveyed on their attitudes toward minorities reacted more negatively to gays than any other group of minorities. In addition, the conservative political climate of the 1990s has encouraged the passing of a number of deliberately discriminatory community and state statutes against the rights of homosexuals. The focus of much of these efforts in states has been to limit the right to marry, to adopt children, and to obtain employment benefits. Growing religious fundamentalism, increasing fear of sexually transmitted diseases, and the tightening economic climate create pressures that conflict with societal concern for equal justice and human rights for all individuals.

The Lambda Legal Defense Fund established the Marriage Project in 1993 after the landmark ruling in the Hawaii marriage case. They maintain a database and represent gays and lesbians involved in legal processes over marriage, custody, and adoption. Their Websites include clear, practical advice on individual options for couples, as well as information of interest to their entire community, such as progress of landmark cases. A large part of their efforts in recent years has been in consulting in states' attempting to pass same-sex marriage bans. As of May 1998, 29 states had enacted laws to prohibit same-sex marriage (Wolfson, 1998). Efforts in states like New Jersey provide a contrast. In 2002 seven gay and lesbian couples sued the state of New Jersey for the right to marry based on the state constitution's equal protection clause. This was the latest in efforts to obtain legal protection in a state that has shown itself to be open to homosexual persons' rights. New Jersey's hate crime law includes sexual orientation, its state legislature repealed the sodomy act in 1979, and four years in a row, the legislature blocked bills introduced to outlaw homosexual marriages. In January 2003 the legislature was developing domestic partner legislation while 55 community organizations planned a series of 10 community town meetings on the theme "Supporting Equality in the Courts, Domestic Partnerships in the Legislature" (Lambda Legal, 2006).

A particularly difficult reality for homosexual families is the continual ambiguity and stress of a lifestyle that carries clear risks for disclosure (Friskopp & Silverstein, 1995). In contrast to ethnic, racial, or physically challenged minorities, homosexual people form a minority that is identified by the behavior choices of individuals themselves. When these behaviors are acted on by adults in a caring relationship, it is difficult to understand how such families can be treated negatively within American society. The homosexual community particularly has reaped the grief and trauma of the AIDS epidemic. In addition, they are often in the position of a "blame the victim" mentality in the wider American society. When AIDS and other sexually transmitted diseases are treated as events that the homosexual community brought on itself, it is difficult for homosexual individuals to feel accepted, respected, or protected. Homosexual couples who parent children need the assistance of the wider community systems to coparent with them.

Religious Communities

The 10 percent (Briggs, 1994) of Americans who are homosexuals include many people with strong religious and spiritual values. McWhirter and Mattison (1984) reported that in their sample of committed gay couples, 60 percent identified themselves as religious, but only one in four attended church (p. 186). For many of them, one of the heaviest burdens has been the lack of support from their religious community. Americans have a strong pattern of public celebration of family events in religious communities. Thus weddings, baptisms, and other family transitions are often shared with a congregation. Yet religion has struggled with theological and political acceptance of homosexual rights. From biblically referenced prejudicial statements against a homosexual lifestyle to investigations of sexual abuse among homosexual members of the clergy, religious communities reveal themselves as very human institutions. Both religious leaders and members of religious communities have struggled to create an open dialogue about religion's role in supporting homosexual couples.

The tragic revelations about the American Catholic Church's record on sexual and psychological abuse has created more open dialogue about sexual orientation. Aside from the appalling charges of abuse toward nuns and female members of the congregation, the stories of young males being abused by priests has created a more realistic recognition that some of us are indeed gay or lesbian. Yet a religious community that requires celibacy of priests while placing them in powerful positions of authority and trust over young people has evidently created an explosive temptation for some individuals. Both the acknowledgment that some priests have homosexual orientations and the recognition that the hierarchy of the church has a moral, legal, and spiritual obligation to create different processes for protecting members of its community are changes long overdue. The most tragic victims of this chapter are the men and women whose own sexual freedom of expression is scarred by a relationship of abuse and manipulation connected with a spiritual community.

Conflicts over how to support homosexual church members have been expressed through clergy leaving their congregation or the ministry entirely, or finding ways to begin changing practices. Sherman (1992) quotes a number of homosexual couples who were married by a member of the clergy known to them but in a location different from where the congregation normally met. Other couples were already members of denominations that provided specific ceremonies and recognition within their faith. Metropolitan Community Church is a religious group that deliberately supports and includes the gay community in its membership (McWhirter & Mattison, 1984; Sherman, 1992). Sherman's research included interviews with rabbis, priests, ministers, and a Wiccan high priestess who had conducted services for homosexual couples in a variety of settings. Roscoe (1998) recommended that the ability to integrate homosexuality within one's own cultural and spiritual history facilitates the resilience of families.

A number of religious leaders have engaged in support for homosexual persons whose partners are dying of AIDS. Their acknowledgment of the importance of spiritual values in this process has challenged conservative religious practices prejudicial towards gay persons.

Some lesbians have been particularly concerned that mainstream religious groups have been marked by male chauvinist practices that conflict with lesbian values. Although some of them, therefore, have resisted engaging in any public practices used by the heterosexual religious community, others have joined alternative religious communities. Native American Indian traditions and ancient Wiccan practices are two examples of other groups that have appealed to the lesbian community.

All of these efforts by traditional and alternative spiritual communities involve support for personal reflection, caring, and choice. The homosexual lifestyle perhaps provides one of the deepest challenges to the effectiveness of religious faith, compassion, love, and community.

CHANGES AND ADAPTATIONS

Some homosexual families have created strong connections to a wider community that is respectful and supportive of their life choices. With the increased publicity surrounding legal challenges and homosexuality, individuals have taken a variety of positions on disclosing their homosexuality to friends and community. The conflict described by gay fathers, who felt that disclosure brought censuring from some individuals in their children's community but that the lack of disclosure robbed fathers themselves of support from the gay community, is a typical conflict for many homosexual families.

There is evidence among the gay community that the AIDS epidemic has resulted in more conservative sexual behavior and more stable relationships. In the context of caring for the terminally ill, a number of homosexual men have reconfirmed the affectionate and supportive elements in their community. Difficult issues remain concerning the need to continue research that results in both the prevention and cure of AIDS. In addition, it is likely that for some time there will be misunderstanding and confusion about the relationship of homosexuality to the AIDS epidemic.

HELPFUL TECHNIQUES FOR SERVING GAY AND LESBIAN FAMILIES

Compassion, sensitivity, and accurate information are resources needed by all professionals supporting and serving the homosexual family (Appleby & Anastas, 1998). Homosexual families engage in their lifestyles at great personal risk and cost, and their commitment to parenting commands respect. Because many members of the homosexual community have experienced death and grief, it is important to be sensitive to the importance of relationships, and to provide comfort and the means of expressing grief with these transitions.

Many of you may find yourself working with a family that has not openly disclosed their sexual orientation to others or at least not to the organization you represent. This is appropriate protective behavior, and your role is to respect their decision and earn their trust. Many gay and lesbian parents will recognize your meaning if you state that yours is a "welcoming" agency/school/organization. State that your goals are to be inclusive and supportive of family choices. In a study by Perrin and Kulkin (1996), homosexual families recommended that helping professionals of the dominant culture give clear cues to signal approval, acceptance, and safety to family members. Explicit discussion of acceptance of the parents' sexual orientation and respect for confidentiality is an important bridge to an effective partnership. When a family is being enrolled in an educational, health, or social services system, ask specifically about legal arrangements regarding medical consent. One parent may have given the other parent formal power of attorney for specific purposes, or if a second parent adoption has occurred, either parent may consent. In counseling sessions or conferences with these parents, you should ask "Who else helps you parent __?" if this information has not been shared. Remember to ask what their children call each member of the homosexual couple, and make certain that all adults who are important to the child's or youth's development are included in information sessions and are invited to significant celebrations. It is not unusual for two to six additional significant adults to be part of a homosexual family's "fictive kin." It is also helpful to give children self-protective behaviors to deal with negative communication regarding their family such as instilling in them ways to "say no" or "throw off" negative messages in early childhood, elementary, or middle school settings.

Most homosexual parents are particularly concerned by society's portrayal of very rigid models of gender behavior and are interested in a broader and more equitable experience for their own children. In a dramatic essay, Rofes (1994) describes our cultural pattern of the hypermasculine "bully" in school. He identifies the harassment of the "sissy" in an educational environment that refuses to acknowledge this reality of male socialization. As professionals working with homosexual families, you can review and consciously select language, illustrations, and activities planned to respect homosexual family interests. Many homosexual persons act out strong values of individual freedom and responsibility through their lifestyle. Therefore, they are concerned that their children learn these same values and have an opportunity to practice them. Rules or regulations may be questioned more frequently than by other parents. A strong sense of justice and sensitivity to prejudice may be evident. In supporting these families, it is important to see opportunities for growth and for expressing more universal values in the nurturing of children and youth.

We have emphasized your role as helping professionals with gay or lesbian couples and parents. Yet for some of you, a challenging service may be interactions with young people or their parents when the younger generation declares their homosexual orientation. Research continues to document the stress such a revelation brings to a family and that a homosexual orientation is now being revealed at younger ages. Ryan and Futterman's (1997) study of lesbian and gay youth documented the average age for disclosure as 16 years, down from earlier studies showing the average age at 19 to 23 years old. Therefore, many gay and lesbian youth will be actively confronting their sexual orientation in junior and senior high schools. A national study of youth in 2005 documented that within the previous year, 65 percent of youth had been verbally or physically assaulted at school because of their sexual orientation and 67 percent related that they never report such incidents (Gay, Lesbian and Straight Education Network, 2001). Clearly, educators, counselors, and other human service providers have significant education and advocacy roles to play for justice and protection of such young people. See references for working with youth at the end of the chapter.

Staff in human service professions *need* to have referral agencies that are sensitive to and have an accepting commitment to the homosexual family. As you provide in-service training to staff, make certain that staff members have an opportunity to talk with homosexual members of their community and ask honest and frank questions that will help them in working with both children and parents. In addition, plan online sessions with staff members to explore the many Internet sources of information and support to homosexual families (see resources at end of chapter).

✦ CONCLUSIONS

People and family structures are diverse, and families are formed in many different ways, a few having been highlighted throughout this book. Families choose to relate to each other, forming alliances that give their members a sanctuary of emotional and economic support; privacy rights protect families from the intrusion of others. Same-sex partnerships are a form of family that has been in the news, and rights associated with these family forms are currently being debated in the courts and the media. Children and adults in such families are entitled, without fear of discrimination, to services of helping professionals. In working with families with a lifestyle that differs from your own, you are obligated to seek understanding, to provide needed services, and to avoid being judgmental.

✦ STUDY QUESTIONS

1. Describe the McCarthy era, when U.S. culture was particularly critical of homosexuality.
2. Do we know how many individuals in the United States are homosexual? Why or why not?
3. Approximately how many homosexual families are there in the United States?
4. Describe some differences between gay and lesbian families.
5. List different ways that gay and lesbian persons can become parents.
6. How can gay or lesbian couples provide legal protection for their rights or the rights of each partner?
7. Define *homophobia,* and suggest some of its causes.
8. Describe two recent landmark decisions regarding homosexual relationships.
9. List unresolved legal issues for the people in gay and lesbian families.
10. Discuss the process of "coming out" to families of origin as a "stressor event."

✦ APPLICATIONS

1. Investigate whether there is a gay and lesbian rights organization on your campus. Arrange an interview with an officer of this organization. Ask your source

to evaluate the institutional support for the organization. Give examples of this support or lack of support.

2. Investigate whether there is a family law committee within the bar association in your state. If such a committee exists, contact the chairperson or an officer of that group and ask how gay and lesbian families legally protect themselves and their rights in this state.

3. Interview five of your fellow students on campus about their views of gay and lesbian families. Have they had any experiences with such families? What do they view as the positive and negative challenges for these families?

4. Contact a member of the local ministerial alliance or council. Ask if there are marriage ceremonies conducted by members of various religious groups for gay or lesbian couples. If possible, talk with a member of the clergy or priesthood about the kinds of ceremonies provided.

5. Write a position paper on the advantages of disclosure of homosexual lifestyle. What are the private, social, and economic implications of disclosure? Would you advocate it or not? For what reasons?

6. Write a list of recommendations for homosexual partners who are also parents. These recommendations should include the following topics:
   a. Disclosure of lifestyle to children
   b. Each partner's parenting role with the children
   c. Economic support for the children
   d. Relationship with extended-family members
   e. Relationships with school systems and youth organizations

7. Recently, some urban newspapers have changed their engagement and marriage social pages to read "celebrations." Write a letter to the editor suggesting the advantages of this policy and encouraging a change in this section of your local newspaper.

8. If there is a chapter of PFLAG in your town, attend a meeting and interview an officer of the organization about the objectives and activities of the chapter.

✦ MEDIA RESOURCES

Silent Pioneers: Gay and Lesbian Elders. (1985). (42 minutes). Pioneer Films. New York, NY: Filmmakers Library.

✦ PERIODICALS

Empathy, an interdisciplinary journal for persons working to end oppression based on sexual identities, P.O. Box 5085, Columbia, SC 29250.

Gay Parent Magazine. P.O. Box 750852, Forest Hills, NY 11325–0852. Bimonthly magazine.

The High School Journal, 77(1–2), special double issue on the gay teenager: October/November, 1993; December/January, 1994.

Journal of Homosexuality, Haworth Press, Inc., 10 Alice Street, Binghamton, NY 13904, (800) 342–9678. Quarterly research journal published on topics related to homosexuality.

Teaching Tolerance. Published twice a year since 1992 by the Southern Poverty Law Center, 400 Washington Avenue, Montgomery, AL 36104. Free to educators, it covers all forms of intolerance.

✦ ORGANIZATIONS

American Civil Liberties Union (ACLU). Lesbian Gay Bisexual Transgender Project, 125 Broad Street, 18th Floor, New York, NY 10004

Lambda Legal Defense and Education Fund (LLDEF), 120 Wall Street, Suite 1500, New York, NY 10005, (212) 809-8585

National Coalition of Grandparents, 137 Larkin Street, Madison, WI 53705, (608) 238-8751

National Federation of Parents and Friends of Gays (NF/PFOG), 8020 Eastern Avenue, N.W., Washington, DC 20012, (202) 726-3223

National Gay and Lesbian Task Force, 1325 Massachusetts Ave. NW, Suite 200, Washington, DC 20005, (202) 393-5177

Parents and Friends of Lesbians and Gays (PFLAG), 1726 M. Street NW, Suite 400, Washington, DC 20036, (202) 467-8180

✦ ORGANIZATIONAL RESOURCES

Friends of Project 10. (1991). *Project 10 handbook: Addressing lesbian and gay issues in our schools* (3rd ed.). Los Angeles: Author. (ERIC Document Reproduction Service No. ED337567)

✦ KEY INTERNET RESOURCES

Alternative Family Magazine
www.altfammag.com/is2toc.jpg.

American Civil Liberties Union Lesbian and Gay Rights
www.aclu.org/lesbiangayrights/lesbiangayrightsmain.cfm

American Psychological Association—Healthy Lesbian, Gay and Bisexual Students Project
www.apa.org/edhlgb/

Children of Lesbians and Gays Everywhere
www.mispedia.org/children_of_Lesbians_AND_Gays_Everywhere.html

Lambda Legal Defense Fund
www.lambdalegal.org/cgi-bin/pages/about

Parents, Families and Friends of Lesbians and Gays (PFLAG)
www.pflag.org/
Partners Task Force for Gay and Lesbian Couples
www.buddybuddy.com/welcome.html

✣ FURTHER READING

Alpert, H. (1988). *We are everywhere: Writings by and about lesbian parents.* Freedom, CA: Crossing Press.

Berzon, B. (1988). *Permanent partners: Building gay and lesbian relationships that last.* New York: E. P. Dutton.

Bozette, F. (Ed.). (1987). *Gay and lesbian parents.* Westport, CT: Perager.

Bozette, F. (Ed.). (1989). *Homosexuality and the family.* New York: Haworth Press.

Brill, S. (2001). *The queer parents' primer: A lesbian and gay family guide to navigating the straight world.* Oakland, CA: New Harbinger Publications.

Brogan, J. (1986). *Casey: The bi-coastal kid.* Salinas, CA: Equanimity Press.

Clifford, D., & Curry, H. (1988). *A legal guide for lesbian and gay couples* (5th ed.). Berkeley, CA: Nolo Press.

Drucher, J. (2001). *Lesbian and gay families speak out: Understanding the joys and challenges of diverse family life.* Cambridge, MA: Da Capo Press.

Fricke, A. (1981). *Confessions of a rock lobster.* Boston: Alyson.

Gantz, J. (1983). *Whose child cries: Children of gay parents talk about themselves.* Rolling Hills Estate, CA: Jolmar.

Garden, N. (1982). *Annie on my mind.* New York: Farrar, Straus and Giroux.

Hicks, S., & McDermott, J. (Eds.). (1998). *Lesbian and gay fostering and adoption: Extraordinary yet ordinary.* Philadelphia, PA: Jessica Kingsley Publishers.

Perrin, E. C., & Kulkin, H. (1996). Pedriatric care for children whose parents are gay or lesbian. *Pediatrics, 97,* 629–635.

Perry, T. (1990). *Don't be afraid anymore.* New York: St. Martin's Press.

Preston, J. (Ed.). (1992). *A member of the family.* New York: E. P. Dutton.

Rafkin, L. (1990). *Different mothers: Sons and daughters of lesbians talk about their lives.* Pittsburgh, PA: Cleis.

Schulenburg, J. (1985). *Gay parenting: A complete guide for gay men and lesbians with children.* Garden City, NY: Anchor.

IV
CONCLUSIONS

→15

Serving Families

→ **Key Concepts**

- Advocacy
- Humility
- Dedication
- Service

Steve Mason/Getty Images, Inc.–PhotoDisc

There are no boundaries in the real Planet Earth. No United States, no Soviet Union, no China, no Taiwan, East Germany or West. Rivers flow unimpeded across the swaths of continents. The Persistent Tides—the pulse of the sea—do not discriminate, they push against all the varied shores on Earth.

—Jacques-Yves Cousteau, Oceanographer and Explorer

As the ocean tides pulse against our shores, we can gain strength from their boundless energy to strengthen families everywhere. Families in America are a mere microcosm of the families of the world. There are many common threads of diversity and of common purpose among all the world's people. . . . As President Clinton said in his proclamation for the International Year of the Family:

> The fabric of the United States and the world is woven together from many diverse ethnic and cultural family threads. Each family's unique traditions and teachings blend together to build the very foundation upon which we, as an international family, have grown and will continue to grow.

In designating 1994 as the International Year of the Family, the United Nations encouraged the people of the world to focus on the hopes and needs of the many diverse families living in their own communities as well as those in the global apartment house, the Earth. The year highlighted the fact that, although diverse, families are the basic social unit of all societies. Although families have structural and value differences, they are the builders of the human capital of the world. You, as a helping professional, have a solemn duty to assist in this noble endeavor.

REMEMBERING GOALS

A major goal for most families is to be together while educating individuals to be self-supporting and learning values and virtues within the family circle. Another important goal of families is to learn to grow and develop together and to relate harmoniously to each other and to the outside world. As you have learned, the family circle is defined differently by various cultural groups. Much of family life is within the home, out of view of neighbors and others. In America, the home is the most private of environments, protected by law and rules of decorum from infringement by others, and especially protected from invasion by governmental authorities.

Family support systems, agencies that serve families, and helping professionals in their many community roles must become attuned to helping where families need help and doing so when called on. Empowering all families to achieve a high-quality life in their community must be the major goal of every helping professional serving families.

FOSTERING A SENSE OF COMMUNITY

As the ideals, goals, and reality of increasing diversity among families permeate societies, the need arises for each individual citizen to take personal responsibility for making community life pleasant, safe, and productive for all who live there. As educated people, you can be of special help, providing leadership where less knowledgeable or thoughtful people might hesitate to take initiatives.

Laws, rules, civil agreements, conventions, and courtesies become part of the fabric of welcoming every family to our communities. Of course, what is everyone's business often becomes nobody's responsibility. Businesses, service providers, and all organizations should coordinate a welcoming effort for new residents and for monitoring other community needs. How gratifying it is to be personally welcomed! As people's status changes this effort can help people adjust. For example, when people age or become disabled they may come to your attention for different services, which you can help them initiate through already established channels.

Citizens in every walk of life can take responsibility for being joyful and pleasant to newcomers and old-timers. Discrimination and any other foul treatment must be constantly monitored by leadership people and nipped in the bud through deliberate effort. A sense of community evolves through the efforts of many individuals each doing small things within the community.

GIVING SERVICE

Service orientation for helping professionals focuses on empowering individuals and families to obtain the best assistance available to meet their needs and to create a harmonious and peaceful society. As graduates entering the professional arena, you will be able to serve diverse people from the youngest to the eldest. An orientation toward service means the clients' needs are paramount, their satisfaction is important, and you will go the extra mile to assist each of them. Although you cannot do for them what they might do for themselves, you must provide a needed high-quality service, as mandated by your employer as well as your personal standards.

An excellent example of a service orientation was observed in a woman selling hot dogs in an airport waiting room. The people waiting for planes were tired and hungry. She took a personal interest in each person who wanted a hot dog, checking to be sure that each had all the mustard, pickles, and catsup desired. She brought smiles to the faces of the tired and hungry passengers and made the wait go more quickly. We've all experienced vendors who seemed to hate doing us the favor of serving us; this woman enjoyed pleasing her patrons and performing a needed service.

Your college years will prepare you to be a professional, developing the skills and expertise to serve families in many respects. Not only will you be professionally prepared as a teacher, social worker, physician, or the like, but you will become skillful in meeting and speaking with clients of many different ages, ethnic backgrounds, and with different challenges. Initially, your education and skill development may be elementary, but throughout your career you will continue to learn and develop new skills. You may already be browsing college catalogs for additional professional and graduate studies. Many of you, wishing to serve families in the years ahead, should plan for further professional education.

You will become an advocate for your clients as you provide needed services. In many respects you must be creative as you seek to pull together the collage of clients' personal characteristics, the family's needs, the professional know-how, the state of the art knowledge, and the resources available. Like an artist weaving a landscape, you will fashion a wonderful tapestry for each client you serve.

WELCOMING DIVERSITY

As you have learned throughout this book, people and their families are diverse in many ways. No two individuals or families are alike. Even clients from your own community will differ from you in many respects. You must learn to recognize differences between yourself and your clients and not let those differences impact the quality of your service. You must serve equally well people of any family, no matter what group—ethnic, racial, age, gender, disabled, regional, religious, or other. Your professional preparation for high-quality service and your commitment to serve with distinction should always be a priority. Upon meeting new clients, make them feel accepted, regardless of their particular group, and remember that although we all have unique aspects, we are all human beings deserving respect.

You may feel uncertain because of your own characteristics, especially if you are new to your job. Will you receive the recognition and acceptance you have rightly earned? The hope is that with your advanced level of knowledge and understanding, people will accept your skills and abilities and disregard the fact that you may not be like them in some ways. A great deal has been learned in recent years about welcoming diverse people into our midst. Of course, there is still much to be learned. Your study of diversity in this book is a step in that direction. What you've learned will allow you to be a role model, welcoming diversity as you conscientiously do your job. Little by little, those clients who have doubts will be persuaded that your skills, abilities, dedication, and human qualities are more important than superficial differences. In other words, the differences won't make a difference—diversity will be accepted and respected!

APPLYING ECOLOGICAL SYSTEM CONCEPTS

In studying about the ecological system that helps us plan services for families, you've learned that one of the three divisions of the ecological system is the natural physical-biological environment, consisting of the various natural resources of a region. The richness of this natural resource base affects the level of goods and services the private and government sectors can provide.

A second part of the ecological system is the human-built environment. This environment includes the accumulation of capital in industrial factories, roads, institutions, and structural systems that a country develops to meet the needs and desires of individuals and families. Although each new person born brings a new pair of hands to produce food and well-being, the output will be meager and life will be bleak and barren of opportunity unless there is an adequate accumulation of private and public capital for those new hands to use in productive work. We've seen examples of the development of systems in government, education, health, social services, business, agriculture, religion, and the like. Understanding how families interact with the various systems gives us important information to help plan services for a particular group.

The third part of the ecological system is the sociocultural environment, which is where the people, their cultural values, and their family structures are considered—including family size and the total numbers of a population in relation to resources available in a given region or country. To ensure that every new birth is a planned one would help reduce violence within families and communities.

In the sociocultural environment, we find what people value, how they operate social systems, and how families learn to use those systems and guide their children to learn to function adequately. Through overt teaching as well as through modeling behavior, families teach their children to use the education or health system.

All areas of the ecological system must be considered as you analyze the services proposed for families. As you endeavor to improve systems, you may interact with policymakers at the local, state, national, and international levels. If you observe barriers that might interfere with a family's access to a system, you can help break up or remove those barriers. Many of your families will be too vulnerable to become activists.

FOCUSING ON ECONOMIC CONCERNS

Your study of various family groups has taught you about some families' economic views. You have your own economic views and knowledge from living your life thus far. All information helps conceptualize one's conclusions about serving families.

The progress made on welfare reform resulting from the passage of the legislation in 1996 (discussed in Chapter 2) had begun to show up in reports of the 2000 U.S. census. The questions on many people's minds were related to how much change in the welfare situation would be evident in the census. Early reports showed that welfare caseloads had been reduced about 50 percent.

The decade of the 1990s, which witnessed the welfare act passage, was a high economic growth period with positive attitudes about the economic future of individuals and families. Unfortunately, the "dot-com" era in the late 1990s that started the rush upward in income levels and in attitudes about economic growth began to turn sour just after the century turned. At the time of the 2000 census, people were already beginning to feel the economic pinch. The percentages of poor in the population changed very little in each state. However, others who had never felt poor began to worry about both income and expenses, particularly health care expenses. The increasing numbers of elderly especially felt this pinch.

The economic fiasco that followed brought sad news to many who had felt they had no economic problems to worry about. Table 15.1 shows how states ranked in the 2000 census with regard to poverty levels, with specific states generally remaining in the same relative position—the low-income states still being low and the high-income states staying high. A practical fact in this era was that college students graduating during the "dot-com" era had high opportunities for jobs, especially in the exciting computer industry. A few years later graduates wondered where to look for work and found it difficult to be positive as they graduated.

In contrast, the teenage mothers discussed in Chapter 10 generally look to the community, state, and nation for economic and emotional support, such as support for housing, health care, food, and education for themselves and their children. When those services are withdrawn, the mothers often face real financial difficulties both in the present and in the future. Many teen mothers have made decisions, including desiring and permitting themselves to become pregnant, causing them and their children to face many trials in life. The human capital—skills, knowledge, abilities, and the like—of these young women must be developed to ensure that they and their children do not spend time on public assistance. Studies show that investing in their education in the present will pay off in their children's future contributions to society.

Poverty and its related problems affect housing, nutrition, health, education, employment, and the social and cultural quality of life. Recalling our ecological system, remember that all systems are linked and that pressure or movement in one system can affect the other systems. The current political climate favors a punitive effort to control the teenage pregnancy phenomenon.

The United States is currently in a period of reducing taxes. No matter how worthy some programs appear, taxpayers are concerned about spending and legislators are voting to hold the line and even make cuts. Such budget constraints have caused many

Table 15.1   U.S. States Ranked by Poverty Rate, 2000

State	Percentage of Population Below Poverty
Louisiana	20.3
West Virginia	19.3
Mississippi	18.2
New Mexico	18.0
District of Columbia	17.7
Arkansas	17.4
Kentucky	16.5
Alabama	16.0
Arizona	15.6
Texas	15.3
South Carolina	14.8
Montana	14.4
Oklahoma	14.4
Tennessee	14.1
California	13.9
New York	13.5
Florida	13.4
North Carolina	13.2
Georgia	13.1
Oregon	13.0
UNITED STATES	12.5
North Dakota	12.3
Washington	11.9
Wyoming	11.9
Idaho	11.6
Missouri	11.5
South Dakota	11.5
Illinois	11.4
Rhode Island	11.3
Ohio	11.1
Vermont	11.0
Iowa	10.7
Pennsylvania	10.6
Indiana	10.5
Michigan	10.4
Maine	10.3
Nebraska	10.3
Nevada	10.1
Massachusetts	9.9
Delaware	9.6
Virginia	9.6
Kansas	9.4
Maryland	9.3
Wisconsin	9.3

(Continued)

Table 15.1 (continued)

State	Percentage of Population Below Poverty
Utah	9.0
Alaska	8.9
Colorado	8.8
Hawaii	8.8
New Jersey	8.2
Connecticut	7.9
Minnesota	7.2
New Hampshire	6.0

Source: U.S. Census Bureau, *Census 2000 supplementary survey.* Retrieved April 4, 2002, from www.census.gov/c2ss/www/Products/Rank/RankPL040.htm

health and social service providers to look elsewhere for funding or find ways to economize and provide services more efficiently (Department of Health and Human Services 1998, 2002).

There is a strong ethic in the country that responsibility for children rests solely with their parents. Many governmental programs today are being designed to help put people to work, in part by providing care for children so parents can become trained to become productive wage earners. Absent parents are being sought so they can assume full financial responsibility for their children. A nationwide computer system now helps track absent parents and records whether they pay child support.

Various social systems are attempting to strengthen families in different ways. Places of worship have a renewed commitment to the families in their midst. Families are being encouraged to save money by doing things at home—cooking, sewing, mending, laundering, as well as entertaining. Urging families to omit items like soft drinks and other junk foods from the grocery cart because of the expense of such items in relation to the lack of useful nutrition they contribute to the diet is another way families can be taught to economize. Family labor is often abundant, and the skills learned in home production sometimes can be transferred to outside employment. Part of children's human capital development should include learning to manage their home services—cooking, cleaning, and child care.

Finding good jobs for the breadwinners of the families is still the best guarantee of adequate services for families. In a full-employment economy, families can purchase needed services with income earned. Most people want to be independent of public welfare. Modern societies are finding, even encouraging, that both men and women become breadwinners in many families. Because many families are financially overextended, parents attempting to raise a family on one paycheck are disadvantaged and especially vulnerable if layoffs occur. The government attempts to create an economic safety net, but there is a growing sentiment that people must face the reality of possible financial difficulties if they don't take responsibility for themselves. The old-fashioned virtues of hard work and personal responsibility are expected of everyone. Children are the economic responsibility of parents. More and more, authorities are requiring both parents to assume this financial responsibility. The double standard in which fathers accept no responsibility for pregnancies or children, and place all blame and burden on mothers, appears to be ending as women demand empowerment and equality.

ACTING WITH HUMILITY

Humility is a characteristic of temperament that every person needs when dealing with people, especially in the helping professions. Science has shown us a great deal about people, and although studies may tell us about averages and norms, they may not give us much insight into a specific individual who may be far from the norm or average. Your role as a professional will be to study each client and apply what you know from science to help solve problems being presented by the individual family. At times you will be forced to admit that there are things you really don't know, that you'll try to find out, or that you may have to try possible solutions for. Feigning knowledge you don't have is both unethical and dangerous.

Some professionals assume guises of authority—authority that is often not warranted by present-day information, especially about individual cases. Readily admit when you are wrong or may not know something. For example, a college counselor once told a young male student that his entrance test scores showed that "people with scores like yours have generally not made it through this college." The student arrived each term and showed his high grades to the counselor. Consequently, the counselor reminded the student that data may not always apply in individual cases. Was the test wrong? Had the student just had a bad day when he took the test? Or had the counselor, by leveling with the student, motivated him to tackle the task of his classes with increased energy and determination to prove the counselor and scores wrong?

It is helpful to bring clients along with you in the discovery process. That is what empowerment means. Clients are the ones whose efforts will most likely bring success to the family. A specified diet is only as good as the decision making of the person eating the food; the disciplinary method only as good as the parent or teacher putting it into operation. Each of your clients can help design the treatment and then be motivated to take pride in its success.

BEING HONEST

You will need to be honest with those you serve. They will be expecting honest, clear, and forthright advice and leadership from you. Many people in difficult circumstances are tough enough to take honest answers. Their imaginations can always conjure up worse scenarios than your honesty might present. Before advising clients, take time to plan your session. Make information clear. Go over it a number of times with clients, perhaps on various days, to be sure they understand. Allow clients to call you on the telephone for information. Parents of children with disabilities, for example, are tired of what they call "the runaround." Make it possible for them to receive honest assistance from you.

BEING ENERGETIC

A great amount of energy is needed in working with families. You will need energy to seek information, inform your clients, and see if they carry out the plan you've worked out with them. You'll need energy to go the extra mile when you recognize that families won't get the assistance they need and deserve unless you help them through the bureaucratic maze. The effort you make will prove tiring but satisfying.

If you recognize that you are having difficulties, you may want to consult with experts or consider more advanced education. Every science and service is progressing so fast that your early college degree will soon become outdated if you don't make plans to attend refresher workshops, do professional reading, and seek advanced degrees along the way. Advanced degrees will take money and energy, especially if you have to work to support yourself, like many graduate students today.

ACTING WITH DEDICATION

Experiencing a satisfied dedication to your career is a pleasant outcome of study, hard work, and commitment. You'll find yourself tackling your work because you enjoy it, rather than merely to satisfy a boss or receive a paycheck. Being dedicated means you'll eagerly look for new information, attend conferences, develop professional connections, and read continuously to be assured of the latest knowledge.

Being dedicated doesn't mean giving up a life of your own, only that you become focused and learn to decide what your priorities are. However, you should also know that every year many people change careers, even after working in one field for a number of years. Technologies change, people reassess their decisions, and family commitments shift, all making it important to confront a decision made earlier. Some career counselors are now predicting that most people will change careers to some extent at least three times during a working lifetime. Every university has career specialists available to guide you in new choices in your world of work. Always seek information and career advice before making career changes.

BEING FLEXIBLE

Your creative spirit and ability to swing with the times may be tested in your service to people. The Lansing, Michigan, group of volunteers teaching English as a Second Language to summer migrant workers is a case in point. Previous summer tutoring projects had been held in a mobile (home) classroom at large farms having large camps for workers. But in 1998 the growers had smaller groups of workers, and it was not feasible for the mobile classroom to be towed. To meet the needs of several farms, the literacy volunteer tutors drove from farm to farm, substituting a few chairs, card tables, and boxes of supplies to give the 30 or so regular participants their desired English lessons each week. (Bader, 1998, 2002).

USING ADVOCACY

Advocating for families may mean championing the cause of a single family as a route to societal improvement. Helping to improve society may mean taking responsibility in a political campaign, such as working for efficiency and equity in needed human services. In that sense, as a committed professional, you'll become an advocate for the families you serve. Dedication to your job and a desire to see a society that works more effectively may prompt you to seek advocacy work as an adjunct to your job description. Advocacy may mean that you take a leadership role in promoting societal improvement.

You may see an inequity in a service that reduces societal productivity. Consequently, you may become an advocate for improving procedures to move toward equity for diverse groups. Advocacy requires you to keep in touch with leaders of your profession, become one of them, and confer as needed to improve societal functioning on the local, national, and global levels.

CORRECTING PROBLEMS OF DISCRIMINATION

Gender, age, race, ethnicity, sexual orientation, disability, religion, and family forms are types of diversity that were discussed in previous chapters. Efforts to achieve equity concerning these diversities have been ongoing for centuries. Many groups have struggled for rights to education, jobs, and equal pay in the workplace. Some of the groups discussed in this book may have made you aware of the powerful male patriarchy that exists in many homes. There may be youths born into those families who are discontented with that situation and wish to change it. Some Americans have succeeded in making changes in oppressive situations in the past. The history of efforts toward equal rights for boys and girls, brothers and sisters, men and women, and husbands and wives, is well worth reading about. Some of the strongest advocates of these efforts to end discrimination are persons who have taken action when they found themselves severely discriminated against.

✦ CONCLUSIONS

Families with many cultural, ethnic, and structural variations will continue to be formed in the United States and around the world. Modern communication has facilitated improved understanding within families, as well as within the entire global human family. Familiarity and understanding will continue to develop over the years ahead with respect to diversity. In a world of diverse peoples, in some situations each of you will be classified as a minority. It is apparent that harmful discrimination and intolerance is not an appropriate response. Let us recognize that diversity adds strength to our global society and is something to be cherished. Peaceful, enlightened dialogue within national and global democratic structures must replace violence and war if the human family is to survive and thrive.

The United Nations, representing all the diverse people of the world, endeavors to promote dialogues, utilizing the talents of all the world's people and bringing to bear new perspectives from all points of the globe. To encourage a peaceful dialogue leading to more harmonious relationships within families and among families all around the world, the United Nations proclaimed the year 1994 as the International Year of the Family. Reflecting the crucial role played by the family in promoting the well-being of society, the year's motto was, "Building the smallest democracy at the heart of society." May we all contribute to that motto at home and abroad as we remember this line from South African Archbishop Desmond Tutu's 1984 Nobel Peace Prize statement:

"My humanity is bound up in yours, for we can only be human together."

✦ STUDY QUESTIONS

1. What was the reason the United Nations designated 1994 as the International Year of the Family?
2. List 10 personal temperament characteristics needed by helping professionals for empowering families. Briefly describe these characteristics in a two-page report.
3. Review the application of the ecological systems framework and tell how it applies to serving families in your community.
4. Read the opening and closing quotations of the chapter, and tell how they apply to the objectives of this book.

✦ APPLICATIONS

1. Ask your librarian to assist you in finding documents of the United Nations and other countries relating to families during the 1994 International Year of the Family. Analyze the content and, in a two-page essay, discuss how the recommendations or major concepts relate to American families.
2. Write a two-page essay on the International Year of the Family motto, "Building the smallest democracy at the heart of society." Discuss how that motto is incongruent or may not be accepted by some of the cultures you have studied and give examples.
3. Study the 10 personal temperament characteristics for helping professionals. Write a two-page essay on how difficult or easy it will be for you to put these characteristics into practice. Give examples of professional people you know, and rate them on these characteristics.

✈ KEY INTERNET RESOURCES

U.S. Census
www.census.gov/

Circle of Inclusion
http://circleofinclusion.org/

Zero to Three
www.zerotothree.org/site/PageServer

National Association of Social Workers
www.socialworkers.org/

✈ FURTHER READING

Brown, L., Kane, H., & Roodman, D. M. (1994). *Vital signs 1994: The trends that are shaping our future.* New York: Norton; Washington, DC: Worldwatch Institute.

Covey, G. (1995). *Theory and practice of group counseling.* Belmont, CA: Brooks/Cole.

Ferencz, B. C. (1991). *Planethood: The key to your future.* Coos Bay, OR: Love Line Books.

Ferencz, B. C. (1994). *New legal foundations for global survival.* Dobbs Ferry, NY: Oceana Publications.

Keyes, K., Jr. (1987). *The hundredth monkey.* Coos Bay, OR: Vision Books.

Lawton, M. P., & Salthouse, T. A. (Eds.). (1998). *Essential papers of the psychology of aging.* New York: New York University Press.

Martin, D. G., & Monie, A. D. (1995). *First steps in the art of intervention.* Belmont, CA: Brooks/Cole.

Riley, N. E. (1998). *Gender, power, and population change.* Washington, DC: Population Reference Bureau.

References

Chapter 1

Andrews, M. P. (2003). Globalization: The role of FCS in shaping the new world community. *Journal of Family and Consumer Sciences, 95*(1), 4–8.

Dority, B. (1992, March–April). Civil liberties watch. *The Humanist, 52*(2), 31.

Havel, V. (1994, 1997). *The art of the impossible.* New York: Alfred A. Knopf.

Jervis, R. (1997). *System effects: Complexity in political and social life.* Princeton, NJ: Princeton University Press.

McFalls, J. A., Jr. (2007). *Population: A lively introduction* (5th ed.). Washington, DC: Population Reference Bureau.

Pinker, S. (1995). *The language instinct: How the mind creates language.* New York: HarperCollins.

Population Reference Bureau. (2002). *2001 Population Data Sheet.* Washington, DC: Author.

Slobin, D. I. (1972, July). They learn the same way all around the world. *Psychology Today.* In Anne Kilbride (Ed.), *Human development 76–77* (p. 272). Guilford, CT: Dushkin.

U.S. Department of Commerce, Bureau of the Census. (2002). *Statistical abstract of the United States 2000.* Washington, DC: U.S. Government Printing Office.

Chapter 2

Ashford, L. S. (2001). *New population policies: Advancing women's health and rights.*

Bianchi, S. M., & Casper, L. M. (2000). *American families.*

Bianchi, S. M., & Spain, D. (1996). *Women, work, and family in America.* Washington, DC: Population Reference Bureau.

Brockerhoff, M. P. (2000). *An urbanizing world.*

Bubolz, M. M., & Sontag, M. S. (1993). *Human ecology theory.* In P. G. Boss, W. J. Doherty, R. LaRossa, W. R. Schumm, & S. K. Steinmetz (Eds.), *Sourcebook of family theories and methods: A contextual approach* (pp. 419–448). New York: Plenum Press.

Cross, E. W., Cantwell, M., & Summers, T. (1993). The Americans with Disabilities Act: Increasing awareness through human ecology/home economics education. *Journal of Home Economics, 85*(2), p. 32. (See also The Americans with Disabilities Act of 1990, P. L. 101–336, 42 U.S.C.A. 12101.)

Federal Register. (1992). Vol. 56, No. 160, p. 61. Washington, DC: U.S. Government Printing Office.

The Guide to American Law. (1983, 1992, 1994). Vols. 2–9, 1983, plus 1987, 1992, and 1994 Supplements. New York: West Publishers.

Himes, C. L. (2001) *Elderly Americans.*

Johnson, L. (1964–1965). *Code of Federal Register.* Executive Orders 11246 and 11375 (1966). Washington, DC: Office of the Federal Register. 1964–1965, pp. 339–348 and 1966–1970, pp. 684–686.

Kent, M. M., Poland, K. M., Haaga, J., & Mather, M. (2001). *First glimpses of the 2000 U.S. census.*

Lichter, D. T., & Crowley, M. L. (2002). *Poverty in America: Beyond welfare reform.*

Martin, P., & Widgen, J. (2002). *International migration: Facing the challenge.*

O'Neill, B., & Balk, D. (2001). *World population futures.*

Ratzan, S. C., Filerman, G. L., & LeSar, J. W. (2000). *Attaining global health: Challenges and opportunities.*

Riche, M. F. (2000). *America's diversity and growth: Signposts for the 21st century.*

U.S. Census. (2001). *Statistical Abstract of the United States.* Washington, DC: Author.

U.S. Government Printing Office. (1996). *Personal Responsibility and Work Opportunity Reconciliation Act of 1996, P. L. 104–193,* August 22, 1996. See also *Weekly Compilation of Presidential Documents,* Vol. 32 (1996): August 22, Presidential remarks and statement.

Population Bulletins published by the Population Reference Bureau, Washington, DC. Read at www.prb.org

Chapter 3

Bronfenbrenner, U. (1979). *The ecology of human development.* Cambridge, MA: Harvard University Press.

Bubolz, M. M. (2002). *Beatrice Paolucci: Shaping destiny through everyday life.* East Lansing, MI: Paolucci Book Committee.

Bubolz, M. M., & Sontag, S. (1993). Human ecology theory. In P. G. Boss, W. J. Doherty, R. LaRossa, W. R. Schumm, & S. K. Steinmetz (Eds.), *Sourcebook of family theories and methods: A contextual approach* (pp. 419–448). New York: Plenum Press.

Dunst, C. J., & Trivette, C. M. (1987). Enabling and empowering families: Conceptual and intervention issues. *School Psychology Review, 16*(4), 451.

Griffore, J. R., & Phenice, L. (2001). *The language of human ecology.* Dubuque, IA: Kendall/Hunt.

Hook, N., & Paolucci, B. (1970). The family as an ecosystem. *Journal of Home Economics, 62*(5), 315–318.

Jervis, R. (1997). *System effects: Complexity in political and social life.* Princeton, NJ: Princeton University Press.

Sarbaugh, L. (1988). A taxonomic approach to intercultural communication. In Y. Y. Kim & W. B. Gudykunst (Eds.), *Theories in intercultural communication* (pp. 22–38). Newbury Park, CA: Sage.

Schultz, T. P. (1994). *Human capital investment in women and men.* San Francisco: Institute for Contemporary Studies.

Schultz, T. P. (1995). *Investment in women's human capital.* Chicago: University of Chicago Press.

Teun, A. D. (1987). *Communicating racism.* Newbury Park, CA: Sage.

Chapter 4

Aguirre, A., & Turner, J. (1998). *American ethnicity.* Boston: McGraw-Hill.

Allen, R. (Ed.). (1988, May/June). Older minorities in work and retirement. *Working Age, 3*(6), 1.

Barrow, L. (1990, November). Yes, cancer kills! But it doesn't have to kill you. *The Crisis Magazine* (pp. 11–15). Baltimore, MD: National Association for the Advancement of Colored People.

Bell, R. (1971). The relative importance of mother and wife roles among Negro lower-class women. In R. Staples (Ed.), *The Black family: Essays and studies* (pp. 248–256). Belmont, CA: Wadsworth.

Bell, R. (1992). *Faces at the bottom of the well.* New York: Basic Books.

Billingsley, A. (1968). *Black families in White America.* Upper Saddle River, NJ: Prentice Hall.

Billingsley, A. (1993). *Climbing Jacob's ladder.* Upper Saddle River, NJ: Prentice Hall.

Black churches on fire (1996, May 5). Associated Press.

Brown, A., & Forde, D. (1967). *African systems of kinship and marriage.* New York: Oxford Press.

Collins, J. David, R., Handler, A., Wall, S., & Andes, S. (2004). Very low birth weight in African American infants: The role of maternal exposure to interpersonal racial discrimination. *American Journal of Public Health 94*(12), 2132–2139.

Coontz, S. (1992). *The way we never were.* New York: Basic Books.

Devore, W., & Schlesinger, E. (1999). *Ethnic-sensitive social work practice.* Needham Heights, MA: Allyn & Bacon.

Edmonds, M. (1993). Physical health. In J. Jackson, L. Chatters, & R. Taylor (Eds.), *Aging in Black America.* Newbury Park, CA: Sage.

Farley, R., & Allen, W. (1991). Education strategies for the 90s. In J. Dewart (Ed.), *The state of Black America, 1991* (pp. 95–110). New York: National Urban League.

Frazier, F. (1932). *The free Negro family.* Nashville, TN: Fisk University Press.

Gamble, V. (1993). A legacy of distrust: African-Americans and medical research. *American Journal of Preventive Medicine, 9*(6), 35–39.

Goodwin, N. (1990, November). Heart disease and stroke—the leading killer of African-Americans. *The Crisis Magazine* (pp. 10, 30). Baltimore,

MD: National Association for the Advancement of Colored People.

Graves, E. (Ed.). (1993, July). No time to rest. *Black Enterprise,* p. 9.

Guess, J. (1990, June/July). Freedom's warriors—The fighting Black clergy: An historical overview. *The Crisis Magazine* (pp. 14–30). Baltimore, MD: National Association for the Advancement of Colored People.

Ho, M. (1992). *Minority children and adolescents in therapy.* Newbury Park, CA: Sage.

Hughes, L., & Bontemps, A. (Eds.). (1951). *The poetry of the Negro, 1746–1949,* Garden City, NY: Doubleday.

Jackson, J., Chatters, L., & Taylor, R. (1993). *Aging in Black America.* Newbury Park, CA: Sage.

Jaynes, G., & Williams, R. (Eds.). (1989). *A common destiny: Blacks and American society.* Washington, DC: National Academy Press.

Joe, T., & Yu, P. (1984). *The "flip side" of Black families headed by women: The economic status of Black men.* Washington, DC: The Center for the Study of Social Policy.

Jones, E. (1993, August). An interview on the topic, "Changing church confronts the changing Black family." *Ebony, 18*(10), 94–100.

Jordan, W. (1962). Modern tensions and the origins of American slavery. *Journal of Southern History, 28,* 18–30.

Kluegel, R. (1975). *Simple justice: The history of Brown v. Board of Education and Black America's struggle for equality.* Hawthorne, NY: Aldine de Gruyter.

Kunjufu, J. (1982). *Counteracting the conspiracy to destroy young Black boys* (Vol. 1). Chicago: African-American Images.

Lindblad-Goldberg, M. (1986). Results of a federal study of Black single parent families. *Behavior Today, 17*(34), 2–3.

Mann, C. R. (1994). The reality of a racist criminal justice system. In R. C. Monk (Ed.), *Taking sides.* Guilford, CT: Dushkin.

Marable, M. (1994). The Black male: Searching beyond stereotypes. In R. G. Majors & J. U. Gordon (Eds.), *The American Black male.* Chicago: Nelson Hall.

Massaquoi, H. (1993, August). The Black family nobody knows. *Ebony,* pp. 28–31.

Mauer, M. (1994). A generation behind bars: Black males and the criminal justice system. In R. G. Majors & J. U. Gordon (Eds.), *The American Black male.* Chicago: Nelson Hall.

McAdoo, H. (1979). *American ethnic family.* Racine, WI: The Johnson Foundation.

McAdoo, H. P., & McAdoo, J. L. (1985). *Black children and social and educational and parental environments.* Beverly Hills, CA: Sage.

McAdoo, J. L., & McAdoo, J. B. (1994). The African-American father's roles within the family. In R. G. Majors & J. U. Gordon (Eds.), *The American Black male.* Chicago: Nelson Hall.

Mindel, C., Habenstein, R., & Wright, R. (Eds.). (1988). *Ethnic families in America.* New York: Elsevier.

National Cancer Institute. (1986). *Cancer among Blacks and other minorities: Statistical profiles.* U.S. Department of Health and Human Services, Public Health Services. Washington, DC: U.S. Government Printing Office.

National Center for Education Statistics. (2003). *Digest of education statistics.* Washington, DC: U.S. Department of Education.

National Center for Health Statistics. (1987). *Vital statistics of the United States.* Washington, DC: U.S. Government Printing Office.

National Center for Health Statistics. (1991). *Health: United States, 1990.* Hyattsville, MD: Public Health Service.

National Center for Health Statistics. (2002). Vital Statistics System. Office of Statistics and Programming, National Center for Injury Prevention and Control, Centers for Disease Control and Prevention.

National Vital Statistics Reports. (2004). *53* (6).

O'Hare, W., Pollard, K., Mann, T., & Kent, M. (1991, July). African-Americans in the 1990s. *Population Bulletin.*

Pierce, C., & Profit, W. (1994). Racial group dynamics: Implications for rearing Black males. In R. G. Majors & J. U. Gordon (Eds.), *The American Black male.* Chicago: Nelson Hall.

Schafer, R. (1993). A class of people neither freemen nor slaves: From Spanish to American race relations in Florida, 1821–1861. *Journal of Social History, 26,* 587–609.

Schiraldi, V. (2006). The juvenile justice system in Black and White. Building Blocks for Youth. Washington, DC: Justice Policy Institute. Available from www.buildingblocksforyouth.org/issues/dmc/schiraldi.html

Smith, A. W. (1998). Survey research on African Americans. In J. Stanfield II & R. Dennis (Eds.), *Race and ethnicity in research methods.* Newbury Park, CA: Sage.

Smith, G. (1992, October 26). There's no Whites only sign but . . . *Business Week,* p. 78.

Staples, R. (1988). The Black American family. In C. Mindel, R. Habenstein, & R. Wright (Eds.), *Ethnic families in America* (pp. 303–324). New York: Elsevier.

Sudarkasa, N. (1993). Female-headed African-American households: Some neglected dimensions. In H. McAdoo (Ed.), *Family ethnicity: Strength in diversity* (pp. 81–89). New York: Sage.

Thomas, S., & Quinn, S. (1991). The Tuskegee syphilis study, 1932–1972: Implications for HIV education and AIDS risk education programs in the Black community. *American Journal of Public Health, 81*(11), 1498–1505.

U.S. Census Bureau, (1992). *Statistical abstract of the United States.* Washington, DC: U.S. Government Printing Office.

U.S. Census Bureau, (1995). *Statistical abstract of the United States.* Washington, DC: U.S. Government Printing Office.

U.S. Census Bureau, (2000, 2004). Department of Commerce, Washington, DC: U.S. Government Printing Office.

U.S. Census Bureau, (2004–2005a). *General demographic characteristics.* Economics and Statistics Administration. Washington, DC: U.S. Government Printing Office.

U.S. Census Bureau, (2004–2005b). *Statistical abstract of the United States.* Washington, DC: U.S. Government Printing Office.

Wilkinson, D. (1993). Family ethnicity in America. In H. McAdoo (Ed.), *Family ethnicity: Strength in diversity* (pp. 15–59). New York: Sage.

Chapter 5

Bianchi, S. M., & Spain, D. (1996). Women, work, and family in America. *Population Bulletin, 51,* 3.

Briggs, D. (1993, November 6). National conference of Catholic bishops. *Houston Chronicle,* p. 1a.

Chavez, L. (1991). *Out of the barrio: Toward a new politics of Hispanic assimilation.* New York: HarperCollins.

Cozic, C. P. (Ed.). (1997). *Illegal immigration: Opposing viewpoints.* San Diego, CA: Greenhaven Press.

del Pinal, J., & Singer, A. (1997). Generations of diversity: Latinos in the United States. *Population Bulletin, 52,* 3.

Diaz-Guerrero, R., & Peck, R. (1976). *Psychology of the Mexican: Culture and personality.* Austin: University of Texas Press.

Falicov, C. J. (1998). *Latino families in therapy: A guide to multicultural practice.* New York: Guilford Press.

Fillmore, L. W., & Britsch, S. (1988, June). *Early education for children from linguistic and cultural minority families.* Paper prepared for the Early Education Task Force of the National Association of State Boards of Education.

Frisbie, W.P. (1993). Variation in patterns of marital stability among Hispanics. *Journal of Marriage and the Family, 48,* 99–106.

Garcia, E.E. (March, 1997). The education of Hispanics in early childhood: Of roots and wings. *Young Children, 52,* 3.

Hudgens, B. (1993). The Relationship of Cognitive Style, Planning Ability and Locus-of-Control to Achievement for Three Ethnic Groups (Anglo, African-American, Hispanic). *Dissertation Abstracts International,* A53 - 08, 2744.

Lyons, J. J. (1993, February 15). The view from Washington: English-only extremism. *National Association for Bilingual Education News,* p. 1.

Martin, P., & Midgley, E. (1999). Immigration to the United States. *Population Bulletin, 54,* 2.

Office of the U.S. Surgeon General. (1993, June). *The surgeon general's report on HIV and AIDS.* Washington, DC: Author.

Olmos, J. E., Ybarra, L., & Monterrey, M. (1999). *Americanos: Latino life in the United States*. New York: Little, Brown.

Houston Chronicle, November 6, 1993.

Richardson, C. (1993, August 23). The border life project. *Houston Chronicle*, p. 10.

Rodriguez, L. (1993, May 3). One vote. One voice. *Houston Chronicle*, p. 10.

Rumbaut, R. G. (1997). Ties that bind: Immigration and immigrant families in the United States. In A. Booth, A. C. Crouter, & N. Landale (Eds.), *Immigration and the family: Research and policy on U.S. immigrants*. Mahwah, NJ: Erlbaum.

Stavans, I. (2001). *The Hispanic condition: The power of a people* (2nd ed.). New York: HarperCollins.

Chapter 6

Asian American Family Services. (2006). *Why a counseling center for Asian-Americans?* Houston, TX: Author. (Available at www.aafstexas.org/)

Barringer, H., Gardner, R., & Levin, M. (1995). *Asian-Americans and Pacific Islanders in the United States*. New York: Russell Sage Foundation.

Biagini, J. (1989). *Issues of mental health and social adjustment for Southeast Asian refugees*. Minneapolis, MN: Upper Great Lakes Multifunctional Resource Center.

Broom, L., & Kitsuse, J. (1956). *The managed casualty*. Los Angeles: University of California Press.

Brown, G. (1988). Issues in the resettlement of Indochinese refugees. *Social Casework, 63,* 155–159.

Burton, E. (1983). *Surviving the flight of horror: The story of refugee women*. Washington, DC: Indochina Project, Center for International Policy.

Cabezas, A., & Kawaguchi, G. (1988). Empirical evidence for continuing Asian-American income inequity: The human capital model and labor market segmentation. In G. Y. Okihiro, S. Hyme, A. Hansen, & John Liu (Eds.), *Reflections on shattered windows: Promises and prospects for Asian-American studies* (pp. 148, 154). Pullman: Washington State University Press.

Carlin, J., & Sokoloff, B. (1985). Mental health treatment issues for Southeast Asian refugee children. In T. Owan (Ed.), *Southeast Asian mental health: Treatment, prevention services, training, and research*. Washington, DC: National Institute of Mental Health.

Chan, S. (1991). *Asian-Americans: An interpretive history*. Boston: Twayne.

Chung, D. (1992). Asian cultural commonalities: A comparison with mainstream American culture. In S. Furuto, R. Biswas, D. Chung, & K. Murase (Eds.), *Social work practice with Asian Americans* (pp. 27–44). Beverly Hills, CA: Sage.

Connor, J. (1977). *Tradition and change in three generations of Japanese Americans*. Chicago: Nelson Hall.

Curb, J., Reed, D., Miller, F., & Yano, K. (1990, September). Health status and life style in elderly Japanese men with a long life expectancy. *Journal of Gerontology, 45* (5), 206–211.

Daniels, R. (1981). *Concentration camps: Japanese Americans and World War II*. New York: Holt, Rinehart & Winston.

DeGenova, M. (1997). *Families in cultural context*. Mountain View, CA: Mayfield.

Devore, W., & Schlesinger, E. (1999). *Ethnic-sensitive social work practice*. Needham Heights, MA: Allyn & Bacon.

Dillard, J. (1987). *Multicultural counseling: Toward ethnic and cultural relevance in human encounters*. Chicago: Nelson Hall.

Gann, H. (1979, January). Symbolic ethnicity: The future of ethnic groups and cultures in America. *Ethnic and Racial Studies*, pp 1–20.

Gim, R., Atkinson, D., & Whitely, S. (1990). Asian-American acculturation, severity of concerns, and willingness to see a counselor. *Journal of Counseling Psychology, 37* (3), 281–285.

Hall, E. T. (1966). *The hidden dimension*. Garden City, NY: Doubleday.

Hall, E. T. (1983). *The dance of life*. Garden City, NY: Doubleday.

Ho, C. (1990). An analysis of domestic violence in Asian-American communities: A multicultural approach to counseling. *Women and Therapy, 9,* 129–150.

Hsia, J., & Nakanishi, M. (1989, November/December). The demographics of diversity: Asian-Americans in higher education. *Change, 21,* 20–27.

Hu, A. (1988). Asian-Americans: A model minority or double minority. *Amerasia, 15* (1), 243–257.

Ichioka, Y. (1988). *The Issei: The world of the first generation Japanese immigrants, 1885–1924.* New York: Free Press.

Jiobu, R. (1988). *Ethnicity and assimilation.* Albany: State University of New York Press.

Kavanaugh, K., & Kennedy, P. (1992). *Promoting cultural diversity.* Newbury Park, CA: Sage.

Kim, P., & Kim, J-S. (1992). Korean elderly: Policy, program, and practice implications. In S. Furuto, R. Biswas, D. Chung, K. Murase, & F. Ross-Sheriff (Eds.), *Social work practice with Asian-Americans* (pp. 227–239). Newbury Park, CA: Sage.

Kinzie, J., & Leung, P. (1993). Psychiatric care of Indochinese Americans. In A. Gaw (Ed.), *Culture, ethnicity, and mental illness* (pp. 281–304). Washington, DC: American Psychiatric Press.

Kitano, H. (1988). The Japanese American family. In C. Mindel, R. Habenstein, & R. Wright, Jr. (Eds.), *Ethnic families in America* (pp. 258–299). New York: Elsevier.

Kitano, H., & Daniels, R. (1988). *Asian-Americans: Emerging minorities.* Upper Saddle River, NJ: Prentice Hall.

Lai, H., Lim, G., & Yung, J. (1981). *Island poetry and history of Chinese immigrants on Angel Island, 1910–1940.* San Francisco: Chinese Historical Society.

Langberg, M., & Farley, R. (1985). Residential segregation of Asian-Americans in 1980. *Sociology and Social Research, 70,* 71–75.

Leadership Education for Asian Pacifics, Inc. (1993). *The state of Asian Pacific America: A public policy report, policy issues to the year 2020.* Los Angeles: LEAP Asian Pacific American Public Policy Institute.

Lee, E. (1982). A social systems approach to assessment and treatment of Chinese American families. In M. McGoldrick, J. Pearce, & J. Giordano (Eds.), *Ethnicity and family therapy* (pp. 527–551). New York: Guilford Press.

Leong, F., & Hayes, T. (1990, December). Occupational stereotyping of Asian-Americans. *The Career Development Quarterly, 39,* 143–153.

Marden, C., Meyer, G., & Engel, M. (1992). *Minorities in American society.* New York: HarperCollins.

Mass, A. (1992). Interracial Japanese Americans: The best of both worlds or the end of the Japanese American community? In M. Root (Ed.), *Racially mixed people in America: Within, between, and beyond race* (pp. 265–279). Newbury Park, CA: Sage.

Mei, J. (1984). Socioeconomic origins of emigration: Guangdong to California, 1850–1882. In L. Cheng & E. Bonachich (Eds.), *Labor immigration under capitalism: Asian workers in the United States before World War II* (pp. 219–247). Berkeley: University of California Press.

Moore, L., & Boehnlein, R. (1991). Treating psychiatric disorders among Mien refugees from highland Laos. *Social Science and Medicine, 32* (9), 1029–1036.

Moore, T., & Gunnison, R. (1994, March 3). Blacks and Asian-Americans say the system is insensitive. *San Francisco Chronicle,* p. A4.

Morrow, R. (1989). Southeast Asian child rearing practices: Implications for child and youth care workers. *Child and Youth Care Quarterly, 18* (4), 273–287.

Nagata, D. (1989). Long term effects of the Japanese American internment camps: Impact on the children of the internees. *Journal of the Asian-American Phychological Association, 13,* 48–55.

Nakanishi, D. (1989, November/December). A quota on excellence. *Change, 21,* 39–47.

Newton, B., Buck, E., Kunimura, D., Colger, C., & Scholsberg, D. (1988). Ethnic identity in Japanese Americans in Hawaii. *International Journal of Intercultural Relations, 12* (4), 305–369.

Nguyen, S. (1982). Psychiatric and psychosomatic problems among South East Asian refugees. *Psychiatric Journal of the University of Ottawa, 7,* 163–172.

Nicassio, P. (1985). The psychosocial adjustment of the Southeast Asian refugee: An overview of empirical findings and theoretical models. *Journal of Cross-Cultural Psychology, 16*(2), 153–173.

Office of Minority Health. (2006). *Asian-American populations.* Retrieved April, 2007 from www.cdc.gov/omh/populations/AsianAm/htm

Office of Refugee Resettlement. (1982, May). *Monthly data report.* Office of Refugee Resettlement. (1984, July 6). Amerasian problems and issues [Memorandum].

Ogawa, D. (Ed.). (1978). *Kodomo no tame ni: For the sake of the children.* Honolulu: University of Hawaii Press.

O'Hare, W., & Felt, J. (1991, February). *Asian-Americans: America's fastest growing minority group.* Washington, DC: Population Reference Bureau,.

Roland, A. (1984). The self in India and America: Toward a psychoanalysis of social and cultural contexts. In V. Kavolis (Ed.), *Design of selfhood* (pp. 170–194). London: Associated University Press.

Roland, A. (1988). *In search of self in India and Japan: Toward a cross cultural psychology.* Princeton, NJ: Princeton University Press.

Shoho, An. (1992, April). *An historical comparison of parental involvement of three generations of Japanese Americans (Issei, Nisei, and Sansei) in the education of their children.* Paper presented at the annual meeting of the American Educational Research Association, San Francisco, CA.

Smith, K. (1983). Social comparison processes and dynamic conservatism in intergroup relations. *Research in Organizational Behavior, 5,* 199–233.

Strong, E. (1934). *The second generation Japanese problem.* Stanford, CA: Stanford University Press.

Suzuki, L., & Yamashiro, C. (1980). *A study of the attitude of third generation Japanese Americans in Hawaii and the mainland.* Master's thesis, University of California, Los Angeles.

Takaki, R. (1993). *A different mirror.* Boston: Little, Brown.

Tang, J. (1991). Asian-American engineers: Earnings, occupational status, and promotions. Paper presented at the annual meeting of the American Sociological Association, Cincinnati, OH.

True, R. (1990). Psychotherapeutic issues with Asian-American women. *Sex Roles, 22*(7/8), 477–486.

Tsuchida, N. (1990). The evacuation and internment of Japanese Americans during World War II: An invaluable lesson on the American judicial system. In R. Endo, V. Chatterzy, S. Chou, & N. Tsuchida (Eds.), *Contemporary perspectives on Asian and Pacific American education* (pp. 160–191). South El Monte, CA: Pacific Asia Press.

Tsui, P., & Schultz, G. (1985). Failure of rapport: Why psychotherapeutic engagement fails in the treatment of Asian clients. *American Journal of Orthopsychiatry, 55*(4), 561–569.

Uba, L. (1994). *Asian-Americans.* New York: Guilford Press.

U.S. Census Bureau. (1995). *Statistical abstract of the United States: 1995.* Washington, DC: U.S. Government Printing Office.

U.S. Census Bureau. (2000). *Population & socioeconomic data.* Washington DC: U.S. Government Printing Office. (Available at www.apiahf.com/cic/state_pop.asp?StateID=00)

U.S. Census Bureau. (2003a). *Asian Pacific American Heritage Month: May 2003.* (Available from www.census.gov.\/Press-Release/www2003/cb03-ff05.html)

U.S. Census Bureau. (2003b, May 28). *United States Department of Commerce News.* Washington, DC: U.S. Government Printing Office.

U.S. Census Bureau. (2004). *Current population reports.* Washington, DC: U.S. Government Printing Office.

U.S. Census Bureau. (2005). *Income/Poverty and health insurance coverage in the United States: 2004.* U.S. Department of Commerce. Washington, DC: U.S. Government Printing Office.

U.S. Commission on Civil Rights. (1992). *Civil rights issues facing Asian-Americans in the 1990s.* Washington, DC: Author.

U.S. Department of Justice. (1964–1980). Immigration and Naturalization Service (1984). Washington, DC: U.S. Government Printing Office.

U.S. Pan Asian-American Chamber of Commerce. (2002). *The Asian-American facts and statistics.*

Yanagisako, S. (1985). *Transforming the past.* Stanford, CA: Stanford University Press.

Young, S-K. (1992). Battered Korean women in the urban United States. In S. Furuto, R. Biswas, D. Chung, K. Murase, & F. Ross-Sheriff (Eds.),

Social work practice with Asian-Americans (pp. 213–226), Newbury Park, CA: Sage.

Chapter 7

Abd al-Auhir al Jurjani. (1972). *The secrets of eloquence.* Cairo, Egypt: Maktabat al-Qahirah.

Ahmed, A. (2001). *Islam today.* New York: I.B. Tauris.

Ahmed, I., & Gray, N. (Eds.). (1988). *The Arab-American family: A resource manual for human service providers.* Ypsilanti, MI: Eastern Michigan University, Children's Bureau, Administration on Children, Youth, and Families, Office of Human Development Services, Discretionary Funds Program.

Amiruddin, B. (1939). Woman's status in Islam: A Moslem view. *Muslim World, 28,* 153–163.

Ashabranner, B. (1991). *An ancient heritage.* New York: HarperCollins.

Aswad, B. (1988). Strengths of the Arab family for mental health considerations and therapy. In I. Ahmed & N. Gray (Eds.), *The Arab-American family: A resource manual for human service providers.* Ypsilanti: Eastern Michigan University.

Berger, M. (1962). *The Arab world today.* Garden City, NY: Doubleday.

Bernado, S. (1981). *The ethnic almanac.* Garden City, NY: Doubleday.

Devore, W., & Schlesinger, E. (1999). *Ethnic-sensitive social work practice.* Needham Heights, MA: Allyn & Bacon.

Fernea, E., & Bezirgan, B. (1977). *Middle Eastern Muslim women speak.* Austin: University of Texas Press.

Germain, C. (1994). Emerging conceptions of family development over the life course. *Families in Society,* pp. 259–267.

Haddad, Y., & Lummis, A. (1987). *Islamic values in the United States.* New York: Oxford University Press. http://faculty.newe.edu/toconnor/soc/355lect14.htm

Kayal, P. (1983). The Syrian-Lebanese in America: A study in religion and assimilation. In S. Abraham & N. Abraham (Eds.), *Arabs in the new world.* Detroit, MI: Wayne State University, Center for Urban Studies.

Leuchtenburg, W. (1977). The American perception of the Arab world. In G. Atiyeh (Ed.), *Arabs and the American culture* (pp. 15–25). Washington, DC: American Enterprise Institute for Public Policy Research.

Naff, A. (1983). Arabs in America: A historical overview. In S. Abraham & N. Abraham (Eds.), *Arabs in the new world* (pp. 8–29). Detroit, MI: Wayne State University, Center for Urban Studies.

Naff, A. (1985). *Becoming American.* Carbondale and Edwardsville, IL: Southern Illinois University Press.

Noakes, G. (1993, April/May). San Francisco spy ring, "The tip of the iceberg." *Washington Report on Middle East Affairs, 11*(9), 19–20.

Patai, R. (1983). *The Arab mind.* New York: Charles Scribner and Sons.

Shabbas, A. (1979, May/June). The child in the Arab family. *The Link.* New York: Americans for Middle East Understanding.

Suleiman, M. (1988). *The Arabs in the mind of America.* Brattleboro, VT: Amana Books.

Willford, C. (1993, April/May). Arab-American activism. *Washington Report on Middle East Affairs, 11*(9), 73–74.

Zenner, W. (1982, October). Arabic-speaking immigrants in North America as middleman minorities. *Ethnic and Racial Studies, 5*(4), 457–477.

Chapter 8

Aguirre, A., & Turner, J. (1998). *American ethnicity.* Boston: McGraw-Hill.

Boyce, W., & Boyce, J. (1983). Acculturation and changes in health among Navajo school students. *Social Sciences and Medicine, 17,* 219–226.

Bureau of Indian Affairs. (1985, January). *Indian service population and labor force estimates.* Washington, DC: U.S. Government Printing Office.

Coles, R. (1977). Eskimos, Chicanos, Native Americans. In *Children in Crisis* (Vol. 4, p. 62). Boston: Little, Brown.

Collier, J. (1947). *The Native Americans of the Americas.* New York: Norton.

Dell, P. F. (1980). The Hopi family therapist and the Aristotelian parents. *Journal of Marital and Family Therapy, 6,* 123–130.

Devore, W., & Schlesinger E. (1999). *Ethnic-sensitive social work practice.* Needham Heights, MA: Allyn & Bacon.

Dobyns, H. F. (1983). *Their numbers become thinned: Native American population dynamics in eastern North America.* Knoxville: University of Tennessee Press.

Farb, P. (1968). *Man's rise to civilization as shown by the Native Americans of North America from primeval times to the coming of the industrial state.* New York: E. P. Dutton.

Feagin, J. R. (1989). *Racial and ethnic relations.* Upper Saddle River, NJ: Prentice Hall.

Fost, D. (1991, December). American Native Americans in the 1990s. *American Demographics,* pp. 26–34.

Funmaker, A. (2005, June). Alexarae Funmaker Grand Traverse Band Member. *Grand Traverse Band News.* Peshawbestown, MI: Grand Traverse Band of Ottawa and Chippewa Native Americans

Gross, E. R. (1989). *Contemporary federal policy toward American Native Americans.* New York: Greenwood Press.

Guillemin, J. (1975). *Urban renegades: The cultural strategy of American Native Americans.* New York: Columbia University Press.

Hungry Wolf, A., & Hungry Wolf, B. (1987). *Children of the sun.* New York: Morrow.

Jaimes, M. A. (Ed.). (1992). *The state of native America.* Boston: South End Press.

John, R. (1988). The native American family. In C. H. Mindel, R. W. Habenstein, & R. Wright (Eds.), *Ethnic families in America* (pp. 325–363). New York: Elsevier.

LaFromboise, T. D., & Graff Low, K. (1989). American Indian children and adolescents. In J. T. Gibbs, L. N. Huang, & Associates (Eds.), *Children of color: Psychological interventions with minority youth,* (pp. 114–147). San Francisco: Jossey-Bass.

Leap, W. L. (1981). American Indian language maintenance. *Annual Review of Anthropology, 10,* 271–280.

Mail, P. D. (1978, March). Hippocrates was a medicine man: The health care of Native Americans in the twentieth century. *Annals, AAPSS,* p. 436.

Manson, S. M., Walker, R. D., & Kivlahan, D. R. (1987). Psychiatric assessment and treatment of American Native Americans and Alaska natives. *Hospital and Community Psychiatry, 38,* 65–173.

Neligh, G., & Scully, J. (1990). Differential diagnosis of major mental disorders among American Indian elderly. In M.S. Harper (Ed.), *Minority aging: Essential curricula context for selected health and allied health professionals.* DHHS Publication No. HRS (P-DV-90-4). Washington DC: U.S. Government Printing Office.

Paige, J. (2006). *Native American demographics.* (Available from www.native-language.org/composition/native-american-demographics.html)

Paniagua, F. (1994). *Assessing and treating culturally diverse clients.* Thousand Oaks, CA: Sage.

Parrillo, V. N. (1985). *Strangers to these shores: Race and ethnic relations in the United States.* New York: Wiley.

Red Horse, J., Lewis, R. G., Feit, M., & Decker, J. (1978). Family behavior of urban American Native Americans. *Social Casework, 59,* 67–72.

Red Horse, J. (1988). Cultural evolution of American Indian families. In C. Jacobs & D. Bowles (Eds.), *Ethnicity and race: Critical concepts in social work* (pp. 86–102). Silver Spring, MD: National Association of Social Workers.

Reyhner, J. (1994). American Native Americans out of school: A review of school-based causes and solutions. In R. C. Monk (Ed.), *Taking sides.* Guilford, CT: Duskin.

Ryan, R. A. (1980). Strengths of the American Indian family: State of the art. In F. Hoffman (Ed.), *The American Indian family: Strengths and stresses* (pp. 25–43). Isleta, NM: American Indian Social Research and Development Associates.

Snipp, C. (1986). The changing political and economic status of the American Native Americans: From captive nations to internal colonies. *American Journal of Economics and Sociology, 45,* 145–157.

Trimble, J. E. (1981). Value differentials and their importance in counseling American Native Americans. In P. Pedersen, J. Draguns, W. Lonner, & J. Trimble

(Eds.), *Counseling across cultures* (pp. 203–226). Honolulu: University Press of Hawaii.

U.S. Census Bureau. (1970). American Native Americans, *1970*. Washington, DC: U.S. Government Printing Office.

U.S. Census Bureau. (1987). Statistical Abstract of the United States, *1986,* Table 32, p. 86. Washington, DC: U.S. Government Printing Office.

U.S. Census Bureau. (1994). *Characteristics of American Native Americans by tribe and language: 1990.* Washington, DC: U.S. Government Printing Office.

U.S. Census Bureau. (1995). *Statistical abstract of the United States: 1995.* Washington, DC: U.S. Government Printing Office.

U.S. Census Bureau. (2000). *Poverty in the United States:2000.* Washington, DC: U.S. Department of Commerce, U.S. Government Printing Office.

U.S. Census Bureau. (2005). *Income, poverty and health insurance coverage in the United States: 2004.* U.S. Department of Commerce. Economic and Statistics Administration. Washington, DC: U.S. Government Printing Office.

U.S. Census Bureau. (2006). *American Native Americans by the number.* Washington, DC: U.S. Government Printing Office.

U.S. Congress, Office of Technology Assessment. (1986). *Indian health care* (OTA-H290). Washington, DC: U.S. Government Printing Office.

U.S. Department of Health and Human Services. (1993). *Health United States 1992 and Healthy people 2000 review.* (Pub. No. 93-1232). Washington, DC: U.S. Department of Health and Human Services.

U.S. Public Health Service. (1974). *Indian health trends and services* (Department of Health, Education, and Welfare Publication No. IISA 74-12, 009, p. 32). Washington, DC: U.S. Government Printing Office.

Vogel, V. (1972). Indian ways with farming and wild foods. In B. Fontana (Ed.), *Look to the mountain top* (pp. 61–66). San Jose, CA: H. M. Gousha.

Walker, R., & LaDue, R. (1986). An integrative approach to American Indian mental health. In C. Wilkinson (Ed.), *Ethnic psychiatry* (pp. 143–199). New York: Plenum.

Washburn, W. (1970). *The Indian in America.* Norman: University of Oklahoma Press.

Yellowbird, M., & Snipp, C. (1998). American Indian families. In R. Taylor (Ed.), *Minority Families in the United States* (pp. 234–248). Upper Saddle River, NJ: Prentice Hall.

Chapter 9

Helman, C. G. (1990). *Culture, health and illness: An introduction to health professionals.* London: Wright.

Hostetler, J. A. (1968). *Amish society.* Baltimore, MD: Johns Hopkins Press.

Hostetler, J. A., & Huntington, G. E. (1971). *Children in Amish society.* New York: Holt, Rinehart & Winston.

Huntington, G. E. (1988). The Amish family. In C. H. Mindel, R. W. Habenstein, & R. Wright, Jr. (Eds.), *Ethnic families in America.* New York: Elsevier Science.

Labi, N. (1998, July 6). Amiss among the Amish. *Time Magazine.*

Locke, D. C. (1992). *Increasing multicultural understanding: A comprehensive model.* Newbury Park, CA: Sage.

Milicia, J. (2005). Rapid growth brings change to Amish community. *The Times Reporter,* May 9, 2004, www.timesreporter.com/left.php?

Redfield, R. (1947, January). The folk society. *American Journal of Sociology,* pp. 292–308.

Ruth, J. (1985). *A quiet and peaceable life.* Intercourse, PA: Good Books.

Scott, S. (1988). *The Amish wedding and other special occasions of the old order communities.* Intercourse, PA: Good Books.

Wittmer, J. (1990). *The gentle people: Personal reflections of Amish life.* Minneapolis, MN: Educational Media Corporation.

Chapter 10

Allen-Meares, P. (1989). Adolescent sexuality and premature parenting: Role of the black church in prevention. *Journal of Social Work and Human Sexuality, 8*(1), 133–142.

Barnes, A. S. (1987). *Single parents in black America.* Bristol, IN: Wyndham Hall Press.

Brooks-Gunn, J., & Furstenberg, F. F., Jr. (1986). The children of adolescent mothers: Physical, academic and psychological outcomes. *Developmental Review, 6,* 224–251.

Bryson, K., & Casper, L. M. (1998). Household and family characteristics: March 1997. *Current Population Reports* (P20-509) Washington, DC: U.S. Census Bureau.

Children's Defense Fund. (1987). *Declining earnings of young men: Their relation to poverty, teenaged pregnancy and family formation.* Washington, DC: CDF Adolescent Pregnancy Prevention Clearinghouse.

Children's Defense Fund. (1993). New child support requirements. *CDF Reports, 14,* 12–13. CDF Adolescent Pregnancy. Washington, DC: Prevention Clearinghouse.

Coles, R. L. (2001). The parenting roles and goals of single black full-time fathers. *Western Journal of Black Studies, 25*(2), 101–116.

Coontz, S. (1992). *The way we never were.* New York: Basic Books.

Coontz, S. (1997). *The way we really are.* New York: Basic Books.

Davis, A. A., Rhodes, G. E., & Hamilton-Leaks, J. (1997). When both parents may be a source of support and problems: An analysis of pregnant and parenting female African-American adolescence relationships with their mothers and fathers. *Journal of Research and Adolescence, 7*(3), 331–348.

DeNavas-Walt, C., & Cleveland, R. W. (2002). Money income in the United States: 2001. *Current Population Reports* (P60218). Washington DC: U.S. Department of Commerce, U.S. Census Bureau.

DeLiere, T., & Kalil, A. (2002). Good things come in threes: Single parent multigenerational family structure and adolescent adjustment. Joint Center for Poverty Research, IL: Working paper, 238. ED.458320.

Dilworth-Anderson, P., Burton, L. M., & Turner, W. L. (1993). The importance of values in the study of culturally diverse families. *Family Relations, 42*(3), 243–248.

Downs, B. (2003). Fertility of American women: June 2002. *Current Population Reports* (P20-548). Washington, DC: U.S. Department of Commerce, U.S. Census Bureau.

Dye, J. L. (2005). Fertility of American Women: June 2004. *Current Population Reports* (P20-555). Washington DC: U.S. Department of Commerce, U.S. Census Bureau.

Dye, J. L. (2002). Fertility and program participation in the United States: 1996. *Current Population Reports* (P70-82). Washington, DC: U.S. Department of Commerce, U.S. Census Bureau.

Edin, K., & Lein, L. (1997). *Making ends meet: How single mothers survive welfare and low wage work.* New York: Russell Sage Foundation.

Fields, J. (2003). Children's living arrangements and characteristics: March 2002. *Current Population Reports* (P20-547). Washington, DC: U.S. Department of Commerce, U.S. Census Bureau.

Fields, J., & Casper, L. M. (2001). America's families and living arrangements: Population characteristics. *Current Population Reports* (P20-537). Washington, DC: U.S. Census Bureau.

Fu, H., Darroch, J. A., Haas, T., & Ranjit, N. (1996). Contraceptive failure rates: New estimates from the 1995 National Survey of Family Growth. *Family Planning Perspectives, 31*(2), 56–63.

Furstenberg, F. F., Jr., Brooks-Gunn, J., & Morgan, S. P. (1987). *Adolescent mothers in later life.* Cambridge, MA: Cambridge University Press.

Golonk, S., Steisel, S., & Ryan, E. (1996). *Analysis of the Personal Responsibility and Work Opportunity Reconciliation of 1996 Conference Agreement for H.R. 3734.* [Unpublished document]. Washington DC: National Governors' Association, National Conference of State Legislatures, American Public Law for Association.

Hamer, J. E. (1997). The fathers of "fatherless" Black children: Families in society. *Journal of Contemporary Human Services, 78*(6), 564–578.

Haub, C. (1993). Births per U.S. woman? *Population Today, 21*(9), 6–10. Washington, DC: Population Reference Bureau.

Hetherington, E. M. (1997). Teenaged childbearing and divorce. In S. S. Luthar, J. A. Burack, D. Cicchetti, & J. R. Weisz (Eds.), *Developmental psychopathology: Perspectives on adjustment risk and disorder* (pp. 350–373). New York: Cambridge University Press.

Lancashire, J., & Smith, S. (1997). *Teen sex down, new study shows: Secretary Shalala announces new teen pregnancy grant program.* (Available at www.hhs.gov/news/pres/1997pres/970501.html)

McAdoo, H. (1980). Black mothers and the extended family support network. In L. Rodgers-Rose (Ed.), *The black woman.* Beverly Hills, CA: Sage.

McAdoo, H. R., & McAdoo, J. L. (1985). *Black children: Social, educational, and parental environments.* Beverly Hills, CA: Sage.

Moyers, B. (1986). *The vanishing family: Crisis in black America* [Television broadcast]. New York: CBS News.

Moynihan, D. P. (1965). *The Negro family: The case for action.* Washington, DC: Office of Policy Planning and Research, U.S. Department of Labor.

Mulroy, E. A. (Ed.). (1988). *Women as single parents.* Dover, MA: Auburn House.

Murray, V. M. (1997). The impact of sexual activity and fertility timing on African-American high school graduates' later life experiences. *Families in Society, 78*(4), 383–391.

Mylod, D. E., Whitman, T. L., & Borkowski, J. G. (1997). Predicting adolescent mothers' transition into adulthood. *Journal of Research on Adolescents, 7*(4), 457–478.

National Commission on Children. (1993). *Just the facts.* Washington, DC: U.S. Government Printing Office.

Nelson, K., & Landsmen, M. J. (1992). *Alternative models of family preservation: Family-based services in context.* Springfield, IL: Thomas.

Newberger, C. M. (1977). *Parental conceptions of children and child rearing: A structural developmental analysis.* Unpublished doctoral dissertation, Harvard University, Cambridge, MA.

Pianta, R. C., Lopez-Hernandez, C., & Ferguson, J. E. (1997). Adolescent mothers and their children's early school performance. *Early Education and Development, 8*(4), 377–387.

Proctor, B. D., & Dalaker, J. (2002). Fertility of American women: June 2000. *Current Population Reports* (P20-543RV) Washington, DC: U.S. Census Bureau.

Raisner, J. K. (1997). Family mediation and never married parents. *Family and Conciliation Courts Review, 31*(1), 90–101.

Rhein, L. M., Ginsburg, K. R., Schwartz, D. F., Pinto-Martin, J. A., Zhao, H., Morgan, A. P., & Slap, G. D. (1997). Teen father participation in child rearing: Family perspectives. *Journal of Adolescent Health, 21*(4), 244–252.

Saluter, A. F. (1989). Changes in American family life. *Current Population Reports, Special Studies* (P-23). Washington, DC: U.S. Government Printing Office.

Scarr, S. (1989a). *Caring for children: Challenge to America.* Hillsdale, NJ: Erlbaum.

Schorr, L. B. (1988). *Within our reach: Breaking the cycle of disadvantage.* New York: Anchor Press.

Scommegna, P. (2002, September). Increased cohabitation changing children's family setting. *Research on Today's Issues, 13.* (Available at www.prb.org/Articles/2002/ Increased Cohabitations Changing Children's Family Settings. www.nichd.nih.gov/about/cpr/dbs/pubs/ti13.pdf)

Simmons, T., & O'Neill, G. (2001). *Households and families: 2000* (C2KBR/01-8). Washington, DC: U.S. Department of Commerce, U.S. Census Bureau.

Solinger, R. (1992). *Wake-up little Susie: Single pregnancy and race before Roe v. Wade.* New York: Routledge.

Sorensen, E., & Zibman, C. (2000). *A look at poor dads who don't pay child support.* Urban Institute.

Stephens, S. A., Wolf, W. C., & Batten, S. T. (2003). Strengthening school-based programs for teen parents: Challenges and solutions. *The Prevention Researcher, 10*(3) 5–8.

Story, M. (1997). Promoting healthy eating and ensuring adequate weight gain in adolescence: Issues and strategies. In M. S. Jacobson, J. M. Rees, N. H. Golden, & C. E. Irwin (Eds.), *Adolescent nutritional disorders: Prevention in treatment* (Vol. 817, pp. 321–347). New York: New York Academy of Sciences.

Strober, M. H., & Dornbush, S. M. (1988). Public policy alternatives. In S. M. Dornbush & M. H. Strober

(Eds.), *Feminism, children, and the new families* (pp. 327–357). New York: Guilford Press.

Taylor, R. J., Tucker, M. B., Chatters, L. M., & Jayakody, R. (1997). Recent demographic trends in African-American family structure. In R. J. Taylor, J. S. Jackson, & L. M. Chatters (Eds.), *Family life in Black America* (pp. 14–62). Thousand Oaks, CA: Sage.

U.S. Census Bureau. (1990). *The black population in the United States: March 1988* (Series P20–442). Washington, DC: U.S. Government Printing Office.

U.S. Census Bureau. (1992). *Poverty in the United States*. Washington, DC: U.S. Government Printing Office.

U.S. Census Bureau. (1996a). Income and poverty status of Americans improve, health insurance coverage stable, Census Bureau reports. *U.S. Department of Commerce News* (20–496). Washington, DC: U.S. Government Printing Office.

U.S. Census Bureau. (1996b). Marital status and living arrangements, March 1994 update. *Current Population Reports: Population Characteristics* (20–484). Washington, DC: U.S. Government Printing Office.

U.S. Census Bureau. (1997a). *Children with single parents—How they fare*. (Census brief CENDR/97-1). Washington DC: U.S. Government Printing Office.

U.S. Census Bureau. (1997b). How we're changing: Demographic state of the nation. *Current Population Reports* (Series P23–193). Washington DC: U.S. Government Printing Office.

U.S. Census Bureau. (1998). Co-resident grandparents and their grandchildren: Grandparent-maintained families. *Population Division working paper no. 26*. Washington, DC: U.S. Government Printing Office.

Ventura, S. J., & Bachrach, C. A. (2000). Non-marital child-bearing in the United States, 1940–99. *National Vital Statistics Reports, 48*(16), 5. Washington, DC: U.S. Department of Health and Human Services, Centers for Disease Control and Prevention, National Center for Health Statistics.

Ventura, S. J., Curtin, S. C., & Mathews, T. J. (1998). *Teenage births in the United States: National and state trends, 1990–1996*. National Vital Statistics System. Hyattsville, MD: National Center for Health Statistics.

Ventura, S. J., Martin, J. A., Curtin, S. C., & Mathews, T. J. (1998). Report of final and natality statistics, 1996. In *Monthly vital statistics report, 46*(11). Atlanta, GA: U.S. Department of Health and Human Services, Centers for Disease Control and Prevention, National Center for Health Statistics.

Ventura, S. J., Mosher, W. D., Curtin, S.C., Abma, J.C., & Henshaw, S. (2001). Trends and pregnancy rates for the United States, 1976–97: An update. *National Vital Statistics Reports, 49*(4). U.S. Department of Health and Human Services, Centers for Disease Control and Prevention.

White House Domestic Policy Council. (1993). *Health security: The president's report to the American people*. Washington, DC: U.S. Government Printing Office.

Williams, C. W. (1991). *Black teenaged mothers: Pregnancy and childrearing from their perspective*. Lexington, MA: Lexington Books.

Wilson, W. J. (1987). *The truly disadvantaged: The inner city, the underclass, and public policy*. Chicago: University of Chicago Press.

Wolf, R. How welfare reform changed America. USA Today. Retrieved July 17, 2006, from www.USAToday.com

Wojtkiewicz, R. A. (1993). Household change and racial inequality in economic well-being, 1960–1980. *Journal of Family History, 18*(3), 249–264.

Chapter 11

Ahrons, C. R., & Rogers, R. H. (1987). *Divorced families: A multidisciplinary view*. New York: Norton.

Applewhite, A. (1997). *Cutting loose: Why women who end their marriage do so well*. New York: HarperCollins.

Arendell, T. (Ed.). (1997). Divorce and remarriage. In *Contemporary parenting: Challenges and issues* (Vol. 9, pp. 154–195). Thousand Oaks, CA: Sage.

Bachu, A., & O'Connell, M. (2001). *Fertility of American women: June 2002* (T20-543RV). Washington, DC: U. S. Census Bureau.

Ballard, P. (1995). *Statement of Travis Mallard to the White House meeting on supporting the role of fathers in families.* Retrieved July 17, 2006, from http://com.timenet.com/ncfc/travwhit.html

Beld, J. M. (2003). Revisiting the Politics of Fatherhood: Administrative Agencies, Family Life, & Public Policy. *Political Science and Politics, 36* (October): 713–718.

Bolgar, R., Sweig-Frank, H., & Paris, J. (1995). Childhood antecedents of interpersonal problems in young adult children of divorce. *Journal of the American Academy of Child and Adolescent Psychiatry, 34*(2), 143–150.

Booth, A., & Amato, P. (1992). Divorce, residential change, and stress. *Journal of Divorce and Remarriage, 18*(1–2), 169–187.

Bramlett, M. D., & Mosher, W. D. (2002). *Marriage, divorce and remarriage in the United States* (23-[22N]). Washington, DC: National Center for Health Statistics, Vital Health Statistics.

Brenner, A. (1993). *Helping children cope with stress.* Lexington, MA: D. C. Heath.

Brown, P., & Fox, H. (1979). Sex differences in divorce. In F. S. Gonsberg & V. Franks (Eds.), *Gender disordered behavior: Sex differences in psychopathology.* New York: Brunner/Nagel.

Buehler, C., & Legg, B. H. (1993). Mothers' receipt of social support and their psychological well-being following marital separation. *Journal of Family Issues, 14*(1), 21–38.

Children's Defense Fund. (1993). Child poverty hits record level. *CDF Reports, 14*(12), 11.

Compher, J. V. (1989). *Family-centered practice: The interactional dance beyond the family system.* New York: Plenum.

Coontz, S. (1992). *The way we never were.* New York: Basic Books.

DeLeire, T., & Kalil, A. (2001). *Good things come in threes: Single parent multi-generational family structure and adolescent involvement.* (Working paper 242.) Chicago: Joint Center for Poverty Research.

DeMaris, A., & Greif, G. L. (1992). The relationship between family structure and parent-child relationship problems in single father households. *Journal of Divorce and Remarriage, 18*(1–2), 55–57.

DeNavas-Walt, C., & Cleveland, R.W. (2002). *Money income in the United States: 2001* (P60-218). Washington DC: U.S. Census Bureau.

Donnelly, D., & Finkelhor, D. (1993). Who has joint custody? Class differences in the determination of custody arrangements. *Family Relations, 42*(1), 57–61.

Dudley, J. R. (1996). Noncustodial fathers speak about their parental role. *Family and Conciliation Courts Review, 31*(3), 410–426.

Duran-Aydintug, C. (1993). Relationships with former in-laws: Normative guidelines and actual behavior. *Journal of Divorce and Remarriage, 19*(3–9), 69–82.

Egan, T. (2000). After seven years, couple is defeated. *New York Times.* p. A22.

Ehrenberg, M. S. (1996). Cooperative parent arrangements after marital separation: Former couples who made it work. *Journal of Divorce and Remarriage, 26* (1–2), 93–115.

Family Support Act of 1988. (1988, October 13, P. L. 100-485). *United States Statistics at Large, 102,* 2343–2428.

Fields, J., & Casper, L. M. (2002). *America's families and living arrangements* (P20-537). Washington, DC: U.S. Census Bureau.

Fine, M. A. (1993). Current approaches to understanding family diversity: An overview of a special issue. *Family Relations, 42*(3), 235–237.

Fine, M. A., & Fine, D. R. (1992). Recent changes in law affecting stepfamilies: Suggestions for legal reform. *Family Relations, 42,* 334–340.

Furstenberg, F., & Teitler, J. O. (1994). Reconsidering the effects of marital disruption: What happens to the children of divorce in early adulthood. *Journal of Family Issues, 15,* 173–190.

Gay, R. F., & Palumbo, G. J. (1998). *The child support guideline problem.* Retrieved February, 2006, from www.acfc.org.html/study.htmlChildSupport

Gigy, L., & Kelly, J. B. (1992). Reasons for divorce: Perspectives of divorcing men and women. *Journal of Divorce and Remarriage, 18*(1–2), 169–187.

Gottleib, D. W., Gottleib, I. B., & Slavin, M. A. (1988). *What to do when your son or daughter divorces*. New York: Bantam Books.

Grall, T. (2002). *Custodial mothers and fathers and their child support* (P60-217). Washington, DC: U.S. Census Bureau.

Gray, M. M., & Coleman, M. (1985). Separation through divorce: Supportive professional practices. *Child Care Quarterly, 14*(4), 248–261.

Hetherington, E. M., Cox, M., & Cox, R. (1985). Long-term effects of divorce and remarriage on the adjustment of children. *Journal of American Academy of Child Psychiatry, 24,* 518–530.

Hepworth, J., Ryder, R. G., & Dreyer, A. S. (1984). The effects of parental loss on the formation of intimate relationships. *Journal of Marital and Family Therapy, 10,* 73–82.

Ingrassia, M. (1993, August 30). Endangered family. *Newsweek,* pp. 17–29.

Johnson, C. L. (1988). *Ex-families: Grandparents, parents, and children adjust to divorce*. New Brunswick, NJ: Rutgers University Press.

Johnston, J. R., & Roseby, V. (1997). *In the name of the child*. New York: Free Press.

Koball, H., & Principe, D. (2002). Do non-resident fathers who pay child support visit their children more? Washington, DC: Urban Institute. www.urban.org/DesireePrincipe

Kramer, L., & Washo, C. A. (1993). Evaluation of a court-mandated prevention program for divorcing parents: The children first program. *Family Relations, 41,* 224–229.

Kuhn, R., & Guidubaldi, J. (1997). Shared parenting: The best parent is both parents. *Child Custody Policies and Divorce Rates in the United States.* Washington, DC: Children's Rights Council.

Kurkowski, K. P., Gordon, D. A., & Arbuthnot, J. (1993). Children caught in the middle: A brief educational intervention for divorced parents. *Journal of Divorce and Remarriage, 20*(3–4), 139–152.

Lansford, J. E., Ceballo, R., Abbey, A., & Stewart, A. J. (2001). Does family structure matter? A comparison of adoptive, two-parent biological, single-mother, step-father, and step-mother households. *Journal of Marriage and Family, 63*(3), 840–851.

Leving, J., & Dachman, K. (1997). *Fathers' rights*. New York: HarperCollins.

Maccoby, E. E., & Mnookin, R. H. (1992). *Dividing the child: Social and legal dilemmas of custody*. Cambridge, MA: Harvard University Press.

McFarlane, A. H., Bellissimo, A., & Norman, G. R. (1995). Family structure, family functioning, and adolescent well-being: The transcendent influence of parental style. *Journal of Child Psychology and Psychiatry and Allied Disciplines, 36,* 847–864.

McLanahan, S. (1994). The consequences of single motherhood. *The American Prospect, 18,* 48–58.

Miller, G. (1993). The psychological best interests of the child. *Journal of Divorce and Remarriage, 19* (1–2), 21–39.

Mulroy, E. A. (Ed.). (1988). *Women as single parents*. Dover, MA: Auburn House.

National Commission on Children. (1993). *Just the facts*. Washington, DC: U.S. Government Printing Office.

Parnell, M., & Bagbee, B. H. (1993). Grandparents' rights: Implications for family specialists. *Family Relations, 42*(2), 173–179.

Powell, B., & Downey, D. B. (1995). Well being of adolescents in single-parent households: The case of the same-sex hypothesis. *Sociological Abstracts, 28,* 413–415.

Rofes, E. (Ed.). (1982). *The kids' book about divorce*. New York: Vintage Books.

Schaefer, S. A. (2002). *Welfare to work: Does it work for kids? Research on work and income welfare experience* [Factsheet]. Washington, DC: National Association of Child Advocates.

Schutter, M. E., Scherman, A., & Carroll, R. S. (1997). Grandparents and children of divorce: Their contrasting perceptions and desires for the post-divorce relationship. *Educational Gerontology, 23,* 213–231.

Scoon-Rogers, L., & Lester, G. H. (1995). Child support for custodial mothers and fathers: 1991. *Current*

Population Reports (Series P 60–187). Washington, DC: U.S. Government Printing Office.

Scoon-Rogers, L., & Lester, G. (1997). Who receives child support? *U.S. Census Bureau Statistical Briefs* (301–457–1221). Washington, DC: U.S. Government Printing Office.

Seltzer, J. A. (1991). Relationships between fathers and children who live apart: The father's role after separation. *Journal of Marriage and the family, 53,* 79–101.

Shim, M.K., Fellner, R.D., & Shim, E. (2000, April 24–28). *The effects of family structure on academic achievement.* Presentation at the annual meeting of the American Educational Research Association, New Orleans, LA.

Simmons, T., & O'Neill, G. (2001). *Hustled in families: 2000* (C2KBR/01–8). Washington, DC: U.S. Census Bureau.

Stamps, L. E., Kunen, S., & Rock-Faucheux, A. (1997). Judges' beliefs dealing with child custody decisions. *Journal of Divorce and Remarriage, 28*(1–2), 3–16.

Stewart, A. (1998). *Separating together: How divorce transforms families.* New York: Guilford Press.

Thomson, E., Mosley, J., Hanson, T., & McLanahan, S. S. (2001). Remarriage, co-habitation, and changes in mothering behavior. *Journal of Marriage and the Family, 63*(2), 370–380.

U.S. Census Bureau. (1992). Family life today . . . and how it has changed. *Statistical Briefs* (P 92–13). Washington, DC: U.S. Government Printing Office.

Wallerstein, J. S. (1998). Children of divorce: The society in search of policy. In M. A. Mason, A. Skolnick, & S. D. Sugarman (Eds.), *All our families: Calling new policies for a new century* (pp. 66–94). New York: Oxford University Press.

Wallerstein, J. S., & Kelly, J. (1980). *Surviving the breakup: How children and parents cope with divorce.* New York: Basic Books.

Whitehead, B. D. (1993, April). Dan Quayle was right. *Atlantic Monthly,* pp. 47–84.

Zinn, M. B. (1992). Family, race, and poverty in the eighties. In B. Thorne (Ed.), *Rethinking the family.* Boston: NYU Press.

Chapter 12

Anderson, E. R. (1999). Sibling, half sibling, and stepsibling relationships in remarried families. *Society for Research in Child Development Monographs, 64,* (4), 101–126.

Annie B. Casey Foundation. (2003). *Kids count.* Baltimore, MD: Annie B. Casey Foundation.

Arendell, T. (1997). Divorce and remarriage. In T. Arendell (Ed.), *Contemporary parenting: Challenges and issues* (pp. 154–195). Thousand Oaks, CA: Sage.

Austin, J. F. (1993). The impact of school policies on noncustodial parents. *Journal of Divorce and Remarriage, 20*(3–4), 153–170.

Baum, K. J. (2000). A comparison of lesbian and heterosexual stepfamilies: Is sex of stepparent or sex of parent the more salient factor in family adjustment? The Wright Institute CA. (Doctoral dissertation, 1990). *Dissertation Abstracts International-B, 60*(09), 4874.

Bramlett, M. D., & Mosier, W. D. (2002). Cohabitation, marriage, divorce, and remarriage in the United States. National Center for Health Statistics. *Vital Health Statistics, 23*(22.2002).

Bray, J. M., & Berger, S. H. (1990). Noncustodial father and paternal grandfather relationships in stepfamilies. *Family Relations, 39,* 414–419.

Brewer, V. E., & Pasley, K. (2000). Family boundary ambiguity, marital status, and child adjustment. *Journal of Early Adolescence, 20,* 281–308.

Brewer, V. E., & Paulsen, D. J. (1999). A comparison of U. S. and Canadian findings on uxorcide risk for women with children sired by previous partners. *Homicide Studies, 13*(4), 317–332.

Ceglian, C. P., & Gardner, S. (2000). Attachment style and the "wicked stepmorther" spiral. *Journal of Divorce and Remarriage, 34*(1/2), 111–129.

Cherlin, A. (1999). Going to extremes: Family structure, children's well-being, and social science. *Demography, 35*(4), 421–428.

Cherlin, A. J. (1992). *Marriage, divorce, and remarriage.* Cambridge, MA: Harvard University Press.

Cherlin, A. J., & Furstenberg, F. F., Jr. (1994). Step families in the United States: A reconsideration. *Annual Review of Sociology, 20,* 359–381.

Christensen, S. (2000). Family definition, family identity: Processes in the lesbian stepfamily (Doctoral dissertation, University of Guelph, CA, 2000). *Dissertation Abstracts International-B 60*(10), 5249.

Church, E. (1999). "I had no idea what I was getting into": Stepmothers' initial expectations about stepfamily life.

Coleman, M., Fine, M. A., Ganong, L. H., Downs, K. J. M., & Pauk, N. (2001). When you're not the Brady Bunch: Identifying perceived conflicts and resolution strategies in stepfamilies. *Personal Relationships, 8*(1), 55–73.

Coleman, M., & Ganong, L. (1990). Remarriage and stepfamily research in the 1980s: Increased interest in an old family form. *Journal of Marriage and the Family, 52,* 925–940.

Coleman, M., Ganong, L. H., & Fine, M. (2000). Reinvestigating remarriage: Another decade of progress. *Journal of Marriage and the Family, 62*(4), 1288–1307.

Coontz, S. (1992). *The way we never were.* New York: Basic Books.

Creider, R. M., & Fields, J. M. (2002). Number, timing and duration of marriages and divorce: 1996. *Household Economic Studies* (P70-80). Washington, DC: U. S. Census Bureau.

Crosbie-Burnett, M., & Lewis, E. A. (1993). Use of African American family structures and functioning to address the challenges of European American postdivorce families. *Family Relations, 42*(3), 243–246.

Daly, M., & Wilson, M. I. (1996). Violence against step children. *Parent Directions in Psychological Science, 5*(3), 77–80.

DeMaris, A., & Greif, G. L. (1992). The relationship between family structure and parent-child relationship problems in single father households. *Journal of Divorce and Remarriage, 18*(1–2), 55–77.

Donnelly, D., & Finkelhor, D. (1993). Who has joint custody? Class differences in the determination of custody arrangements. *Family Relations, 42*(1), 57–61.

Duran-Aydintug, C. (1993). Relationships with former in-laws: Normative guidelines and actual behavior. *Journal of Divorce and Remarriage, 19*(3–9), 69–82.

Einstein, E., & Albert, L. (1987). *Pitfalls and possibilities.* Ithaca, NY: The Step-Family Living Series.

Ephron, D. (1986). *Funny sauce: Us, the ex, the ex's new mate, the new mate's ex, and the kids.* New York: Viking Press.

Erera-Weatherley, P. I. (1996). On becoming a step parent: Factors associated with the adoption of alternative step parenting styles. *Journal of Divorce and Remarriage, 25*(3–4), 155–174.

Fields, J., & Caspar, L. M. (2001). America's families and living arrangements: Population characteristics. *Current Population Reports* (P20-537). Washington, DC: U.S. Census Bureau.

Fine, M. A., & Fine, D. R. (1992). Recent changes in law affecting stepfamilies: Suggestions for legal reform. *Family Relations, 41,* 334–340.

Furukawa, S. (1994). *The diverse living arrangements of children: Summer 1991.* U.S. Bureau of the Census (Series P70-38). Washington, DC: U.S. Government Printing Office.

Ganong, L., & Coleman, M. (1986). A comparison of clinical and empirical literature on children in stepfamilies. *Journal of Marriage and the Family, 48,* 309–318.

Ganong, L., & Coleman, M. (1993a). An exploratory study of stepsibling subsystems. *Journal of Divorce and Remarriage, 19*(3–4), 125–141.

Ganong, L. H., & Coleman, M. (2004). *Stepfamily relationships: Development, dynamics and interventions.* New York: Springer.

Ganong, L., Coleman, M., Fine, M., & Martin, P. (1999). Stepparents' affinity-seeking and affinity-maintaining strategies with stepchildren. *Journal of Family Issues, 20*(3), 299–327.

Gerrard, I. (2001). Disenfranchised grief in stepfamilies. Stepfamily Association of Victoria, Inc. Retrieved May 2, 2007 from www.stepfamily.org/au/articles.asp?view=7

Gerrard, I. (2001). Disenfranchised grief in stepfamilies. *Victorian Association of Family Therapists VAFT News, 23*(4), 6–9.

Giles-Sims, J., & Finkelhor, D. (1984). Child abuse in step families. *Family Relations, 33,* 411.

Glick, P. C. (1989). Remarried families, stepfamilies, and stepchildren: A brief demographic profile. *Family Relations, 38,* 24–27.

Greene, S. M., & Anderson, E. R. (1999). Observed negativity in large family systems: Incidents and reactions. *Journal of Family Psychology, 13*(3), 372–392.

Grizzle, G. L. (1999). Institutionalization and family unity: An exploratory study of Cherlin's (1978) views. *Journal of Divorce and Remarriage, 30*(3/4), 125–141.

Hans, J. D., & Fine, M. A. (2002) Children of divorce: Experiences of children whose parents attended a divorce education program. *Journal of Divorce and Remarriage, 36*(1/2), 1–26.

Hetherington, E. M. (1999). Family functioning in nonstepfamilies and different kinds of stepfamilies: An integration. *Society for Research in Child Development Monographs, 64*(4), 184–191.

Hetherington, E. M., & Henderson, S. H. (1997). Fathers in stepfamilies. In M. E. Lamb (Ed.), *The role of the father in child* development (pp. 212–226). New York: Wiley.

Jones, S. E. (2001). Impact of change in quality of stepfamily relationships on older-adolescent adjustment: A longitudinal study. (Doctoral dissertation, The University of Miami, 2001). *Dissertation Abstracts International-B, 62*(05), 2536.

Johnson, H. C. (1980). Working with stepfamilies: Principles of practice. *Journal of Social Work, 50,* 304–308.

Johnston, J. R., & Roseby, V. (1997). *In the name of the child: A developmental approach to understanding and helping children of conflicted and violent divorce.* New York: Free Press.

Karsky, J. L. (1999). The relationship between stepmothers' social structure and self-structure: A use of symbolic interactionism and role theory. South Dakota State University (1999). *Dissertation Abstracts International-A, 60*(04), 1347.

Kempe, H. C. (1980). Incest and other forms of sexual abuse. In H. C. Kempe & R. E. Helfer (Eds.), *The battered child* (pp. 41–53). Chicago: University of Chicago Press.

Kennedy, G. E., & Kennedy, C. E. (1993). Grandparents: A special resource for children in step-families. *Journal of Divorce and Remarriage, 19*(3-4), 45–68.

Kheshgi-Genovese, Z., & Genovese, T. A. (1997). Developing the spousal relationship within step families. *Families in Society: The Journal of Contemporary Human Services, 78*(1), 255–264.

Ludwig, T. E. (2001). A longitudinal examination of stepfamily: Cohesion from a normative-adaptive perspective. (Doctoral dissertation, The University of Miami, 2001). *Dissertation Abstracts International-B, 61*(10), 5623.

Maglin, N. B. (1989). Reading stepfamily fiction. In N. B. Maglin & N. Schneidewind (Eds.), *Women and stepfamilies: Voices of anger and love* (pp. 67–85). Philadelphia: Temple University Press.

Maglin, N. B., & Schneidewind, N. (Eds.). (1989). *Women and stepfamilies: Voices of anger and love.* Philadelphia: Temple University Press.

Mason, M. A. (1998). The modern American step family: Problems and possibilities. In M. A. Mason, A. Skolnick, & S. D. Sugarman (Eds.), *All are families: New policies for a new century* (pp. 95–116). New York: Oxford University Press.

Mason, M. A., & Mauldon, J. (1996). The new step family requires a new public policy. *Journal of Social Issues, 52*(3), 11–27.

National Commission on Children. (1993). *Just the facts.* Washington, DC: U.S. Government Printing Office.

Newman, B., Skopin, A. R., & McKerry, P. C. (1993). Influences on the quality of stepfather-adolescent relationships: Views of both family members. *Journal of Divorce and Remarriage, 19*(3–4), 181–196.

Nielsen, L. (1999). Stepmothers: Why so much stress? A review of the research. *Journal of Divorce and Remarriage, 30*(1/2), 115–148.

Orchard, A. L., & Solberg, K. B. (1999). Expectations of the stepmother's role. *Journal of Divorce and Remarriage, 31* (1/2), 107–123.

Pappernow, P. L. (1980). *A phenomological study of the developmental stages of becoming a stepparent—a gestalt and family systems approach.* Ann Arbor, MI: University Microfilms International.

Pappernow, P. L. (1988). Step parent role development: From outsider to intimate. In N. W. Beer (Ed.), *Relative strangers* (pp. 54–82). Totowa, NJ: Rowman and Littlefield.

Peterson, J. L., & Nord, C. W. (1990). The regular receipt of child support: A multistep process. *Journal of Marriage and the Family, 52*, 539–551.

Rush, F. (1980). *The best kept secret: Sexual abuse of children.* Englewood Cliffs, NJ: Prentice-Hall.

Sanders, G. F., & Trygstad, D. W. (1989). Stepparents and grandparents: The view from young adults. *Family Relations, 38,* (1) 71–75.

Scommegna, P. (2002, September). Increased cohabitation changing children's family setting. *Research on Today's Issues, 13.* (Available from www.nichd.nih.gov/about/cpr/dbs/pubs/til3.pdf)

Sevier, S. F. (2000). The stepmother: In search of self. (Doctoral dissertation, Syracuse University NY, 2000). *Dissertation Abstracts International-A, 60*(09), 3282.

Smith, W. (2000). The experience of being a member of a stepfamily: A heuristic investigation. (Doctoral dissertation, The Union Institute, 2000). *Dissertation Abstracts International-B, 60*(12), 6384.

Spanier, G. (1988). Foreword. In W. R. Beer (Ed.), *Relative strangers.* (pp. ix–xi). Totowa, NJ: Rowman and Littlefield.

Stewart, S.D. (2001). Contemporary American stepparenthood: Integrating cohabiting and nonresident stepparents. *Population Research and Policy Review, 20*(4), 345–364.

Stump, B. (1999, November). How to raise another man's kids: A dozen rules for being a better stepdad. *Men's Health,* pp. 106–108.

Thompson, P. (1999). The role of grandparents when parents part or die: Some reflections on the mythical decline of the extended family. *Ageing and Society, 19*(4), 471–503.

U.S. Census Bureau. Children's living arrangements and characteristics: March 2002. Annual Demographic Supplement to the March 2002 Current Population Survey, *Current Population Reports* (Series P20-547). Washington, DC: Author.

Visher, E. B., & Visher, J. S. (1980). Stepfamilies are different. *Journal of Family Therapy, 7,* 9–18.

Vogt, T. R. (1999). The relative importance of living in a stepfamily and its effects on the development of cynicism toward marriage and family. *Master's Abstracts International, 37*(02), 505.

Vurgoyne, J., & Clark, D. (1982). Parenting in step families. In C. P. Diggory & M. Sutherland (Eds.), *Changing patterns of child bearing and child rearing* (pp. 133–147). London: Academic Press.

Watson, P. A. (1995). Ancient stepmothers: Myths, mysogony and reality. *Mnemosyne Supplement, 143,* xii, 288.

White, L. K. (1994). Co-residence and leaving home: Young adults and their parents. *Annual Review of Sociology, 20,* 81–102.

White, L. (1999). Contagion in family affection: Mothers, fathers and young adult children. *Journal of Marriage and Family, 61*(2), 284–294.

White, L., & Gilbreth, J. G. (2001). When children have two fathers: Effects of relationships with step-fathers and non-custodial fathers on adolescent outcomes. *Journal of Marriage and Family, 63*(1), 155–167.

Widmer, E. D. (1999). Contexts as cognitive networks: A structural approach to family relationships. *Personal Relationships, 6*(4), 487–503.

Chapter 13

Applequist, K. (2005). Special education litigation. In E. Fletcher-Janzen & C. R. Reynolds (Eds.), *The special education almanac, 2005* (pp. 537–562). Hoboken, NJ: Wiley.

Bearn, A. & Smith, C. (1998). How learning support is perceived by mainstream colleagues. *Support for Learning, 13*(1), 14–20.

Beavers, J. (1989). Physical and cognitive handicaps. In L. Combrinck-Graham (Ed.), *Children in family contexts* (pp. 193–212). New York: Guilford Press.

Bennett, T., DeLuca D., & Bruns, D. (1997). Putting in clusion into practice: Perspectives of teachers and parents. *Exceptional Children 64*(1), 115–131.

Brotherson, S. E., & Dollahite, D. C. (1997). Generative ingenuity in fatherwork with young children with special needs. In A. J. Hawkins &

D. C. Dollahite (Eds.), *Generative fatherins: Beyond deficit perspectives* (pp. 89–104). Newbury Park, CA: Sage.

Casper, L., & Bryson, K. R. (1998). Co-resident grandparents and their grandchildren: Grandparent maintained families. Population division working paper No. 26. Washington, DC.: U.S. Bureau of the Census.

Connor, M. J. (1997). Parental motivation for specialists or mainstream placement. *Support for Learning, 12*(3), 104–110.

Couples with ill children more likely to split up. (1993, September 27). *Wall Street Journal,* p. 14.

D'Amato, R. K., & Rothlisberg, B. A. (1997). How education should respond to students with traumatic brain injury. In A. D. Bigler, E. Clark, & J. E. Farmer (Eds.), *Childhood traumatic brain industry: Diagnosis, assessment, and intervention* (pp. 213–237). Austin, TX: Pro-Ed.

Dawson, A. (1997). Parent-to-Parent Link Program. *Canadian Journal of Rehabilitation, 10*(4), 333–334.

Derman-Sparks, L., & ABC Task Force. (1989). *Antibias curriculum: Tools for empowering young children.* Washington, DC: National Association for the Education of Young Children.

Frye, K. S., Greenburg, M. T., & Fewell, R. R. (1989). Stress and coping among parents of exceptional children: A multidimensional approach. *American Journal on Mental Retardation, 94,* 3.

George, M. C. (1997). Tossed salad: Diversity considerations in adoptions. *Law and Psychology Review 21,* pp. 197–219.

Gilbert, N. (1998). Working Families: Help Hearth to Market. In M. Mason, A. Skolnick, & S. Sugarman (Eds.), *All our families: New policies for a new century* (pp. 193–216). New York: Oxford University Press.

Greenfield, J. (1970). *A child called Noah.* New York: Pocket Books.

Greenspan, M. (1998). Exceptional mothering in a normal world. In C. Garcia Cowles & J. L. Surrey (Eds.), *Mothering against the odds: Diverse voices of contemporary mothers,* (pp. 34–60). New York: Guilford Press.

Groze, V. (1996). A one- and two-year follow-up study of adoptive families and special needs children. *Children and Youth Services Review, 18*(1–2), 57–82.

H. R. 5, An Act to Amend the Individuals with Disabilities Education Act to Reauthorize and Make Improvements to That Act and For Other Purposes. (1997). Washington, DC: U.S. Congress.

Hudgens, L., Hobfall, S. E., & Lerman, M. (1989). Predicting receipt of social support: Longitudinal study of parents' reaction to their children's illness. *Health Psychology, 8,* 61–77.

Isbell, M. T. (1992). *HIV and family law: A survey.* New York: Lambda Legal Defense and Education Fund.

Kavale, K. A., & Forness, S. R. (2000). History, rhetoric and reality: Analysis of the inclusion debate. *Remedial and Special Education 2*(5), 279–296.

Lamb, M. E., & Billings, L. H. L. (1997). Fathers of children with special needs. In M. E. Lamb (Ed.), *The role of the father in child development* (pp. 1–18). New York: John Wiley & Sons.

May, J. E. (1991). *Fathers of children with special needs: New horizons.* Bethesda, MD: Association for the Care of Children's Health.

McNurlen, G. (1996). Resiliency in single and dual parent families with special needs children. *Infant Toddler Intervention, 6*(4), 309–323.

Mickelson, K. D. (1997). Seeking social support: Parents in electronic support groups. In S. Kiesler (Ed.), *Culture of the Internet* (pp. 157–178). Mahwah, NJ: Lawrence Erlbaum Associates.

Mullins, J. B. (1987). Authentic voices from parents of exceptional children. *Family Relations, 36,* 30–33.

Murray, J., & McDonald, L. (1996). Father involvement in early intervention programs: Effectiveness, obstacles and considerations. *Developmental Disabilities, 24*(2), www.ualberta.ca/~jpdasddc/bulletin/articles/murray1996.html

National Information Center for Children and Youth with Disabilities. (1991). *Partners: A manual for family-centered respite care.* Washington, DC: Author.

Pruett, K. (1989). *The promise of fatherhood: Fathers in their relationships with infants, toddlers and service providers*. Plenary session presented at the National Center for Clinical Infant Programs, Sixth Biennial. National Training Institute, Washington, DC.

No Child Left Behind Act, Public Law 107–110, 20 U.S.C. Sec. 6301 (200) (enacted January 8, 2002).

Individuals with Disabilities Act (IDEA), 20 U.S.C. Sec. 1412.

Simons, R. (1987). *After the tears: Parents talk about raising a child with disabilities*. New York: Harcourt Brace Jovanovich.

Singer, G. H. S., & Irvin, L. K. (Eds.). (1989). *Support for caregiving families: Enabling positive adaptation to disability*. Baltimore, MD: Paul H. Brookes.

Snell, S. A., & Rosen, K. H. (1997). Parents of special needs children mastering the job of parenting. *Contemporary Family Therapy, 19*(3), 425–442).

Special ed's special costs. (1993, October 20). *Wall Street Journal*, p. 10.

U.S. Census Bureau. (1997). *One in 10 Americans reported a severe disability in 1994–95*. Washington, DC: U.S. Census Bureau, Public Information Office.

Ward, M. J. (1946). *The snake pit*. New York: Gosset and Dunlap.

Warfield, M. E., & Hauser-Cram, P. (1996). Child care needs, arrangements, and satisfaction of mothers of children with developmental disabilities. *Mental Retardation 34*, 294–302.

Wyche, K. F., & Lobato, D. J. (1996). Minority mothers: Stress and coping when your child is in special education. In K. F. Wyche & F. Crosby (Eds.), *Women and Ethnicity: Journeys Through Psychology*. Boulder, Co: Westview.

Chapter 14

ACLU. (1997). *New Jersey becomes first state to allow joint adoption by lesbian and gay couples*. Retrieved February, 2007 from www.aclu.org/news/n121797a.html

Allen, M., & Burrell, N. (1996). Comparing the impact of homosexual and heterosexual parents on children: Meta-analysis of existing research. *Journal of Homosexuality, 32*(2), 19–35.

Appleby, G. A., & Anastas, J. W. (1998). Social work practice with lesbian, gay, and bisexual people. In A. T. Morales & B. W. Scheafer (Eds.), *Social work: A profession of many faces* (pp. 313–345). Boston: Allyn & Bacon, 313–345.

Belcastro, P. A., Giamlich, T., Nicholson, T., Price, J., & Wilson, R. (1988). A review of data based studies addressing the effects of homosexual parenting on children's sexual and social functioning. *Journal of Divorce and Remarriage, 20*(1–2), 105–122.

Benkov, L. (1994). *Reinventing the family*. New York: Crown.

Bigner, J. J. (2002). *Parent-child relations: An introduction to parenting*. Upper Saddle River, NJ: Merrill-Prentice Hall.

Boyer, P. (1985). *By the bomb's early light: American thought and culture at the dawn of the atomic age*. New York: Pantheon Books.

Bozette, F. (1988). Social control of identity by children of gay fathers. *Western Journal of Nursing Research, 10*, 550–595.

Bozette, F. (1989). Gay fathers: A review of the literature. In F. Bozette (Ed.), *Homosexuality and the family* (pp. 137–162). New York: Haworth Press.

Braschi v. Stahl Association Company. (1989). New York Court of Appeals, WL. 73109.

Briggs, J. R. (1994). *A Yankelovich monitor perspective on gays/lesbians*. Norwalk, CT: Yankelovich Partners.

Brooks, D., & Goldberg, S. (2001). Gay and lesbian adoptive and foster care placements: Can they meet the needs of waiting children? *Social Work, 46*(2), 146–157.

Butler, A. C. (2000). Trends in same gender sexual partnering, 1988–1998. *Journal of Sex Research, 37* (4), 333–343.

Buxton, A. P. (1991). *The other side of the closet: The coming out crisis for straight spouses*. Santa Monica, CA: IBS Press.

Collins, R., & Coltrane, S. (1991). *Sociology of marriage and the family* (3rd ed.). Chicago: Nelson Hall.

Crosbie-Burnett, M., & Helmbrecht, L. (1993). A descriptive empirical study of gay male stepfamilies. *Family Relations, 42*(3), 256–262.

Downing, C. (1991). *Myths and mysteries of same sex love.* New York: Continuum.

Duran-Aydintug, C., & Causey, K. A. (1996). Child custody determination: Implications for lesbian mothers. *Journal of Divorce and Remarriage, 25*(1–2), 55–74.

Elia, J. P. (1993). Homophobia in the high school: A problem in need of resolution. *The High School Journal, 77*(1–2), 177–185.

Ellis, L., & Ames, M. A. (1987). Neurohormonal functioning and sexual orientation: A theory of homosexuality-heterosexuality. *Psychological Bulletin, 101,* 233–258.

Fields, J. (2001). Normal queers: Straight parents respond to their childrens' coming out. *Symbolic Interaction, 24*(2), 165–187.

Friskopp, A., & Silverstein, S. (1995). *Straight jobs, gay lives.* New York: Scribner's.

Gay, Lesbian and Straight Education Network. (2005). *From teasing to torment: School climate in America—A national report on school bullying.* Retrieved April 2, 2007 from www.glsen.org/cgi-bin/Iowa/all/library/1859.html

Golombok, S., Tasker, F., & Murray, C. (1997). Children raised in fatherless families from infancy: Family relationships in the social-emotional development of children of lesbian and single heterosexual mothers. *Journal of Child Psychology and Psychiatry in Allied Disciplines, 38,* 783–791.

Gottman, J. S. (1989). Children of lesbian and gay parents. *Marriage and Family Review, 14*(3/4), 177–196.

Griffin, C. W., Wirth, M. J., & Wirth, A. G. (1996). *Beyond acceptance: Parents of lesbians and gays talk about their experiences.* New York: St. Martin's Press.

Guggenheim, M., Lowe, A. D., & Curtis, D. (1996). *The rights of families.* Carbondale: Southern Illinois University Press.

Hall, L. S. (2000). Dermatoglyphic analysis of total finger ridge count in female monozygot twins discordant for sexual orientation. *Journal of Sexual Research, 37*(4), 315–320.

Hare, J., & Richards, L. (1993). Children raised by lesbian couples: Does context of birth affect father and partner involvement? *Family Relations, 42*(3), 249–253.

Harry, J. (1989). Parental abuse and sexual orientation in males. *Archives of Sexual Behavior, 18,* 251–261.

Herek, G. M., & Berrill, K. T. (Eds.). (1992). *Hate crimes: Confronting violence against lesbians and gay men.* London: Sage.

Hoeffer, B. (1981). Children's acquisition of sexual behavior in lesbian-mother families. *American Journal of Orthopsychiatry, 51,* 536–544.

Human Rights Campaign. (1998). *Continued high rate of anti-gay hate crimes points to need for federal law, HRC asserts.* Washington DC: Author. (Available at www.hrc.org)

Kirkpatrick, M. (1987). Clinical implications of lesbian mother studies. *Journal of Homosexuality, 14,* 120–211.

Koepke, L., Hare, J., & Moran, P. (1992). Relationship quality in a sample of lesbian couples with children and child-free lesbian couples. *Family Relations, 41,* 224–229.

Lambda Defense and Education Fund. (2001). Partial summary of domestic partnership listings.

Lambda Legal Defense and Education Fund. (2002a). Facts and figures about marriage, family, and same sex couples. New York: Author.

Lambda Defense and Education Fund. (2002b). *Facts: Gay and lesbian youth in schools.* Retrieved February, 2006, from www.lambdalegal.org/egi=bin/iowa/documents/record/?record=1120

Lambda Defense and Education Fund. (2002c). New New York State law giving spousal benefits to gay partners of 9/11 victims is a significant step forward but gay families still unprotected in tragedies. Retrieved March 20, 2007, from www.lambdalegal.org/egi=bin/iowa/documents/record/?record=1138

Lambda Legal Defense and Education Fund. (2003a, June). Landmark ruling for gay civil rights: U.S. Supreme strikes down Texas Homosexual Conduct Law. Retrieved from www.lambdalegal.org.

Lambda Defense and Education Fund. (2003b). New Jersey civil union watch. Retrieved March, 2007 from www.lambdalegal.org/take-action/campaigns/nj-civil-union-watch.

Lambda Legal Defense and Education Fund. (2003c, November 18). Praising Massachusetts' court ruling allowing same sex couples to marry. Lambda Legal vows to push forward. Retrieved February, 2007 from www.lambdalegal.org

Lambda Legal Defense and Education Fund. (2006a). Status update on the "next frontier" of pending cases on marriage and relationship recognition same-sex couples. Retrieved February 12, 2006, from www.lambdalegal.org.

Lambda Legal Defense and Education Fund. (2006b). Background and pending cases seeking full equality for gay couples. Retrieved February 2006, from www.lambdalegal.org.

Marcus, E. (1992). *Making history: The struggle for gay and lesbian equal rights.* New York: HarperCollins.

McWhirter, D. P., & Mattison, A. M. (1984). *The male couple: How relationships develop.* Englewood Cliffs, NJ: Prentice Hall.

Mercer, L. R., & Berger, R. M. (1989). Social service needs of lesbian and gay adolescents: Telling it their way. *Journal of Social Work and Human Sexuality, 8*(1), 75–95.

Miller, B. (1979). Gay fathers and their children. *The Family Coordinator, 28,* 544–552.

Millic, J. H., & Crowne, D. T. (1986). Recalled parent-child relations and need for approval in homosexual and heterosexual men. *Archives of Sexual Behavior, 15,* 239–246.

More, A. (2003). Law of the land, high court to give "gays" their own "row": Case could establish constitutional right to homosexual conduct. Retrieved February 23, 2003, from Worldnet Daily.com

Moses, A., & Hawkins, R. (1982). *Counseling lesbian women and gay men.* Englewood Cliffs, NJ: Merrill/Prentice Hall.

Osborn, T. (1996). *Coming home to America.* New York: St. Martin's Press.

Oswald, R. F. (2002). Resilience within the family networks of lesbians and gay men: Intentionality and re-definition. *Journal of Marriage and Family, 64*(2), .

Patterson, C. J. (1994a). Children of a lesbian baby boom. In N.B. Green & G. M. Herek (Eds.), *Lesbian and gay psychology: Theory, research, and clinical applications* (pp. 156–175). Thousand Oaks, CA: Sage.

Patterson, C. J. (1994b). Lesbian and gay families. *Contemporary Directions in Psychological Science, 4,* 6–64.

Patterson, C. J., Hunt, S., & Mason, C. (1998). Families of the lesbian baby boom: Children's context with grandparents and other adults. *American Journal of Orthopsychiatry, 68,* 390–399.

Patterson, C. J., & Redding, R. E. (1995). Lesbian and gay families with children: Implications of social science research for policy. *Journal of Social Issues, 52,* 29–50.

PFLAG. (1997). *Annual report, 1996–97.* Washington, DC: Author.

Rila, M., & Reed, B. (1980). *100 bisexual women.* San Francisco: Institute for the Advanced Study of Human Sexuality.

Rofes, E. E. (1994). Making our schools safe for sissies. *The High School Journal, 77*(1–2), 37–40.

Roscoe, W. (1998). *Two-spirit people: Gay American Indians changing ones: Third and fourth genders in Native North America.* London: Macmillan.

Ryan, C., & Futterman, D. (1997). Lesbian and gay youth care and counseling. *Adolescent Medicine: State of the Art Review, 8*(2), 207–374.

Sears, J. T. (1994). Challenges for educators: Lesbian, gay and bisexual families. *The High School Journal, 77*(1–2), 138–156.

Seligman, J. (1993). Variations on a theme. *Newsweek* [special issue on the family], pp. 38–41.

Sherman, S. (Ed.). (1992). *Lesbian and gay marriage: Private commitments, public ceremonies.* Philadelphia: Temple University Press.

Tanner, D. (1978). *The lesbian couple.* Lexington, MA: D.C. Heath.

The 21st century family. (1990, July 4). *New York Times,* pp. 1, 10.

Thorne, B. (1993). *Gender play: Girls and boys together.* New Brunswick, NJ: Rutgers University Press.

U.S. Census Bureau. (1998). Household and family characteristics: March 1997. *Current Population Reports* (pp. 20–509). Washington, DC: U.S. Government Printing Office.

U.S. Census Bureau. (2002, July). *Technical note on same-sex, unmarried partner data, from the 1990 and 2000 censuses.* Washington, DC: U.S. Census Bureau, Population Division, Fertility and Family Statistics Branch.

Westin, K. (1991). *Families we choose: Lesbians, gays, kinship.* New York: Columbia University Press.

Westin, K. (1992). The politics of gay families. In B. Thorne (Ed.), *Rethinking the family: Some feminist questions* (pp. 119–139). Boston: Northeastern University Press.

Whitam, F. L., & Zendt, M. (1984). A cross-cultural assessment of early cross-gender behavior and familial factors in male homosexuality. *Archives of Sexual Behavior, 13,* 427–439.

Wisenkale, S. K. (1992). *Domestic partnerships: Issues and legislation.* New York: Lambda Legal Defense and Education Fund.

Wisenkale, S. K., & Heckart, K. E. (1993). Domestic partnerships. *Family Relations, 42,* 199–204.

Wolfson, E. (1996a). *Bibliography of equal marriage rights for lesbians and gay men.* New York: Lambda Legal Defense and Education Fund.

Wolfson, E. (1996b, January). Why should we fight for the freedom to marry? *Journal of Gay, Lesbian, and Bisexual Identity, 79,* 41–49.

Wolfson, E. (1998). *Anti-marriage measures 1998: A state by state status report.* (Available at www.freedomtomarry.org/archive/lldef/bibliography.html)

Chapter 15

Bader, L. (1998, 2002). *Migrant literacy program report 1998.* [and subsequent reports]. Lansing, MI: The Reading People.

Department of Health and Human Services. (1998). "Changes in Welfare Caseloads, 1993–1998," and "Welfare Caseloads: Families and Recipients, 1960–1998." Washington, DC. (Available at at www.acf.dhhs.gov)

Name Index

A

Abbey, A., 252
ABC Task Force, 306
Abd al-Auhir al Jurjani, 157
Abma, J. C., 211
Aguirre, A., 67, 78, 180
Ahmed, I., 151, 154, 156
Ahrons, C., 254
Akiko, Y., 112
Albert, L., 278
Allen, M., 345
Allen, R., 78–79
Allen, W., 70
Allen-Meares, P., 212
Amato, P., 261
American Civil Liberties Union (ACLU), 344
Ames, M., 338
Amiruddin, B., 154
Anastas, J., 349
Anderson, E. R., 280, 283
Andes, S., 76
Andrews, M. P., 5
Annie B. Casey Foundation, 278
Appleby, G., 349
Applequist, K., 303
Applewhite, A., 250
Arbuthnot, J., 267
Arendell, T., 250, 253, 275, 277, 282
Ashabrannar, B., 157
Asian-American Family Services, 120
Asian Task Force, 136
Aswad, B., 152–153, 154
Atkinson, D., 131

B

Bachrach, C. A., 209, 210, 212, 215, 216, 217, 219, 225
Bachu, A., 248
Bader, L., 367
Bagbee, B., 255
Ballard, P., 263
Barnes, A. S., 217

Barringer, H., 118, 132
Barrow, L., 75, 76
Batten, 232
Baum, K. J., 293
Bearn, A., 306
Beavers, J., 305
Beld, J. M., 263
Bell, D., 80
Bell, R., 70
Bellisimo, A., 252
Benkov, L., 340, 345
Bennett, T., 306
Berger, M., 155
Berger, R. M., 335
Berger, S. H., 290
Berrill, K., 347
Bezirgan, B., 154
Biagini, J., 135
Bigner, J. J., 339, 341
Billings, L., 307, 324
Billingsley, A., 66, 69
"Black Churches on Fire," 72
Boehnlein, R., 119
Bolgar, R., 252
Booth, A., 261
Borkowski, J., 235
Boyce, J., 173
Boyce, W., 173
Boyer, P., 333
Bozette, F., 345
Bozetty Gay, 345
Bramlet, M. D., 247, 248, 277
Bray, J. M., 290
Brenner, A., 253
Brewer, V. E., 278
Briggs, J., 334, 337, 348
Britisch, S., 91
Bronfenbrenner, U., 46–47
Brooks, D., 343–344
Brooks-Gunn, J., 209, 225
Broom, L., 124
Brotherson, S. E., 307

Brown, A., 70
Brown, G., 134
Brown, P., 260
Bruns, D., 306
Bryson, K., 222, 309
Bubolz, M. M., 24, 47, 48
Buck, E., 129
Buehler, C., 249
Burrell, N., 345
Burton, E., 141
Burton, L., 236
Butler, A. C., 334, 337
Buxton, A., 336

C
Cabezas, A., 122, 131
Carlin, J., 135, 136
Carroll, R., 256
Casper, L., 209, 215, 218, 222, 225, 250, 252,
    257, 309
Causey, K. A., 346
Ceballo, R., 252
Ceglian, C. P., 280, 293
Chan, S., 114
Chatters, L., 223
Chavez, L., 103
Cherlin, A., 278, 279, 280, 283
Chief Joseph, 165, 180
Children's Defense Fund, 223, 233, 246, 261, 264
Christensen, S., 293
Chung, D., 116
Church, E., 280
Cleveland, R. W., 229, 249
Coleman, M., 268, 274, 275, 277, 281, 282, 285
Coles, R., 172, 223
Colger, C., 129
Collier, J., 184
Collins, J., 76
Collins, R., 335
Coltrane, S., 335
Compher, J., 264
Connor, J., 129
Connor, M., 305
Coontz, S., 70, 73, 212, 214, 219, 222–223, 229,
    258, 262, 268
"Couples with Ill Children," 308
Cousteau, J.-Y., 358
Cox, M., 254
Cox, R., 254

Cozic, C. P., 90
Creider, R. M., 277
Crosbie-Burnett, M., 285, 345
Crowne, D. T., 338
Curb, J., 130
Curtin, S., 211, 212, 213, 227
Curtis, D., 345

D
Dachman, K., 249
Dalaker, J., 218, 220, 224, 230
Daly, M., 279
D'Amato, R. K., 301
Daniels, R., 124, 128, 131
Darroch, J. A., 227
David, R., 76
Davis, A., 222
Dawson, A., 319
Decker, J., 169
DeLeire, T., 233, 255
Dell, P., 178
Del Pinal, P., 88, 90, 94, 105
De Luca, D., 306
DeMaris, A., 249, 281
DeNavas-Walt, C., 229, 249
Derman-Sparks, L., 306
Devore, W., 136, 137, 139
Diaz-Guerrero, R., 100
Dillard, J., 134, 135
Dilworth-Anderson, P., 236
Dobyns, H., 177
Dollahite, D., 307
Donnelly, D., 252, 253, 278
Dority, B., 16
Dornbush, S., 231
Downey, D., 250
Downing, C., 337
Downs, 210, 211
Dreyer, A., 260
Dudley, J., 252
Due, 227
Dunst, C., 51
Duran-Aydintug, C., 251, 289, 346
Dye, J. L., 230

E
Edin, K., 229
Edmonds, M., 75
Egan, T., 255

Ehrenberg, M. S., 255
Einstein, E., 278
Elia, J., 347
Ellis, L., 338
Engel, M., 125
Ephron, D., 274
Erera-Weatherley, P., 282

F
Falicov, C. J., 87, 92, 97, 105
Farb, P., 179
Farley, R., 70, 131
Feagin, J., 175, 176
Federal Register, 33
Feit, M., 169
Fellner, R. D., 260
Ferguson, J., 224, 233
Fernea, E., 154
Fewell, R. R., 308
Fields, J., 209, 215, 216, 218, 222, 225, 230, 236,
　　250, 252, 257, 276, 277, 341
Fillmore, L., 91
Fine, M. A., 248, 262, 264, 275, 281
Fine, D. R., 262
Finkelhor, D., 252, 253, 278
Forde, D., 70
Forness, S. R., 301
Fost, D., 181
Fox, H., 260
Frazier, F., 72
Freeman, 75
Frisbie, W., 94
Friskopp, A., 347
Frye, K. S., 308
Fu, H., 227
Funmaker, A., 183
Furstenberg, F., 209, 225, 229, 233, 234, 236,
　　251, 278, 280
Furukawa, S., 277
Futterman, D., 350

G
Gamble, V., 75
Gann, H., 128
Ganong, L., 274, 275, 281, 282, 285
Garcia, E. E., 91
Gardner, R., 118
Gardner, S., 280
Gay, R., 246

Gay, Lesbian and Straight Education Network, 350
Genovese, T., 289
George, M. C., 324
Germain, C., 150
Gerrard, I., 291
Gibran, K., 146, 157
Gigy, L., 249
Gilbert, N., 299
Gilbreth, J. G., 283
Giles-Sims, J., 278
Gim, R., 131
Glick, P. C., 274
Goldberg, S., 343–344
Golombok, S., 345
Golonk, S., 220
Goodwin, N., 75
Gordon, D., 267
Gottleib, D., 249
Gottlieb, I., 249
Gottman, J. S., 338
Graff Low, K., 176, 178
Grall, T., 246, 261
Graves, E., 78
Gray, M., 268
Gray, N., 151
Greenburg, M., 308
Greene, S. M., 280
Greenfield, J., 312
Greenspan, M., 306
Greif, G., 249, 281
Griffin, C. W., 341
Griffore, J. R., 49
Grizzle, G. L., 275
Gross, E. R., 167
Guess, J., 71
Guggenheim, M., 345
Guide to American Law, The, 31–33
Guidubaldi, J., 255, 265
Guillemin, J., 170
Gunnison, R., 122

H
Haas, T., 227
Habenstein, R., 65
Haberstroh, 284
Haddad, Y., 150, 155
Hall, E. T., 123, 130
Hall, L. S., 338
Hamer, J., 223

Hamilton-Leaks, J., 222
Handler, A., 76
Hanson, T., 253
Hare, J., 334, 342, 343
Harry, J., 334, 338
Haub, C., 212
Hauser-Cram, P., 324
Havel, V., 4–5
Hawkins, R., 334
Hayes, T., 121
Hayslip, 284
Heckart, K., 340, 344
Helman, C., 199
Helmbrecht, L., 345
Henderson, S., 281, 282
Henshaw, S., 211
Hepworth, I., 260
Herek, G., 347
Hetherington, E., 210, 223, 233, 236, 254, 278,
     281, 282
Ho, C., 115, 134
Ho, M., 80
Hobfall, S. E., 298–299
Hoeffer, B., 334
Hook, N., 47
Hostetler, J. A., 188, 190, 194, 197
Hsia, J., 118
Hu, A., 117
Hudgens, B., 96
Hudgens, L., 298–299
Hughes, L., 64, 72
Human Rights Campaign, 336
Hungry Wolf, A., 175
Hungry Wolf, B., 175
Hunt, S., 346
Huntington, G., 188, 191, 192, 193, 194, 196,
     197, 199

I
Ichioka, Y., 123, 127
Immigration and Naturalization Service, 124
Ingrassia, M., 248
Irvin, L., 305
Isbell, M. T., 309

J
Jayakody, R., 223
Jaynes, G., 68, 76
Jervis, R., 4, 46

Jiobu, R., 132
John, R., 169, 170, 171
Johnson, C. L., 256
Johnson, H. C., 279
Johnston, J. R., 253, 266, 292
Jones, E., 71–72
Jones, S. E., 282
Jordan, W., 65
Joseph. *See* Chief Joseph
Juarez, B., 101

K
Kalil, A., 233, 255
Kavale, K. A., 301
Kavanaugh, K., 139
Kawaguchi, G., 122, 131
Kayal, P., 151
Kelly, J., 249, 251, 253, 254, 260
Kempe, H., 279
Kennedy, C., 284
Kennedy, G., 284
Kennedy, P., 139
Kent, M., 67
Keung Ho, 176
Kheshgi-Genovese, Z., 289
Kim, J.-S., 140
Kim, P., 140
Kinzie, J., 136
Kirkpatrick, M., 338
Kitano, H., 120, 125, 126, 127, 128
Kitsuse, J., 124
Kivlahan, D., 178
Kluegel, R., 72
Koball, H., 252
Koepke, L., 342, 343
Kohlberg, L., 224
Kramer, L., 253
Kuhn, R., 255, 265
Kulkin, H., 349
Kunen, S., 254
Kunimura, D., 129
Kunjufu, J., 74
Kurkowski, K., 267

L
Labi, N., 196
LaDue, R., 182
LaFromboise, T., 176, 178
Lai, H., 113

Lamb, M., 307, 324
Lambda Legal, 334, 339, 340, 347
Lancashire, J., 227, 234
Landsmen, M. J., 235
Langberg, M., 131
Lansford, J. E., 252
Leadership Education for Asian Pacifics, Inc. (LEAP), 119, 122, 133
Leap, W., 166
Lee, E., 116
Legg, B., 249
Lein, L., 229
Leong, F., 121
Lerman, M., 298–299
Lester, G., 261, 262
Leuchtenburg, W., 159
Leung, P., 136
Levin, M., 118
Leving, J., 249
Lewis, E. A., 285
Lewis, R. G., 169
Lim, G., 113
Lindblad-Goldberg, M., 69
Lobato, D. J., 324
Locke, D. C., 200
Lopez-Hernandez, C., 224, 233
Lowe, A., 345
Ludwig, T. E., 291
Lummis, A., 150, 155
Lyons, J., 92

M
Maccoby, E., 244, 246, 255
Maglin, N., 280, 281, 286
Mail, P., 177
Mann, T., 67
Manson, S., 178
Marable, M., 70
Marden, C., 125
Martin, J. A., 212, 213
Martin, P., 87, 90, 281
Mason, M., 278, 287, 288, 346
Mass, A., 129
Massaquoi, H., 68, 69
Mathews, T. J., 211, 212, 213, 227
Mattison, A., 332, 346, 348
Mauer, M., 68
Mauldon, J., 288
May, J., 306
McAdoo, H. P., 70, 222, 223, 234

McAdoo, J. B., 66
McAdoo, J. L., 66, 70, 222, 234
McDonald, L., 307
McFarlane, A., 252
McKerry, P., 282
McLanahan, S. S., 253
McNurlen, G., 319
McWhirter, D., 332, 346, 348
Mei, J., 113
Mercer, L., 335
Meyer, G., 125
Mickelson, K., 324
Midgley, E., 87, 90
Milicia, J., 196, 198, 200
Miller, B., 334
Miller, F., 130
Miller, G., 264
Millic, J. H., 338
Mindel, C., 65
Mnookin, R., 244, 246, 255
Monterrey, M., 93
Moore, L., 119
Moore, T., 122
Moran, P., 342
Morgan, S. P., 225
Morrow, R., 135
Moses, A., 334
Mosher, W. D., 211, 247, 248
Mosier, W. D., 277
Mosley, J., 253
Moyers, W., 223
Moynihan, D. P., 218, 222, 226
Mullins, J., 305
Mulroy, E., 230, 231, 258
Murray, C., 345
Murray, J., 307
Murray, V. M., 220, 226, 234
Mylod, D., 235

N
Naff, A., 149, 159
Nagata, D., 135
Nakanishi, D., 118, 121
National Cancer Institute, 75
National Center for Education Statistics, 73, 74, 175
National Center for Health Statistics, 68, 75
National Commission on Children, 220, 225, 226, 229, 232, 247, 261
National Indian Council on Aging (NICA), 171

National Information Center for Children and Youth
 with Disabilities, 310
National Institutes of Health, 68
Neigh, 178
Nelson, K., 235
Newberger, C., 224
Newman, B., 282
Newton, B., 129
Nguyen, S., 119
Nicassio, P., 119
Nielsen, L., 280
Noakes, G., 161
Nord, C. W., 278
Norman, G. R., 252

O
O'Connell, M., 248
Office of Minority Health, 119
Office of Refugee Resettlement, 133
Office of the U.S. Surgeon General, 105
Ogawa, D., 126
O'Hare, W., 67, 79
Olmos, J. E., 93, 94
O'Neill, G., 230, 251
Orchard, A. L., 280
Osborn, T., 337, 341, 342, 345, 346
Oscarson, 293
Oswald, R. F., 346

P
Paige, J., 166
Palumbo, G., 246
Paniagua, F., 174
Paolucci, B., 47
Pappernow, P., 275, 290
Parillo, V., 175, 181
Paris, J., 252
Parnell, M., 255
Patai, R., 157
Patterson, C., 343, 345, 346
Paulsen, D. J., 278
Peck, R., 100
Perrin, E. C., 349
Peterson, J. L., 278
Phenice, L., 49
Philip, 151
Pianta, R., 224, 233
Pierce, C., 71
Pinker, S., 13
Pollard, K., 67

Population Reference Bureau, 8
Powell, B., 250
Principe, D., 252
Proctor, B. D., 218, 220, 224, 230
Profit, W., 71
Pruett, K., 307

Q
Quinn, S., 75

R
Raisner, J. K., 239
Ranjit, N., 227
Rawlings, S. W., 214
Redfield, R., 190
Red Horse, J., 169–170, 171
Reed, B., 334
Reed, D., 130
Reyhner, J., 167
Rhein, L., 234
Rhodes, G., 222
Richards, L., 334, 343
Richardson, C., 93
Rila, M., 334
Rock-Faucheux, A., 254
Rofes, E., 258, 350
Rogers, R., 254
Roland, A., 129, 141
Roseby, V., 253, 266, 292
Rosen, K. H., 311
Rothlisberg, B., 301
Rumbaut, J., 93
Rush, F., 279
Ruth, J. R., 192
Ryan, C., 350
Ryan, E., 220
Ryder, R., 171, 260

S
Saluter, A., 218
Sanders, G. F., 290
Sarbaugh, L., 44
Schachtman, T., 189
Schaefer, S. A., 251
Schafer, R., 65
Scherman, A., 256
Schiraldi, V., 77
Schlesinger, E., 136, 137, 139
Schneidewind, N., 280, 281, 286
Scholsberg, D., 129

Schorr, L., 213, 235
Schultz, G., 116
Schultz, T. P., 54, 55–56, 57
Schutter, M., 256
Scommegna, P., 216, 284
Scoon-Rogers, L., 261, 262
Scott, S., 190, 196
Scully, J., 178
Sears, J., 345
Seligman, J., 332
Seltzer, J., 253
Sevier, S. F., 281
Shabbas, A., 155, 156
Sherman, S., 331, 336, 340, 341, 343, 348
Shim, E., 260
Shim, M. K., 260
Shoho, A., 130
Silverstein, S., 347
Simmons, T., 230, 251
Simon, R., 312
Singer, A., 88, 90, 94, 105
Singer, G., 305
Skopin, A., 282
Slavin, M., 249
Slobin, D., 13
Smith, A. W., 66
Smith, C., 306
Smith, G., 78
Smith, K., 129
Smith, S., 227, 234
Smith, W., 275
Snell, S. A., 311
Snipp, C., 169, 170, 171, 180
Sokoloff, B., 135, 136
Solberg, K. B., 280
Solinger, R., 208, 212, 217, 218
Sontag, S., 24, 47, 48
Sorensen, E., 222, 223
Southern Poverty Law center, 336
Spanier, C., 278
"Special Ed's Special Costs," 317
Stamps, L., 254
Staples, R., 70, 71
Stavans, I., 87, 89, 90, 91, 92, 103
Steisel, S., 220
Stephens, S. A., 232
Stewart, A. J., 248, 252
Stewart, S. D., 284
Story, M., 228, 229

Strober, M., 231
Strong, E., 125
Stump, B., 282
Sudarkasa, N., 69
Suleiman, M., 161
Suzuki, L., 123
Sweig-Frank, H., 252

T
Takaki, R., 113
Tang, J., 122
Tanner, D., 336
Taylor, R., 223
Teitler, J., 251
Tesker, 345
Teun, A. D., 45
Thomas, S., 75
Thompson, P., 284
Thomson, E., 253
Thorne, B., 343
Trimble, J., 178
Trivette, C., 51
True, R., 116, 120
Trygstad, D. W., 290
Tsuchida, N., 120
Tsui, P., 116
Tucker, M., 223
Turner, J., 67, 78, 180
Turner, W. L., 236
Tutu, D., 368
"21st Century Family, The," 331

U
Uba, L., 119, 120, 129, 134
U.S. Bureau of Indian Affairs, 166, 175
U.S. Commission on Civil Rights, 118, 120
U.S. Department of Health and Human Services, 168, 177, 178, 364
U.S. Department of Housing and Urban Development, 231
U.S. Department of Justice, 124
U.S. Government Printing Office, 33
U.S. Pan Asian-American Chamber of Commerce, 114, 121
U.S. Public Health Service, 177

V
Ventura, S. J., 209, 210, 211, 212, 213, 215, 216, 217, 219, 225, 227
Visher, E., 279

Visher, J. S., 279
Vogel, V., 177, 183
Vogt, T. R., 279, 283

W
Walker, R., 178, 182
Wall, S., 76
Wallerstein, J. S., 251, 253, 254, 260, 264
Ward, M., 300
Warfield, M. E., 324
Washburn, W., 177
Washo, C., 253
Watson, P. A., 280
Westin, K., 336, 346
White, L., 280, 282, 283
Whitehead, B. D., 249
White House Domestic Policy Council, 229
Whitely, S., 131
Whitman, T., 235, 338
Widmer, E. D., 274
Wilkinson, D., 65
Willford, C., 161
Williams, C. W., 212, 222, 223, 224, 226, 232, 234
Williams, R., 68, 76
Wilson, M. I., 279
Wilson, W. J., 218, 219

Wirth, A., 341
Wirth, M., 341
Wisenkale, S., 340, 344
Wittmer, J., 193
Wohl, 284
Wojtkiewicz, R. A., 214
Wolf, R., 221
Wolf, W. C., 232
Wolfson, E., 336, 347
Wright, R., 65
Wyche, K. F., 324

Y
Yamashiro, C., 123
Yanagisako, S., 126, 127
Yano, K., 130
Ybarra, L., 93
Yellowbird, M., 169, 170, 171
Young, S.-K., 138
Yung, J., 113

Z
Zendt, M., 338
Zenner, W., 160
Zibman, C., 222, 223
Zinn, M. B., 250

Subject Index

A

Aboriginal Americans. *See* Native American families
Abortion, 210, 217, 219, 226, 227, 232
Abstinence, 226
Acculturated Native American family, 170
Acculturation
    Arab American families, 150, 151, 153, 154, 156
    Asian Americans, 113, 115, 116, 122, 142
    Japanese Americans, 123, 125–129, 130, 131
    Native American families, 169, 170, 171, 175, 176
    Vietnamese Americans, 136
Adaptation, 48–49
    families with children with special needs, 319–321
    gay and lesbian families, 349
    stepfamilies, 290–291
    teenage single-parent families, 233–235
Adolescence, in Amish culture, 195–196
Adolescent parents. *See* Teenage single-parent families
Adoption, 216–217, 337, 343, 344, 347, 350
Adult education, 28
Adulthood, in Amish culture, 196–197
Advocacy, 367
Aesthetics
    divorced single-parent families, 258
    families with children with special needs, 312
    stepfamilies, 285–286
Affirmative action, 32, 76
African American families, 64–65, 80
    criminal justice system and, 77
    demographic information, 67–68
    divorced single-parent families, 247, 250
    economic system and, 77–79
    educational system and, 72–74
    family ecosystem, 68–71
    governmental system and, 76
    health care system and, 74–76
    historical background, 65–66
    serving, 79–80
    stepfamilies, 276, 277, 284, 285
    teenage single-parent families, 211–212,
      217, 218–219, 222, 223, 226, 232
    values, 71–72
Age Discrimination in Employment Act, 33

Ageism, 26
Agency forms, inadequacy of, 291
Agriculture
    Amish families, 192, 200
    Native Americans, 180, 183
Aiding Leukemia Stricken American Children, 159
AIDS Memorial quilt, 333
Aid to Families with Dependent Children (AFDC),
    33, 219, 230, 231, 232, 246
Alcohol consumption, 228
Alien Land Laws, 126
ALSAC, 158–159
Amerasian Homecoming Act, 133
Amerasian Immigration Act, 133
Amerasians, 119, 133, 135
American Arab Anti-Discrimination Committee, 161
American Bar Association, 316
American Civil Liberties Union (ACLU), 335–336
American Indian Citizenship Act, 167
American Indians. *See* Native American families
American Lebanese Syrian Associated Club, 159
American Psychiatric Association, 338
American Psychological Association, 338
Americans with Disabilities Act, 32, 33, 309,
    315–316, 321
Amerinds. *See* Native American families
Amish families, 188
    agricultural enterprises, 192
    background, 188–191
    behavior codes, obedience to, 192–193
    community organization, 193
    conclusions, 201–202
    demographic information, 191
    economic system and, 200
    educational system and, 198
    family ecology, 191–197
    family service, 200–201
    family structure, 193–194
    governmental system and, 200
    health care system and, 199
    historical background, 189–191
    language, 193
    life stages, 194–197

religious system and, 198–199
respect for, 201
Amish High German, 193
Amman, Jacob, 189
Analytic parental style, 224
Angel Island, 113
Anglos, 87, 88, 93, 100
Arab American families, 146
conclusions, 161–162
economic system and, 159–160
educational system and, 157–158
family ecology, 150–156
governmental system and, 159
health care system and, 158–159
historical background, 146–150
serving, 160–161
values, 156–157
Arabic language, 147, 148, 160
Arab–Israeli conflicts, 151
Articles of Confederation, 179
Asian American families, 112
conclusions, 141–142
demographic information, 114–115
divorced single-parent families, 248
economic system and, 121–122
educational system and, 117–118
family ecology, 115–116
governmental system and, 120–121
health care system and, 119–120
historical background of, 113–114
Japanese Americans, 122–132
Korean Americans, 122, 137–140
serving, 140–141
stepfamilies, 276, 277
teenage single-parent families, 212, 213, 218
values, 116–117
Vietnamese Americans, 122, 132–137
Assimilation, of Native Americans, 166, 168, 169, 175, 176, 178, 179. See also Acculturation
Assimilation period, 182
Association for Retarded Citizens of the United States (ARC), 324

B
Baehr v. Mike, 339
Baptism, in Amish families, 188, 190, 195, 196, 199
Barrios, 97
Beachy Amish, 190, 191
Behavior codes, in Amish families, 192–193

"Best interests of the child" doctrine, 254–255
Bicultural attainment, 103
Biculturalism, 103, 106, 127–128, 132
Bicultural Native American family, 170
Bifocal family, 254
Bigotry, 16
Bilingual attainment, 103
Bilingual Education Act, 91
Binuclear families, 254. See also Stepfamilies
Biological families, 45
Biological parents, parenting classes and education for, 238
Birthrates, 209, 210, 211–213, 214, 215, 218, 219
Bisexual, 334, 335, 342, 347
Blended families, 277, 280, 285, 294
Boat people, 132
Boricua label, 90
Braschi v. Stahl Association Company, 340, 344
Brown v. Board of Education of Topeka, Kansas, 25, 72
Budget Reconciliation Act, 223, 261
Bumblebee generation, 128. See also Sansei
Bush, George W., 76, 226

C
Career goals, 34–35
Careers
family service and, 6–7
family service, 28–29
globalization and, 6
See also Economic factors
Caregiving function, 52–53
Caribbean Hispanics. See Hispanic Americans
Castro, Fidel, 89, 104
Celebrations, 269
Central American Hispanics. See Hispanic Americans
Chicano label, 90
Child care, 28
Child Find, 318
Children
African American, 70–71
Amish families, 194–195
Arab American families, 152–153, 155–156, 157–158
Asian American families, 115, 116
divorced single-parent families, 246–248, 250–251, 253–256, 259–260
gay and lesbian families, 345
Hispanic American families, 96–98, 99

Children (*Continued*)
 Korean American families, 138
 Native American families, 171–173
 stepfamilies, 278, 282–283
 teenage single-parent families, 224
Children Act of 1989, 288
Children's Defense Fund, 246
Children with special needs. *See* Families with children
 with special needs
Child Support Enforcement Division, 264
Chinese Exclusion Act, 113
Chinese immigrants, 113. *See also* Asian American
 families
Civil rights. *See* Rights
Civil Rights Act of 1964—Title VII, 31, 57
Clinton, William Jefferson, 161, 303, 333–334,
 342, 358
Cohabitation
 divorced single-parent families, 247, 248, 253
 stepfamilies, 275, 284, 293
 teenage single-parent families, 215–216, 217, 236
Colonias, 97
Columbus Day celebrations, 176
Communal cohesion, in Arab American families, 157
Communication, 44–45
 Arab Americans, 160–161
 Asian American families, 141
 divorced single-parent families, 256
Community
 Amish families, 193
 Asian American families, 129
 family service and, 359
 Hispanic families, 97–98
 resources, 51
Conference on the Family (1990), 333
Conflict, 17
Conflict resolution, 27
Conservative Arab Americans, 150
Context, 129–130
Continuing education, 26
Contraceptives, 212, 227, 229, 234
Conventional parental style, 224
Conversion therapy, 338
Cooperation, 51, 99, 101, 198
Criminal justice system, African American families, 77
Cuban Hispanics. *See* Hispanic Americans
Cuban revolution (1959), 89
Cultural values. *See* Values
Culture, 13

Cuomo, Mario, 161
Current Population Survey (CPS), 276
Custodial parents, 281, 289, 291
Custody. *See* Joint custody

D
Daughters, impact of divorce on, 250–251
Daughters of Bilitus, 333
Death rituals, in Amish culture, 197
Decision making, 50–51
Dedication, 366
Defense of Marriage Act (DOMA), 333–334, 339
Deficit model, 311–312
Democratic Party, 76, 118, 121, 131
Demographics, 8–11, 12
 African American families, 67–68
 Amish families, 191
 Asian American families, 114–115, 142
 divorced single-parent families, 248, 256–258
 families with children with special needs,
  309–311
 Hispanic American families, 86–88, 93–94
 Native American families, 167–168
 stepfamilies, 284–285
 teenage single-parent families, 211–219, 225
Diet, 228, 229
Differential birthrates, 212–213
Disabilities. *See* Families with children with special
  needs; Individuals with disabilities
Discipline, 116–117, 194
Discrimination, 16, 26
 African American families, 65
 Arab American families, 146, 158
 communication and, 45
 criminal justice system and, 77
 family service and, 359, 367, 368
 federal laws, 31, 32, 33
 gay and lesbian families, 333, 335, 337, 339,
  342, 347, 351
 Native American families, 166, 176, 182
Dissent, 16
Diversity, 7–8, 15
 demographics and, 8–11, 12
 discrimination and, 26
 family definitions and, 24
 family service and, 360–361
 human capital and, 57–58
 minority group membership, 14–15
 peaceful accommodation and, 16–17

workforce, 25–27
See also African American families; Amish fami-
    lies; Arab American families; Asian American
    families; Gay and lesbian families; Hispanic
    American families; Native American families
Divorce
    no-fault, 245, 246, 251, 262
    stages of, 265
Divorced single-parent families, 244
    aesthetics, 258
    children, 246–248, 253–256, 259–260
    conclusions, 269
    demographics, 256–258
    economic impacts, 261–263
    education and reeducation, 258–260
    family ecology, 256–264
    governmental policies and agencies, 263–264
    health care impacts, 261
    historical background, 245
    housing impacts, 263
    kinship networks and interactions, 264–266
    laws, 262–263
    no-fault divorce, 245
    property settlement, 245–246
    religion, 260–261
    serving, 267–269
    sociocultural foundations, 248–253
Domestic partnerships, 335, 337, 339, 340, 347
Due process, 30

E

Early Intervention Act, 301
Early intervention program, 301, 302, 321
Early Intervention Services, 302
Economic development, on reservations, 181
Economic factors
    African American families, 77–79, 218
    Amish families, 200
    Arab American families, 159–160
    Asian American families, 115, 121–122
    divorced single-parent families, 246, 247,
        249–250, 261–263, 264
    families with children with special needs,
        315–317
    family service and, 362–365
    Hispanic American families, 104
    Japanese American families, 131–132
    Native American families, 179–181
    stepfamilies, 278, 287–288

teenage single-parent families, 220–222, 224,
    229–230, 230, 234, 235
Economic function, 53–54
Education for All Handicapped Children Act, 32, 300
Education of the Handicapped Act, 301
Education of the Handicapped Amendments, 299
Education, 6, 26, 28
    African American families, 72–74
    Amish families, 198
    Arab American families, 157–158
    Asian American families, 117–118
    divorced single-parent families, 258–260
    families with children with special needs, 313–314
    Hispanic American families, 96–97, 101–103
    human capital and, 54–55
    Japanese American families, 130
    Korean American families, 139
    Native American families, 175–177
    stepfamilies, 286
    teenage single-parent families, 225–226
    Vietnamese American families, 135
Egotistical parental style, 224
Elderly
    African American families, 75–76, 78
    Amish families, 197
    Arab American families, 155
    Asian American families, 116, 119, 142
    divorced single-parent families, 256–257
    family service, 28
    family types, 42, 43
    Hispanic American families, 97
    Japanese American families, 129, 131
    Korean American families, 139–140
    Native American families, 171, 174, 178
    socialization and caregiving, 52–53
    Vietnamese American families, 134, 136
Emotional divorce, 265
Emotional support function, 53
Employers, family-friendly, 28–29
Employment. *See* Economic factors; Workforce
Employment rates, 24, 25
Employment-related laws, 31, 32, 33
Empowerment, 50–52, 57–58
Endurance, 157
Energy, 366
English-only legislation, 92
E Pluribus Unum, 14
Equal Pay Act, 31, 56–57
Ethnic, definition of, 65

Ethnic diversity. *See* African American families; Amish families; Arab American families; Asian American families; Diversity; Hispanic American families; Native American families
Ethnocentric ideas, 45
Evangelical Arab Americans, 150
Excommunication, 196, 199
Executive Order 9066, 120
Executive Order 11246, 32, 76
Executive Order 11375, 32
Exosystems, 46, 47
Expression, literary, 157
Extended families
    Arab Americans, 151
    divorced single-parent families, 255–256, 264–266
    families with children with special needs, 308–309, 318–319
    gay and lesbian families, 346
    Hispanic Americans, 97–98
    Native American families, 170–171
    stepfamilies, 280, 281, 284, 289, 290
    teenage single-parent families, 222, 229, 232–233

F
Fair Housing Act, 31
Fair Labor Standards Act, 32
Families
    adaptation, 48–49
    biological, 45
    deficits of, 36–37
    defining, 24–25
    demographics and, 8–11, 12
    federal laws and, 30–33
    functional, 45
    globalization and, 5
    interpersonal, 45
    legal, 45
    rights of, 29–30
    similarities between, 13
    state and local laws, 34
    strengths of, 36–37, 50
    types of, 42–43
    uniqueness of, 11–13
    values, 49–50
    See also African American families; Amish families; Arab American families; Asian American families; Divorced single-parent families; Gay

and lesbian families; Hispanic American families; Native American families; Stepfamilies; Teenage single-parent families
Families with children with special needs, 298
    aesthetics, 312
    changes and adaptations, 319–321
    conclusions, 325
    deficit model, 311–312
    demographics, 309–311
    economic factors, 315–317
    education, 313–314
    family service, 298–299, 321–325
    government policies and agencies, 318
    health care system, 314–315
    historical backgrounds, 300–304
    housing, 317
    kinship networks and interactions, 318–319
    religion, 314
    sociocultural foundations, 304–309
Family and Medical Leave Act, 33
Family ecology, 47
    African American families, 68–71
    Amish families, 191–197
    Arab American families, 150–156
    Asian American families, 115–116
    divorced single-parent families, 256–264
    family service and, 361
    gay and lesbian families, 346–349
    Hispanic American families, 92
    Japanese American families, 122–124
    Korean American families 137–139
    Native American families, 168–174
    stepfamilies, 284–289
    Vietnamese American families, 132–135
Family ecosystem, 47–48, 50, 57–58
Family-friendly employers, 28–29
Family functions, 52–54
Family planning, 227, 229, 240, 261, 315
Family practices, of Native American families, 169–170
Family-related sciences, 35–36
Family relationships. *See* Relationships
Family service, 358
    advocacy, 367
    African American families, 79–80
    Amish families, 200–201
    Arab American families, 160–161
    Asian American families, 140–141
    career goals, 34–35

careers and, 6–7
community, 359
conclusions, 367–368
dedication, 366
discrimination and, 367
diversity, 360–361
divorced single-parent families, 267–269
economic factors and, 362–365
energy, 366
families with children with special needs,
    298–299, 321–325
family ecology concepts and, 361
flexibility, 366–367
gay and lesbian families, 349–350
giving, 359–360
goals, 359
Hispanic American families, 105–106
honesty, 365
humility, 365
Native American families, 182–183
professional, 35
stepfamilies, 291–293
teenage single-parent families, 235–238
Family structure
    African American families, 68–70
    Amish families, 193–194
    Arab American families, 151–153
    Asian American families, 115–116
    Hispanic American families, 93–94
    Japanese American families, 123–124
    Korean American families, 137–139
    Native American families, 168–169
    stepfamilies, 274–276
    Vietnamese American families 133–135
Family Support Act of 1988, 262
Family systems, 43–44, 45–48
Farming. See Agriculture
Fecundity, 212
Federal Bureau of Investigation (FBI), 333, 336
Federal Insurance Contributions Act, 32
Federal laws, 30–33, 301–302, 321. See also specific
    legislation
Federation of States, 179
Feedback, 49
Fellowship, 196
Female roles
    Arab American families, 153–155
    families with children with special needs,
        306–307

gay and lesbian families, 342–343
Hispanic American families, 95–96
Japanese Americans, 129
Korean American families, 138, 139
stepfamilies, 280–281
teenage single-parent families, 222
Vietnamese American families, 134
See also Gender roles; Women
Feminists, 333, 342
Feminization of poverty, 233
Fetal alcohol syndrome (FAS), 228, 305
Fictive kin, 236
Field-sensitive learning style, 96–97
First Amendment, 29, 30
Fisher, Barbie, 189
Fisher, Marian, 189
Five Pillars of Islam, 148–149
Flexibility, 366–367
Flextime, 28–29
Food Stamp program, 228, 231, 232
Ford Foundation, 77
Forms, inadequacy of, 291
Four circles, 178
Fourteenth Amendment, 29, 30
Franklin, Benjamin, 179
Friends. See Kinship networks and interactions
Functional families, 45
Funmaker, Alexarae, 183

G
Gay Activist Alliance (GAA), 333
Gay and lesbian families, 331–332
    changes and adaptations, 349
    children, 345
    conclusions, 350
    extended families, 346
    family ecology, 346–349
    female roles, 342–343
    historical background, 332–335
    legal status, 339–340
    male roles, 343–345
    public disclosure, 340–341
    religion, 348–349
    serving, 349–350
    sociocultural foundations, 335–342
    status, 337
    support groups, 341–342
Gay and Lesbian Parents Coalition International
        (GLPCI), 335

Gay Rights Project, 335
GED (General Equivalency Diploma), 221, 225,
    232, 240
Gender differences, related to divorce, 249–250,
    251–252
Gender roles
    African American families, 70
    Amish families, 194
    Arab American families, 153–155
    Asian American families, 115–116, 118
    families with children with special needs,
        306–308
    gay and lesbian families, 342–345
    Hispanic American families, 93, 94–96
    Japanese American families, 129
    Korean American families, 138, 139
    stepfamilies, 280–282
    teenage single-parent families, 222–223
    Vietnamese American families, 134, 135–136
    See also Women
Generational model, 125–128
"Gentleman's Agreement, A," 124
Geographic information. See Demographics
GI Bill, 55
Giving, 359–360
Glass, David H., 218
Glass ceiling, 27
GLBT, 342
Globalization, 4–6, 17
Goals, of family service, 359
Government contracts, 32
Government in the Sunshine Act, 33
Governmental system
    African American families, 76
    Amish families, 200
    Arab American families, 159
    Asian American families, 120–121
    divorced single-parent families, 263–264
    families with children with special needs, 318
    Hispanic American families, 103–104
    Japanese American families, 131
    Native American families, 179
    stepfamilies, 288–289
    teenage single-parent families, 231–232
    Vietnamese American families 136–137
Grandparents, as substitute parents, 309. See also
    Extended families
Grief, 254, 263, 267, 323–325
Guttmacher Institute, 223, 234

H
Hate crimes, 72
Head Start, 12, 231, 237
Head Start Parent Advisory Councils, 237
Health care system
    African American families, 74–76
    Amish families, 199
    Arab American families, 158–159
    Asian American families, 119–120
    divorced single-parent families, 261
    families with children with special needs, 314–315
    Hispanic American families, 105
    Japanese American families, 130–131
    Korean American families, 139–140
    Native American families, 173, 177–178
    stepfamilies, 287
    teenage single-parent families, 226–229
    Vietnamese American families 135–136
High-context culture, 123, 129–130
Higher education, 102–103
Hispanic American families, 85, 106
    children's roles in, 96–98
    divorced single-parent families, 247, 248
    economic system and, 104
    education, 101–103
    family ecology, 92
    family structures, 93–94
    female roles in, 95–96
    geographic information, 86–87
    governmental system and, 103–104
    health care system and, 105
    history, 85–88
    male roles in, 94–95
    migration, 88–89
    population data, 87–88
    prejudice against, 89–90
    religious foundation of, 92–93
    serving, 105–106
    similarities and differences between, 90–92
    Spanish language, 90–92
    stepfamilies, 276, 277
    teenage single-parent families, 211–213, 214,
        215, 216, 218, 219, 222, 223, 224
    values, 98–101
Historical background
    African American families, 65–66
    Amish families, 189–191
    Arab American families, 146–150
    Asian American families, 113–114

divorced single-parent families, 245
gay and lesbian families, 332–335
Hispanic American families, 85–88
Native American families, 167
stepfamilies, 276–277
families with children with special needs,
    300–304
Holism, 65
Homophobia, 336, 344
Homosexual families. *See* Gay and lesbian families
Homosexuality, reasons for, 337–338
Honesty, 365
Honor, 153, 154, 156, 157
Horizontal relationships, 115
House Bill 479, 218
Housing
    divorced single-parent families, 263
    families with children with special needs, 317
    teenage single-parent families, 230–231
Housing designs, 231
Human-built environment, 47, 48
Human capital, 54–57
Human ecological system, 46–47
Human ecosystem, 47
Human rights, 4, 5, 15, 17, 18
Humility, 365
Hwas-byung, 139

I

Immigration
    Arab American families, 146, 149–150, 153,
        159, 161
    Asian Americans, 113–114, 117, 122, 141, 142
    Hispanic Americans, 88–90
    Japanese Americans, 123, 124, 125
    Korean Americans, 137, 138–139
    Vietnamese Americans, 132, 133
Immigration Act (1924), 124
Immigration and Naturalization Act, 137
Incest, 227
Inclusive environments, 313–314
Indian Child Welfare Act, 182
Indian Health Care Improvement Act, 182
Indian Religious Freedom Act, 182
Indian Removal Bill, 179
Indian Self-Determination Act, 182
Indian Territory, 179
Indigenous peoples, 165, 166. *See also* Native
    American families

Individualized education program (IEP), 300, 301,
    302, 303, 306, 313
Individualized family service plan (IFSP), 299, 302,
    306, 308, 309, 323
Individualized Functional Assessment (IFA), 316
Individual rights, 29–30. *See also* Rights
Individuals with disabilities, laws related to, 32, 33.
    See also Families with children with special
    needs
Individuals with Disabilities Education Act (IDEA),
    299, 301–302, 303, 304, 305, 313
Infancy, in Amish families, 194
Infanticide, 154
Information gathering, about teenage single-parent
    families, 237–238
In loco parentis, 287
Inouye, Daniel, 131
Institutional racism. *See* Racism
Insurance. *See* Health care system
Integration, 25
Interagency councils, 302
Intercultural communication, 44–45
    Arab Americans, 160–161
    Asian American families, 141
International Year of the Family, 358
Internment, of Japanese Americans, 122, 123, 124,
    126, 127, 128, 131
Interpersonal families, 45
Iroquois Nation, 179, 183
Islam, 147–149, 150, 153, 154. *See also* Religion
Issei, 125–127, 128, 130

J

Japanese American families, 122
    acculturation, 125–129
    economic system and, 131–132
    educational system and, 130
    family ecology, 122–124
    family structure, 123–124
    gender roles, 129
    generational model, 125–128
    governmental system and, 131
    health care system and, 130–131
    values, 129–130
    World War II internment, 120, 122, 123, 124,
        126, 127, 128, 131
    See also Asian American families
Job sharing, 29
Johnson, Lyndon B., 32, 218

Joint legal custody, 251–252, 253, 255, 262, 264
Joint physical custody, 249, 250, 252, 255, 266

K
Kennedy, John F., 6
Kinsey Report, 332–333
Kinship networks and interactions
    divorced single-parent families, 264–266
    families with children with special needs,
        318–319
    stepfamilies, 289
    teenage single-parent families, 232–233
Korean American families, 122, 137–140
    educational system and, 139
    family ecology, 137–139
    health care system and, 139–140
    religious system and, 140
    See also Asian American families

L
Labor force. *See* Economic factors
Lamba Legal Defense and Education Fund, 335, 347
Languages
    Amish, 193
    Arabic, 147, 148, 160
    Native American, 166, 175
    Spanish, 90–92
La Raza, 90
Latino label, 90
Lawrence v. Texas, 339
Laws
    divorced single-parent families, 262–263
    federal, 30–33, 301–302, 321
    state and local, 34
    See also specific legislation
League of Arab States, 147
League of the Iroquois Confederacy, 179, 183
Learning Disabilities Association (LDA), 324
Learning environments, for children with special
        needs, 305–306
Least restrictive environment (LRE), 300
Legal custody, joint, 251–252, 253, 255, 262, 264
Legal divorce, 265
Legal families, 45
Legal guardians, 238, 288, 292
Legal issues, in divorced single-parent families,
        262–263
Legal rights, 29–33, 154
Legal status, of gay and lesbian families, 339–340

Lesbian families. *See* Gay and lesbian families
Liberal Arab Americans, 150
Life expectancy, 56–57
Life stages, in Amish families, 194–197
Literary expression, 157
Local laws, 34
Loyalty, 100

M
MacArthur Foundation, 77
Macrosystems, 46, 47
Mainstreaming, 300–301
Male roles
    divorce and, 250–251
    families with children with special needs,
        307–308
    gay and lesbian families, 343–345
    Hispanic American families, 94–95
    Japanese Americans, 129
    Korean American families, 138, 139
    stepfamilies, 281–282
    teenage single-parent families, 222–223
    Vietnamese American families, 134
    See also Gender roles
Manford, Jeanne, 335
Manifest Destiny, 182
March on Washington for Gay and Lesbian Rights
        (1987), 340
Marriage
    Amish culture, 196
    patterns, 213–216, 217
    See also Demographics; Gender roles
Marriage Project, 347
Marvin v. Marvin, 340
Matriarchal tribes, 169
Matriarchy, 218
Matrilineal tribes, 168, 169
Matrilocal tribes, 169
McCarthy era, 333
Meaning, shared, 44
Medicaid, 228, 264
Meidung (shunning), 191, 196, 199
Mennonite Church, 190, 191
Mental health care
    Arab American families, 159
    Asian American families, 119–120, 131, 135, 139
    divorced single-parent families, 261
    Native American families, 173, 178
    See also Health care system

Mesosystems, 46, 47
Metropolitan Community Church, 348
Mexican Americans. *See* Hispanic Americans
Microsystems, 46, 47
Migration, of Hispanics, 88–89
Minority, definition of, 65
Minority groups, membership in, 14–15. *See also*
     African American families; Amish families;
     Arab American families; Asian American fami-
     lies; Diversity; Hispanic American families;
     Native American families
Miss Indian World Pageant, 183
Monogamy, 154
Morales, Pablo, 101
Moyers, Bill, 223
Moynihan Report, 218

N

National Center for Health Statistics, 248
National Commission on Children, 232
National Committee for Amish Religious Freedom, 200
National Conference of Catholic Bishops, 93
National Congress for Fathers and Children, 263
National Consumer Expenditure Surveys, 246
National Federation of Parents and Friends of
     Gays, 346
National Gay and Lesbian Task Force (NGLTF),
     335, 347
National Indian Council on Aging, 171
National Rehabilitation Information Center, 316
National Research Act, 33
National Stepfamily Resource Center, 293
National Study of Family Growth, 234
Native American families, 165
     background, 165–168
     children and youth, 171–173
     conclusions, 183–184
     demographic information, 167–168
     economic system and, 179–181
     educational system and, 175–177
     elders, 171
     extended families, 170–171
     family ecology, 168–174
     family practices, 169–170
     family service, 182–183
     family structures, 168–169
     governmental system and, 179
     health care system and, 177–178
     historical background, 167

stepfamilies, 276, 277
     teenage single-parent families, 212, 213, 236
     values, 173–174
Native peoples, 183
Natural physical–biological environment, 47
Negative feedback, 49
Neonormative Arab Americans, 150
Neotraditional Native American family, 170
Never-married parents, 208, 209–211
     change and adaptation, 233–235
     children, socialization of, 224
     conclusions, 238–239
     demographics, 211–219, 225
     economic factors, 229–230
     economic status, 220–222
     education, 225–226
     family service, 235–238
     female roles, 222
     governmental policies and agencies, 231–232
     health care system and, 226–229
     housing, 230–231
     kinship networks and interactions, 232–233
     male roles, 222–223
     religion, 226
     societal concern and debate, 208–209
     sociocultural foundations, 219–220
Nisei, 125, 127–128
Nixon, Richard M., 167
No Child Left Behind (NCLB), 303, 304
No-fault divorce, 245, 246, 251, 262
Nonconfrontation, 174
Noninterference, 174
Nonresident stepparents, 281, 284
Nonviolence, 190
Nursing homes, 75–76
Nutrition, 55–56, 228, 229

O

Observation, of teenage single-parent families, 237
Occupational Safety and Health Act, 32
Office of Faith-Based Initiatives, 226
Official Weighted Poverty Thresholds (U.S. Census
     Bureau), 67
Old Order Amish, 189–190. *See also* Amish families
Open system, 47
Oppression, 65
Ordnung, 190, 191, 193, 199, 201
Original Americans. *See* Native American families
Other-centeredness, 99

P

Pacific Islanders. *See* Asian American families
Pacifism, 190, 200
Palestine-Israeli Accords, 161
Pan-Indianism, 167, 169, 179
Pan-renaissance Native American family, 170
Parenting alliances, 266
Parents. *See* Custodial parents; Divorced single-parent families; Never-married parents; Nonresident stepparents; Stepfamilies; Teenage single-parent families
Parents, Families and Friends of Lesbians and Gays (PFLAG), 335, 341, 346
Pathway Publishers, 193
Patriarchy
    Amish families, 194, 197
    Arab American families, 151
    Asian American families, 112, 115, 126, 137
    Native American tribes, 169
Patrilineal families, 151, 152–153
Patrilocal families, 151
Peace, of the Amish, 190
Peace Corps, 6
Peaceful accommodation, 16–17
Penn, William, 190
Pennsylvania Dutch, 193
Personal relationships. *See* Relationships
Personal Responsibility and Work Opportunity Reconciliation Act, 33, 210, 258
Phonetic syllabary, 175
Physical custody, joint, 249, 250, 252, 255, 266
Physical divorce, 265
Plain People, 189–190. *See also* Amish families
Pluralism, 179
Pluralistic society, 14, 16
Political criticism, of African American families, 218
Polygamy, 154
Population changes. *See* Demographics
Population data. *See* Demographics
Positive feedback, 49
Poverty, feminization of, 233. *See also* Demographics; Economic factors
Powell, Colin, 76
Powwow, 182, 185
Precontact period, 182
Pregnancy, 56. *See also* Health care system
Pregnancy Discrimination Act, 31
Pregnancy prevention, 226–227

Prejudice, against Hispanic Americans, 89–90, 106
Preschool children, in Amish families, 194–195
Prestige
    Amish elders, 197
    Arab American elders, 155
Professional service, 35
Profiling, 77
Property settlement, 245–246
Prostitution, 227
Psychological divorce, 265
Public disclosure, 340–341
Public Law 9838-387, 262
Puerto Rican Hispanics. *See* Hispanic Americans

Q

Qur'an, 147, 148, 149, 154, 155

R

Racism, 45
    African American families, 75, 77, 80
    Asian Americans, 117, 140
    Native American families, 182
    teenage single-parent families and, 217, 218
Rape, 227, 278
Reagan, Ronald, 231
Reductionism, 65
Reeducation, 258–260
Refugees, 132–133, 135, 142
Rehabilitation Act, 32
Relationships
    Asian American families, 115
    divorced single-parent families, 264–266
    Hispanic families, 99–100
    Korean American families, 137
    stepfamilies, 289
    teenage single-parent families, 232–233, 234, 236, 237
    See also Extended families
Religion
    African American families, 71–72, 79–80
    Amish families, 188, 189, 191, 198–199
    Arab American families, 147–149, 150, 151, 153, 154
    Asian American families, 116
    divorced single-parent families, 260–261
    families with children with special needs, 314
    gay and lesbian families, 348–349

Hispanic American families, 92–93
Korean American families, 140
stepfamilies, 287
teenage single-parent families, 226
Relocation Act, 168
Remarriage, 248, 253, 258, 262, 266. *See also*
   Stepfamilies
Reorganization Act, 167
Reproductive function, 52
Republican Party, 76, 118, 121, 131
Reservations
   economic development on, 181
   economic system and, 180, 181
   educational system and, 175, 176, 177
   extended families, 170
   family practices, 169
   family service and, 182
   governmental system and, 179
   health care system and, 178
   historical background, 165–166, 168
Residence order, 289
Respect
   Amish elderly, 197
   Amish families, 201
   Arab American families, 155
   Hispanic American families, 99, 100–101
   Native American families, 174
Responsibility
   Arab American families, 153–155
   Asian American families, 129
   Hispanic American families, 99, 101
   teenage single-parent families, 219
Rice, Condoleezza, 76
Rights
   Arab American women, 154
   human, 4, 5, 15, 17, 18
   individual and family, 29–30
   legal, 29–33, 154
Rivera, Sylvia, 333
Roberts, Charles Carl, IV, 189
Rockefeller Foundation, 77
Roosevelt, Franklin D., 120, 179
Rounds, 178
Rumschpringes, 195

S
Sansei, 119, 123, 125, 128–129, 130
Schoolchildren, in Amish families, 195

School shootings, 189
Science, 5, 6
Sciences, family-related, 35–36
Second-parent adoption, 337, 343, 344, 347, 350
Segregation
   African Americans, 65, 69
   children with special needs, 300
   Native Americans, 179 (*see also* Reservations)
Self-Determination period, 182
Self-reliance, 174
Separation, 265
Separatism, 14, 17
Sequoyah, 175
Service. *See* Family service
Serving families. *See* Family service
Sexism, 70
Sex-role ambiguities and abuse, 278–280
Shachtman, Tom, 189
Shalala, Donna, 227
Shared meaning, 44
Shi'ite Muslims, 149
Shunning (*meidung*), 191, 196, 199
Single-parent families. *See* Divorced single-parent
   families; Teenage single-parent families
Slavery, 65, 66, 69, 72, 80, 82
Smoking, 228, 229
Social divorce, 265
Socialization
   divorced single-parent families, 253–256
   families with children with special needs, 308
   gay and lesbian families, 345
   stepfamilies, 283
   teenage single-parent families and, 224
Socialization function, 52–53
Social Security, 200
Social Security Act, 32
Social Security Administration, 316
Social Services Act, 245
Sociocultural environment, 47, 48
Sociocultural foundations
   divorced single-parent families, 248–253
   families with children with special needs,
      304–309
   gay and lesbian families, 335–342
   teenage single-parent families, 219–220
Sodomy, 339, 347
Sons, impact of divorce on, 252–253
Sorrow, 323–325

South American Hispanics. *See* Hispanic Americans
Spanish-American War, 89
Spanish language, 90–92
Special needs children. *See* Families with children with special needs
Staff training, 268
State Interagency Coordinating Council, 302
State laws, 34
Status
    divorced parents, 249
    gay and lesbian families, 337
Stepfamilies, 274
    aesthetics, 285–286
    change and adaptation, 290–291
    children, 278, 282–283
    conclusions, 293–294
    demographics, 284–285
    economic factors, 287–288
    education, 286
    extended families, 284
    family ecology, 284–289
    family structure, 274–276
    female roles, 280–281
    governmental policies and agencies, 288–289
    health care, 287
    historical background, 276–277
    kinship networks and interactions, 289
    male roles, 281–282
    religion, 287
    serving, 291–293
    sex-role ambiguities and abuse, 278–280
Stepfamily Association of America, 293
Stepfamily Foundation, 293
Stereotypes, 22–23, 26, 45
    African Americans, 65, 69, 77
    Arab Americans, 150, 154, 158, 159–160, 161
    Asian Americans, 117, 121, 132, 141, 142
    Hispanic Americans, 93
Sterilization, forced, 218
Stonewall riot, 333
Subfamilies, 214, 220, 230
Subjective parental style, 224
Substance abuse, 195–196, 228, 309
Sufis, 150
Sunni Muslims, 149
Supplemental Security Income (SSI), 32, 316
Support groups, 291–292, 341–342
Survey of American Families and Households, 252
Survey of Business Owners, 181

Survey of Family Growth (1995), 227
Survey of Income and Program Participation (SIPP), 276
Sweat lodge ceremonies, 178
Synergy, 16
System effects, 46
Systems approach, 43–44, 45–48

T
Talking circle, 178
Tanomoshi, 125
Taxes, 200
Technology, 5–6
Teenage single-parent families, 208
    change and adaptation, 233–235
    children, socialization of, 224
    conclusions, 238–239
    demographics, 211–219, 225
    economic factors, 229–230
    economic status, 220–222
    education, 225–226
    family service, 235–238
    female roles, 222
    governmental policies and agencies, 231–232
    health care system and, 226–229
    housing, 230–231
    kinship networks and interactions, 232–233
    male roles, 222–223
    never-married parents, 209–211
    religion, 226
    societal concern and debate, 208–209
    sociocultural foundations, 219–220
Temporary Assistance to Needy Families (TANF)
    divorced single-parent families, 258–259, 261, 262, 263, 264
    stepfamilies, 288
    teenage single-parent families, 220–221, 223, 232, 235, 239
Terrorists, 159, 161
Thomas, Danny, 158
Time-out, 195
Title VII. *See* Civil Rights Act of 1964—Title VII
Traditional Native American family, 169–170
Trail of Tears, 179
Transgendered, 333, 342
Transitional Native American family, 170
Transportation, 6
Travel, 6
Tribalism, 17

Troxel et vir. v. Granville, 255
Tutu, Desmond, 368
Two-family model, 254

U
United Nations, 4, 5, 17, 358, 368
U.S. Bureau of Indian Affairs (BIA), 175, 177, 180
U.S. Constitution, 29–30, 37
U.S. demographics, 8–11, 12
U.S. Department of Health and Human Services, 177, 178
U.S. Department of Health, Education, and Welfare, 177
U.S. Department of Housing and Urban Development, 231
U.S. Equal Employment Opportunity Commission, 131
United Way, 12
Universal Declaration of Human Rights, 4
Universal Grammar, 14

V
Vacations, 319
Values, 49–50
    African American families, 71–72
    Arab American families, 156–157
    Asian American families, 116–117
    families with children with special needs, 323
    Hispanic American families, 98–101
    Japanese American families, 129–130
    Korean American families, 137–139
    Native American families, 173–174
    Vietnamese American families, 134–135
Vertical relationships, 115
Vietnam Era Veterans' Readjustment Assistance Act, 32
Vietnamese American families, 122
    educational system and, 135
    family ecology, 132–135
    family structure, 133–135
    governmental system and, 136–137
    health care system and, 135–136
    See also Asian American families
Vietnam War, 114, 132, 133
Violence, 17, 279–280
Visha, Emily, 293
Visha, John, 293
Vocational Rehabilitation Act, 315–316
Volunteering, 12
Voter Registration Act, 31
Voting Rights Act of 1965, 31, 76

W
Wage and Hour Law, 32
War, 17
War Department, 177
Weddings, in Amish culture, 196
Welfare Reform Act, 24, 33
    divorced single-parent families, 258, 264
    families with children with special needs, 316–317
    teenage single-parent families, 210, 219, 220, 222, 223, 229, 232
Wheeler-Howard Act, 167
White House Conference on the Family, 333
White House Office of Faith-Based Initiatives, 226
Whole school plan, 301, 305, 311, 313–314
Wilder, Lawrence Douglas, 76
Williams, Robert, 246
Wilson, Woodrow, 16
Wisconsin Model, 245–246
Women
    Amish families, 194
    Arab American families, 153–155
    Asian American families, 118, 141
    divorce and, 249–250
    employment and, 24, 26, 27
    Equal Pay Act and, 31, 56–57
    human capital and, 56–57
    Infants and Children (WIC) program, 228, 231
    Korean American families, 137–138, 139
    life expectancy, 56
    Vietnamese Americans, 135–136
    See also Gender roles
Work, Hispanic attitudes toward, 101
Workforce
    diversity, 25–27
    employment-related laws, 31, 32, 33
    family service, 28–29
    home life, 27–28
    teenage single-parent families and, 222–223
    See also Economic factors
World War II internment, 120, 122, 123, 124, 126, 127, 128, 131

X
Xenophobia, 117

Y
Yellow Peril, 117
Yonsei, 125
Youths. *See* Children